CAMPAIGNING FOR THE POOR
CPAG AND THE POLITICS OF WELFARE

CAMPAIGNING
FOR
THE
POOR

CPAG and the Politics of Welfare

MICHAEL McCARTHY
Foreword by
Peter Townsend

CROOM HELM
London • Sydney • Dover, New Hampshire

© 1986 Michael McCarthy,
Croom Helm Ltd, Provident House, Burrell Row,
Beckenham, Kent BR3 1AT
Croom Helm Australia Pty Ltd, Suite 4, 6th Floor,
64-76 Kippax Street, Surry Hills, NSW 2010, Australia

British Library Cataloguing in Publication Data

McCarthy, Michael
    Campaigning for the poor: CPAG and the
    politics of welfare.
    1. Child Poverty Action Group – History
    I. Title
    362.5'8'D6041   HC260.P63

    ISBN 0-7099-4606-6
    ISBN 0-7099-3593-5 Pbk

Croom Helm, 51 Washington Street, Dover,
New Hampshire 03820, USA

Library of Congress Cataloging-in-Publication Data

McCarthy, Michael.
    Campaigning for the poor.

    Bibliography: p. 368
    1. Poor–Great Britain. 2. Child poverty action
group. 3. Welfare state. 4. Great Britain–politics and
government–1979–   . I. Title.
HC260.P6M34   1986   362.8'282'0941   86-8822
ISBN 0-7099-4606-6
ISBN 0-7099-3593-5 (pbk.)

Printed and bound in Great Britain
by Billing & Sons Limited, Worcester.

CONTENTS

Foreword
Dedication
Acknowledgements

Foreword

"DEMOCRACY FOR THE POOR"

Peter Townsend

The history of the Child Poverty Action Group and other similar organisations in the late twentieth century is essentially one about the failings of British democracy. For all the trumpeting of principles of representation, social responsibility and respect for the views of others political practice has been a very different thing. There are several minorities, adding up to many millions of people, who have been, and remain, poorly represented. Many among them do not believe their needs and difficulties are understood - or even conscientiously examined. Most of the institutions of the British state - Parliament, Government departments and local authorities, the judiciary and the police, the military and the Church - are seen as remote and authoritarian. Either these institutions seem to be disguised by outmoded trappings which foster mystery, awe and subservience, or they depend upon procedures and regulations which seem intended not so much to protect rights and provide efficient services as induce dependence and feelings of inferiority so that officials and their masters can remain in entire charge of events.

The creation of new kinds of pressure groups like Shelter, the Disablement Income Group and the Campaign Against Racial Discrimination, as well as the Child Poverty Action Group, in the mid-1960s, was more than a sign of the times. It was a reaction to what was perceived to be the fraudulent character of British democracy. There were of course special conditions which explained the new expressions of protest. Public expectations had been running high. The policies of successive Governments had been built on relatively full employment and steadily increasing national wealth. This meant that the views and interests of workers, pensioners and others were

believed to weigh more heavily than they had done
before the war in the conduct of national affairs.
But class divisions and inequalities in income proved
to be more entrenched than many had supposed after
the victories of war and the post-war Welfare State.
Further social reforms which were promised or
anticipated turned out to be paper tigers, and the
new arrivistes among the rich, along with the
traditional owners or property, came to be seen by
many as confirming and even augmenting their
ascendancy.

At best new policies seemed capable of being
interpreted cynically as methods of preserving the
status quo in a rapidly changing world. Or they could
be interpreted, equally cynically, as forms of mild
compensation for those on the losing side of new
development. Confidence in Government administration
declined. Such administration came to be seen as
reinforcing instead of counterbalancing market
forces. Some groups - like the elderly, one-parent
families and sick and disabled people - were observed
to have been left behind in the race for prosperity.
There was growing concern at revelations of
substantial residual poverty.

All this was made worse when the Labour Party
took office and failed to deliver the changes which
party and non-party radicals optimistically hoped
for. There was a want of national planning and of
radical strategic planning. Attention was not given
to the need to change structures, spread the
ownership of wealth and construct programmes for
social development. Political education and
organisation to meet the objectives of a more
participative democracy were underrated and
disappeared from national agendas. Political status
inside and outside Parliament reflected a scale of
values which gave low priority to the problems of the
poor.

With some qualifications this picture remains
true. The efforts of the last twenty years have not
brought categorical or universal improvement.
Examples abound. Even in 1986 there are fewer than a
dozen Members of Parliament who can speak with
authority about the operation of the social security
system. Yet that system provides all or most of the
livelihood of a quarter of the population of the
United Kingdom. And there are authoritive bodies
other than representatives of the social sciences who
call attention anxiously to the condition of Britain.
During 1985 one bishop after another took up the
refrain. Some reiterated the declamatory style of

"Darkest England", in the 1880s. The wheel of privation and misery seemed to have gone full circle. And the Archbishop of Canterbury's Commission on Urban Priority Areas stated, in its Report, Faith in the City, at the end of 1985 "Social disintegration has reached a point in some areas that shop windows are boarded up, and there is a pervading sense of powerlessness and despair".

The problem of social representation (and participation) does not stop just with social security or with the seventeen or eighteen million people who primarily depend on social security. It spreads into many related issues. Racism has become institutionalised without sufficient, sustained opposition from Parties, professions and administration. The needs of a million and a half people in Northern Ireland have been transposed into the problems of military policing and management. The mass deprivation of the inner cities has been accepted fatalistically instead of being resolutely opposed by everyone with any claim to power. The writing of the authoritarian state is very much on the wall.

So the pressure groups founded in the Sixties and early Seventies find they now have an even bigger role to play. Let me try to give some sense of what this means. In 1965 the Child Poverty Action Group was formed in the crucible of outrage - particularly by Quakers and social workers with first-hand acquaintance with poverty and by social scientists whose research demonstrated comprehensively that the phenomenon was as unnecessary as it was widespread. The first step was to publicise the evidence. Michael McCarthy recounts the history below.

Despite the initial success in demontrating the huge scale of poverty and the need to redistribute resources to the young family, these ideas came to be resisted by Departments of State (especially the Treasury), Government Ministers and many agencies of the media. When the chips are down there are a lot of people who are not prepared to surrender a significant part of their wealth or income to assist the living standards of millions of poor people. And there are many vested interests, including politicians in all political parties, who are ready to back them up. An integral part of people's unwillingness to give up income is explained by the position they hold in society and their belief that they have earned and thoroughly justify any elevated status and wealth which they currently enjoy. People's view of society therefore often reflects a self-righteous claim to any advantage they already hold. Perceptions of others' needs and rights is partly a function of the position people themselves hold. So resistance to the surrender of income gets translated into an ideological resistance to the evidence of poverty and even to a more generous or social definition of poverty.

Only by some such theory does it become possible to explain many of the events of the late sixties, seventies and early eighties, which Michael McCarthy so scrupulously describes. How otherwise can the Thatcher Government's determination to cut, and go on cutting, total expenditure on social security, withdraw some groups entirely from benefit, substitute less expensive but less effective means-tested benefits for benefits as of right, and fail to include child benefit as a necessary part of the tax threshold of families, be adequately explained? How otherwise can the clumsy opposition of many trade unionists and much of the Labour Cabinet to the child benefit scheme in 1975, or the fact that in the run up to the election of 1970 the Labour Cabinet came within a hair's breadth of introducing the derisory Family Income Supplement scheme, which was subsequently enacted by the Conservative Government, also be adequately explained?

The stakes are higher than they were in 1965. There are twice as many people in poverty or on the margins of poverty – even by Government standards of low income. Many more communities are wracked by long-standing and multiple deprivation, bitter social divisions and the threatening knowledge that standards of personal and family security as well as safety have collapsed. The gentleness and decency of British culture are becoming hard to discern. This is no time for glum reflections on the failure of small pressure groups to influence the course of national events. On the contrary, the surprising thing is how much, despite their puny incomes and staffing, they have been able to influence opinion and secure fractional resources for their causes during the most unfavourable period of this century, politically, for the poor. What they have learned above all else is the supreme importance of building constituencies of opinion and especially new alliances not just in a defensive war against encroachments upon the post-war Welfare State but in the necessarily long haul towards a society where poverty might not exist. Governing Ministers, and other governing elites, are no longer thought to hold the answers. These elites are no longer believed to hold the key to the adoption of policies favourable to the poor. More consequential are the groups, organisations and agencies upon whom these elites depend for their power. And that is another historical twist in the pursuit of democracy.

The term "democracy" goes back to the classical Greek polis, when it represented a constitution in which the poor (demos) exercised power in their own interests as against those of the rich aristocracy. But it was not until after the French Revolution that the idea of democracy came into its own and began to include representative parliaments, the rule of law, the separation of powers and civil rights. With the passing of time some of these elements have become divorced from their original promise. New methods are being devised to breathe life into the ageing ideals of majority rule, protection of minorities, constitutional liberty, accountability, egalitarianism, participation and much else.

There are a number of ways by which organisations like the Child Poverty Action Group have been, and can continue to be, fertile instruments of popular democracy. They have been "representative" of poor people only in particular senses. Thus, they cannot pretend to organise or establish the needs of millions of people or consult the entire complex of national opinion responsibly – though they can and do learn a lot about the results of survey research and, through welfare rights activities, keep in first-hand touch with the realities of poverty. They cannot arrange many conferences and other meetings for large numbers of people and set up generously staffed branches up and down the country. But what they can do is commit themselves unreservedly to the interests of millions of poor people, call representative injustices to public notice and exchange blow with blow in an expert struggle with the Government over the effects, implications and constitutional niceties of policy.

One relatively new feature of this democratic strategy is collaboration with sympathetic fellow organisations. In the early 1970s the Child Poverty Action Group helped to pioneer joint action by voluntary bodies to impress Government and public with the need to take particular anti-poverty measures. In 1986 such action takes many forms and even the most traditionally soft-spoken bodies are aware of the dangers of not establishing their independence of both State and party in power. If they were not sufficiently sensitive to that independence they realise they would soon lose all credibility with the people on whose behalf they are supposed to act. Different minorities have begun to find their voices in a social revolution against exclusion and condescension. With the support of women's groups and libertarian local councils that revolution will be taken a lot further in the next decade. One of the marvellous developments of the last ten years has been the growing assertion of independence on the part of people with disabilities, encouraged by such bodies as the British Council of Organisations of Disabled People, the Campaign for Mentally Handicapped People and the Disability Alliance. The future rests with more representative and participative specialist organisations, acting in concert with each other. Together they show signs of taking many of the more important democratic initiatives, which Party politicians will often be obliged to adopt. They will comprise the "middle-men" (and women) of democratic reform. That will be the central strategy to secure equality of respect and lay the basis for an effective anti-poverty strategy.

But there is an addendum to this argument. The social polarisation which lies behind growing poverty is attributable ultimately to the excessive powers of wealthy and affluent people in key institutions of state and market. Those institutions are rapidly becoming internationalised and that poses the biggest threat to the frail threads of national democracy. More attention must be given to the exposure of excessive and unnecessary privilege, as much as excessive and unnecessary power. It is impossible to raise the poor without simultaneously diminishing the rich. The wealthy are treated as an enviable secret society. Far too little is known about the sources of their wealth and the machinery which maintains and multiplies that wealth. Democrats need to learn that poverty is created by a system which includes wealth and that the description and explanation of the one must include the description and explanation of the other. When it existed in the late 1970s the Royal Commission on the Distribution of Income and Wealth was circumspect, indeed, unadventurous in its documentation of wealth. That did not save it from being abolished by the Thatcher Government. No attempt has been made, so far as I am aware, by any of the so-called independent Foundations or Institutes to set up a corresponding programme of national research and information. The investigative traditions of the serious media seem also to have been abandoned – except for occasional flurries of interest in corruption in high places, as in banks and insurance companies in 1985 and early 1986. But in these instances the purpose of the investigation seems generally to be aimed at discrediting personalities instead of exposing long-standing institutional disservices to democracy. For consistent, illuminating evidence about the origins and practices of institutional power people have to fall back on the reports of small organisations like Counter Information Services or the legal and procedural challenges of the National Council of Civil Liberties.

Democratic enquiry into wealth is fundamental because it reveals the extent of the potential resources to abolish poverty as well as the potential obstacles to the reconstruction of the institutions of distribution and redistribution. The statistics published by the Central Statistical Office continue to reveal that the richest 20 per cent of the population would need to have their incomes cut by only £1 in every £6 to double the incomes of the poorest 20 per cent. Of course that would not be easy to fulfil. In practice it would involve an elaborate democratic exercise designed to obtain public support for a programme of raising benefits, introducing a minimum wage, redistributing income from single and married people without dependants to those with families, reducing inequalities between men and women, redistributing resources from middle-aged people both to young families and the elderly, extending personal income taxation to income currently freed from taxation - like mortgage interest payments covered by income tax relief, introducing wealth taxation and increasing capital transfer taxation, increasing the rate of taxation at the higher rates of income, and placing a ceiling on the growth of earnings at higher levels. There would necessarily be changes in relationships and responsibilities at work and in social relationships outside work. But this is what the creation of democracy for the poor would entail.

Michael McCarthy has produced a remarkably faithful history of the struggles on behalf of poor families to which the Child Poverty Action Group has contributed over the span of a generation. The story is one of collaborative effort in common cause, in which the indictment of human construction of anti-poverty policies has been overwhelmingly more important than the trivia of personal publicity and squabbles within the Cabinet. This book in itself represents a fine tribute to that principle. It also poses all the searching questions about a future strategy - for pressure groups as much as Governments to confront. I hope I have stated enough in outline at least to suggest that members of these pressure groups may be aware of the nature of the challenge. More important, we have to hope there are those in Government or who will shortly enter Government who will be prepared to respond to that challenge.

Peter Townsend
London, February, 1986.

To Mum and Dad
and to Rosalind for the future
thank you.

ACKNOWLEDGEMENTS

In 1976 I first approached the Child Poverty Action Group with a view to undertaking an extended piece of academic research that would document their work and analyse and assess their role as a pressure group for the poor. Nearly ten years later, that work produces its second fruit with the publication of <u>Campaigning for the Poor</u>. Originally scheduled elsewhere for production in 1983, those efforts now seem doubly worthwhile as publication coincides with the most timely of events, CPAG's twenty-first year. If there is any time to reflect for a moment in what will prove yet another difficult year for the poor and one in which CPAG's energies will be stretched to the limit, then I trust this record and assessment of the Group's work over the last two decades will add a further dimension to its coming of age. Over the various phases of research for the book I have come to owe considerable debts of gratitude to all those who have given me their time, their interest and their guidance. Generally, I owe a great debt to all the staff of CPAG over the years who so kindly and willingly endured my endless questions, interviews, telephone conversations and quests for dusty files and minutes languishing in forgotten corners of Macklin Street. I owe particular debts to a number of CPAG leaders and members without whose help and guidance this undertaking would no doubt have foundered in the late seventies - Peter Townsend, Tony Lynes, Henry Hodge, Malcolm Wicks, Marigold Johnson, Jane Streather, David Piachaud, Jo Tunnard, Nick Bosanquet, Jonathan Bradshaw. I owe a strong and more recent debt to Ruth Lister and Fran Bennett for their support in my efforts to bring my earlier work on CPAG up to date and for the comment and sense of direction they gave me in writing on the work of the Group in the eighties. I owe that same debt to Peter

Townsend and a sense of great pleasure in his agreement to write the preface.

I would like to record my thanks also to John Stancer and Jeremy Richardson who both did so much to spur me on during the academic life of this work and to friends and colleagues at Trent Polytechnic who helped me shape the political arguments. Naturally, I owe the Polytechnic an important vote of thanks for the use of its resources and support during my tenure there.

I owe special gratitude to many friends and colleagues at the British Association of Social Workers in Birmingham who have done so much to encourage and assist me in completing this book in the last year. To Mary Nunes, Kiran Chauhan, Maureen Thrupp and Stephen Blackwell yet another thank you for spinning the magic of the Alphatronic. I owe a very special debt of gratitude at BASW to David Swaysland who encouraged me on my arrival at the Association in January 1985 to resurrect an earlier venture and helped arrange the means to do it. Thank you.

That brings me to the bridge between 1983 and 1985. To Anne Beech, formerly of Junction Books, I owe a considerable debt. I have not forgotten it. Once more, thank you.

It was in 1985, however, that Campaigning For the Poor became reality and the credit for that is overwhelmingly due to the interest and efforts of Jo Campling. I hope the book proves a just reward for her support and endeavour and that it repays the faith also of my publisher David Croom.

Of all the debts I owe in the course of my work on CPAG none is greater than that to Frank Field. It is enough to say that this venture could never have been realised without the support and encouragement he first gave to it nearly ten years ago and in the many years since.

Michael McCarthy
Holymoorside
Derbyshire

Chapter One

POVERTY AND THE PLURAL SOCIETY

It has been argued that 'the real source of
innovations in public policy is new information, new
ideas, and new interpretations of old problems' and
that 'Given the high level of uncertainty that
characterises governmental decision-making, policy-
makers depend heavily on the steady flow of policy
responses. Those who contribute to this flow exercise
real influence' (1). This view may be seen as
particularly relevant to the field of social policy
where the limited availability and use of effective
social and economic indicators, the impingement of
economic and fiscal policy, and the complexity of
individual and group interests have conspired to
produce a tradition of fragmentation and immobilism.
    The ability of those who contribute to the 'flow
of policy responses' to exercise 'real influence',
however, depends upon a range of factors other than
the ability to communicate ideas and information.
The value of those ideas and information is
important, as is the willingness of policymakers to
accept external inputs. Also crucial are the climate
of public opinion, the relative strengths and
weaknesses of the client groups conveying and
resisting ideas, the attachment of government to
notions of consensus, the dynamics of departmental
pluralism and, of course, the nature of the issues at
stake. Where issues are seen to affect or concern
relatively small or poorly-defined publics, and
where they are regarded as contentious or
controversial, those contesting them may encounter
serious difficulties in effecting policy innovation
or change.
    This book considers one such issue, that of
family poverty, and attempts to offer some insight
into how the issue progressed in status from relative

1

obscurity to the centre of the political stage during the twenty years from 1965 to 1985. The study seeks, in particular, to examine and assess how a small promotional group may influence events: it documents both the group's progress and that of the issue concerned against the backcloth of political events and change in the period of the Wilson, Heath, Callaghan and Thatcher Governments.

Efforts to win both public and governmental support for a strategy to end family poverty were hindered from the outset, as Chapter 2 shows, both by the general belief that poverty had been largely eliminated through post-war advances in the provision of social welfare and by the absence of a 'pressure-group for the poor'. The campaign to eradicate family poverty, with the statutory provision of some sort of 'family allowance' as its chief aim, had originated with the establishment of the feminist 1917 Committee which took its name from the year of its formation. In the following year the National Union of Societies for Equal Citizenship, a suffragette body with Eleanor Rathbone as one of its guiding lights, was instrumental in the reconstitution of the 1917 Committee as the Family Endowment Society (2). The latter also took as its chief target the need to bring about some state provision for families with children.

It is an irony of later campaigns that the most entrenched obstacles to reform and change in family policy and provision have largely been either the legacy or the oversight of the 1945 Family Allowances Act for which the Family Endowment Society had so energetically campaigned. The Act had, for example, excluded the family's first child from the benefits of state provision. A further problem for latter-day campaigners was the failure of the 1945 Labour government to provide for any regular or systematic review of family allowance levels with the result that on only two occasions in the period 1945-64 was the issue of benefit 'erosion' raised (3).

To compound this situation, the provision of family allowances has been popularly and somewhat narrowly associated with the need to reverse Britain's falling birth rate, so that when the rate rose once more support for the scheme seriously waned. Indeed, the public opinion survey of 1944, Britain and Her Birth Rate (4), had already revealed that family allowances as an attack on poverty had only a secondary or tertiary importance for most people. In addition, the exclusion of the first child from the scheme was interpreted as an indication that family allowances were really designed for large rather than small families.

A major theme of this study is the apparent fragmentation of social policy and its isolation from economic and fiscal policy. This, too, may be seen to have had its origins in the 1945 Act. Family allowances were introduced in isolation from other social security reforms, an indication of the differing objectives that different groups saw them fulfilling, and were, rather vaguely, to be supplemented at some later, specified date with free school meals and milk. Neither were measures over which the Minister of National Insurance exercised any control, falling, as they did, within the education budget (5). Control and accountability were further obscured by a lack of discussion and consensus about the future of the scheme. For others, significantly, the primary aim of the scheme was not even to alleviate family poverty but instead to curb inflation or maintain work incentives.

Any plans for a post-war campaign to secure regular reviews of the new family allowance scheme were effectively ended with the death of Eleanor Rathbone and the subsequent demise of the Family Endowment Society in 1946. Their passing left a vacuum in welfare politics which was not filled until the emergence of the Child Poverty Action Group (CPAG) in 1965.

Not only did interest in family allowances and the cycle of family poverty itself subside, but other issues were forced onto the political agenda to occupy the attention of government to the exclusion of others. The task for any future family allowance campaigner was therefore twofold - to make up for lost ground and time, and to dislodge entrenched interests in favour of their own issue.

The influence of social scientists in documenting the problems which had either ensued from or which had not been met by the 1945 Act, and in defining a new conceptual approach to the understanding of both the nature and extent of poverty in a society which generally believed itself free of the problem, was to become the most crucial force for policy innovation. Their role as 'policy-watchers' in filling gaps in the government's knowledge of family poverty created a climate of debate which sparked the emergence of a plethora of groups, including CPAG and Shelter, concerned to politicise their findings and promote the policy alternatives they advanced. The role of the social scientists was not to end there, however. Until 1965 their role had largely remained one of problem definition and the specification of alternatives. Significantly, as it became clear that their own definition of priorities was not matched by the government's, these 'policy-watchers' were moved to adopt more political and organised means of communicating their views and the need for change.

CPAG AND THE PLURALIST ORDER

The value in studying a group like CPAG is considerable and this study takes as its overall theme a question which this group has wrestled with since its inception - how might a small group, lacking political sanctions, influence policymakers? This question, in turn, poses a further series of questions concerning the nature of the CPAG. Is it promotional or defensive? Is it a cause group or a sectional group? How is it organised, how resourceful is it, does it have a useful network of contacts, is it part of or outside the recognised policy community in its field? Important questions must also arise in any analysis of the Group's 'clients' and of the nature of the issues it confronts. Do the 'clients', for example, form part of a recognised and well-defined 'public'? Do they possess a useful level of political consciousness? Do they or could they exert political influence or latent power? Are the issues which affect or determine the life-chances of this public recognised as important political issues, calling for effective political action by policymakers and/or by other publics? To what extent will the resolution of these issues, and the tackling of the problems that underpin them, threaten other interests in society? Do such interests prosper socially, culturally or politically from the disadvantages experienced by this client group?

The pattern of pressure-group politics in Britain from the mid-sixties to the mid-eighties indicates that small, impoverished, sometimes poorly-established groups, often articulating interests related to fundamental social issues such as poverty, mental health, homelessness and unemployment, are invariably disadvantaged vis a vis economic, industrial and professional groups in terms of political access. Often, like CPAG, they seek to represent publics whose interests or welfare are difficult to define - let alone secure - and which rarely exert any influence upon the stability of government or the adversary politics of the Party system. For the most part they are the type of issues which Schattschneider spoke of as being 'organised out' of politics (6). The reasons why this should be are not always clear or consistent. Generally, they are likely to be a combination of poor organisation and value-laden preferences which are at variance with the prevailing norms and values of the group process.

At least one observer has equated the poor political impact of such interest groups with their apparent lack of voting power. Enoch Powell, for instance, has criticised a political system that has produced a welfare state which fails to provide serious and sustained cognisance of issues like mental health, child poverty, prison reform and homelessness. It is Powell's view, and it is one which is closely examined throughout this study, that the importance or relevance of issues is not established through moral or social criteria but through Party calculation of precise electoral advantage. His comment on the fortunes of the mentally ill, that 'no significant voting power is involved ... (because) ... the voting power of mental affliction is in the bottom range' (7), may be judged to be equally relevant to the poor. The electoral significance of expenditure strategies to alleviate poverty has figured particularly prominently in the sensitivity of Labour governments to the problem, and has culminated in something of a credibility gap betwen the radical symbolism of Labour in opposition and the policies it adopts within the constraints of governmental office. By contrast, Mrs Thatcher's victories in 1979 and 1983 made a virtue of tax cuts to facilitate wealth generation that were always going to be financed from cuts in services and welfare expenditure.

As a result of government or Party inertia, and as a consequence of their own shortcomings, groups like CPAG, representing politically-weak client publics, may be obliged to articulate their interests through one of the group establishment, or, as some writers refer to them, 'Insider groups' (8) — those groups with consultative status as a major goal. To a large extent the shortcomings of such interests reflects their cause-group status (9) and may be organisational, financial, educational or articulatory. Each may impose a severe constraint upon the group's ability to achieve its goals (10).

The inequality experienced by such groups is essentially twofold. On the one hand non-established groups may be obliged and encouraged to seek the patronage and resource' support of the established groups, in what Richardson and Jordan have termed the 'policy community', to enhance their chances of goal achievement (11). As Truman notes 'the weaker the means of direct action available to a ... group, the more ready has it been to work through such mediating institutions ... unaided by the wider powers of some more inclusive group, they cannot achieve their objectives'. Crucially, Truman asks, 'why must this institution be the Government' (12) and suggests, instead, that the Church, trade unions, employers' organisations and professional associations may readily acquire this role.

The importance of an alliance with the trade union movement for social cause-groups has been accentuated as other avenues of influence have closed and as the idea of a social contract has gained support. CPAG's efforts to forge an alliance with the trade unions and to promote an interest in welfare rights among rank-and-file workers are discussed later. It is important at this point, however, to acknowledge the growing interest of the trade union movement in non-work place issues and its development of a firm societal role. This role has important implications for conventional pluralist theory.

In offering this view, Truman was, in part, echoing ideas expressed earlier by E. Durkheim and J.R. Commons. The latter had even gone so far as to argue that 'the preservation of the economic system against a totalitarian world and against its own internal disruption, consists mainly in the collective bargaining between organised capital and organised labour, as against Government by the traditional parties. Other organisations, whether farmers, merchants, bankers or the professions, must conform their policies and methods to this major economic issue of capital and labour' (13).

In similar fashion it is Truman's belief that this insider network or 'established-group stratum' could adopt the role of monitor and patron of those emerging interests requiring a helping-hand to secure government attention. For Truman, the group process reflects the equilibrate nature of social and economic forces in society at a given point in time. For Commons, the group process constitutes a social and occupational 'parliament' with a quasi-messianistic role to play in ensuring the stability and continuance of society. Indeed, Commons found this view so compelling that he could conclude prophetically in 1951 that 'both political science and economic science are beginning to recognise a transition from territorial governments to economic governments' (14).

In adopting this view Commons was offering an economic refinement of the theory of group equilibrium propounded by Arthur Bentley at the turn of the century. It was Bentley's view that, seen in isolation, groups are in conflict, and some will dominate others because of their superior resources or their occupational advantage (15). However, an overview of the process of group politics reveals that domination and subordination may be less pronounced than at first assumed. Instead, both may be cyclical experiences for most groups, so that at a given point some groups will be in the ascendancy and some in decline in terms of their influence. As circumstances change and new issues arise the situation of such groups also begins to alter so that groups at the periphery of the critical centre of power move into temporary ascendancy. Bentley's methodology, and the orthodox tradition of pluralism that has followed from him, was based, therefore, upon concepts of symmetry, balance and equilibrium.

Where writers like Commons, Galbraith, Connolly, and Bachrach and Baratz in the USA, and Smith, Middlemass, Miliband and Cawson in the UK have broken with this tradition in varying degree is in their insistence in the existence of a fixed, permanent, established stratum of groups embedded at the core of the so called equilibrate order where all other groups/issues around them remain characterised by Bentley's notion of flux and mutability. These may be viewed as the insider groups of which Grant talks or those groups which have come to make up the 'policy communities' and 'policy networks' to which Richardson, Jordan, Gustaffson and Heclo variously refer (16).

Bentley himself had argued that there is no basic difference between the representatives of interest groups and the structural organisation of the government (17). All social phenomena are in some way connected to government, and government can be seen as little more than an organisation of interests combined into a single coherent system. Bentley's functional theory of the state is that all interests and all potential or, as Truman terms them, 'latent' interests are part of the governing process, since each interest is represented in proportion to its pressure. What Bentley did not foresee was the development of a highly complex, technologically interdependent economy and society in which basic social values might be subordinated to the demands of post-industrialisation and in which certain issues and publics might become increasingly organised out of politics as the powerful, resourceful groups increasingly organised themselves in. This is an important observation and raises a theme that will recur.

Truman touched upon the dangers of viewing 'might as right' in his own reformulation of Bentley concluding, rather uncomfortably, that his own analysis of the representativeness and fairness of the pluralist system might be flawed by its deference towards the economically strong and well-organised and its tendency to overlook the inarticulate, the malorganised and the impoverished. Perhaps what both Bentley and Truman, unlike Commons and his followers, failed to develop was the idea that the more complex society became on the economic-industrial level the more the state would need to incorporate groups active in these spheres, the more the state would seek to secure new forms of legitimacy like functional representation, the more the so-called equilibrium of groups could be rationalised and reduced to a form of elite accommodation.

Ultimately they might have foreseen a situation in which government might develop a series of exclusive partnerships with corporate groups dominating various issue areas to create powerful and recognisable policy communities. Those groups wishing to gain influence through entrance to such communities are faced with two primary choices. Either they opt to gain influence through their own independent action, in which case they might contribute directly to the 'overcrowding' and 'immobilism' that many writers have seen as a feature of the contemporary policy-making process; or they may themselves contribute to the process of rationalisation and elite accommodation by working through major groups already entrenched in the policy-making process.

Trevor Smith has attempted to document both these trends - elite accommodation and immobilism - and takes the creation of the National Economic Development Council (Neddy) as the classic catalyst in this process of incorporation. He notes of the tripartite consultative framework established in the early 1960's that 'the new agencies were an authoritative acknowledgement ... that a two-tier system of representation existed. Membership of NEDC indicated the granting of a superior franchise: it was an exercise in elite accommodation' (18). One of the reasons why, perhaps, even during the harsh anti-trade union realities of Mrs Thatcher's second term of office the TUC has clung to its 'new-realism' and chosen not to abandon its membership of the Council. He also talks of the 1960s as witnessing 'a tropical growth in interest groups catering for the under-enfranchised elements in society: these included the Consumers' Association, Shelter, the Child Poverty Action Group, the Claimants and Unemployed Workers Unions, and many others seeking to influence the contents of the public agenda.' (19).

Writing in the mid-70s, Smith suggested, arguably, that the creation of the National Consumer Council in 1975 illustrated the success of this consumer movement of the 1960s, and concludes that the Council 'goes some way to enfranchising consumers in the court politics of the neo-corporate state' since the Secretary of State for Prices and Consumer Protection has chosen 'indirectly (to) elect' representatives from such organisations as CPAG, Shelter, Age Concern, the National Council for Social Service, Citizens Advice Bureaux and the Claimants Union. Yet it must be said that these representatives do not sit as formal delegates of their respective groups, the Council itself has only advisory powers and early hopes of establishing a powerful and articulate consumer movement have not been fulfilled. Indeed, rare references to 'consumerism' are now largely confined to the 'New Rights' protagonism of privatisation in Welfare as the only viable guarantee of choice and efficient delivery of service.

Crucially, of course, many of these groups are in competition for scarce resources and their emergence may only have served to further the trend towards policy overcrowding. Ultimately, if consumers are to influence events it may make greater strategic sense to range themselves <u>with</u> rather than against their more resourceful and powerful producer counterparts. Indeed, a major section of this book is devoted to a discussion of the Child Poverty Action Group's attempts to do just that, by liaising with and working through the trade union movement.

Smith argues that such trends show 'the drift of government thinking towards a corporatist system of interest representation' and that this 'drift' reveals the intention, in the first place, of governments to 'shore up the legitimacy of central control' (20). The need to do so may stem from what Volker Ronge sees as the 'administrative dilemma' of modern pluralist-capitalist systems – that is, the growing necessity to act qualitatively and concretely without achieving corresponding support. Ronge assumes a specific interdependence between the political and the economic subsystem in the sense that the interdependence is determined economically by the capitalist mode of production and politically by the pluralist ordering of interests. His view is that not only is the political system controlling or trying to control its social environment, but that that environment and especially the economy in turn, are controlling or restricting the political system (21).

Government's growing responsibility for managing economic crises, controlling and alleviating the effects of unemployment, and for financing and administering a complex welfare system, has required at least until 1979 the generation of new types of support dependent upon consensus and participation (22). The need to act qualitatively and confidently may be seen to have obliged the state to enter partnership with an elite stratum of private interest groups offering advice, expertise, information and guarantees of support or non-impedance (23). The old abstract, general mechanisms of support have thus become obsolete in a post-industrial society; non-elected interest groups have come to occupy the role of 'semi-executive agents'.

It is Ronge's view that the test of a good policy is no longer in its legal-bureaucratic process of conversion, but in its _functional_ qualities. Political consent, he asserts, can no longer be presupposed as was the case in the liberal model, policies now depend increasingly on social participation. Inevitably, the issue of who does participate arises. Governments may welcome and facilitate the participation of some publics and seek to discourage or impede the involvement of others, particularly where they represent issues or grievances regarded by the government as politically 'inconvenient' (24). As Schattschneider has commented, 'In politics as in everything else it makes a great difference whose game we play. The rules of the game determine the requirements for success' (25).

Schattschneider sees politics as the domination and subordination of conflicts. A pluralist democracy will secure its survival by managing conflict through the establishment of priorities among a multiplicity of potential conflicts. Indeed, it was his view that there is no more certain way of destroying the meaning of politics than to treat all issues as if they were free and equal. Politics may only become meaningful when governments establish

priorities. Increasingly, post-war British governments have either chosen, or have been obliged, to
place economic growth at the top of the political
agenda with the result that welfare reform has been
subordinated to the vagaries of increased national
productivity (26).

Schattschneider, and more recently Wootton and
Richardson and Jordan, have raised the problem of
immobilism, of too many groups 'getting in on the
act'. They each have suggested that the system may
only work 'by being selective and biased; if
everybody got into the act the unique advantages of
this form of organisation would be destroyed, for it
is possible that if all interests could be mobilised
the result would be a stalemate' (27). Indeed,
Wootton has spoken of the accommodation of too many
interests as leading to 'pluralist stagnation', a
situation of impasse (28). The result, then, is that
'probably about 90 per cent of the people cannot get
into the pressure system ... the system is skewed,
loaded and unbalanced in favour of a fraction of a
minority' (29). If the view is accepted that it is
the executive, the bureaucracy and the various policy
communities which largely determine the procedural
norms and values of the policy-making process and
that this is largely dominated by economic factors
and economic/occupational associations, then it is
reasonable to conclude that 'whoever decides what the
game is about decides also who can get into the game'
(30).

A major task of groups such as CPAG then, is to
undermine the exclusivity of the 'game' either by
breaking into it themselves, through a reformulation
of the 'rules' achievable by the injection of new
values or by forging co-operation with established
'players' of the game. It is clear that the existing
pluralist order in Britain is already under attack by
those excluded from it. The attack may take various
forms depending on the goals and values of the
protagonists. Some, such as the Claimants Union, have
chosen to reject the current order altogether and
have devoted their energies to its replacement.
Others, like CPAG, have chosen to remain critical but
largely to work from within. Either way, outsiders,
by choice or by necessity, share a common cause in
their representation of publics organised out of the
mainstream of politics. As Ronge notes:

> the chief values of pluralist democracy -
> maintenance of the political and social system
> in principle, acceptance of the 'rules of the

11

game' in social interactions, use of limited and
legal power only, negotiation and compromise as
dominant and accepted methods of political
action - are increasingly questioned and even
violated by social groups because of their
discontent with the concrete outcome of those
rules and their belief of being structurally
under-privileged. (31)

CPAG - INSIDER OR OUTSIDER?

The Child Povery Action Group seeks to represent one
such social group, the poor, whom most observers
would see as structurally underprivileged. As part of
a strategy to overcome this underprivilege CPAG has,
over the last 21 years, employed most of the
conventional tactics open to interest groups -
parliamentary lobbying, the raising of parliamentary
questions and adjournment debates, media campaigns,
petitions, detailed policy submissions to central
government departments. Two strategies employed by
the Group stand out above the rest. The first is
CPAG's relationship with the Labour Party, the second
is that with the trade union movement.
    The insider-outsider dichotomy favoured by
Grant as an explanation of the influence of the group
process upon government provides a useful framework
within which the role-play and activity of CPAG may
be considered. Grant speaks of two types of outsider
or non-established group - those who are outsiders by
choice, and those who are outsiders by necessity.
While the findings of Bill Jordan make clear that the
Claimants Union has deliberately chosen and upheld
its outsider status (32), the identity of the Child
Poverty Action Group is less clear and may well be
something of a hybrid. Grant says, for example, that
'Those groups which are outsider groups by choice are
careful not to become too closely entangled with the
politico-administrative system because they wish to
challenge accepted authority and institutions.
Rather than becoming part of the existing system,
they wish to replace it or alter it in some
fundamental way' (33). While it will become clear
that CPAG has frequently advocated sweeping reform of
social and economic policy, often, in the process,
resorting to strong moral attacks upon vested
interest, the Group has never seriously raised or
considered wholesale replacement of the existing
order. Instead, it has favoured a strategy of reform
which has, to some extent, become interlinked with

its own desire to enter the 'game'.

CPAG's apparent hybrid role may be explored further if one considers its response to what Grant sees as the two principal strategies open to outsiders: those of bringing about fundamental change 'by attempting to change public attitudes towards certain problems' and the adoption of 'more militant strategies such as demonstrations aimed at administratives agencies' (34). While it will be shown that the educative role implicit in the first strategy has been strongly favoured by CPAG, the conflict-confrontational alternative has been largely eschewed and has, instead, become the hallmark of the Claimants Union and more localised groups urging and employing direct action.

Study of the Child Povery Action Group becomes especially fruitful in that Grant largely confines his classification to the relationship between groups and government and perhaps underplays the equally revealing relationships between interest groups themselves and between interest groups and opposition parties. Taking the latter relationship first, it is important to note that many of those who later came to found and work for or through CPAG had already long been active in the policy-making structure of the Labour Party, most notably the Party's Social Policy Sub committee. While the representatives of interest groups other than the TUC may not be officially co-opted onto such committees, CPAG staff and members have long constituted an active caucus within the Social Policy Sub committee: the Group's ideas have enjoyed a continuing currency. In some sense, then, CPAG has enjoyed a modified insider status within the Labour Party though not, as will be seen, within Labour governments. Indeed, the Group's failure to develop that status when the Party came to power or, perhaps, its rather naive belief that it could do so, may have had some influence upon the type of role CPAG developed for itself between 1965 and 1969.

Secondly, we may note CPAG's relationship with the trade union movement. It is here that the relationship between groups themselves, rather than between groups and government, is explored. Significantly, it is a relationship that could be viewed as that between an outsider group in the shape of CPAG and an insider group in the form of the TUC, at least in the case of Labour governments, and, to a lesser extent, individual trade unions. If we accept that structures of social and political inequality are inherently resistant to change then it may be argued that the members of the established or insider stratum have the motivation and, in general, the resources to sustain their position and transmit the advantages it brings to others that they favour, i.e. those groups obliged or determined to articulate their own preferences via the patronage of the insider groups in the hope of achieving back-door access to a government which has otherwise chosen to overlook them (35).

Crucially, of course, questions arise as to how and why CPAG found itself having to seek liaison with what it viewed as insiders after 1974, and why it was not able to develop such a status itself. The answer may partly lie in the nature of poverty as an issue and in the ability of groups to force it onto the political agenda and, secondly, in the role played by the poor themselves in contemporary British politics. Frequently, however, the fate of poverty as a political priority, and of the poor as a structurally underprivileged group, will be determined by the demands and influence of other publics and issues. For example, the interests of both the trade union movement and the business community in the sphere of taxation policy may well conflict with that of claimant groups whose material welfare is inextricably bound up with the level of tax revenue flowing into government. A reversal or stemming of the flow may easily develop a justification on the part of governments for effecting the sort of cuts in welfare expenditure that were in evidence between 1970-3, 1976-8, and which we are now experiencing once again in the mid-eighties in the wake of massive unemployment, demographic change and the fiscal redefinition of Beveridge by Normal Fowler. Ultimately, the ability of a group to influence policy comes down to its resources, its skills, its representativity and its capacity to apply sanctions against an unsympathetic or intransigent administration.

The dangers of powerful interest groups, often representing relatively small publics, entrenching themselves at the critical power centres are considerable. The location of power is increasingly shifted from the legislature to the executive and the bureaucracy; the representative claims and responsiveness of group leaders to their own members may diminish as they become more institutionalised. Furthermore, the intensity of group competition and the standards of political morality and social priority may decline as some issues are not given definition or adequate recognition because of the

system's prevailing bias towards certain interest
groupings. Indeed, the phenonmenon of group
institutionalisation has been described as 'a
remarkable contracting out of general political
responsibilty ... interested groups are becoming
less and less inclined to hold a general opinion or
attitude and to seek to persuade public opinion to
support it as they grow more and more determined (and
organised) to secure the best terms for themselves,
within the framework of a government's (any
government) policy' (36).

There is a danger, then, of powerful publics
arrogating too much power to themselves and usurping
the functions of the legislature. Private interest
groups have now largely superseded the Commons'
former function of supplying information and
expertise to both the bureaucracy and the general
public. Interests and publics formerly represented
by Parliament are now more and more the focus and
prerogative of structured group demands with the
result that the representative and informative
functions of Parliament have been seen as virtually
defunct. 'The primary function of the politician –
the adjustment and reconciliation of different
interests and ideas - is abruptly terminated at the
point where it is most important: the adjustment and
reconciliation of the industrial and commercial
interests - capital, management and labour - on which
the prosperity and future of the country depend.
(37)'

It is against this trend towards what some
writers have described as 'corporatism' (38) that the
'tropical growth in consumer groups', detailed by
Smith, has taken place. Their emergence and
subsequent attempts to break into the insider stratum
poses the dilemma of increasing immobilism in the
policy-making process. However, their general
failure to do so lends growing support to the belief
that British policy-making is, and will continue to
be, dominated by a system of elite pluralism. The
emergence of this order has been assisted and
consolidated by the emergence of what may be termed
'technocracy' and by the dramatic shift in the
location of power to the executive and administration
in the post-war period. Inevitably, the extent to and
way in which political influence may be achieved is
largely determined by a group's capacity to adapt its
organisation and its values to a bargaining framework
constructed by these institutions. It may be argued
that the group which does or can adapt its style and
preferences to suit the rules and values imposed by

the policy-making process and which does or can reflect prevailing norms and values has a much greater chance of achieving its goals than does a group unwilling or unable to meet these requirements.

Significantly, many of the publics which resort to direct action do so for one of two key reasons: (a) they are unable to gain consultative access to government and direct action remains the only feasible alternative for influence; or (b) they are unwilling to compromise their principles and interests by submission to a bargaining process that favours incrementalism and demands acquiescence and trade-off. It may well be that some groups prefer not to involve themselves in the consultative and bargaining process for fear that, once involved, the superior institutional resources of the bureaucracy, the executive and other interest groups will be brought to bear thus adversely affecting the effective placement of their own preferences.

With these factors in mind, Benewick and Smith have concluded that 'although it is a sad commentary, it is often through forms of direct action that the moral basis of politics is kept before the government and the public' (39). Direct action now characterises political activity on such fundamental issues as homelessness, poverty, abortion, environmental degradation, unemployment, apartheid, nuclear power, industrial closures and women's rights. The relationship between effort expended and success achieved in these areas is adversely disproportionate. The inevitable question is, why?

DIFFERENTIAL ACCESS AND THE OBSTACLES TO REFORM

The structural changes which are thought to have consolidated the corporatist trend, and which have partially or wholly excluded the interests of smaller groups, have already been noted. It now remains briefly to identify the other reasons why these groups remain largely unsuccessful. Most striking is the overwhelming differential access to resources enjoyed by various interest groups. The term 'resources' may be seen to cover finance, expertise, contacts, leadership skills and familiarity with the rules of the game (40).

More fundamental than any of these, however, is the problem of self-identification; the ability or willingness of those with shared interests or values to perceive that they constitute a group, potential or otherwise. It is similarly difficult to frame

issues for popular or governmental consumption when
dealing with those like poverty, which can be both
vague and specific and absolute and relative at the
same time. Overcoming both obstacles is crucial to a
group's development and its propensity for success.
In addition, problems of this sort are further
compounded by the nature of many social or moral
issues which militate against the mobilisation of
support and the building of a permanent, coherent
membership. Apart from the clear social barriers to
mobilisation caused by the stigma attached to certain
issues, many problems affect individuals for a short
time only - unemployment and homelessness may be
useful examples - and the rapid turnover in
membership that may occur within a group as
individual problems are resolved may prove
disruptive and demoralising for activists. The
Claimants and Unemployed Workers Unions, for
example, have found it difficult to sustain their
activities and their representative base because of
the highly transient or 'intermittent' nature of
their memberships (41).

On the other hand, social stigma has been an
important constraining factor in the Campaign for
Homosexual Equality's efforts to mobilise interest
and support among both homosexuals and hetero-
sexuals. Stigma, combined with the media's
'scrounger-phobia', has also hindered the mobilisation of the poor in particular, and welfare claimants
in general. Even allowing for a reasonable degree of
expertise, resources and articulation some publics
will inevitably regard themselves as the victims of
the prevailing biases within the political system and
their sense of social deprivation and structural
underprivilege may lead them to conclude that they
have only two alternative responses open to them -
passivity leading to alienation or direct action
which may lead to their denunciation as deviants
employing illicit political tactics.

There is a third alternative, of course - one
which may well require little or no participation
from these publics themselves. That is the
intervention of middle-class activists on their
behalf, activists possessing the skills and
organisational requirements for political influence
that their clients lack (42). The Child Poverty
Action Group is one such group whose traditional role
has been to articulate both the statistics of poverty
and the sense of deprivation experienced by the poor.
In 1965, when the Group was established in response
to evidence of a startling increase in child poverty,

most observers might have been forgiven for expecting it to have an early influence in social policy matters. After all, a so-called 'reformist' Labour government had just come to power, many of the Group's leading members and supporters had been influential in the Party during its period in opposition, and the abolition of poverty had figured at the hustings during the 1964 General Election.

Yet the Child Poverty Action Group has encountered a number of serious obstacles to its progress over the last two decades. Some of these have been the direct shortcomings of post-war legislation, some have been of its own making and have resulted from its own political misjudgement, from its uneasy and constraining relationship with the Labour Party and from its own lack of representativity and effective sanctions. These include what some have seen as a poorly judged 'election campaign' in 1970 when the Group alienated support within the Labour Party, and rather more recent and fragmented attempts to secure influence by liaison with bodies such as the TUC. Even so it must be said that the 1970 election campaign genuinely represented the opinions of many associated with the group and, looking back, clearly consolidated its reputation for integrity and independence – a fact which no doubt enabled it to work across the party political spectrum in the years to come and which signalled that it would not operate in the pocket of one party or another. Other obstacles have not been of the Group's making, and have seriously impeded its efforts to bring about an effective strategy to alleviate poverty. Notable among these were the effects of the deflationary package of measures presented by the Labour government in July 1966, the apparent reversal of Labour's priorities during the Wilson governments, the failure of Labour's review of social services, the Conservative public expenditure cuts of 1970-3; the debacle over family allowance increases in 1967-8, and the introduction of child benefits in 1975-7. Perhaps the most striking Achilles heel of CPAG in its role as a 'pressure group for the poor' is the relatively low level of regular, formal contact it enjoys with departmental civil servants, a fact which further requires that the emphasis of this study be upon Group-Party Group to Group and Group-trade union relations. Given the structural underprivilege of the poor, the type of role CPAG claims for itself and the pledges made by successive governments since 1964 in the field of social policy, a study of the activities, aims and the changing political strategy of CPAG would seem to provide a useful opportunity to consider recent trends in interest-group politics in Britain in a more specific context. That is all the more timely given the current governments plans in 1986 for a far-reaching and controversial reform of social security.

We first consider therefore, the publication of an important study of poverty in the mid-1960s that prompted the emergence of CPAG and which, initially at least, galvanised Party thinking on the problem.

NOTES

1. Banting, K., Poverty, Politics and Policy, (Macmillan, 1979), p.5.
2. Land, H., 'The Introduction of Family Allowances: An Act of Heroic Justice', in Hall, P., Land, H., Parker, R. and Webb, A., Change, Choice and Conflict in Social Policy (Heinemann, 1978), pp.164-6.
3. Ibid., pp.227-30.
4. Mass Observation, Britain and Her Birth Rate (Curwin Press, 1945). See also Report on the Royal Commission on the Population, Cmnd. 7695 (1949).
5. Land, op.cit., p.223.
6. He notes, 'All legislative procedure is loaded with devices controlling the flow of explosive materials into the governmental apparatus. All forms of organisation have a bias in favour of the exploitation of some kind of conflict and the suppression of others because organisation is the mobilisation of bias. Some issues are organised into politics while others are organised out'. Schattschneider, E.E., The Semi-Sovereign People: A Realist's View of Democracy in America (Holt, Rinehart & Winston, New York, 1960), p.69.
7. Powell, E., in Six Essays on the Welfare State (Granada Television, 23 January 1977).
8. Wyn Grant, for example, argues that 'insiders' are characterised in one of two ways: (1) They may be established by government or with government encouragement; or (2) They may have a permanent staff 'Who have a vested interest in maintaining and developing their existing network of contacts with the civil services'. Grant says that 'The most important distinguishing characteristic of insider groups is their tendency to adopt a 'strategy of responsibility'.' Grant, W., 'Insider Groups,

19

Outsider Groups and Interest Group Strategies in Britain' (unpublished, University of Warwick, 1977), p.5. See also, Peters, B.G., 'Insiders and Outsiders', Administration and Society, Vol. 9, No.2 (1977).

9. As Stewart notes 'the cause group represents only a point of view about the way in which government and Parliament should act, in many cases a point of view very far from being generally accepted. But even when its viewpoint is accepted the group cannot expect to be automatically consulted. It is not necessary to the conduct of affairs'. Stewart, J.D., British Pressure Groups (Clarendon, 1958), p.26.

10. David Truman has argued that the extent to which a group achieves effective access to the institutions of government is the result of a complex of interdependent factors, which may be simplified into three broad categories: (1) factors relating to a group's strategic position in society; (2) factors associated with the internal characteristics of the groups; and (3) factors peculiar to the governmental institutions themselves. Truman, D., The Governmental Process (Alfred Knopf, New York, 1966).

11. Richardson, J.J. and Jordan, G., Governing under Pressure (Martin Robertson, 1979), pp.43-4.

12. Truman, op.cit., p.105.

13. Commons, J.R., The Economics of Collective Action (Macmillan, New York, 1951), p.262.

14. Ibid.

15. Bentley, A.F., The Process of Government (1908) in Odegard, P. (ed.) (Bellknap Press, Harvard, 1967).

16. See, for example, Richardson, J.J. and Gustafsson, G., 'Concepts of Rationality and the Policy Process', European Journal of Political Research, No.7 (1979), pp.415-36.

17. Commenting on Bentley's analysis, Mackenzie has concluded that 'Government is the resultant and is wholly the resultant of group pressures in this sense and so is "law in the broadest sense" which is "one form of statement of the equilibrium of interests, the balancing of groups". Government "in the narrowest sense" is defined as "a differentiated, representative group, or set-up of groups (organ or set of organs)" performing specified governing functions for the underlying groups of the population'. Mackenzie, W.J.H., 'Pressure Groups: The Conceptual Framework', Political Studies, Vol. 3 (October 1955), p.249.

18. Smith, T., The Politics of the Corporate

Economy (Martin Robertson, 1979).

19. Ibid. See also Seyd, P., 'Shelter: The National Campaign for the Homeless', Political Quarterly, No. 46(4) (1975), pp.418-31.

20. Smith, T., Trends and Tendencies in Reordering the Representation of Interests in Britain, paper to the PSA conference (Nottingham, 1976), p.8.

21. Ronge, V., 'The Politicisation of Administration in Advanced Capitalist Societies', Political Studies, Vol. 22 (March 1974).

22. See Rokkan, S., 'Numerical Democracy and Corporate Pluralism', in Dahl, R.A., Political Oppositions in Western Democracies (Yale University Press, New Haven, 1966).

23. Charles Andrain comments that 'pluralism represents a society of privileged groups; not one where several different groups have relative equality. Consistent with this finding, pluralistic governments often seem controlled not by a balance of diverse groups but rather by a few powerful groups. Not all groups have the resources to participate in the group equilibrium'. Andrain, C.F., Political Life and Social Change (Wadsworth Press, California, 1970), p.114.

24. David Ricci notes 'certain important interests are persistently weak, continually ineffective and repeatedly disregarded in the process of political bargaining. Consumers are in this category, since they lack powerful organisations, as do migrant farm labourers, white-collar workers, the poor and the multitudes with an interest of peace'. Ricci, D.M. Community Power and Democratic Theory: The Logic of Political Analysis (Random House, New York, 1971), p.79.

25. Schattschneider, op.cit., p.47.

26. See Haniff, G.H., 'Politics, Development and Social Policy: A Cross-National Analysis', European Journal of Political Research, No.4 (1976), pp.361-76. Thomas Dye notes that 'most comparative, cross-national policy studies indicate that wealth and welfare policies, regardless of political systems are clearly associated with costs of economic development'. Dye, T.R., Policy Analysis (University of Albama Press, 1976), p.51.

27. Schattschneider, op.cit., p.34.

28. Wootton, G., Pressure Politics in Contemporary Britain (D.G. Heath, 1978), ch.10.

29. Schattschneider, op.cit., p.35.

30. Ibid., p.102.

31. Ronge, op.cit.

32. Jordan, B., Paupers: The Making of the New Claiming Class (Routledge & Kegan Paul, 1973), pp.20-1.

33. Grant, op.cit., p.9.

34. Ibid.

35. There are considerable dangers here as Ricci, op.cit., has noted: 'the danger in such relationships, which became symbiotic between private interest groups and public agencies, is that established groups acquire some of the power of the state and can use it to discipline their own members and prevent the rise of groups with opposing interests and alternative policies' (p.79).

36. Fairlie, H., The Life of Politics (Methuen, 1968), p.231.

37. Ibid.

38. Corporatism has been defined as 'a system of interest representation in which the constituent units are organised into a limited number of singular, compulsory, non-competitive, hierarchically differentiated categories, recognised or licensed (if not created) by the state and granted a deliberate representational monopoly within their respective categories in exchange for observing certain controls on their selection of leaders and articulation of demands and supports'. Schmitter, P.C., Corporatism and Public Policy in Authoritarian Portugal (Sage, London, 1975), p.9.

39. Benewick, R., and Smith T., Direct Action and Democratic Politics (George Allen & Unwin, 1972), p.13.

40. Graeme Moodie and Gerald Studdert-Kennedy include control over the possession of access to decision-makers as 'a possible resource', bearing in mind the frequently substantial power of confidants, secretaries, acquaintances, etc. Indeed they regard access to decision-makers as so important in the UK that 'For lack of it, a group may be driven to disaffection from the political system, and if control of significant resources is allied to denial of access, the situation is ripe for rebellion'. Opinions, Publics and Pressure Groups (George Allen & Unwin, 1970), p.68.

41. Rose, H., 'Up Against the Welfare State', in Miliband, R. and Saville, J. (eds.), Socialist Register (Merlin, London, 1974).

42. Saul Alinksy notes: 'These types of ... people, usually by virtue of education, background and personal manners, have much more in common with the representatives of the formal agencies than do the rank and file'. He notes, further, that officials

themselves 'feel much more at home with these people and find them more articulate and more able to talk in terms and values that ... they are comfortable with'. Alinsky, S., <u>Reveille for Radicals</u> (Random House, New York, 1969), p.66.

Chapter **Two**

THE REDISCOVERY OF POVERTY

In December 1965 Brian Abel-Smith and Peter Townsend wrote in their study, The Poor and the Poorest:

> Two assumptions have governed much economic thinking in Britain since the war. The first is that we have 'abolished' poverty. The second is that we are a much more equal society; that the differences between the living standards of the rich and poor are much smaller than they used to be. These assumptions are of great practical as well as theoretical importance. They form the background to much of the discussion of social and economic policy. But are they true? (1)

This was the principal question the authors sought to answer in their comparative study of the nature and extent of poverty in the years 1953 and 1960. The significance of their study lay in its fresh interpretation and rather disturbing analysis of existing data from the Ministry of Labour's Family Expenditure Surveys for 1953-4 and 1960, and it did much to undermine conventional wisdom about the extent of poverty in Britain. As much of their work was devoted to exploding the contemporary myths regarding the incidence of poverty among children it is appropriate that present interest is confined to that section of the population.

Between 1953 and 1960 the proportion of children increased by approximately 0.5 per cent in both the total population and in the samples used in the two Ministry of Labour surveys. The proportion of children in households with 'low levels of living' increased by 1 per cent. However, as the authors noted, such apparently insignificant changes concealed much larger increases in family size. In the 1953-60 period the total population increased by

about 4 per cent. Yet the number of families with
four dependent children increased by about 20 per
cent, those with five children by about 26 per cent
and those with six or more children by 45 per cent.

Compounding this increase in family size was
their equally important observation that the
economic position of such families was in relative
decline in the same period. Although general levels
of income rose by just over 50 per cent in money
terms, the family allowance for the second child
remained at its 1953 level of 8 shillings (40p),
while that for a third or subsequent child increased
a mere 25 per cent, from 8 to 10 shillings (40-50p).
The combined effects of inflation and rising consumer
expectations led the authors to comment: 'No doubt
the failure of family allowances to keep pace with
the living standards of the community contributed to
the higher proportion of households found to have low
levels of living in 1960 than in 1953-54' (2). In
1960 alone there were nearly 1 million individuals
who received pensions or other state benefits and
whose incomes still remained below the assistance
rates plus rent.

Townsend and Abel-Smith's analysis revealed
that not only were a substantial minority of the
population, in addition to those receiving National
Assistance, living at or below National Assistance
standards, but also that a substantial minority were
not receiving National Assistance who appeared to
qualify for it. For perhaps the first time, then, the
phenomenon of low or no take-up of benefits was
clearly and coherently exposed. The authors' own
reaction was hardly surprising: 'The legitimacy of
the system of National Assistance is therefore called
in question'.

The most significant of their findings was the
extent of poverty among children. It had been
generally assumed by politicians and academics alike
that the problem of poverty was largely confined to
the aged section of the population. Abel-Smith and
Townsend discovered, however, that there were more
people who were not aged than there were aged among
the poor households of 1960. They estimated that
there were about 2.25 million children in low-income
households in 1960.

Thus quantitatively the problem of poverty
among children is more than two-thirds of the
size of poverty among the aged. This fact has
not been given due emphasis in the policies of
the political parties. It is also worth

observing that there were substantially more
children in poverty than adults of working age.
There is a simple, if relatively expensive,
remedy for the problem of poverty among children
- to substantially increase family allowances,
particularly for the large family. (3)

Their study concluded with the revelation that some
5-6 per cent of the population were in low-income
households because wages, even where supplemented by
family allowances, were insufficient to raise them
above the minimum level; an additional 4 per cent
lived in households receiving insufficient social
insurance benefits (usually pensions); while a
further 4-5 per cent of the population were in
low-income households because of their non-entitle-
ment to full National Assistance grants. The authors
ended with a challenge to government: 'the fact that
nearly a third of the poor were children suggests the
need for a readjustment of priorities in plans for
extensions and developments'.
    There were, then, two inextricably related
factors in the Abel-Smith-Townsend strategy for
alleviating poverty. First, they had identified the
apparent need for government action in increasing
both the level and the application of family
allowances. Secondly, they established a clear
causal relationship between poverty and low pay, made
all the more evident in a period of general
prosperity and rising expectations. The sense of
deprivation felt by this stratum of the work force
was, therefore, likely to be more acute in the
affluent 1950s and early 1960s than in the 1940s when
the exigencies of both war and post-war
reconstruction ensured that most of the population
experienced deprivation in some form or another.
    Abel-Smith and Townsend's emphasis on the
extraction and interpretation of extant government
data on poverty is wholly consistent with the
development of informed opinion preceding the
publication of their study. Academics and Labour
politicians, often meeting under the umbrella of the
Party's Social Policy Sub-Committee, had been slowly
converging on the issue of poverty since the late
1950s. In its 1950 manifesto, the Party had claimed
to have eliminated destitution, and the following
year had echoed this self-congratulation in a further
manifesto:

    Now we have a National Health Service scheme
    which is the admiration of the post-war world.

Then, we had the workhouse and the poor law for the old people. Now we have a national insurance system covering the whole population with greatly improved pensions and a humane National Assistance Scheme. (4)

Initially, the Labour Party's claims appeared to have some substance. Rowntree and Lavers' third social survey of York appeared the same year and revealed, certainly in that locality, that the proportion of the working-class population living in poverty had fallen from 31.1 per cent in 1936 to 2.77 per cent in 1950 (5). In 1936 the two chief causes of poverty had been unemployment of the chief wage earner (28.6 per cent) and low wages (32.8 per cent); by 1950 the former did not even figure as a cause, and the latter accounted for only 1 per cent of those in poverty. The two new principal causes were old age (68.1 per cent) and sickness (21.3 per cent) (6). However, the York survey did stress that while poverty in absolute terms may have appeared to diminish, poverty as a relative concept had not. There remained an increasing number of families only marginally above the levels used to define the survey poverty line. Therefore, while giving some support to Labour's claims, the survey made important qualifications of its findings - though politicians and the media chose to interpret them rather selectively.

In 1957 Townsend had been among the first to question the complacency of Labour's manifestos and to dispute the popular notion that real poverty had been largely eliminated. His study of the aged in Bethnal Green, <u>Family Life of Old People</u> (7), revealed that one-third of his sample of old people had a personal income below the National Assistance Board's subsistence minimum, and that between a fifth and a quarter of all old people were not receiving the assistance to which they were entitled. By the mid-1950s the realities of post-war poverty had become of increasing concern to Labour ideologues. The influence of Labour academics like Richard Titmuss, Townsend and Abel-Smith through the Party's social policy-making committees had forced a critical re-appraisal of Labour's post-war outlook. Labour's 1955 election manifesto, for example, claimed that the 1945-51 Labour government had not actually 'abolished' poverty, but that it had, instead, 'begun to abolish the fear of old age, sickness and disablement which haunted working-class life before the war'.

The role of academics in assisting what Stringer
and Richardson have termed 'problem definition' (8)
and in helping to get the poverty issue onto the
political agenda was particularly crucial during
this period when both the major parties appeared
unclear and ambivalent as to the nature and extent of
poverty. Nowhere was this more important than in the
publication of The Poor and the Poorest. The work of
academics in raising the issue of poverty within the
Labour Party and in providing information about it,
largely generated by their own research, helped
initiate an intra-party debate that persuaded Labour
to incorporate 'an attack on poverty' into its own
political agenda. In 1959, influenced by Townsend's
Bethnal Green survey, the Party hastened to make the
problem of poverty among the aged a key election
issue: 'the living standards of more than half of our
old-age pensioners are a national disgrace. About a
million are driven by poverty to seek National
Assistance and another 500,000 would be entitled to
receive it but are too proud to do so' (9). The
Party's leader, Hugh Gaitskell, raised expectations
further when he declared, 'the real challenge to us
is whether we're going once and for all to abolish
poverty in old age. The Labour Party is the only
party that can do that' (10).

NATIONAL ASSISTANCE AND PROBLEM DEFINITION

Events immediately preceding the 1964 General
Election raised further hopes that social reform was
imminent. The years 1962-3 witnessed a concerted
attempt by some academics to advance the frontiers of
research by persuading the National Assistance Board
to improve its irregular and meagre statistical
output on the nature and extent of poverty.
Throughout these years a largely LSE-based ginger
group numbering Titmuss, Townsend, Tony Lynes, David
Donnison, Michael Young and Dorothy Wedderburn
within its ranks, most of them committed Labour
supporters, continuously pressed the National
Assistance Board (NAB) Chairman, Lord Ilford to
increase the Board's output of data so that a
coherent, national picture of poverty could be drawn
up.
Hugh Heclo has referred to such groups as
'policy-watchers' and notes that it is through their
scrutiny of, and interaction with, government 'that
public policy issues tend to be refined, evidence
debated, and alternative options worked out' (11). In

essence, their campaign was aimed at making a complete jigsaw for which each held only a small piece. It was hoped that this sustained lobbying would persuade the Board to release a wealth of data as yet unseen by academics and would, subsequently, enable academics to test their suspicions of the government's failure or reluctance to perceive the full implications of that data (12).

This lack of freely available government information was an important obstacle to problem definition. Until an improved and increased flow of information took place any critique of government policy on poverty was weakened by resort to generalisation. The limiting of information, a serious blow to the policy-watcher, can be a useful tactic in controlling the political debate and keeping the government's agenda to manageable proportions. Stringer and Richardson note, for example, that

> from the point of view of the politicians and
> Civil Servants yet another issue forcing itself
> onto the political agenda may appear as an
> unwelcome intrusion into an already overburden-
> ed system which has not the capacity to respond
> positively. Far better, perhaps, to so arrange
> things that it is very difficult for anyone to
> claim that there is a problem in the first
> place. (13)

Wedderburn and Townsend had already shown in 1962 that the NAB was gathering and collating information, but was publishing selective and incomplete conclusions (14). Using the findings of the Ministry of Labour's Household Expenditure Surveys, Townsend found that in 1953-4 about 8 per cent of the population (nearly 4 million people) were living at a standard no higher than the average family on National Assistance. His preliminary comparisons for 1960 showed that the numbers had nearly doubled. Some $7\frac{1}{2}$ million people were now to be found in households with incomes at or below the average amount allowed to similar families on National Assistance: 'As many as two million had less than the "basic" National Assistance scale on which, it has been officially stated, nobody is expected to live' (15). Using the same Expenditure Surveys, Wedderburn found similar anomalies, and concluded that there were twice as many people living at or below National Assistance level than there were receiving assistance. Confirming both the findings of the 1951 York survey and Townsend's Bethnal Green study, Wedderburn revealed that one-third of those old people who appeared eligible for National Assistance in 1959-60 were not receiving it, and that one-eighth of <u>all</u> old age pensioners were living on incomes below National Assistance level. It was left to Tony Lynes, research assistant to Professor Richard Titmuss, to collate these findings and ask why the Welfare State's attack on poverty had failed and, most disturbing, why poverty had apparently increased. Superficially, the correlation between non-take-up of assistance and the socio-psychological overtones of stigma provided a ready answer for apologists of the Beveridge plan.

However, this could hardly detract from the failure of institutions to fulfil their prescribed roles in the welfare system. A prime target for Lynes, therefore, was the agency charged with the responsibility of measuring and alleviating poverty - the National Assistance Board. A principal criticism concerned the Board's ineffectual efforts in the public relations field. Lynes, amongst others, felt that the Board had failed to present itself to the claimant as either sympathetic or helpful. Instead it had become 'extremely conscious of its role as guardian of the public purse' (16). Its publicity tended to be so discrete as to be inaudible; its impact upon the press was invariably confined to accusations that it was paymaster to 'scroungers' and the idle. Its vulnerability and resulting ineffectuality was aptly described by Howard Glennerster: 'It seems afraid to raise its voice too much in case too many people hear' (17). The kind of publicity the Board attracted from a popular press given to sensationalism and exaggeration was unlikely to encourage it to advertise its services too widely or with more enthusiasm (18). In short, the NAB felt it was on a hiding to nothing.

However, there may have been a more rational, administrative explanation for the Board's apparent reticence. Michael Hill has argued that NAB officials were obliged to reconcile two conflicting objectives (19). On the one hand, they had a clear duty to meet needs and to promote the welfare of claimants. On the other hand, they also had a duty, often pointed out to them by the press, to protect public funds from abuse and fraudulent applications. As R.G.S. Brown has commented: 'This implied reasonable conscient-iousness in verifying the applicant's statements ... The way of life of some of these cases was not at

first sight likely to command a great deal of
sympathy from a hard-working white-collar worker.
The investigating officer could be under some social
pressure from his fellow officers not to be taken for
a ride' (20).
   The role and attitude of the NAB and its
officials were influenced by a further example of
conflicting interest. Michael Hill has shown that the
alternative to leaving some measure of discretion to
officials is to enforce a stricter definition of
entitlement, which may result in some needy cases not
being met, or to define it so liberally that there is
a real danger of over-expenditure and waste. The
result, says Brown, was that the NAB was reluctant to
publicise the full range of exceptions that could be
made to the normal rates because it would then become
very difficult to deny extra, discretionary payments
to cases that were not exceptional (21). Inevitably,
the NAB may have seen its hybrid role as a limiting
factor in the development of a more generous,
sympathetic and better advertised approach to the
claimant.
   Lynes also pointed to another handicap from
which the Board suffered. Its officers received very
little specialised training for a job demanding much
tact and patience. Of its staff's capacity to
discharge their duties effectively, sympathetically
and without undue prejudice, he observed: 'some have
recently attended courses in human relations, but
most still rely largely on skills and attitudes
passed on by their predecessors, whose apprentice-
ship was served under the old Poor Law. A person who,
on his first application for assistance, happens to
meet a tactless officer may be permanently deterred
from applying again' (22).
   It is useful to consider here a view that will
be discussed at some length later. Hilary Rose has
suggested that difficulties of the sort described by
Lynes persist because of the conditions of employment
experienced by welfare staff and the perceived
disparity between their low <u>earned</u> income and the
<u>unearned</u> assistance dispensed to claimants. She
charges that staff were often paid little above, and
sometimes considerably below, the benefit levels of
some of the claimants with whom they deal. In some
cases, then, the victim of the dehumanising ritual of
the claiming and dispensing of benefits may not be
the claimant but the dispenser, a fact which was not
lost upon those DHSS staff protesting about
conditions of employment in the Department's
Birmingham offices in 1982. She notes: 'The low-paid

bureaucrat behind the desk of the Social Security
Office or the Housing Department stands at the abyss
of poverty he confronts daily, held back only by his
respectability' (23).

Perhaps the most serious criticism levelled at
the NAB was its highly discriminatory practice of
applying the 'wage-stop ruling' (24) against
unemployed claimants so that they could not receive
more out of work than they could earn in full-time
employment. For many, a disturbing feature of the
wage-stop was its tendency to keep a large number of
families below the prescribed minimum National
Assistance rates laid down in statute by Parliament,
because the chief wage-earner had earned less than
those rates in full-time employment (25). Writing in
1963, Lynes pointed out, 'The heavy unemployment of
last Winter drew attention to the "wage-stop" rule
under which the allowance paid by the NAB to an
unemployed person is not allowed to exceed his normal
earnings. The number of cases in which, under this
rule, families receiving less than the normal rates
of Assistance rose to 25,000 - one in eight of the
200,000 unemployed persons on National Assistance'
(26). Most disturbing, he felt, were the effects the
ruling had on the most vulnerable sections of the
population. 'After the recent increase in the
Assistance rates, the numbers affected by the
wage-stop rose still more. It is the families with
several children that suffer under this rule, and it
is little comfort to know that these families and
their children are below the National Assistance
level even when the father is in full-time work.'
(27)

In addition to the shortcomings of the Board
itself, Townsend, Lynes and Wedderburn had each
demonstrated the need to account for the phenomenon
of 'relative poverty' in any future discourse on the
incidence of poverty, 'the realisation that what any
society understands by poverty must depend on the
living standards of the population as a whole ... In
retrospect it is surprising that for so many years we
were content to leave the poorest groups among the
aged, the sick and the unemployed at a static level
of income while most other people were growing
richer' (28). This emphasis on the 'relative' nature
of poverty was important for a number of reasons, not
the least of which was the implication that the
tendency of post-war governments to view poverty as a
once-and-for-all, absolute social problem constituted an inaccurate definition of the problem.

Such inaccuracy may derive unintentionally from

unreliable information or an incomplete picture of
what is happening in a given policy area. An
important object of academic research in this period
was to correct such inaccuracy and to emphasise the
long-term, dynamic nature of poverty as a social
problem - a problem that could not be tackled in the
mopping-up fashion popularly prescribed in the early
1950s. The corollary of this emphasis on relative
poverty, of course, was the possibility that poverty
may not have been tackled in the early 1950s because
academics themselves, whose research is an important
source of information for government, had not
properly grasped the real nature of the problem.

Lynes' solution to the problems he and his
colleagues had identified was a five-point plan to
lift most of the poor above the NAB-defined poverty
line. Principally, he advocated a rise in National
Assistance rates and, where the NAB was shown to pay
less than the rates approved by Parliament,
investigation of the maladministration or 'misadmin-
istration'. Secondly, he saw improved National
Insurance benefits related to individual earnings
and an income guarantee to supplement the low incomes
of pensioners as a right. To assist families with
more than one child, he proposed an increase in
family allowances to an average of £1 8s (£1.40) per
child and the abolition of child tax allowances,
which had largely favoured higher income taxpayers.
This, he estimated, would cost about £290 million a
year but would be offset by the abolition of the tax
allowances which would net £350 million - more than
enough to fund the scheme. However, the interests of
other groups in society, combined with the possible
electoral impact such a sweeping change in fiscal
policy would have upon Party fortunes, ensured that,
at this stage at least, this would remain a
pipe-dream (29). Of contemporary significance were
his suggestions for periodic adjustments of all
social security payments to ensure that they reflect
rising living standards, a proposal favoured by both
the Labour and Liberal Parties. Finally, Lynes
called for a determined attempt to raise wages in
low-paid occupations. This, he felt, would partly
help to offset the punitive structure of the
wage-stop.

It is difficult to assess the full impact of
this rather short-lived tirade against the NAB. It is
tempting to argue that the anomalies and injustices
he and others exposed may have contributed directly
to the abolition of the NAB and its replacement by
the Supplementary Benefits Commission, which one of

these policy-watchers, David Donnison later came to chair. However, the most tangible outcome of this period was the shared experience of this academic coterie in translating their professional interest into political objection - an experience that was drawn upon and reapplied shortly afterwards when the need for a more permanent and structured pressure group was acknowledged. It is possible to detect among the activities of these policy-watchers the foundations for the development of a more sophisticated policy community at a later stage. Heclo observes that 'what they all (policy-watchers) have in common is the detailed understanding of specialised issues that comes from sustained attention to a given policy debate' (30). Ultimately, however, if policy-makers continue to resist or largely ignore information inputs or feedback from policy-watchers, an alternative course of action open to the latter will be the organisation of themselves or others into a structured interest group determined to enter and compete within the recognised policy community (31). It is to this next stage of development that we now turn.

NOTES

1. Abel-Smith, B. and Townsend, P., The Poor and the Poorest, Occasional Papers in Social Administration, No. 17 (Bell & Co., December 1965).
2. Ibid.
3. Ibid.
4. Quoted in Craig, F.W., British General Election Manifestos 1918-66, Political Reference Publications (1970), pp.132, 149.
5. Rowntree, B.S. and Lavers, G.R., Poverty and the Welfare State: A Third Social Survey of York Dealing Only With Economic Problems (Longman, 1951), ch.4.
6. MacFarlane, L.J., Issues in British Politics Since 1945 (Longman, 1975), p.55, Table 3.1.
7. Townsend, P., The Family Life of Old People: An Inquiry in East London (Routledge, 1957), pp.163-4.
8. Stringer, J. and Richardson, J.J., 'Managing the Political Agenda: Problem Definition and Policymaking in Britain', Parliamentary Affairs (Winter 1980).
9. MacFarlane, op.cit., p.56.
10. Butler, D. and Rose, R., The British General Election of 1959, Nuffield Election Studies

(Macmillan, 1960), p.55.

11. Heclo, H., 'Issue Networks and the Executive Establishment', in King, A., The New American Politics (American Enterprise Institute, 1978).

12. Indeed, Lynes, increasingly cast in the post of the group's Secretary, had complained in a letter to Douglas Houghton, Opposition spokesman on social services, on 13 February 1963 that 'discussion of the board's work is serious interrupted by lack of detailed information'. Commenting on this type of dilemma, Stringer and Richardson have noted 'When criticising governments for their failure adequately to define a problem or for deliberately attempting to manage its definition, we labour under the difficulty in many instances of lack of knowledge. When knowledge is confined in this way, how much easier it is for governments to control the emergence of issues; to define or redefine problems out of existence, with a view only to short-term expediency. A more open system, we might hope, would expose just what the government is up to' (op.cit., p.36).

13. Ibid., pp.23-4.

14. Poverty in Britain Today, Paper to Conference of the British Sociological Association (Brighton, 1962).

15. See Lynes, A., 'Poverty in the Welfare State', Aspect (August 1963), p.8.

16. Ibid.

17. Glennerster, H., National Assistance: Service or Charity? Young Fabian Pamphlet (Fabian Society, 1962).

18. For an analysis of the phenomenon of 'Scroungerphobia', See Golding, P. and Middleton, S., 'Why is the Press so Obsessed with Welfare Scroungers?', New Society (26 October 1978). The authors note that David Donnison, chairman of the SBC until its demise in 1981 'has repeatedly claimed that anti-claimant stories in the press contribute to stigma and the low take-up of benefits' and they comment themselves that 'The potency of the myth is discovered by its victims. The rhetoric and ideology of news in the British press about the welfare state is more often openly hostile to a broad-based welfare and social security system'.

19. Hill, M., 'The Exercise of Discretion in the National Assistance Board', Public Administration (1969), pp.75-90.

20. Brown, R.G.S., The Management of Welfare (Fontana, 1975), pp.94-5.

21. Ibid., p.96.

22. Lynes, op.cit., p.9.

23. Rose, H., Rights, Participation and Conflict, Poverty Pamphlet No. 5 (CPAG), p.13.

24. The introduction of the wage-stop actually pre-dates both the Conservative governments of 1951-64 and what might be termed the modern welfare state which has largely developed since 1945. Laurie Elks has noted that 'the rule has existed since the beginning of Unemployment Assistance in 1935 and can be traced back to the Poor Law Commissioners of 1834 and their rule of "less eligibility". At all times, the principle has remained that no man should be able to escape, through resort to the assistance of the state, from the hard facts of poverty at work'. Elks, L., The Wage-Stop, Poverty Pamphlet No. 17 (CPAG). The Labour government inherited the ruling in 1964 and gave it further life by incorporating it in Schedule 2, para. 5, of the Ministry of Social Security Act, 1966.

25. Ibid. See also Lynes, A., 'The Wage-Stop', Poverty, No.2 (Spring 1967), pp.4-6.

26. Lynes, 'Poverty in the Welfare State', p.9.

27. Poverty, No. 6 (Spring 1968), pp.6-7.

28. Lynes, 'Poverty in the Welfare State', p.10; and Townsend, P., 'The Meaning of Poverty', British Journal of Sociology, No.13 (1962), pp.210-27.

29. Unaware of some of the limitations and influences at work upon government efforts to establish priorities and formulate policy, the alternatives put forward by academics working in the field may appear one-dimensional, unrealistic and perhaps naive. Conversely, governments may deliberately obscure the influences at work to keep unwelcome issues off the agenda. R.G.S. Brown notes, for example, that 'Government-sponsored research can never wholly answer the criticism (however undeserved) that it can be steered away from politically inconvenient issues. There is also a fundamental point that internal research cannot, by definition, be expected to cover problems of which those who commission it are themselves aware. Per contra, the policy recommendations of academics who carry out independent research on social problems may lack realism or balance ... the outcome of which is in turn influenced by the policy preferences of the researchers' Brown, op.cit., p.197.

30. Heclo, op.cit., p.99.

31. See Gustafsson, G. and Richardson, J.J., 'Concepts of Rationality and the Policy Process',

European Journal of Political Research, No. 7 (1979),
pp.415-36.

Chapter Three

A PRESSURE GROUP FOR THE POOR

The Labour Party's apparent acceptance of the
'rediscovery' of poverty in the late 1950s may have
given some encouragement to those expecting early and
resolute action on the issue when and if the Party
came to power. Yet it was clear well before the 1964
General Election that the Party was moving in other
directions and was likely to establish expenditure
priorities which might preclude an early solution to
the problem. Birch has suggested that the Labour
initiative had been exhausted even before the
outbreak of the Korean War and that the Party's
leaders 'would, clearly, be more sympathetic to
demands for more freedom both in the economy and in
the social services, provided society still met its
basic needs, and they would ... be more inclined to
rely upon material improvement as the surest way to
raise the general standards of the people' (1). In
retrospect, the optimism expressed at the hustings in
1959 for Labour's plans to eradicate poverty seems
misplaced. Paul Foot has noted that the radical,
reforming tone of Labour in opposition in the mid- to
late 1950s may have been rather superficial at
leadership level and that by the 1964 election it had
shifted to an emphasis on 'efficiency', 'dynamism'
and the ability to produce and compete (2). One
student of the Party, David Coates, notes, for
example, that during the 1964 Election

> The 'problem' which the party placed before the
> electorate was not that of capitalism against
> socialism, but one of 'a sluggish and fitful
> economy' which had fallen behind its
> international competitors, which was ineffic-
> ient, whose management was drawn from too
> socially restricted a background, and which had
> failed to invest with sufficient vigour in the

new scientific and technological industries ...
and the 'solution' which they offered,
inevitably, was the election of a Labour
Government 'to energise and modernise our
industries' and 'to make Britain up-to-date,
vigorous, and capable of playing her full part
in world affairs'. (3)

It is Coates' view that Labour went to the hustings
in 1964 'behind a rhetoric of "science" and
"modernisation" that served both to unite the party
in the wake of Gaitskell's death, and to express in a
highly ambigious fashion the Wilson leadership's
overriding priorities of economic growth, a strong
currency, and an interventionist state' (4).
    Increasingly, Harold Wilson's emphasis on the
'white heat of the technological revolution' came to
displace the 1959 theme of closing the gap between
rich and poor. Wilson's highly administrative style
of politics, and his preoccupation with the theme of
economic growth as the prerequisite for social action
(5), had convinced many Labour activists that an
initiative in the welfare field must perforce come
from outside the Party leadership. This preoccupation with growth may well have been a genuine attempt
at agenda management. Clearly, Wilson saw a sound
logic in using economic growth as a platform for the
social transformation of society. If growth was
genuinely seen as the panacea for society's ills, it
was reasonable for that issue to dominate the
political agenda to the exclusion of others -
provided, of course, that expectations of growth were
realistic. It is clear, however, that Labour had not
investigated the problem of achieving growth as
thoroughly as may have been assumed (7). Accordingly,
the framework and focus of policy debate in
opposition assumed a wrong emphasis. The Party's
efforts at problem definition, and its scaling of
priorities, may well have been inconsistent with
predictions of an economic recession taking place
after the post-Korean War boom. The strategy it
brought with it into office may therefore have been
inappropriate in the economic climate of 1964. As
Coates pointed out,

    in the 1950s, as in the 1930s, the Labour Party
    had spent its period in opposition discussing
    the wrong problems, i.e. not discussing the
    problems which an incoming Labour Government
    would face. They entered office equipped to run
    a high-growth economy, anticipating that the

barriers to growth would be technological and
scientific. They in fact inherited a low-growth
economy, where the barrier to growth was
primarily a financial and a competitive one. (8)

Commenting on Wilson's stage-management of
Party priorities in the eighteen months preceding the
1964 General Election, Christopher Price, a Labour
MP, noted that 'this progress from false teeth to
technology, from soft hearts to hard heads, as has
been evident from recent Labour Party Conferences,
has set up very real tensions among the ordinary
party members' (9). The ideological commitment of
1951 had given way to the intense pragmatism of 1964.
Social reform, once an exalted icon embedded at the
core of the Party's socialist doctrines, was now
subordinated to the vagaries of Labour's plans for
sustained economic growth. Price went on to note:

the issue has been to an extent softened so far
by the fact that the Labour Party is led by a
Prime Minister who is firmly respectable on both
counts; having resigned office to protect a free
Health Service in 1951, he was almost solely
responsible for launching and developing the
modernising technical stance on which the 1964
election was won. Since then, however, the flood
of political technologists into the party, the
inevitable constant emphasis on efficiency and
productivity in the ministerial and party
pronouncements, could endanger the delicate
balance between head and heart which is
essential to the party if it is to survive.
(10)

The dangers of an intra-party split as the party
leadership suspended its interest in traditional
goals and values in favour of an emphasis on
'scientific socialism' and modernity were quite
clear (11). What was equally clear was that the
initiative for social reform had now passed out of
the Party's hands: 'policy statements there have been
in plenty - but by and large the job of pointing out
the gaps in the Welfare State and planning the future
of social policy has been bequeathed to left-wing
academics like Professors Titmuss and Townsend'
(12).
     The tone for academic-inspired change had
already been set by Lynes in 1963, effectively
demonstrating that the problem of poverty was a
dynamic one, endemic to any developed society. He,

too, had lamented the inertia which appeared to dog
the issue. 'The fact that, after 15 years of more or
less full employment and social security for all, the
poor are still with us has forced us to the
realisation that poverty must be continually
re-defined, as the standards of the community rise.'
(13)

THE EMERGENCE OF A PRESSURE GROUP FOR THE POOR

In 1965, in the wake of Labour inaction and growing
academic frustration, an attempt was made, somewhat
inadvertently, to cohere the disparate contributions
to the poverty debate into a programme for action. In
March of that year, Brian Abel-Smith was invited to
address a meeting of the Social and Economic Affairs
Committee of the Society of Friends on 'a number of
aspects of poverty' at Toynbee Hall. The impact of
his talk was such that a follow-up was arranged 'to
consider what action ought to be taken to increase
public awareness of poverty and to draw up a
programme of action which would prevent and relieve
it' (14). A positive outcome of the meeting was the
drafting of the group's first memorandum on poverty
which was despatched in June to Douglas Houghton,
Chancellor of the Duchy of Lancaster (15), who had
recently been appointed by Harold Wilson as the new
overlord of the Social Services.

On assuming office, the Party's leadership had
attemped to meet criticism of the declining priority
of social reform by translating a number of its
manifesto commitments into legislative action. Old
age pensions were increased, National Insurance and
National Assistance rates were improved, prescription charges were abolished early in 1965, and a
Redundancy Payments Act was passed later the same
year. In addition, the government had announced in
November 1964 that a major review of the social
security system would be undertaken under Houghton's
guidance (16). His task was to examine the problems
of the five groups disproportionately represented
among the poor: (1) the long-term unemployed; (2) the
chronically sick and disabled; (3) fatherless
families; (4) the elderly; and (5) low-paid
wage-earners and their families. The review lasted
three years yet failed to produce any substantive
published outcome or to establish firm guidelines for
future social policy. Its announcement also managed
to surprise and confuse many observers who were under
the impression that Labour's social policies had

41

already been thrashed out and reshaped by the Party's committees some years earlier (17).

The basis of the memorandum submitted on 30 June 1965 to Houghton was Tony Lynes' article, 'A Policy for Family Incomes' published in The Listener in March 1965. Lynes had documented the interrelationship between incomes policy and taxation and its effect upon families, the inequities produced by the wage-stop, the effects of perinatal mortality, nutrition and diet, and sizes of family related to educational achievement. His principal recommendation for the alleviation of distress was an increase in family allowances. By the time Houghton received his memorandum, the group had named itself the Family Poverty Group. It proposed two main reforms: the abolition of child tax allowances, and the replacement of the existing family allowance by a tax-free allowance of 10 shillings (50p) for the first child and £1 5s 0d (£1.25) for subsequent children. Secondly, the group proposed an alternative system based on the extension of tax allowances to those below the tax threshold by adaptation of the PAYE machinery. Tax adjustments could be added to the weekly wage packet and recovered from the Inland Revenue by the employer.

Broadly, the aims could be summarised as, first, to achieve an increase in the income of poorer families with dependent children when the head of the household was either employed or unemployed; and secondly, to accomplish this without encouraging increases in family size and without creating a disincentive to work. By mid-July a reply from Houghton was still not forthcoming and the second part of the group's strategy now came into force. At a meeting on 15 July the group agreed to write to 'a group of selected influential people sending them a copy of the memorandum, drawing their attention to the problem and asking if they would support an appeal to the Government to take action to alleviate it by signing an endorsed letter to the Prime Minister' (18). Securing the patronage of well-known figures at the inception or during the course of a campaign is a well-tried and orthodox tactic for interest groups seeking to attract attention. Famous individuals add an aura of prestige and respectability to a group, and may serve to give impetus to the group's efforts in both the parliamentary and public relations fields. Apart from the 'associational' value of such individuals to a nascent group, they may also possess certain skills, and, perhaps, useful contacts which the group

may seek to exploit. In the case of the Family
Poverty Group, the letter attracted the signatures,
among others, of Baronesss Wootton of Abinger, Sir
John Maud, Arthur Morton, Director of the NSPCC,
leading members of the Family Service Unit and some
twenty-four eminent professors, many in the social
policy field.

In the interim there had been a further
development. The members present at a meeting on 29
October decided that the group should remain in
existence after the appeal to the Prime Minister had
been sent and should be formally constituted to
enable it to raise money and acquire a permanent
staff 'to give publicity to the problem of family
poverty'. The name of the group was also changed to
the more emotive Child Poverty Action Group (CPAG, or
Group) (19). Its continued existence received strong
support for a number of reasons: (1) Houghton's
stance on the issue of family poverty was clearly
ambivalent (20); (2) Labour's plans to reform social
security still appeared to be in a state of flux
despite claims in its 1966 manifesto that in 1964
'our plans for a far reaching reconstruction of
social security were well-advanced when we took
office' (21); (3) Wilson's emphasis on sustained
economic growth as the prerequisite of social reform
had indicated that the alleviation of poverty had
been relegated from the Party's list of key
priorities; (4) adoption of the comprehensive
national superannuation scheme outlined by Richard
Crossman and Peggy Herbison at the 1963 Party
Conference also appeared remote; and (5) piecemeal
repair rather than radical change now characterised
Labour's efforts in the field. The protraction of the
Group's 'watchdog' function and a strengthening of
its role as the unofficial 'social conscience' of the
Labour Party became inevitable.

Timing was a critical factor. The Group's new
emotionally-charged name, and its connotations with
the approaching Christmas season, were seen as a
powerful combination for attracting sympathetic
publicity. To coincide with Wilson's receipt of the
memorandum the Group called a press conference on 22
December to herald the publication of Abel-Smith and
Townsend's The Poor and the Poorest. Its emphasis on
the rediscovery of child poverty, in particular,
ensured that the name Child Poverty Action Group
would remain in the public eye over Christmas (22).
The following day a second conference, chaired by
Lady Wootton, and coinciding with the screening on
television of two major documentaries on poverty was

called to publicise the aims and activities of the
Group itself and invite support. A week later,
Townsend helped maintain interest by adding a
rejoinder to an article on poverty in the New
Statesman by the Labour MP Lena Jeger and asked those
interested to subscribe to the Group and pledge their
support.

The publication of The Poor and the Poorest by
two leading academics was perhaps the catalyst in
focusing attention on the problem of poverty. The
combined effect of the Group's memorandum, and the
assessment of poverty offered by Abel-Smith and
Townsend, was instrumental in bringing the issue
back, at least temporarily, into the forefront of
political debate (23). Yet they failed to evoke any
positive response from the Labour government for
another eighteen months. Wilson replied to CPAG's
initiative on 24 January 1966 thus: 'I can make no
promises ... as with so many desirable activities it
is, of course, necessary for priorities to be
established within the available resources - and one
of the purposes of our review of the Social Services
is to establish the proper priorities as between one
social need and another'. And at least one Labour MP
was moved to remind his leader of the Party's
historic socialist commitment to eradicating poverty
and inequality, warning him that 'only a social
policy which received a constant high priority beyond
the nicely calculated limits of exact electoral
advantage will preserve for the party that soul which
is ... the mainspring of work and effort for the
strongest and loyalest of its supporters' (24).

Since it was clear that the Labour government
was in no particular hurry to complete its
much-vaunted review of the Social Services, CPAG were
obliged to accept the fact that any new initiative on
the issue must come from them. The Group's chairman,
had already spoken of the likelihood of this
development. Anticipating a more permanent structure
for the Group, he had argued that 'If it is to be
effective, the group needs to be the major concern of
one person' (25). His analysis set the tone for the
appointment of Tony Lynes on 1 August 1966 as CPAG's
secretary.

At this stage, and given the impasse on the
poverty issue, Lynes was a most appropriate choice.
The Group required a change of direction, a greater
degree of politicisation, and it needed the sustained
and energetic involvement of someone working
full-time. In particular, it required 'inside
knowledge' of the workings of government departments

and guidance as to which access points it should direct its efforts and, given its limited range of resources, how influence might be most effectively achieved. Lynes' background was ideal. For some time he had been a leading member of Titmuss's social administration group at the London School of Economics. He had effectively orchestrated academic efforts to elicit a greater statistical output from the NAB and was a member of the Labour Party's Social Policy Sub-Committee. As a result he was on close terms with leading Party figures like Crossman, Houghton, Herbison and Kenneth Robinson, the Minister of Health. In 1965 he was among a group of experts seconded to the Civil Service by the Party as ministerial policy advisers. In Lynes' case the secondment was to the Ministry of Pensions where the Minister, Peggy Herbison, is said to have seen his role as that of an 'irritant to stimulate ideas' (26). Lynes had also contributed to Crossman's New Frontiers of Social Security; and before arriving at the Ministry of Pensions fulltime he had held a part-time advisory post which he combined with his teaching at the LSE.

His efforts in achieving influence for CPAG were also aided by events elsewhere. First, the General Election of March 1966 produced an overall majority of 97 for Labour and was notable for its influx of new and generally young Labour members. The prospect of a potentially reformist second Wilson administration seemed further enhanced by the realisation of one of Wilson's election 'ploys': 'the announcement by Margaret Herbison, the Minister of Pensions and National Insurance, that National Assistance was to be abolished and replaced by Supplementary Benefit, as of right' (27). In August 1966, in keeping with his pre-election promise, Wilson created the new Ministry of Social Security with Herbison at the helm, so that Lynes' former chief was now head of a new department which appeared, at face-value, to have a reforming brief. There was every reason to suppose, from CPAG's viewpoint, that Lynes would continue to enjoy access to the Minister.

However, some members of the Group remained sceptical of both Labour's record to date and of its plans for the future. Townsend for example, was concerned that Labour had failed to close the gap between Britain's gross expenditure on social cash benefits and that of other OECD countries. A survey of 62 countries with family allowance systems, by the USA government, had revealed that fifty of them paid some allowance for the first child. Townsend was particularly concerned that Labour had not taken any initiatives to include Britain among them. He contended that Labour had still to measure up to the 'two big problems of poverty', among the old and among families with children (28). Though welcoming Herbison's appointment, he remained unconvinced that Labour's new initiatives were anything more than old ideas reworked; and assessing Herbison's first address to the Labour Party Conference, he added:

> I do not believe that alternative sources of finance to economic growth are being exploited. The Minister ended her speech this morning by saying that further substantial improvements in social security depended on productivity. She called conference to give her the wherewithal. But quite apart from the relatively poor provision for Social Security made in the National Plan there are two other sources open; aggregate and individual income redistribution. There are ways of redistributing Government expenditure. There are also possibilities of redistributing income by adjusting the tax and social security systems ... economic difficulties provide insufficient excuse for not taking immediate action to improve the living standards of the poorest sections of the population. (29)

On 5 August 1966 CPAG took Herbison to task over the continued abuses suffered by many claimants subject to the wage-stop. Aware that the Minister was taking stock of her new duties and was keen to establish early priorities, the Group pressed its anxieties home:

> The new Ministry will have many urgent tasks to face, but none more urgent than that of bringing relief to the very large number of wage-earners' families now living below the minimum National Assistance level ... This rule condemns thousands of families to 'statutory poverty' during sickness or unemployment ... It is a severe disappointment to find this bitterly resented relic of the Poor Law preserved in the new scheme of supplementary allowances which are to replace National Assistance ... According to the estimates you yourself have quoted, there may be 300,000 of these families, and this could mean over a million

children. (30)

By late December it seemed that CPAG had made some progress. Lynes was invited by Richard Hayward, Chairman of the new Supplementary Benefits Commission (SBC), to discuss with him CPAG's proposals for a revision of the Supplementary Benefit system. Shortly after, Hayward wrote to the Group suggesting that such meetings could, in future, take place on a regular basis. One channel of influence, at least, appeared to be open.

The creation of the SBC and the abolition of the NAB, together with the Commission's new insistence upon the payment of benefit as a 'right' was entirely consistent with CPAG demands. An additional filip to the Group's morale came with the appointment of Richard Titmuss to the board of the SBC. Here, it was felt, was the appointment to a position of considerable influence of someone who shared their goals.

THE FAILURE OF THE REVIEW

By early 1967, however, the government's review of social services had been under way for two years without any apparent progress. Consequently, a third memorandum was despatched, this time to the Chancellor of the Exchequer. The Group now made it clear that it would not shrink from denouncing the inertia of a government with whom it was widely held to have close ties. 'One thing must be made clear. If this year's Budget does not give really substantial help to the 200,000 families below the official poverty line, the Government will face a storm of criticism from its supporters as well as its opponents.' (31)

Perhaps Labour's apparent inertia lay in the nature of poverty as an electoral issue. As a reformist party with major social priorities Labour has often found itself in a dilemma. Its traditional socialist values suggest that it should look to the poor and the disadvantaged in society and take positive action to improve their lot. In office, however, Labour has too readily succumbed to counter-pressures from those sections of the electorate whose interests it perceives as antipathetic to particular forms of public expenditure. Indeed, Coates has suggested that the evidence for this is now so overwhelming that

> Labour Party policies cannot, and will not,
> culminate in the creation of a genuinely
> Socialist society ... on the contrary, the
> Labour Party and its claims are a major blockage
> in the struggle to create the kind of party and
> the kind of labour movement that the struggle
> for Socialism requires ... there is now very
> little hope that Labour Governments can deliver
> substantial and sustained packages of social
> reform ... Far from embodying in its political
> practice the actual interests of its
> predominately working class electorate, the
> Labour Party when in power seems fated to come
> ever more into conflict with groups of workers
> who are forced to defend their living standards,
> job control and even job security <u>against</u> the
> policies of the very Labour politicians that
> they helped to elect into office. (32)

Houghton commented upon this dilemma some time later
at a CPAG 'teach-in'. The emphasis of his
explanations of legislative inertia was very much
upon the political difficulties involved in
mobilising electoral support for welfare action. 'It
is most significant that Governments for ten years
have been able to neglect family allowances without
any political repercussions. Why? Because it is the
most unpopular social benefit to a very large number
of people.' (33)
Recognising the problems involved, CPAG's
attack upon the Party's record assumed an
increasingly critical tone. Labour had not only
failed to intervene in aid of the poor, it had
allowed the position of the poor to deteriorate.

> Nothing has yet been done, however, and the
> situation has become steadily worse. The
> erosion of Family Allowances by rising prices
> has continued. The rise in unemployment has
> added greatly to the numbers in poverty. The
> Ministry of Social Security Act has not only
> presented the wage-stop rule, under which many
> thousands of unemployed and disabled men and
> their families are deliberately kept in
> poverty; it has given statutory approval to the
> practice of applying the wage-stop to the sick.
> There is, moreover, increasing evidence of a
> failure to inform families of available sources
> of aid. (34)

In mid-July the SBC made some minor concessions

governing the administration of the wage-stop, but an ensuing Cabinet crisis over the future direction of social security policy and the consequent resignation of Peggy Herbison as Minister confirmed that the concessions would only be pallatives.

LABOUR'S SOCIAL PRIORITIES RECONSIDERED - THE CABINET STRUGGLE

Peggy Herbison's resignation as Minister of Social Security may be seen both as the culmination of a revisionist process in Labour's thinking on social security and as a catalyst for reinforcing that process. It is important, therefore, that the circumstances of her decision be considered in some detail. The change in Labour Party thinking on the issue in the years after 1963 has already been outlined and it was against this new mood that Herbison was obliged to stage a rearguard action. In attempting to assess this mood, James Kincaid has noted that

> tentatively under Gaitskell, then decisively under Wilson, it became Labour policy that extra resources for welfare would be found, not by redistributive taxation, but out of the proceeds of economic growth. Many loyal Labour Party supporters are under the impression that the failure of Mr Wilson's government to reverse the trend to greater social inequality is to be explained by economic difficulties since 1964. What should be more widely appreciated is the prior and fundamental devaluation of social equality in the political philosophy of the party leadership. (35)

It was from this so called 'devaluation of social equality' that Herbison's difficulties largely stemmed and her non-Cabinet rank did little to enhance her situation. Those difficulties were compounded further by the excessive departmental pluralism that characterised the Wilson governments - the second in particular - as the threat of devaluation and public expenditure cuts loomed.

The events leading to her resignation began at the first full meeting of the new Labour Cabinet called on 28 October 1964 to discuss the Queen's speech. Despite his own commitments at the Ministry of Housing, Richard Crossman made it clear that he, among others, was prepared to sacrifice, or at least

defer, his own departmental priorities whilst Labour
fulfilled its election pledges to the poor, the old
and the infirm. Yet he made it equally clear that the
Chancellor, James Callaghan, was intransigent on the
matter and was determined to stage some sort of
economic recovery <u>before</u> social priorities could be
met. The impasse has been drily recorded by Kincaid:
'Welfare reform had become the sugar on the pill of
economic rationalisation, the bleeding heart worn
prominently on the technocrats' sleeve' (36).

A year later the clash between expenditure and
recovery was more marked. Callaghan and Houghton had
already, on the advice of the 'Economic Ministries',
compelled Herbison to abandon her 'big all-in scheme'
of national superannuation; because of that, she was
forced to concede her proposals for the introduction
of a new pension scheme and introduce instead
short-term measures like earnings-related sickness
and unemployment benefits. With her priorities
already under attack and her plans in disarray,
Herbison was invited to attend a Cabinet meeting,
chaired by George Brown, Deputy Prime Minister and
head of the Department of Economic Affairs, on 20
October 1965. On this occasion she was, as Crossman
puts it, 'pleading' to be allowed an extra £7 million
so that she might extend the scheme to widows (37).
It was, however, to be yet another principled
rearguard action against the tide of 'economic
necessity', Herbison's own overlord, Douglas
Houghton, was the first to attack her calculations
and question her political timing, and Anthony
Crosland, Minister of State for Economic Affairs, and
John Diamond, Chief Secretary to the Treasury,
weighed in against her too. Administratively, her
position was quite untenable. As Crossman recalls 'In
Cabinet Peggy was in a weak position because she was
pre-empting money and anybody who does that makes all
his other spending colleagues jealous' (38). Barbara
Castle encountered similar difficulties during her
experiences in Cabinet as a 'spending minister' and
has since concluded that the popular image of Cabinet
as a rational and strategic policy-making forum
obscures the reality of excessive departmental
pluralism, of ministerial in-fighting and competition for a larger slice of the cake (39). Yet, as
Jeremy Richardson and Grant Jordan note,
departmental pluralism of this type may be seen as an
inevitable outcome of the British policy-making
process. 'At the very minimum, ministers tend not to
be impartial in judging between the claims of
departments for resources. Increased allocation for

his (or her) Department indicates political power and abilities, establishes a personal reputation and impresses client groups.' (40)

Herbison was thus disadvantaged on three counts. First, she was requesting extra resources which were either seen as not available or, ultimately, as having to be 'transferred' from other departmental budgets. Secondly, her opportunities to sustain and reinforce her arguments were notably hampered by her junior ministerial status; her appearances in Cabinet were thus intermittent. Finally, unlike some of the larger or more prestigious departments dealing with industry, commerce and the professions, Herbison's own client-groups were largely weak, unorganised and, to some extent, alienated from the mainstream of British politics. This theme will be discussed shortly.

On 27 October, however, and much to the irritation of Houghton, the Cabinet's Social Services Committee agreed to allow Herbison to spend the £7 million at her own discretion as it was proven that this amount was actually already allocated within her Department's budget (41). The next day Houghton was obliged, against his own view, to report the decision to the full Cabinet and approval was secured. Yet by 1 December Herbison was again under pressure. Her proposals for wages-related benefits had gone before the Cabinet on 25 November but Ministers had failed to reach agreement and once more had referred the issue to the Social Services Committee. It was clear on this occasion that Herbison's proposals would not be safeguarded by a budgetary fait accompli.

The 'Economic Ministers' had some time earlier forced the Minister for Pensions and National Insurance to agree to a two-stage reform of social security. First, the plan for short-term benefits, like those already implemented on sickness and unemployment, would be implemented and this would be followed, as economic recovery got under way, by the national superannuation scheme. The problem now was that the 'Economists' had miscalculated. They had favoured the short-term measures first because they were considered essential to the mobility of labour and an antidote to mass unemployment. By December, however, their fears of mass unemployment had proven groundless and the priority given to short-term benefits appeared inept. The commitment, however, could not be reneged upon and Crossman, among others, was seriously worried about the effects of Herbison's proposals for integrating civil servants into the

scheme as they would contribute a great deal but
receive virtually nothing in return because they
rarely suffered redundancy or unemployment (42). A
week later Crossman, too, felt obliged to desert
Herbison's cause.

> The final discussion and decision on
> wage-related sickness and unemployment benefits
> didn't take long. Cabinet accepted the Social
> Services Committee recommendation and I found
> myself reluctantly voting against Peggy
> Herbison. I do hate being on the same side as
> the Treasury but on this occasion John Diamond
> was right; and, anyway, Departmentally I needed
> to do it. (43)

This latter justification was clearly the most
salient one.

On 14 December Herbison was again summoned to a
meeting of the full Cabinet to put the case for a
reform of Social Security. Again, according to
Crossman, 'Douglas Houghton and James Callaghan got
into a sinister combination trying to wreck it' (44).
Herbison had done some thorough research, however,
and produced by all accounts a masterful scheme which
won not only support but praise. At this point she
had twice met with entrenched opposition to her plans
from Houghton and Callaghan and had, on both
occasions, successfully outmaneouvred them - a fact
that failed to stand her in good stead when she
required their support in later skirmishes.

Labour went on to increase its parliamentary
majority in the General Election of March 1966 and,
for a time, Herbison's hand seemed strengthened by
the announcement in the Queen's speech that the Party
was to introduce a new superannuation scheme to be
administered by the new Ministry of Social Security.
However, the creation of the new ministry was
cosmetic, and Herbison's title merely token. By June
the 'surgeons' of the 'Economic Ministries' had so
carved up Herbison's proposals that Crossman was
moved to comment: 'Even our big Social Security
measures are disappointing. All we have got is Peggy
Herbison's little Social Security Bill, by which we
change the name of the National Assistance Board and
don't do much more. We have had to scrap the incomes
guarantee and we have had to postpone national
superannuation' (45).

In February 1967, with the economic situation
deteriorating rapidly and the clamour for
devaluation increasing, any further plans Herbison

proposed were weighed directly against Treasury proposals for cutbacks in public expenditure (46). Wilson has since revealed that in the autumn of 1966 he and Callaghan had drawn up and approved the expenditure estimates for the financial year 1967/8 (47). Economic necessity dictated that although an increase in pensions could be approved it would have to be far below the level desired by Peggy Herbison. For the Minister of Social Security this could only be viewed as yet another stage in the steady undermining of her position. On this occasion the Chancellor's intransigence was politically and administratively unacceptable to her and she tendered her resignation. Wilson, invoking ministerial responsibility, insisted that she should not publicise the event and should continue with her work until the formal announcement on pensions was made the next year (48).

On 23 February 1967 Herbison, rather than acquiescing in Wilson's decision as he hoped she might, was able to out-manoeuvre Callaghan for the last time before her formal resignation took effect. Crossman paints a compelling picture of Cabinet in-fighting on the issue of family allowances that supports the analysis of departmentalism offered by Richardson and Jordan. In particular, Crossman reveals the tensions and conflict at the highest levels of the party that even 'well-connected' groups like CPAG could not begin fully to anticipate. He notes,

> We next turned to Social Security and here there was a great tension and excitement because Peggy Herbison and the Chancellor were presenting their rival proposals. Since January the Chancellor had postponed this week after week in order to ensure that nothing can be done in 1967. Meanwhile, he has been putting tremendous pressure on members of the Cabinet who know that if there is a big increase in family allowances their own Departments will suffer. (49)

The Chancellor had made it clear that in Cabinet government was very much to do with the winning and allocation of resources by spending Departments. Any attempt to pre-empt the normal course of that process with a scheme of expenditure not costed in current estimates would necessarily require that other Departments would have to forfeit some of their resources in order to finance that scheme. It was an appeal to the basic instincts of Cabinet Ministers –

53

the maximisation of rational self- or departmental interest within the constraints imposed by collective goals. As Castle has since noted of the efforts of Ministers in Cabinet: 'The demands of the department must always be paramount ...' (50). Similarly, Bruce Headey has noted that from the point of view of the individual Minister

> the Cabinet is a forum in which he fights for his department's policy proposals, for Treasury money and for Parliamentary time. Since many proposals affect the interests of more than one department a sponsoring Minister is always likely to have to defend his proposals against damaging amendments proposed by Cabinet colleagues. Conflicts between some departments are almost endemic ... and conflicts between the main spending departments and the Treasury occur every year when the estimates are brought to the Public Expenditure survey Committee and the Cabinet. (51)

Yet, if the Chancellor's tactics were perceptive, Herbison's were astute. The Chancellor's alternative to increases in family allowances was to propose the introduction of a means-tested benefit, a family income supplement. This represented a clear volte face, an inversion of all previous promises to eliminate selectivity and discrimination. However, Herbison had already done some sounding out of the type of reception such a scheme would receive from the Labour movement and, almost as a parting gesture, blocked the Chancellor's alternative. Crossman's own reaction was evident: 'Our side had had one stroke of luck ... the TUC Delegation had seen Miss Herbison and as a result the General Council had met yesterday and gone on record as opposing means-tested Family Allowances. Peggy was able to end her speech with this Statement' (52).

FROM SUPPLICANT TO CRITIC - REACTION TO THE CABINET DEBATE

While it is difficult for a comparatively nascent group to acquaint itself fully with the complexities and vagaries of Cabinet politics, familiarity with Herbison's own principled views on social policy and recognition of her political impotence in the face of strong economic forces had prepared the Group for the inevitability of her defeat and resignation.

Throughout the first half of 1967, against the backdrop of this Cabinet struggle, CPAG had continued to press for an increase in family allowances, but Wilson, in the wake of what Frank Field has since termed 'savage deflation' (53), continued to insist that the problem of poverty would remain unassailed until after the completion of the review of social services in July 1967.

In January and February the Group had continued to publicise the facts of poverty to a press eager to adopt a 'pundit role' with the Budget only weeks off (54). In February, the Group sent its now customary memorandum to the Chancellor, calling for the abolition of all tax allowances, the making of all cash benefits tax-free, and proposing that cash benefits be raised to a level that would compensate the standard rate taxpayer for the loss of his tax allowance. Throughout the early months of 1967 the group's anti-wage-stop campaign continued to develop, achieving, as New Society pointed out, an important milestone in politicising social workers:

> the campaign had had a sizeable influence in the resurgence of social workers belief in social and political action as a vital means of helping their clients. The CPAG has come up with a particularly striking example of how social workers might intervene through a campaign against the wage stop ... By encouraging social workers to bombard officials with letters asking how allowances are computed, to assist with appeals to the tribunals and to urge the widest application of the 'exceptional circumstances'; under which the stop need not be applied, the action group is asking social workers to harry officialdom - legally, but none the less awkwardly. (55)

CPAG's growing frustration with what it saw as the Wilson government's fragmented approach to policy-making and its consequent legislative inertia had passed the threshold of polite rebuke by April 1967. On 12 April, Townsend, Abel-Smith and Lynes began a short correspondence with Wilson in which they criticised the Labour government's 'narrow and unimaginative approach to social policy' (56). Their reasoning, they claimed, illustrated a classic failure of government departments to match their traditional fields of responsibility to the corresponding fields of policy. In particular they criticised the failure of the government to recognise

that poverty was experienced by a number of quite
different groups and could only be eradicated by a
coherent and extensive programme of action; a
programme that would attack the roots of the
inequalities which produced poverty in its many forms
– homelessness, low pay, single parenthood, old age,
child poverty, and unemployment. It was their view
that 'the responsibilities of government departments
are too narrowly circumscribed. Taxation policy is
still isolated from social policy in general and
policy for social security in particular' (57).

In taking this view the writers were not making
an isolated criticism of central policy-making, nor
could their criticism be confined to the social
sphere alone. As Richardson and Jordan have noted,

> The traditional criticism of the centre of
> government is ... that policy is made through
> the competition of departments and Ministers
> rather than through the imposition of
> consistent priorities by a team of political
> leaders. The 'rational' allocation of
> priorities is frustrated because departmental
> boundaries do not correspond to the problem
> boundaries and this defective structure
> produces time-consuming negotiations that
> prevent rational analysis. (58)

Forced on the defensive, Wilson replied two weeks
later.

> I do not accept your view that Cabinet is not
> offering prompt and just solutions to these
> problems because it is not being presented with
> the right questions. There is abundant evidence
> that this Government has done more than any to
> study problems, particularly social problems,
> without regard to departmental boundaries and
> where necessary to shape the machinery of
> Government to the end of policy. (59)

While he could reasonably argue that Houghton's
review of the social services verified his claim that
the Labour government had studied problems there was,
as the next chapter will show, only superficial
evidence to suggest that fresh inter-departmental
approaches had been initiated and that new machinery
had been created to implemented them.

Kincaid commented at the time,

> There has been a certain "appearance" of dynamic

activity since 1964. A great many Acts of
Parliament have been passed. Numerous commiss-
ions and committees have made inquiries and
published reports. The Ministry of This has had
its name changed to the Ministry of That and
been merged with the Ministry of Something Else.
But no emphatic break with the lines of policy
inherited from the previous period of
Conservative rule. (60)

More significantly, the manifesto promise of a
'dramatic redeployment of resources in favour of the
underprivileged' had not been realised: the reasons
for this clearly lay either with inherent faults in
the government's taxation, welfare and economic
policies or, as CPAG were suggesting, an
administrative reluctance to coordinate these.
       In making this sort of criticism CPAG were
arguing for significant, and perhaps unrealistic,
changes in policy style that were largely against the
grain of the traditional policy-making process. In
particular, they were overlooking the very powerful
pressures exerted upon Ministers in Cabinet by the
demands of Departmental pluralism and those of their
client-groups. They were also underestimating the
tendency towards policy sectorisation or compartmentalisation that is a clear product of that
pluralism. As Richardson and Gustafsson conclude:
'policy-making systems in Western democracies are
essentially broken down into relatively autonomous
policy segments. Each policy sector (or policy area)
is populated by a policy community and these
communities usually operate relatively independently
of each other' (61). Their view is that under an
administrative regime emphasising sector rationality
'policy-makers and implementers would think in terms
of objectives and goal attainment for their own
areas' (62). If policy-making is carried out in this
'sectorised/segmented' fashion then the principal
feature of the process will be its emphasis upon each
policy sector remaining rational in terms of its own
objectives. In other words, returning to the poverty
debate, social policy, fiscal policy and taxation
policy may all be constructed quite rationally in the
narrow departmental or sectoral sense but may be
viewed overall as potentially in conflict, as
competitive and, in some areas, as irrational. This
tendency to make policy in a vacuum is to a great
extent dictated and reinforced by Departmental
prestige, by aggrandisement and a pervasive process
of bureaucratic socialisation that emphasises the

paramountcy of the departmental interest above all else.

In June, with little to show for its May onslaught, CPAG took the Prime Minister to task again. The theme of 'fragmentation' and policy incoherence was driven hard:

> What disturbs us is that the reform of social security and taxation still appears to be seen in terms of piecemeal changes which are neither adequate in themselves nor indicative of a coherent philosophy ... In Labour's 1964 manifesto, plans for a complete reconstruction of social security were set out (but) ... In place of this comprehensive reform, the Government has introduced a number of separate measures which have inevitably created new anomalies and in many cases have failed to benefit those most in need. (63)

Gone now was the polite dismay with which CPAG had earlier greeted the government's decision to undertake a social services review when most within or associated with the Group assumed this had already been done in opposition. The necessity of the review, specifically in terms of policy revision and amendment was accepted; the objection now was to its vague and protracted nature.

> We fully accept that some of the ideas worked out by the Labour Party in the years of opposition have had to be adapted and amended. But it is more difficult to understand the delays in implementing the undertaking, which appeared for the first time in the 1966 manifesto, to 'see ways of integrating more fully the two quite different systems of social payment - tax allowances and cash benefits'. The recent Budget was all the more disappointing in the light of this undertaking given a year ago when the Labour government has already been in power for 17 months. (64)

It was CPAG's view that the government had reneged on this commitment to rationalise the two policy approaches into a single strategy to tackle poverty. The Group's attitude revealed a growing and increasingly bitter, rift between it and the Labour government. Tactically, it also demonstrated not only the growing willingness of CPAG to question the record of a party formerly regarded as something of an 'ideological bed-fellow' but also a gradual assertion of independence which enabled the Group to shed its overt partisanship and to condemn Labour's ambivalence in a way it would have done if another party had been in office. It may also show, in retrospect, that CPAG's decision, during the 1970 General Election campaign, to sever overt links once and for all with the publication of a strong attack upon Labour's record in office in 1964-70 (65) was not an isolated act of political frustration, but the culmination of a long process of disenchantment and disillusionment with the Party, and a recognition of the Group's early and rather naive perception of its own capabilities.

While it is clear that Labour's efforts in the field of social security had been a great disappointment to many of its supporters, it is equally clear that CPAG's own strategy for helping the poor had its limitations, not the least of which was its over-reliance on the Labour Party. While the Party was a convenient and likely vehicle for the Group's early efforts in conveying the 'problem' of poverty, CPAG largely failed, as the next chapter shows, to seek out other allies capable of tackling the problem. As Keith Banting points out:

> A problem revealed is not a problem solved. CPAG were not rich in conventional political resources ... (but) Through astute use of the resources that they did possess - information, the academic status of their leaders, their contacts in the Labour Party - they were able to change political perceptions of social problems. But they could not command a specific response. The fate of the poor depended not only on their data but, more importantly, on the reaction to that data amongst politicians, civil servants and the wider society. (66)

This raises an additional question: was the Group entirely realistic in the demands it made upon the Labour government in this period? Certainly expectations were high when Labour took office in 1964 and many observers expected early and far-reaching changes from what was considered to be a potentially reformist administration (67). However, it is easy to overlook the wider political and economic situation of the time. Labour did, indeed, come to power with a reformist bent but one, as has been noted, that was already under pressure of change as a result of a revision of priorities that had taken root under Gaitskell's leadership and which acquired an even greater impetus under Wilson's. By mid-1964 the balance of payments deficit had reached the alarming figure of £800 million per annum, the highest in history (68). The government itself was largely inexperienced, most of its members untried in any major office of state. Thirteen years of unbroken Conservative rule had also provided a climate of government appropriate to incrementalism and policy continuity. Labour Ministers thus entered office with massive economic problems to solve, with relatively little shared experience of office to draw upon, with the prospect of having to overcome civil service resistance to change, and with the burden of a manifesto commitment to wide-ranging social reforms, the prospective cost of which was clearly at variance with the type of fiscal strictures the Treasury wished to employ to reduce trading deficits - ultimately with the spectre of devaluation lurking in the background.

It is possible that Labour Ministers were seriously embarassed by the stringency of the economic situation vis a vis the rather sweeping promises made in opposition. It is also possible that CPAG's demands were viewed as sometimes naive and often impracticable. Fabian ideals might not have been as easily transposed into the bargaining - administrative vernacular of mid-1960s <u>realpolitik</u> as some CPAG figures might have supposed (69).

Harold Wilson's reply to CPAG illustrated the pragmatism that characterised his own leadership and offers some insight into the other constraints and demands placed upon his government. 'It is, of course, true that large increases in benefits of all kinds would help eliminate need. But there are many competing claims and there is a limit to what we can do and the speed with which we can do it. We shall, nevertheless, and of course continue to, pursue our social objectives as fast as the growing strength of the economy will permit' (70). In expressing this view, Wilson was perhaps offering an explanation of the dilemmas faced when politics and administration are synthesised. The dilemma is essentially one of reasonably 'satisficing' the political preferences of organised interests while, at the same time, achieving some degree of administrative rationality. The problem lies of course in the fact that 'there may be a fundamental conflict between a system that stresses the accommodation of group demands and a system of policy-making that stresses rationality in some objective sense.' (71)

There are reasons to support this explanation. Certainly Wilson would not have wished to alienate a publicity-oriented group like CPAG which was, after all, considered to be 'sympathetic' to the Party and which was campaigning on a very emotive issue. Accusations of inertia, moreover, could be very damaging to a new government ostensibly committed to the retention and strengthening of the welfare state. For those reasons, at least, as the following chapter shows, it was not politic for the Wilson government to delay action beyond July 1967.

NOTES

1. Birch, R., The Shaping of the Welfare State (Longman, 1974), p.66.
2. Foot, P., The Politics of Harold Wilson (Penguin, 1968), pp.146-8.
3. Coates, D., The Labour Party and the Struggle for Socialism (Cambridge University Press, 1965), p.97.
4. Ibid., pp.97-8.
5. Wilson, H., The New Britain (Penguin, 1964), p.23; and Foot, op.cit., pp.135-9.
6. A further advantage of talking in specific terms of achieving growth as the prerequisite for wider action was that a popularly understood 'target' could be held up as a gauge or 'indicator' of the success of government action. The use of 'policy indicators', or manageable target figures, can assist public comprehension of government policy and, if achieved, win important electoral kudos. As Stringer and Richardson note, 'When Ministers commit themselves to specific targets it is likely that ways will be found of managing indicators in order to show that the policy has "succeeded" (op.cit., p.32).
7. Pryke, R. 'The Predictable Crisis', New Left Review, No. 39 (September-October 1966), p.3.
8. Coates, op.cit., p.101.
9. Price, C. 'The Welfare State: Reform and Development', in Whitaker, B. (ed.), A Radical Future (Jonathan Cape, 1967), p.137.
10. Ibid.
11. See Harold Wilson's address to the Party Conference in 1963, in Labour Party Annual Conference Report 1963, pp.134-40.
12. Price, op.cit., p.137.
13. Lynes, 'Poverty in the Welfare State', p.15.
14. Field, F., 'A Pressure Group for the Poor',

in Bull, D. (ed.), <u>Family Poverty</u>, 2nd edn.
(Duckworth, 1972), p.146.

15. Harold Wilson described Houghton as a
'pensions expert and Chairman of all the Cabinet
Committees concerned with the Social Services'.
Wilson, H., <u>The Labour Government 1964-70 - A
Personal Record</u> (Pelican, 1964), p.84. A much less
enthusiastic assessment of Houghton's 'expertise'
may be found in Crossman, R., <u>The Diaries of a
Cabinet Minister</u>, Vol. 1 (Hamish Hamilton and
Jonathan Cape, 1975), pp.410-11.

16. Houghton was to have the task 'of co-
ordinating the work of the Social Services to ensure
that no longer do we have the scandal of poverty in
the midst of great potential abundance or of an
unbalanced social service sector'. Foot, <u>op.cit.</u>,
p.157.

17. In 1963 the Labour Party's Study Group on
Social Security and Old Age, headed by Douglas
Houghton and Richard Crossman, produced a working
document entitled <u>New Frontiers for Social Security</u>.
The Study group included Titmuss, Townsend, Abel-
Smith and Lynes. Its aims were threefold: (1) to
improve and extend National Insurance and provide
subsistence benefit as a right without recourse to
the NAB; (2) to build a new structure of graded
benefits related to individual savings and needs; (3)
to finance the improved benefits by replacing flat-
rate contributions with wage-related contributions.
The report was introduced to the Party's 1963
Conference, amid considerable enthusiasm, by Peggy
Herbison, who became Minister of Pensions and
National Insurance in 1964. See March, D.C., 'The
Future of the Welfare State: Whither or Wither?', in
Winkler, H.R. (ed.), <u>Twentieth-Century Britain -
National Power and Social Welfare</u> (New Viewpoints,
1976), pp.196-215. The schemes to assist the
chronically sick and the widowed, the proposals to
increase and extend benefits, and the inclusion of a
progressive scheme for retirement pensions had
created optimism among the Party's supporters. It
came as some surprise then when, in November 1964,
James Callaghan announced plans for the new review.
Most observers, Townsend among them, had considered
this already achieved before the Party took office.
Townsend speaks of the announcement as an 'outrage'
which took the Party's policy-makers by surprise
despite their recognition of the problems that Labour
was forced to contend with in the early days of
office. Interview with Peter Townsend, 19 December
1979.

18. Minutes of the Family Poverty Group (15 July 1965).

19. The choice of the word 'child' had been influenced by Dr Harriet Wilson, a founder-member of the group, who had taken the view that 'when considering poverty one must focus on children because they are the most affected. And even the most bigotted person will usually agree that the needs of children should be viewed in a different way from those of the parents'. Summary of Oral Evidence by CPAG to Members of the Committee on Voluntary Organisations (9 December 1975).

20. Lena Jeger, MP, an active supporter of CPAG in the Commons, wrote 'Douglas Houghton has been working on the new concept of social security for Labour. In some ways it is surprising that this is taking so long because during the locust opposition years a sub-committee of the National Executive (with experts like Professors Titmuss, Peter Townsend and Brian Abel-Smith) worked on the plans and some thought that a blueprint had been produced. Whether it is the Economists or the officials who sent Houghton back to square one remains an unanswered question. But it was certainly with the backing of detailed research that the last Labour Election Manifesto was allowed to say ..: "we stress that, with the exception of the early introduction of the income guarantee, the key factor in determining the speed at which new and better levels of benefit can be introduced, will be the rate at which the British economy can advance". 'Labour and the Poor', New Statesman (31 December 1965).

21. Craig, op.cit., pp.266-86.

22. See, for example, 'Many British Children Living in Hardship and Poverty', (The Times); 'Wilson told: Aid Poor Children' (Daily Mirror); 'Poverty Plea to Wilson' (Daily Express); and 'Poverty Brings a Christmas Story to Mr. Wilson' (Guardian). (All 24 December 1965.) See also the reviews of The Poor and the Poorest, in The Economist (1 January 1966) and Tribune (31 December 1965).

23. See Abel-Smith, B., 'Below the Affluent Society', Guardian (2 February 1966); and 'National Insurance and the National Plan', New Society (3 February 1966).

24. Price, op.cit., p.138.

25. Minutes of the Family Poverty Group (21 May 1965).

26. Guardian (26 July 1966).

27. Wilson, H., The Labour Government 1964-70 (Penguin, 1974), p.281.

28. <u>Poverty</u>, No. 1 (1966), p.6.
29. Ibid.
30. A.F. Philp to Margaret Herbison, 5 August 1966.
31. <u>Poverty</u>, No.2 (Spring 1967), p.2.
32. Coates, D. <u>The Labour Party and the Struggle for Socialism</u> (Cambridge U.P., 1965) V & VI (Preface). See also Jordan, B., <u>Freedom and the Welfare State</u> (Routledge & Kegan Paul, 1976) chapters 10 and 14.
33. <u>Poverty</u>, No. 2, p. 7 and Banting <u>op.cit.</u>, pp. 74-82.
34. CPAG, <u>Memorandum to the Chancellor of the Exchequer</u> (Spring 1967), p.1.
35. Kincaid, J., 'Social Policy and the Labour Government', <u>International Socialism</u> (April-May 1970), pp.21-32. See also Coates, <u>op.cit.</u>, pp.89-96.
36. Kincaid, <u>op.cit.</u>, pp.21-2.
37. R. Crossman, <u>Diaries</u>, Vol. 1, pp.361-2.
38. Ibid., p.362.
39. Castle, B., 'Mandarin Power', <u>Sunday Times</u> (10 June 1973).
40. Richardson, J.J. and Jordan, G., <u>Governing Under Pressure</u> (Martin Robertson, 1979), p.27.
41. Crossman, <u>op.cit.</u>, p.365.
42. The situation was further aggravated by the fact the government was attempting to introduce this scheme at a time when it was also turning down civil service wage claims in order to preserve its incomes policy. Crossman, <u>op.cit.</u>, p.397.
43. Ibid., p.403.
44. Ibid., pp.410-11.
45. Ibid., p.533; and Kincaid, <u>op.cit.</u>, pp.27-31.
46. Peter Townsend has concluded that, since the 1950s, the most important instrument for planning social policy has been 'public expenditure planning'. Describing this process he notes 'Despite protestations from some government departments, like the DHSS, that their planning is "needs" conscious, the fact is that the exigencies of the economy, as decided by the Treasury, have led to the adoption of public expenditure control as the dominant form of planning approved by the Cabinet and imposed by Whitehall'. 'Social Planning and the Treasury', in Bosanquet, N. and Townsend, P. (eds.), <u>Labour and Equality</u> (Heinemann, 1980), pp.8-9.
47. Wilson, <u>The Labour Government</u>, p.537. Townsend comments: 'In recent years, it has come to be realised that most of the key decisions in social policy are taken during the sequence of discussions

leading up to the Budget in April of each year ... It is preceded by the review of public expenditure. This takes place in the Summer, is approved in the Autumn, and published the following January. The Public Expenditure Survey Committee is chaired by a Treasury Deputy Secretary and consists of the Finance Officers from different departments and Treasury officials ... The Committee makes estimates of the likely growth of the economy, revenue and departmental spending over the next 5 years ... neither the Committee nor the Cabinet engages in exhaustive discussion of all the major departmental proposals which may be put up. Instead, Treasury intimations of what can be afforded are communicated to the departments which, in turn, attempt to get departmental estimates agreed with the Treasury representatives on the Committee before the estimates are put to Cabinet for broad approval. The system is therefore cost and not needs-oriented and has the effect of maintaining the status quo'. Bosanquet and Townsend, Labour and Equality, p.9.

48. Wilson, The Labour Government, p.537.
49. Crossman, Diaries, Vol. II, p.252.
50. Sunday Times (10 June 1973).
51. Headey, B., British Cabinet Ministers, (George Allen & Unwin, 1974), pp.48-9.
52. Crossman, op.cit., Vol. II, pp.251-3.
53. Bull (ed.), op.cit., p.147.
54. See the Observer (19 February 1967) and The Economist (13 February 1967).
55. New Society (6 April 1967).
56. Poverty, No. 4 (Autumn 1967), p.10.
57. Ibid.
58. Richardson and Jordan, op.cit., p.29.
59. Poverty, No. 4, p.11.
60. Kincaid, op.cit., p.31.
61. Gustafsson and Richardson, op.cit., p.423.
62. Ibid., p.424.
63. Poverty, No. 4, p.12.
64. Ibid.
65. CPAG, Poverty and the Labour Government (June 1970).
66. Banting, op.cit., p.73.
67. Coates (op.cit.), notes, 'The Labour Party returned to power in 1964 on the promise of a "new Britain" and, after so long in opposition, returned with a renewed faith in their own ability to create it ... In such a society ... there would no longer be that incompatibility of interests between conflict- ing social classes to which Labour leaders in the 1930s had alluded in their analysis of capitalism,

but rather a common pursuit of a "national interest"
of ever greater material production ... under a
"dynamic and purposeful" Labour Government that
would control "the commanding heights of the economy"
in such a way as to stimulate investment, efficiency
and growth' (pp.97-8).

68. Harold Wilson describes the period of
office 1964-70 as 'a government all but a year of
whose life was dominated by an inherited balance of
payments problem which was nearing a crisis at the
moment we took office; we lived and governed during a
period when that problem made frenetic speculative
attack on Britain both easy and profitable. In our
last year of power that balance of payment problem
had been seen to be overcome. But the harsh measures
which we had to take, and from which we did not
shrink, bit deep'. Wilson, <u>The Labour Government</u>,
foreword and pp.27-9.

69. For a similar and more recent assessment of
the expectations that Labour supporters have of their
Party in power, see Bosanquet and Townsend, <u>op.cit.</u>,
pp.3-6.

70. <u>Poverty</u>, No. 4, p.13.
71. Richardson and Jordan, <u>op.cit.</u>, p.29.

Chapter Four

LABOUR, POVERTY AND PARTY MYTH

On 16 July 1967 Patrick Gordon Walker (1), the new
social services overlord, confidently boasted that
the government would resolve the problem of family
poverty by the end of the year; and a week later
announced Labour's package of measures for
eradicating the problem. The first was an increase in
family allowances which CPAG described as 'so
ludicrously small that it can only have been intended
as a sop to the Minister of Social Security, Margaret
Herbison, who had fought the Treasury for so long and
with such little effect' (2). A further six-month
delay was to occur before the full increase of 7
shillings (35p) would come into effect. Even that
would still bring only half of the poorest families
up to the basic supplementary benefit level -
regarded by CPAG as insufficient anyway to meet long-
term family needs. The government also sought to
offset the cost of these measures by raising the
price of school meals and welfare milk, the
assumption being that all families below the means-
test limit would receive meals and milk free of
charge. Not surprisingly, CPAG were highly critical
of the measures and sceptical about their effect:

> As the Ministry of Social Security's Survey
> confirms, most families living below supplemen-
> tary benefit level do not get free school meals
> and very few get free welfare foods. The reasons
> are unknown but certainly complex. Ignorance,
> attitudes to the means-test and the bodies
> administering it, official apathy and
> incompetence probably all play a part. To
> overcome all these in 8 months will require
> determination, ingenuity and willingness to
> disregard departmental boundaries and override
> local authority susceptibilities. (3)

In what was their most vociferous attack to date upon Labour's record, the Group went on at length to challenge the fragmented administrative solutions that had provoked Peggy Herbison's resignation and which had resulted in the isolation of social policy from taxation policy, the political and administrative interdependence of which the Group saw as axiomatic to any solution to poverty. In calling for greater public expenditure on family support and unemployment benefit, and in asking for significant redistributive changes in the tax structure, CPAG was, however, not only creating a scenario for further competition between the relatively weak Ministry of Social Security and the powerful Inland Revenue and Treasury, but for the bringing to bear of the resources and influence of their respective client groups (4). Tax changes having a redistributive effect away from the higher taxpayer to the low and non-tax-paying groups might be expected to produce articulate resistance from such diverse groups and organisations as the Inland Revenue Staff's Federation (who would probably oppose the considerable extra work involved in restructuring), the British Institute of Managers, the Building Societies Association, those trade unions representing the better-paid worker, professional associations, ratepayers' action groups and the plethora of groups which constitute the middle-class lobby, such as the National Association for Freedom and the National Federation of the Self-Employed. It is only in considering the wider implications of such policy changes that the fact of an anti-poverty lobby emerges (5). Such groups do not, of course, intentionally or arbitrarily seek to make or keep people poor, but their influence and effort in retaining an economic status quo which 'requires' the existence of poverty, low pay and unemployment does represent an interest which may be perceived as antithetical to that of the poor (6).

The ability of some interests to limit the scope of policy-making and determine which issues will be politicised, which preferences sustained, and which publics heard, is well documented (7). It is appropriate to note Crenson's observation that 'Decision-making is channelled and restricted by the process of non-decision-making (and that) the power reputations of people within a community may deter action on certain sensitive or politically unprofitable issues' (8). This restriction can be enforced by private interests and government departments acting both separately or jointly.

Whichever alternative obtains, the fact remains that the campaigning group which raises the issue initially may well find its control or influence over the destiny of the issue diminished or removed entirely as it goes behind closed doors, into government machinery. It is here that the interaction and influence of more powerful vested interests, both private and governmental, come into play. In proposing policies that affected interests within adjacent policy communities CPAG found itself disadvantaged by both its exclusion from the policy-making process and by the subsequent diminution of its influence over the issue. Banting notes of this period:

> Within Whitehall the battle lines had formed. The conflict centred, not on fundamentally different definitions of the nature of poverty, but on the specifics of the policy response. The process of designing the choices had been a closed one; social scientists campaigning in public were able to influence the range of options considered, but the final choices were developed within the secret world of officials and ministers ... It was a hidden battle, fought out in the corridors of power, its ebb and flow invisible to all but the most perceptive outside observers. Only in the final stages did conflict radiate outwards and only then as the internal contestants sought to mobilise political support for their cause. (9)

The choice and details of policy were thus to be worked out between the Ministry of Social Security and those Departments which saw increased expenditure on family allowances through reduction of child tax allowances as contrary to their own interests. CPAG clearly identified the Inland Revenue and the Treasury as the most powerful and vociferous of these counter-interests.

> The Chancellor, prompted by the backwoodsmen of the Inland Revenue, insisted that changes in the tax system must be considered in isolation from all other aspects of social policy. If tax allowances were to be cut, therefore, it was for him to announce it in his Budget, not for Mr Gordon Walker in a statement on child poverty. This was more than a procedural quibble. It meant that the tax saving would not be set off against the cost of higher family allowances,

the whole of which would count as social security expenditure, reducing the amount of money available for other advances in the social security field. (10)

The influence of the Inland Revenue upon economic and fiscal policy is perhaps not as widely appreciated as it should be. Writing as the Wilson government came to power, Samuel Brittan stressed its importance as a key factor in any analysis of taxation policy, and particular tax reform. A significant outcome has been that even the powerful Treasury has found it difficult to overcome Inland Revenue opposition to change. The Board remains inherently conservative in its approach to policy initiative and, as Brittan noted, the role of the Treasury has been one of 'honest broker between the more hair-raising tax ideas put forward by the economists and the hardened conservatism of the Revenue Departments' (11).

Thus it has been argued that from the beginning of the family allowance debate CPAG were confronted by three powerful forces - the Board of Inland Revenue, the Treasury, and a Chancellor determined to articulate his Party's fears of a possible electoral backlash should family allowances rise. From the outset Callaghan was implacably opposed to the claw-back proposals favoured by CPAG as a method of financing an increase in family allowances.

Callaghan's position reflected the congruence of two powerful forces: administrative resistance to 'claw-back' from the Inland Revenue and the Treasury, and his own reading of the electoral dangers of income redistribution. The Inland Revenue Board rejected the entire CPAG case. According to tax orthodoxy, the child tax allowance was not a social benefit like family allowances, but simply a mechanism for adjusting tax to the capacity to pay. (12)

THE OPPOSITION TO CLAW-BACK

A principal feature of CPAG's proposals to claw back some of the cost of financing a rise in family allowances by abolishing child tax allowances was its apparent equity. Tony Lynes has explained this reasoning:

As a method of subsidising families with

children ... tax allowances for children seem
remarkably inefficient, since they are worth
most to those least in need of such a subsidy,
while the poorest families derive little or no
benefit from them. Family Allowances, on the
other hand, are payable at the same rates to
rich and poor alike. In some countries, they are
not subject to income tax. In others, of which
Britain is one, they are taxed so that only
families with very low incomes get the full
benefit of them. Their net value falling by
stages as the family's income rises. It is
understandable, therefore, that those concerned
with the abolition of poverty, rather than with
equity as between families further up the income
scale, should regard family allowances as a more
sensible way of redistributing income in favour
of families with children than tax allowances.
(13)

The Inland Revenue's interpretation of equity,
however, differed markedly. Its justification for
retaining child tax allowances stemmed partly from
the nature of the tax system itself. The tax
structure has evolved gradually over the last 300
years and its basic form has never been wholly
abandoned. As a result, new tax codings, measures and
instruments have been added as appendages to the core
- for example, company tax, surtax, value added tax
and capital transfer tax - and fundamental reform to
accommodate new rulings has never taken place. This
in itself has bred a strong sense of resistance to
change. Furthermore, the tax system reflects certain
beliefs and values held by those who administer it.
Brittan noted in the early 1960s that 'the root of
the Inland Revenue's opposition to many reforms goes
deeper still, to a rather limited notion of equity
... behind a great deal of its talk of equity is the
unchallenged assumption that the status quo is
"fair"'. When the Treasury, or a Department like the
Ministry of Social Security (DHSS) suggests,
therefore, that this group should have tax allowances
or that group should forfeit them, the Board, in its
assumption of maintaining equity, asks whether those
affected will regard the changes as 'fair'. If it
comes up with an answer in the negative opposition is
likely to be entrenched. It is at this point that the
support of the client lobby can be mobilised in
defence of the status quo. Brittan cites the case of
the CBI's predecessor, the Federation of British
Industry, whose tax experts 'so far from exercising a

71

reforming influence have been some of the chief obstacles to change - indeed they have occasionally made the Inland Revenue seem radical by comparison' (14).

The Board's implacable opposition to the CPAG proposals for claw-back, adopted by the Ministry of Social Security, centred on what it saw as an unacceptable distribution of tax liability within the more affluent tax paying categories. In contrast with CPAG's 'redistributive' approach to tax, officials of the Inland Revenue concerned themselves primarily and almost exclusively with the concept of equity - was the system of taxation fair?

An across-the-board increase in allowances was seen as undermining such equity, by penalising some families for the benefit of others. Moreover, the Board's officials held the view that family allowances did not concentrate support on those most in need. In short, they regarded claw-back as both inefficient and inequitable. More pointedly, perhaps, they rejected the governments' use of the tax system as a tool of social reform.

There was also strong opposition to claw-back from the Treasury. Treasury officials saw in claw-back an attempt to pre-empt or undermine a tradition in policy-making that had won for their Department the right to determine tax changes and general economic strategy in the preparation of Budgets. As Banting notes:

> The claw-back violated those prerogatives completely. It would formally link a tax with an expenditure change, thereby reducing the Chancellor's flexibility in the future; in addition, it would involve a collective cabinet decision on a tax issue and its announcement some 8 months before the Budget. From the first cabinet discussion of the issue in November 1966, Callaghan objected that claw-back usurped a budget decision and represented an intolerable fiscal procedure. (15)

Callaghan opposed claw-back on three further counts. It was his view that family allowance increases would be highly unpopular with large sections of the working class and that this would pose a serious threat to Labour's ability to maintain electoral support in what was seen as its natural constituency (16). The scheme would be additionally unpopular, he felt, by virtue of its transfer of income from the husband, who paid the higher tax, to the wife, who collected the higher family allowance - an issue that was to reappear, with Callaghan again closely involved, when Labour next came to power in 1974. Finally, he opposed claw-back on broad economic grounds as he sought to spark an industrial revival and achieve growth by placing restrictions on public expenditure.

It was against this backdrop that Peggy Herbison was instructed to arrive at a solution to child poverty which, in resource terms, could only be at the expense of the old, the sick and the unemployed - her own Department's client groups. Cut-backs were to take place within areas of social services expenditure instead of within other expenditure spheres with less immediate or apparent human need. The chief outcome, of course, was that the 'discovery' of a financial solution to child poverty from the existing social services budget would mean that the Chancellor would be free to syphon off any revenue from a later cut in tax allowances for other governmental projects. This was a prospect which the Group regarded as anathema. Commenting upon Herbison's resignation they complained: 'that she was right to resign in these circumstances is beyond question. The pity of it is that she did not feel free to reveal the whole disgraceful story, thus laying the blame where it belongs - on Mr Callaghan and the Board of the Inland Revenue' (17).

The Wilson government was also under attack from other quarters, most notably from among its own backbenches (18). In an alternative policy statement, <u>Change Gear</u>, David Marquand, John Mackintosh and David Owen, among the prominent parliamentary supporters of CPAG, called upon the government to institute, inter alia, a coherent and systematic poverty programme. In a critique which quite clearly questioned the leadership's emphasis on economic growth as the precondition of welfare expenditure they warned, 'it is easier to put socialist principles into practice when the rate of growth is high, but that is no excuse for failing to put them into practice when it is low'. The authors advocated the allocation of a higher proportion of GNP to the social services, to be achieved either by increases in taxation or by a wider use of charges, or by a combination of both. Their proposals included, significantly, a tax on wealth and a value added tax of the kind already in force in the EEC. In keeping with CPAG initiatives, they also advocated a greater tax burden falling on single people so that families would be relatively less penalised.

73

Nevertheless, they appeared to offset some of their more radical proposals by supporting the orthodox Institute of Economic Affairs' argument that direct charges should be extended because 'users may be more willing to pay for the social services if they see a direct connection between the payment they make and the service they receive'. In doing so, they closely anticipated Tory and Alliance thinking in the mid-80s.

Herbison had also made personal efforts to mobilise backbench support for a rise in family allowances during her final weeks in office. Backbench opinion in favour of the rise figured prominently during sessions of question time early in February 1967 and culminated in an early day motion on the issue signed by thirty MPs. While the support was vociferous it was, nevertheless, limited, and in the same month all but twenty-five of these MPs deserted a meeting of the Parliamentary Labour Party when the agenda turned to social security matters. Lewis Minkin, in a study of Labour Party Conferences, has shown that constituency opinion also favoured early and resolute action on this issue and notes that the constituency parties 'were concerned at the Government's inability to tackle the problem of poverty and opposed the imposition of the wage-stop. They were also overwhelmingly opposed to the re-introduction of prescription charges' (19). It is clear, however, that while outside forces were influential in setting and adjusting the tone of the poverty debate its outcome was largely determined in Cabinet when Ministers came to play roles assigned to them by their departmental responsibilities.

THE WAGE-STOP

Whilst the family allowance/claw-back issue had largely passed out of CPAG's hands by mid-1967, the Group had continued to press for reform or abolition of the wage-stop. By the summer its concern with the ruling had intensified to the extent that for a while it became the key issue around which the poverty debate sparked. One of the Group's chief concerns was the claimant's ignorance of how his or her entitlement was calculated. While this lack of knowledge, and a reluctance on the part of the Ministry of Social Security to resolve it, persisted the claimant's position remained excessively weak and his economic security stood threatened.

This apparent information breakdown obscures a

much more important and rather cynical belief which, it is claimed, is at the core of administrative thinking on the dispensation of welfare to claimants and their dependents. Party political inertia, the historically-strained relationship between official and claimant, and the hard facts of non-take-up of entitlement would seem to confirm Hilary Rose's view that, in the field of welfare, administrative caution, perhaps even reticence, is not simply expected, it is actively encouraged. Rose and Brown share the view that there may exist institutional and procedural pressures to minimise discretionary payment and discourage take-up. Those pressures may be further compounded by the view society takes of claimants with large families. The economist, Harry G. Johnson, has argued that there has been a reluctant and tardy acknowledgement in Britain of people, and children in particular, as a 'resource'. The failure to perceive children in this way disadvantages the child and its family in the short run and the economy in the long run. 'Refusal to recognise the investment character of a problem because people are involved may result in people receiving worse treatment than machines. (20)'

Margaret Wynn also supports the view that a society's industrial and economic future is, to some extent, dependent upon the continuation of the larger family. As she points out: 'Family policy must always be bounded by traditions and the extent of public support. Family policy like all forward-looking policies will always be threatened by the demands of the immediate future, by the pressures of short-term expediency, by the pressures for immediate consumption at the expense of longer-term investment' (21). Her analysis of the family as a resource is particularly pertinent when it is recalled that in the early 1970s some 75 per cent of the next generation was being raised in only 22 per cent of the UK households (22), with the result that the burden of a social investment likely to benefit most of future society was born by a minority of households. Ultimately, Wynn's view points to the problems of the short life of governments which encourage short-term expediency. The politicians' sense of survival is more likely to influence the selection of policies that satisfy the preferences of insider-groups and important vested interests who have sanctions to employ if ignored, than those with large families who are disproportionately repres-ented among the poor. Clearly, there is a long way to go before the larger family's contribution to economic growth and social progress is acknowledged and compensated. Indeed, the paradox emerges that the Wilson government was denying extra cash assistance to those with families in the mid-1960s until economic growth took-off yet was, at the same time, expecting them to make a significant contribution to that growth. As Wynn points out: 'whatever abstract philosophy is preached, government measures that are, in fact, biased against the family undermine a nation's vision of the future subtly, and often imperceptibly and unintentionally' (23).

The resource argument is one that CPAG seems largely to have failed to exploit in this period. Instead of swimming with the tide of government opinion in favour of growth, and attempting to locate increased family support as an integral factor in the achievement of that growth, the Group chose to argue the case for greater cash aid largely in terms of need, rights and equity - all admirable reasons in their own right, but perhaps over-played, and therefore of diminishing attraction to party leaders. A more aggressive, less Fabian, presentation of the family as a key factor in economic recovery and growth, with greater comparative emphasis on developments in other countries would have given some useful variation to the poverty debate and some 'new material' with which CPAG's parliamentary supporters could organise a fresh assault on government policy.

An obvious obstacle to the radicalisation of family policy in Britain, and to its closer integration with policy sectors whose own outcomes have some influence upon it, is the highly incremental style of British central administration. Demands for the application of continental practice to British social policy-making are strikingly at variance with the procedural norms and values of the British incremental model (24). Richardson and Jordan have commented that:

> The process of policy-making is one of selecting between the (comparatively) few alternatives that suggest themselves. In comparing these limited numbers of alternatives one does not dwell overlong on values or goals; instead one starts from the problem and considers a manageable range of alternatives. In choosing which option to adopt, one has reference to values, but ... the choice of policy instrument is combined with the ranking of values. In this approach there is a tendency for policy

innovations to be small-scale extensions of past efforts with an exception that there will be a constant return to the problem to make further extensions and to reconsider the problem in the light of new data. (25)

Ultimately, where the style of administration dictates that the policy-making process will not simply be a means of producing gradual changes in policy but will also be a means whereby the preferences of a number of often competing groups will be articulated, adjusted and accommodated, the very plurality of the interests with a concern in a policy will militate against radical innovation and, as the Cabinet discussion on claw-back shows, against a break with the status quo.

The wage-stop ruling provides a further example of an issue on which there was a clear status quo. In this case the status quo represented an apparently popular belief that an individual should not receive more when unemployed than when in full-time employment, regardless of the fact that his full-time employment wage was below the official poverty line (26).

In July 1967 Richard Haywood had already given Tony Lynes an implicit confirmation that instructions were to be issued by the Supplementary Benefits Commission to its local offices to explain to wage-stopped claimants how their benefit was calculated. CPAG pressure on the issue contributed, at least in part, to a situation in the autumn where both the SBC and the Ministry of Social Security became involved in a detailed review of wage-stop with the firm intention of softening its impact.

It is appropriate to note here Richard Titmus's comments on the role of the SBC and its relationship with pressure groups in the field. Titmuss described the Commission's task as creating dilemmas of choice for public debate. It was his view that the SBC's quasi-independent status enabled it to raise policy issues which had clear political overtones, and, in doing so, it could often find itself at variance with its 'parent' department, the DHSS. Nevertheless, its status did enable it to act as something of an internal pressure group within that Department and in this role he saw it being closely assisted by external pressure groups when they co-operated in attacking selected problems for mutual benefit. In the cases of both the wage-stop and child benefits, as will be shown later, CPAG may be judged to have played such a supportive role.

One of the difficulties the SBC faced in the introduction of the new rulings was that its staff were both underpaid and undermanned; it was believed that any additional burden would only pressurise them further. Nevertheless, the dialogue between CPAG and the Commission did give some indication that the latter was prepared to respond actively to the former's criticisms. One response took the form of a report, Administration of the Wage-Stop, published in December 1967 and distributed early in 1968. The report brought with it some important reforms, including the gauging of a labourer's potential earnings by local authority wage rates, and the abolition of the arbitrary deduction from earnings of 7s 6d (37½p) for 'intangible' expenses, which made some families up to £2 per week better-off (27). However, the disabled, the temporarily sick and short-term prisoners' families remained wage-stopped. CPAG's proposal for abolition of the ruling – or at least the suspension of it during the winter months of 1967-8 – was rejected.

Reluctance to abolish the wage-stop, despite grass-roots support for the measure, was also apparent at the Labour Party Conferences in both 1967 and 1968. In response to grass-roots anger at apparent government inertia on the issue, Crossman admitted the punitive and anomalistic nature of the wage-stop but tried to obscure the issue by claiming that the problem of low pay was the more salient one and the one upon which criticism should focus: 'we think that a national minimum wage has much more to do with the issue than Social Security. We cannot deal with the fundamental evil of low wages by Social Security regulations' (28). For CPAG this view represented no more than an uncomfortable attempt by the government to shift the burden of criticism and the source of blame from itself to the vagaries of the economic system – a convenient scapegoat for an embattled government.

The pattern was repeated the following year when the issue of the wage-stop was raised once more from the Conference floor. Minkin concluded from his observations of Labour Party Conferences that the prior disposition of both the Party's Social Policy Sub-Committee and the research department towards a particular issue raised on the floor was crucial in determining how far the issue, or resolution, would progress 'when the Conference passed a resolution which the Committee and the Department head both regarded as "impractical" there was no push at all for its implementation. This was shown in response to the Conference decisions on the wage-stop in 1968' (29). He went on to describe the Party's response to the issue in 1968:

> A resolution calling for the abolition of the wage-stop was carried on a hand vote against 'the platform' but it had little support, either on the Social Policy Advisory Committee or the Home Policy Sub-Committee. For all practical purposes, the resolution simply disappeared from view. It does not appear to have been seriously advocated by party representatives with Ministers. There was no reference to it in the Research Department's Section of the NEC Report of 1969 ... and there was no commitment to it in any of the programmatic documents produced that year by the party. (30)

Essentially, CPAG had fought the wage-stop ruling on two levels. They had launched their campaign calling for nothing less than the abolition of the ruling and the acceptance of their view that there should be a minimum official poverty line below which no one, regardless of what he earned in full-time employment, must be allowed to fall. However, it is often useful for a campaigning group to establish an ambitious target for itself, frequently in the foreknowledge that its achievement is unlikely: this strategy creates room to manoeuvre, and the opportunity to accept a lower target at a level which it may already have perceived as its 'real' target. In CPAG's case its ambitious demand was the abolition of the wage-stop. Its secondary level demand was to bring about administrative changes in the ruling, on the assumption that wage-stop was likely to continue to exist. Here the Group achieved some degree of success.

CLAWBACK - THE ADMINISTRATIVE DEBACLE

By April 1968 the Group's hopes for a new era in social policy had largely faded. The recent small increases in family allowances proved to be of marginal significance only and failed to assist the majority of families receiving supplementary benefit. Their total income was determined by the supplementary benefit scale and unless that scale was raised in line with the increase in family allowances they found that what they had gained was immediately taken away by the SBC. Little effort was made on the part of government to explain this apparently anomalous relationship between family allowances and supplementary benefits with the result that many families felt confused and penalised.

There had been a growing indication throughout the latter period of 1967 that claw-back might finally prevail as a method of financing the new rise in family allowances. In May, Wilson resisted opposition calls for a widening of means-testing. In June a Bill to increase national insurance benefit carried with it a clause giving the government temporary powers to raise family allowances in case it decided in favour of increasing the benefits in the autumn. Furthermore, the clause gave no hint that the government was still considering a means-tested approach - an indication that the government was moving in the claw-back direction. By mid-July, with Cabinet patience almost exhausted over what had been a bitter dispute, claw-back had prevailed. The final details concerned the level and timing of payment, and it was here that the government ran into difficulties.

The confusion following the 1967 and 1968 announcements on family allowances increases, and the government's acceptance of the claw-back proposal only after part of the first increase had been paid to families, did much to alienate public support for the government (31). For those families with four or more children 5 shillings (25p) of the 7 shillings (35p) increase for the fourth and subsequent children came into operation in October 1967. The total increase was planned for April 1968 and, in the Budget of that year, the new Chancellor, Roy Jenkins, was to study the method by which the necessary revenue could be raised. By the end of the year, however, devaluation had taken place, and in January Wilson announced a further increase of 3 shillings (15p) as a protective measure (32). At the same time, Wilson committed the government to simultaneous adjustments in tax allowances so that much of the 1967 and 1968 increases would be funded by a claw-back of tax from better-off families. However, a serious anomaly occurred because some families drew part of the increase from October 1967 and those who paid the standard rate of tax had their tax codes adjusted in such a way that from April to October 1968 they were losing more than the weekly family allowance increase. As Lynes has since noted, the difficulties of explaining what had taken place to irate taxpayers were considerable (33).

Banting has concluded that no single factor can

explain the crucial division in favour of claw-back at the Cabinet meeting of 23 February 1967 which, paradoxically, saw Peggy Herbison outmanoeuvre James Callaghan for the last time before her resignation, and which gave the proposal an impetus that gathered strength in the latter part of the year. He concludes instead that those favouring claw-back were influenced by a range of factors, the most prominent of which were party tradition, by feedback from those in the social administration and academic professions, and by the efforts and arguments of CPAG. Those opposed to claw-back, he contends, were more influenced by administrative factors, by possible electoral consequences, and by what they saw as the need for expenditure restraint (34). Ultimately, 'The final decision turned on the attitudes and perceptions of policy-makers: their party traditions, their administrative concerns, their electoral fears. Outside social constraints were real and potent. But they were present as estimates in the minds of policy-makers rather than demonstrations on the steps of Parliament' (35).

GROWTH AND WELFARE EXPENDITURE

The marginal increases failed to satisfy critical opinion. Comparisons with European developments were inevitable. The British system of social insurance and welfare assistance had long been distinctive in its method of funding, in its financial structure and in its level of provision. Unlike the income-based contributions common in the EEC, the British system, like that of the USA, is based mainly on flat-rate contributions and, as William Shepherd has noted, 'Apart from the regressivity this entails, it has prevented growth in revenues and consequently restrained the rise in benefits. Despite a rapid increase in the last decade, benefits are accordingly a smaller share of GNP in Britain than in comparable countries' (36). Shepherd also attempted an historical explanation of the failure of British governments in the 1960s to advance the level of social welfare provision significantly. This may serve to place CPAG's efforts in their proper and wider context. 'At the outset any diagnosis of Britain's economic difficulties must include the prolonged lapse from 1914 to 1945 of investment and adjustment in many sectors of economic and social infrastructure' (37). The massive redirection of funds in the early 1960s away from other priorities

in order to create the long overdue motorway network,
to bolster the NHS, and to capitalise the reorganisation of the coal and railway industries
resulted in deprivation in sectors like the social
services where the relationship between investment
and a return on capital was less clear.

It is also important to note that any reduction
in Social Services expenditure was further
exacerbated in the 1960s by the projected increases
in the number of young children and the aged in the
population issued in 1960 by the Central Statistical
Office. The latter, of course, is a major factor in
social services investment and a declining 'real'
level of services in the mid-80s also. For the period
1960-75 the 'probable increase' forecast in the
under-9 age group, for example, was a startling 33
per cent; in the 10-19 age group 13 per cent was
forecast; and in the pensionable age group 26 per
cent (38). Yet such projections, despite their
apparently significant implications for consumption,
had little effect on the Treasury's 'sectoral bias'.
Procedural improvements in forecasting the return on
investment in the nationalised industries for
example, meant that a bias would occur in the
Treasury's decisions among economic and social
programmes in favour of the former because economic
indicators of success or failure had been formulated
(39). The fact that the application of economic
forecasting to social service programmes was still
rudimentary and generally piecemeal served merely to
strengthen this bias (40).

By the mid-1960s the Treasury was approving
virtually all investment in the nationalised
industries which promised at least the 8 per cent
test rate of return. However, Shepherd noted that 'No
such economic case is made for social programmes,
most of which is current expenditure. Instead a
variety of technical standards, rules of thumb and
political factors - "needs" and "requirements" -
appears to prevail' (41).

Shepherd's independent analysis offers much
support for CPAG's view that not only was planning
and expenditure in the social services piecemeal and
fragmented, but that there was a clear Treasury bias
against the expenditure beyond certain levels. He
added, for example,

> Even in housing, education and, to some extent,
> health services, where economic appraisal is
> possible, little research has been done, either
> in Whitehall or independently, and what has been

> done does not always influence Treasury
> decisions. This may cause random imbalance
> among these programmes ... more important, it
> may systematically favour the programmes of the
> nationalised industries in the competition with
> social services for public funds. (42)

The result is that the Treasury may too easily
succumb to the facility of existing economic
indicators in making decisions which may
subsequently pre-empt resources which would have
more immediate social uses (43). It is beyond the
scope of this study to comment further upon the
possible economic rationale for Treasury responses
to increased family support in this period, but the
influences and factors outlined above are likely to
have contributed significantly to that rationale.
Ultimately, as Brittan has noted, 'reality' may lie
in the amount a country can afford to give claimants
in a harsh economic climate. 'If the country were to
grow richer more quicky, it would be easier to raise
the real value of pensions, even if prices rose
faster as a result. A policy of rapid growth is in
fact more in the interest of those who are dependent
on the Welfare State than a policy of price stability
at all costs. (44)'
   In adopting this 'growth as a prerequisite of
expenditure' approach the Labour government and the
Treasury were following what some writers have
considered to be a universal trend in social policy-
making. In 1965, for example, Philip Cutright
demonstrated that the variance in social security
coverage and the level of benefits dispensed by
governments could be directly linked with their
country's economic development and that this
economic factor was far more influential in the
formulation of social security programmes than, for
example, the degree of political representativeness
(45). A decade later, in 1976, G.M. Haniff showed
that economic factors, especially the level of
economic development, outweigh political ones in
determining social policy (46). This, in turn, led
Thomas Dye to conclude that 'most comparative cross-
national policy studies indicate that health and
welfare policies, regardless of political systems,
are closely associated with levels of economic
development' (47).
   British political scientists have taken a less
economic view of the public welfare commitment and
have equally stressed the importance of political
factors, not the least of which is the type of system

(i.e. federal or unitary) prevalent in a particular state. Frank Castles and Robert McKinlay conclude, for example, that 'it is clear that differences in political organisation, defined in terms of political structure and ideology, play a critical role in explaining differentials in commitment to public welfare in advanced democratic states'. However, having made this useful qualification they, too, recognise the importance of economic development:

> once we have taken account of such (political) differences, economic development also contributes to public welfare. Since in the short term the political factors do not vary, we can suggest that economic development provides the dynamic for public welfare ... It must be emphasised, however, that the dynamic role of economic development only becomes apparent once we have taken political factors into consideration. (48)

CONSULTATION AND CONSULTATIVE STATUS

In Britain, while the demands for economic growth may have been popularly viewed as pre-eminent in Labour's rhetoric, the whole question of the timing and sizes of a rise in family allowances was ultimately influenced by the response the government expected from other interests affected by the increase. Richard Crossman had already warned in November 1966 that 'in peace-time the gap between private affluence and public squalor cannot be corrected without a fairly rapid rate of economic growth' (49). Callaghan, sensing the tide of public opinion turning against further expenditure on social security, warned that middle-income groups and skilled manual workers were unwilling to sacrifice any further erosion in their standard of living for this purpose (50). The general fears of Ministers about interfering with the tax allowances of middle-income groups were such that by February 1967 one newspaper was moved to comment, 'Government opinion is now moving in favour of a straight increase in family allowances. One major reason for this is the fear of political repercussions among middle class and professional families who have been expressing strong resentment at the prospect of losing tax reliefs to benefit a minority of large families' (51).

This view was endorsed by the Institute of Economic Affairs in March in a sample survey on the issue of family allowances which revealed that 57 per cent of those surveyed approved of selective family allowances, and 53 per cent preferred means-tested rather than free prescriptions (52). This lent further support to a Labour government already teetering on the brink of non-decision. Findings of this sort simply served to nudge it over the edge in favour of those with the 'loudest' voice, though some sections of the press were concerned to articulate the grievances of those least likely to be heard (53).

Responding to a speech by the Prime Minister at the Labour Party Conference in 1967, in which he had talked of the 'great social advance' which had taken place under the Labour government, and in which he had produced figures to show the apparent increases in social services expenditure, Peter Townsend wrote:

> much of the increased expenditure is going to middle-income groups, the new managers, the children of the middle-classes, who largely account for the growing cost of higher education, and the educated consumers who expect high standards in medical care. The real test of social advance is how far a substantial proportionate shift of resources to the lowest income groups has occurred. There is little evidence that this has yet happened in Britain. (54)

If CPAG's influence seemed tenuous in terms of countervailing that of other interests, it appeared even weaker in terms of its broader impact upon some government institutions. In December 1967, for example, in the wake of the government's failure to reform housing policy and alleviate the plight of the homeless, the new overlord for social services, Michael Stewart, announced that he was to convene a conference of academic experts and departmental civil servants at Lancaster House to discuss the problems faced by the social services. Principally, the conference was designed to offer some constructive alternative to the fragmented and generally negative co-operation between the Home Office and the Health and Housing Departments, which was seen as a major factor contributing to government inertia.

Stewart did not, however, choose to invite

representatives of the main pressure groups active in
the fields presided over by these Departments; though
it is Peter Townsend's view that, in giving one of
the two key addresses to the Conference, it was very
much uppermost in Stewart's mind that he was
'representing' the Group. In not doing so he
established a firm precedent for future reliance upon
academic observation and proposition rather than
political feedback. This was all the more important
because the conference provided a clear opportunity
for the type of improved public participation the
Party had so often talked about in opposition. Why
then was the suggestion ignored? Stewart's own view
of the meeting was that it was designed to examine
and establish priorities within the social services
against the backdrop of economic stringency.
Clearly, he felt that academics, politicians and
civil servants, rather than pressure-group activists
(whom one might suppose could be regarded as
'emotionally involved' and too partisan in their
arguments) would provide the type of knowledge and
objectivity the conference required. He commented in
his introductory speech:

> the task of operating the social services was
> limitless, but the nation's economic resources
> were limited, this Government inevitably faced
> a problem of priorities. The solution to this
> problem lay partly in the expansion of the
> Country's economic resources, but it was even
> more important to have the right political
> choices ... among the social services
> themselves. It had therefore been decided that
> the conference should concentrate on those
> problems - the demographic and economic factors
> affecting policy, and the manner in which, in
> the light of those factors, priorities should be
> chosen and resources deployed.

The government line was again supported by an
independent economic forecaster, on this occasion
the Director of the NIESR, who backed the view of the
'Economic Ministries' that growth of public
expenditure programmes could only be maintained by
restricting the growth of personal consumption - his
view being the politically emotive one that stasis
had set in in the economy while public expenditure
and services continued to expand.

CPAG's non-attendance at the Lancaster House
conference raises further questions about its status
in the eyes of government. It may have been the case

that the Labour government felt it already had a fairly accurate idea of the extent of the social problems raised at the conference without resorting to practical feedback from what were comparatively nascent groups anyway. Furthermore, it may have considered it politic to defuse the issues in question by confining discussion of them to academic and administrative observers. In doing so, the prospect of non-incrementalist solutions being offered would be largely obviated. The debate on social policy thus became, once more, internalised, confined to government policy-makers and those that they identified as part of what Heclo has termed the 'issue-network', which he defines as 'a shared-knowledge group having to do with some aspect (or, as defined by the network, some problem) of public policy' (55). Two points are important here. First Helco suggests that the network may be distinguished from conventional pressure groups by its overriding and non-emotive concern with the technical and informational aspects of an issue or problem. Secondly, the network, by its very exclusivity and 'control' over an issue, appears to retain the right to define that problem. He notes: 'Increasingly, it is through networks of people who regard each other as knowledgeable, or at least as needing to be answered, that public policy issues tend to be refined, evidence debated, and alternative options worked out ...' (56). It is clear that the Labour government either felt it did not need to answer groups like CPAG, Shelter and the Disablement Income Group, or perhaps that the timing and style of the conference was not appropriate to such an answer (57).

It is likely that the government did not see itself as having to consult or confer with a group like CPAG for three key reasons. CPAG was not representative of the poor in the membership sense; much of the information it generated could possibly have been supplied by civil servants anyway and a decision to overlook the Group in consultations was unlikely to have the sort of repercussions that could result if an economic or industrial group was overlooked. CPAG was clearly not regarded as the sort of insider group to which Grant has referred. Indeed, as he notes, 'a useful distinction can be made between those interest groups which are accepted by central government departments as legitimate spokesmen which have to be consulted on a continuous basis and those groups which are not consulted on a regular basis' (58). This does not necessarily imply, of course, that the government will cease consultation with such a group, it may simply regulate it in such a way that both sides gain some benefit from their occasional meetings without a hard and fast relationship developing. It seems clear, for example, that the Labour government was still willing to maintain a dialogue of sorts with CPAG on specific issues. The SBC's willingness to consider CPAG initiatives has already been noted, though even here Grant suggests that semi-autonomous government agencies have as a function, the creation of 'a kind of phoney "insider" status for some groups in order to reassure them that they have a sympathetic point of access within the government machine' (59).

Early in February 1968 Stewart met with CPAG and undertook to investigate anomalous practices in the refunding of rate rebates which the group had uncovered, although he ruled out other CPAG requests for extending the provision of free school meals and free welfare foods on the grounds of cost. Two weeks later, representatives of the Group were invited to discuss their proposals for a reform of the tax structure with the Chancellor in advance of his April Budget. They urged him not to reduce tax reliefs without increasing family allowances correspondingly and pressed for the abolition of the government's option mortgage scheme and tax relief on mortgage interest, asking that they be replaced by subsidised mortgages for everyone' (60).

The Group's qualified success in helping to influence Cabinet discussion and acceptance of the claw-back proposal has already been noted. Acceptance of claw-back meant that future increases in family allowances were to be concentrated on low income families by reducing the tax allowances for the better-off and this was included in Jenkins' April Budget, though the scheme remained a temporary measure and was not carried through to 1969-70. Jenkins also promised to keep the Group informed about Treasury progress on negative income tax schemes. The Treasury in turn envisaged a more active role for the Group in the study of negative income tax proposals:

> Treasury Ministers would ... be glad to have a considered statement of your group's views on those aspects of the problem of low incomes with which your group is primarily concerned. When they and the officials concerned have had an opportunity to examine this, the Chief Secretary, who is in charge of the study, will

probably want to discuss it with some members of
your group. (61)

In March Lynes had written to the Minister of
Housing, Anthony Greenwood, to suggest that his
Department consider sponsoring a joint CPAG-
Departmental Study Group on the take-up of rate
rebates among low wage-earners with families, though
nothing appears to have come of this. On 4 March, he
also had a further meeting with Judith Hart, Minister
of Social Security, on the vexed issue of
prescription charges though, again, he was
unsuccessful. Juxtaposed, this series of meetings
and incidents may have created some impression that
the Group was acquiring a growing influence in
government. Yet, if CPAG's important but temporary
success on claw-back was isolated, we are left with
Grant's less flattering assessment that 'The crucial
distinction is between those groups which are invited
by Central Government Departments to submit their
views on topics relevant to their concerns and those
which are at best tolerated to the extent that they
are allowed to send occasional deputations to the
relevant departments (62).

THE REVIEW OF PUBLIC EXPENDITURE 1968

Against the backdrop of other events taking place in
1968 much of this consultation can be viewed as
cosmetic - a palliative to distract from the coming
storm. If the origins of the 1970 rupture in CPAG-
Labour Party relations lie elsewhere than in the
debacle which surrounded the resignation of Peggy
Herbison, then spring 1968 is the crucial period.
Paul Foot has written that Harold Wilson knew
beforehand, in the wake of devaluation of the pound
and pressure from employers, workers and foreign
governments alike, that 1968 would be the year of
harsh economic cutbacks. 'By January 1968 he was
sufficiently cleansed of reformist sentiment to
agree with Jenkins, unequivocally, that what was good
for the balance of payments was good for Labour.
(63)' It is interesting to add, by contrast, that
only three years later Anthony Crosland was arguing
that the Party's preoccupation with economic growth
and stabilising the balance of payments as
prerequisites of increased social services
expenditure had stultified Party 'thinking'
throughout the period 1964 to 1970 (64).

In December 1967 Wilson and Jenkins had reached

agreement that major reductions would be required in defence and overseas expenditure and, more significantly, in the 'planned growth of social expenditure' (65). This meant that as pressure on social services accelerated in accordance with projected demographic changes the provision of resources and facilities would remain relatively static and, in some areas, would be actually reduced. At a Cabinet meeting on 4 January the Chancellor and Prime Minister introduced their package of cuts. As Wilson noted, the political implications were farreaching:

> It was a major exercise in restraining the growth of public expenditure. The task of getting it through cabinet without sensational resignations was the most formidible task I had attempted in over 3 years of Government. My greatest asset was the firmness and determination of the Chancellor in the presentation of his balanced package. (66)

In the event, only one Minister resigned – Lord Longford over deferment of the raising of the school leaving age. By 15 January the package had gone through. In an extraordinary statement to the Commons the next day, Wilson, taking over responsibility from his Chancellor, announced reductions in the existing expenditure programme of £325 million in 1968/9, and £441 million in 1969/70. Turning his attention to social security the Prime Minister stated that in the year 1967/8 total expenditure was £2909 million (48 per cent above 1963/4) and by 1968/9 would be £3106 million, and £3216 million in 1969/70. 'There were no cuts. Indeed, our pledge to shelter the least well-off families against the effect of post-devaluation price increases was to be honoured by a second increase in family allowances, and a further increase in the next reconsideration of supplementary benefits. (67)'

There are two important points to consider here. First, given inflation and the highly marginal nature of the family allowance increases, the position of the poor with large families hardly altered. Secondly, even a scheme as limited as this in its provision of cash aid could not have been achieved had not CPAG, Herbison and a small group of parliamentary supporters waged a long campaign to win the Chancellor's support for the claw-back principle. Consequently, Wilson was able to announce that 'to match the higher family allowances the

Chancellor would recover the value of the increase from the better-off by corresponding reductions in child allowances under income tax - the so-called 'claw-back' principle which had been advocated by many concerned with child poverty' (68). Additionally, Labour's package of cuts must have raised questions regarding the future pattern of public expenditure and income in Britain. Taking defence cuts as an example, Wilson announced that by 1972 the defence budget, in real terms, would be £350 million less than originally planned. The key question CPAG now sought to raise, of course, was just how the 'savings' would be spent.

> Will it be used to reduce the so-called 'burden' of taxation? or will it be to increase the amount spent on Social Services and Welfare benefits? The question is a long-term one, but an important one. To use the money saved on defence to reduce taxation will inevitably increase income differences and widen the gap between the poorest and the remainder of the community. (69)

What was now needed, argued CPAG, was a long-term economic plan in which the new opportunities created by the defence cuts would be used for the pursuit of social justice. This would be the 'real test of the Government's system of priorities'. It was Labour's failure to respond satisfactorily to this challenge that marked a re-think in CPAG's relationship with the Party. By spring 1968, the Labour government had re-introduced prescription charges (and where free prescriptions <u>could</u> be obtained, CPAG claimed publicity was poor); it had introduced the lowest possible increase in family allowances politically acceptable; public expenditure had been savagely cut and, despite Wilson's promises to the contrary, Michael Stewart had warned the Group in February that the Cabinet could not give any assurance that the poor could be shielded from the effects of devaluation by the 'special measures' Wilson had talked of.

CPAG's emphasis on the importance of taxation as an instrument for achieving greater social equality was particularly crucial. Kincaid has noted that the proportion of national resources directly controlled by public authorities is now so great that even apparently minor changes in the taxation structure, especially if they are made at the higher income levels, can have considerable effects upon the social

distribution of income and wealth. The Labour
government had clear opportunities to do this since
it had raised the overall rate of taxation with quite
remarkable speed since coming to office. In the
period 1964-7, central and local government taxation
rose from 36.2 to 41.5 per cent of GNP. Thus, argues
Kincaid, the state had been drawing in extra spending
power of approximately £600 million per year. The
implications of this to groups like CPAG were clear.

> Had tax increases of this magnitude been made
> primarily at the expense of wealthier groups in
> society, their impact upon the pattern of social
> class inequality would have been substantial.
> Yet nothing of the sort had occurred. Rather, it
> has been those social groups, mainly manual
> workers, with incomes at or below, the average
> national wage level, who have borne the brunt of
> Labour's fiscal attack on living standards.
> (70)

This was the situation brought about by Labour
policies by mid-1968. By November, Lynes had become
sufficiently disillusioned both with the government's record and the Group's impact to tender his
resignation. It is to this event, a watershed in
CPAG's development, that we turn in the next chapter.

NOTES

1. Describing the background to the
appointment of Patrick Gordon Walker, Harold Wilson
commented 'Concurrently, we were working on a fresh
attack on poverty. All that we had done in successive
increases in pensions and National Assistance had
been directed towards relieving poverty in the main
sectors - retirement pensioners, the sick and
disabled and war pensioners. But there was
accumulating evidence that once these groups had been
helped, the principal area of poverty was to be found
in large families, whether or not the head of the
household was at work. Patrick Gordon Walker had been
charged with the responsibility for working out means
of help'. Wilson, The Labour Government 1964-70,
p.356.
2. Poverty, No. 4 (Autumn 1967), p.2.
3. Ibid.
4. Michael Meacher MP notes, for example,
that 'spending ministers' opposing the 'Whitehall
consensus' may find themselves the victims of 'the

close interlock with establishment interests outside, which often means officials are acting in concert with the extra-parliamentary power structure against ministers rather than in support of the political manifesto of the governing party'. 'The Men who Block the Corridors of Power', Guardian (14 June 1979).

5.   Miliband notes: 'Lincoln was entirely wrong when he said that a society cannot live half-slave and half-free. It depends first and foremost on the respective strength of conflicting forces operating in society. Some making for the persistence of poverty, and others working against its persistence; and the trouble for the poor is that the forces operating against them are very much stronger than those working in their favour ... there are many other claimants upon public funds, with far more powerful and compelling voices, from large enterprises (which are voracious and effective applicants for public assistance) to the struggling middle classes. The simple fact of the matter is that the poor enter the pressure market, where they enter it at all, from the weakest possible position: that, of course, is one of the main reasons, if not <u>the</u> main reason, why they remain poor'. Miliband, R., 'Politics and Poverty', in Wedderburn, D. (ed.), <u>Poverty, Inequality and Class Structure</u> (Cambridge University Press, 1974).

6.   See Kellner, P. and Schott, K., 'The Un-affluent Society', New Statesman (26 October 1979) and Hill, M., <u>The State, Administration and the Individual</u> (Fontana, 1976), pp.53-4.

7.   Gustafsson and Richardson note 'policies are agreed within professionalised policy commun-ities. Politics, from the viewpoint of the citizen, has gone underground. It has disappeared into a relatively closed world where governments negotiate with interest groups ... The policy community within each segment is in fact a rather restricted community - a policy elite which determines the policy outcomes'. op.cit., p.32.

8.   Crenson, M., <u>The Unpolitics of Air Pollution</u> (Johns Hopkins University Press, Baltimore, 1971), p.178.

9.   Banting, K., <u>Poverty, Politics and Policy</u> (Macmillan, 1979), pp.98-9.

10.   <u>Poverty</u>, No. 4, pp.2-3.

11.   Brittan, S., <u>The Treasury Under the Tories 1951-64</u> (Pelican, 1964), p.118.

12.   Banting, op.cit., p.94.

13.   Lynes, A., 'Clawback', in Bull, D. (ed.),

Family Poverty (Duckworth, 1972), pp.119-20.
14. Brittan, op.cit, p.120.
15. Banting, op.cit., pp.95-6.
16. *Guardian* (27 July 1967).
17. *Poverty*, No. 4, p.3.
18. Richard Crossman spoke of the government's problems in contending with 'the growing disillusionment of our own backbenchers', and added 'This Government had dramatic successes when it only had a majority of three. Now it has a majority of a hundred it has relaxed its efforts; and as a result it has created a sense of impatience and disillusionment among the new intake of able, vigorous, intelligent but politically naive MPs. Quite legitimately many of them are beginning to feel that this is not a Socialist Government, not even a leftist Government, but just any old government teetering along and carrying out its election programme in a rather uninspired way'. Crossman, *Diaries*, Vol. I, pp.532-3.
19. Minkin, L., The Labour Party Conference (Allen Lane, 1978), p.90.
20. See Blaug, M. (ed.) The Economics of Education No. 1 (Penguin, 1968), p.39.
21. Wynn, M. Family Policy (Pelican, 1972), p.264.
22. Wynn notes 'the infertility of about half the adult population has to be compensated for by the greater fertility of a minority. At any one time less than 9% of all households in the UK include 3 or more children dependent upon them; these households are bringing up over 40% of the next generation. Over 40% of all adults alive today (1970) were brought up in the minority households of the last generation which contained three or more dependent children ... Most of the time, trouble and money expended on rearing the next generation fall on the shoulders of a minority of all adults or earners or taxpayers in the community at any one time'. Ibid., pp.26-7. Wynn's analysis makes all the more contentious the comments made by Douglas Houghton in a speech in July 1968 in which he talked of the 'social irresponsibility of large families'. *Guardian* (4 July 1968).
23. Wynn, op.cit., p.267.
24. Brown (op.cit.) notes, for example, that 'There is clearly a risk that a department like the DHSS will see its role as that of integrating the interests of a limited range of powerful groups and minimising conflict among them ... (however) the disadvantages of incrementalism are first that incrementalist decisions are not so much made as

merge from a series of bargains between different participants in the policy process, all attempting to pursue their own goals with adjustments where necessary to avoid serious conflict with other partisan groups. Radical changes are to be avoided, since they would encounter too much resistance. The second disadvantage is that interests which are not central to the discussions tend to be left out. Typically it is the general public that gets overlooked'. p.208. See also James, E. and Laurent, A., 'Social Security: The European Experiment', Social Trends 1974 (CSO), pp.26-34.

25. Richardson and Jordan, op.cit., p.22.
26. It is significant that even by the mid-1970s, in the wake of fifteen years of parliamentary, press and public debate on the causes and injustices of poverty, a study by the EEC Commission discovered that 43 per cent of respondents polled in Britain felt that poverty occurred 'because of laziness and lack of will power', while only 16 per cent attributed it to the view that 'there is much injustice in our society'. The weighted average across the whole EEC in support of the indolence theory was, by contrast, only 25 per cent (ranging from 11 per cent in Denmark to 31 per cent in Luxembourg). For the injustice theory the EEC average was a broadly similar, 26 per cent (ranging from 40 per cent in Italy to a low of 11 per cent in the Netherlands). Table 29, 'The Perception of Poverty in Europe', The Commission of the European Community Expose (1977).
27. Poverty, No. 5, p.13.
28. Ibid., p.14.
29. Minkin, op.cit., p.304.
30. Ibid.
31. Talking Points, No. 9 (Labour Party, July 1968).
32. Wilson, The Labour Government, pp.613-14.
33. Bull, op.cit., pp.122-8.
34. Banting, op.cit., p.104.
35. Ibid., p.105.
36. Shepherd, W.G. 'Alternatives for Public Expenditure', in Caves, R.E. (ed.), Britain's Economic Prospects (George Allen & Unwin, 1970), p.441. For an alternative assessment of public expenditure in the area of Social Service provision, see Abel-Smith, B., Public Expenditure on the Social Services', Social Trends (CSO, 1970).
37. Shepherd, op.cit., p.384.
38. Annual Abstract of Statistics 1966 (CSO), pp.12-13.

39. See, for example, a discussion of the role of the Public Expenditure Survey Committee in Clarke, R., Public Expenditure, Management and Control: The Development of PESC. (Macmillan, 1979), and Richardson and Jordan, op.cit., pp.31-5.

40. Glennerster, H., Social Service Budgets and Social Policy (George Allen & Unwin, 1975).

41. Shepherd, op.cit., p.386.

42. Ibid.

43. Self, P., Econocrats and the Policy Process (Macmillan, 1975), pp.120-4.

44. Brittan, op.cit., pp.148-9.

45. Cutright P., 'Political Structure, Economic Development and National Security Programmes', American Journal of Sociology, No. 70 (1965), pp.537-50.

46. Haniff, G.M., 'Politics, Development and Social Policy: A Cross-National Analysis', European Journal of Political Research, No. 6., pp.361-76.

47. Dye, T.R., Policy Analysis (University of Alabama Press, 1976), p.51.

48. Castles, F. and McKinlay, R.D., 'Does Politics Matter? An Analysis of the Public Welfare Commitment in Advanced Democratic States', European Journal of Political Research, No. 7 (1979), p.181.

49. Crossman, R., Socialism and Planning, Fabian Tract No. 375 (1967), pp.21-2.

50. Guardian (27 July 1967).

51. Sunday Times (5 February 1967). See also The Times (3 February 1967), and Observer (15 January 1967).

52. Seldon, A. and Gray, H., Universal or Selective Social Benefits (IEA, March 1967).

53. The Guardian, for example, said of the April Budget 'Once again the Government has done nothing to mitigate the scandalous poverty of low wage families. Higher family allowances across the board would have cost more than the Chancellor could afford this year. But it should be possible to give help selectively to those in need without upsetting the balance of the economy. For the Government to say that it is still looking for the best way to relieve this hardship is not good enough' (12 April 1967).

54. Townsend, P., Sociology and Social Policy (Allen Lane, 1975), pp.304-5.

55. Heclo, H., 'Issue Networks and the Executive Establishment', in King, A. (ed.), The New American Politics (American Enterprise Institute, 1978), p.103.

56. Ibid., p.104.

57. The fact remains, however, that if we

accept Heclo's view that 'Instead of power commensurate with responsibility, issue networks seek influence commensurate with their understanding of the various, complex social choices being made' (p.103), then groups like CPAG and DIG, which had acquired hybrid roles as promotional pressure groups <u>and</u> repositories of expertise and knowledge, would seem to have been appropriate candidates for membership of any such issue network and, therefore, worthy of participation at the Lancaster House Conference.

58. Grant, <u>op.cit.</u>, p.3.
59. Ibid., p.4.
60. 21 February 1968.
61. D.E.J. Dowler, Principal Secretary at the Treasury, to Tony Lynes 18 April 1968. This reply concluded a short correspondence on the subject of NIT between Lynes and R.T. Armstrong, Private Secretary to the Chancellor (18 March 1968) and with Roy Jenkins, Chancellor of the Exchequer (9 April 1968).
62. Grant, <u>op.cit.</u>, p.3.
63. Foot, <u>op.cit.</u>, p.194.
64. Crosland, A., <u>A Social Democratic Britain</u>, Fabian Tract No. 404 (1971).
65. Wilson, <u>The Labour Government</u>, p.608.
66. Ibid.
67. Ibid., p.613.
68. Ibid., p.614; and <u>Poverty</u>, No.6 (Spring 1968), pp.13-14.
69. <u>Poverty</u>, No.6, p.2.
70. Kincaid, <u>op.cit.</u>, p.21. See also <u>Economic Trends</u> (HMSO, February 1969), p.xxx.

Chapter Five

POLITICISING THE POOR

At no point up to 1969 had poverty, and its alleviation through increased family allowances, become a major party political issue. Certainly, a number of sympathetic MPs and journalists and one or two Ministers had championed the increases from time to time, but CPAG failed to develop child poverty as an issue that would attract strong public support and provoke coherent and sustained administrative action. This might seem all the more depressing in the context of Butler and Stokes' 1964 findings that 77 per cent of their electoral sample favoured more governmental expenditure on pensions and the social services (1). Superficially, such findings may have suggested that the public mood would be responsive to the educative campaigns of public interest groups like CPAG and that it would be unwise of such groups to overlook this avenue of political influence. Ultimately, however, groups with limited resources are more likely to be guided in their approach to the general public by MacFarlane's view 'For many people an issue is an issue because it deeply and immediately affects them' (2).

Additionally, CPAG may have been constrained at this time by the close relations between senior figures in the Group and members of the Labour government and Party. Unlike his successor Frank Field, Tony Lynes largely eschewed a dramatic, mass publicity-oriented approach to poverty, preferring, instead, to remain low-key and selective. This style may well have been influenced by Group-Party relations. As Heckscher notes: 'If a given pressure group is acting through a political party, public relations activities will be moderate since, otherwise, the group would get little sympathy from an opposing political party' (3). Similarly, one of the reasons why Field resorted to a 'dramatisation' of poverty after the Group's 1970 critique of Labour's record in office may have been that 'if the pressure group is operating outside of a party, it will give increased attention to its public relations' (4). Field himself has said that the two principle tactics in CPAG's strategy have been regular attempts to raise issues through the use of questions and debate on the floor of the Commons and keeping the press constantly interested in the poverty issue. 'By operating both these options ... it is possible to create an impression of a groundswell in favour of a particular reform. With civil servants groomed, and politicians forced, to be conciliatory and to move in line with public opinion, both tactics play an essential part in a reformist group's campaign. (5)'

However, Field's use of the term 'public opinion' is rather misleading and is equated wrongly with 'CPAG opinion'. Clearly, during Lynes' period of office, CPAG had undertaken an important and valuable educative role in the dissemination of information on poverty, but it had not directed its campaign towards the general public, nor had it attempted to translate its findings into a form and vernacular easily understood by the general reader. Instead, it was upon the 'informed public' - MPs, academics and civil servants - that CPAG's efforts were concentrated. While these groups may well have been receptive to the 'rediscovery of poverty' in the late 1950s, it was over-optimistic to expect a similar attentiveness in the mid-1960s when economic issues and prices and incomes policy dominated the political stage. Any groundswell that had been achieved, then, was exaggerated, and largely confined to a body of opinion leaders whose sympathies and interests lay in policy areas which now appear to have been antipathetic to increased expenditure on the social services. It could be argued that CPAG had too narrowly committed itself to sections of the government and the Party for whom poverty was a peripheral issue of diminishing interest. In confining the debate in this way, the Group largely set aside the prospect of rank-and-file involvement in the issue from both the trade union movement and the poor themselves. It should be noted, however, that the range of issues on which CPAG fought in this period and the selective style adopted by Lynes to politicise them were consistent with the Group's limited resources. A mass educational/political campaign directed at the general public was neither logistically nor financially possible. Lynes and his colleagues saw the selective use of their resources to influence a small group of opinion leaders as potentially the most effective short-term means of raising poverty to the status of a major political issue on which action would then be forthcoming (6).

POLITICISING AN ISSUE

It is useful to draw some broader comparison between poverty and other social issues against this backdrop of politicisation. Anthony Downs has suggested that issues invariably progress through a series of stages which takes them from relative obscurity to banner headlines and thence to obscurity again. This he refers to as an issue-attention cycle. It begins in the 'pre-problem stage', that is, when some highly undesirable social condition exists but has not as yet captured significant public attention. He notes: 'Many specialised experts or interest groups may already be alarmed about the issue. But somehow they have not succeeded in dramatising it or otherwise bringing it to the centre of the stage of public attention' (7). From this initial, pre-problem stage an issue might progress, as child poverty appears to have done in 1965-6, to stage two; that of 'alarmed discovery and euphoric enthusiasm'. At this point, usually as a result of a dramatic series of events, the public suddenly becomes aware of, and alarmed about, the evils of a particular problem. In the case of child poverty the publication of The Poor and the Poorest, the subsequent media campaign and the formation of CPAG were the catalysts in the formation of public awareness. This alarmed discovery on the part of the public (evidently not those affected by the problem) is accompanied, Downs claims, by 'euphoric enthusiasm about society's ability to "solve this problem" or "do something effective" within a relatively short time period' (8).

In the case of child poverty, in the mid-1960s there was a good deal of optimism that the new, 'reformist' Labour government might similarly be able to 'do something effective'. Drawing broadly on Downs' analysis of American expectations of their own propensity for reform, the belief emerges that 'every such obstacle can be eliminated and every problem solved without any fundamental reordering of society itself, if only we devote sufficient effort to it'. Of course, where such a belief is at fault is in its serious failure to recognise that society as such, or those who have come to dominate it, may well lack the

will to eliminate such 'problems' for a variety of
reasons, not the least of which is that in doing so
they may well weaken their own social and economic
advantage and undermine a process of socialisation
that accords them considerable status and deference.
What Downs loosely terms the 'democratisation of
privilege and opportunity' will invariably
jeopardise the social, economic and, ultimately, the
political advantage of those who have historically
presided over, or prospered in, a system of social
and economic injustice. Some groups may thus have a
vested interest in ensuring that others remain
deprived in one sense or another, and they may be
expected either to oppose or to refrain from
supporting the 'economic liberation' of the poor
(10).
      Peter Self notes that the 'ultimate rationale'
of a democracy lies in the equity of its rules and
norms for reaching public decisions, rather than in
the actual content of those decisions. In practice,
however, the acceptability of rules and norms will
depend upon concrete results and the individual may
find it difficult to accept the degree of
satisfaction he receives (11). What Self seems to
suggest, then, is that even if privilege and
opportunity were 'democratised' in the Downsian
sense there is no guarantee that the 'newly
enfranchised' will be any better-off. This
introduces a classic dilemma of pluralism, i.e. that
the individual or the group may acquire the
opportunity to enter the system (which in itself may
justify pluralism) but may lack the skills and
resources fully to exploit that opportunity (which
may not justify it). Self makes this dilemma
abundantly clear:

> It is not clear that an increase of political
> pluralism, for example, of the number of
> organised groups or agencies that can influence
> decisions, will of itself improve the
> 'transmission belt' function of democracy.
> This is not only because the groups in question
> may be relatively wealthy or privileged ... but
> also because more specialised 'wants' may be
> achieved in this way at the expense of more
> generalised wants ... so that while the whole
> system may be gaining in terms of the number and
> variety of shared wants that are effectively
> articulated, and also in terms of the total
> quantum of political participation, the net
> effect could still be adverse upon the total sum

of want-satisfactions. (12)

The basic tenet of a pluralist society in a state of economic stagnation, as in Britain in the mid-1960s, and now again in the Eighties, is that the cake from which all expect a slice is not growing: in relative terms, given rising expectations, it may well be shrinking. If deprived publics are to be allocated extra resources in the form of increased public expenditure then the resources allocated to the more prosperous sections of the community must be reduced to finance that redistribution. Otherwise, redistribution takes place between deprived groups or resources are held back temporarily with the promise of an increased bounty when the economic miracle, for which that restraint is vital, is finally worked. The situation bears strong resemblance to events between 1964 and 1969. When Lynes, and later Field, went cap-in-hand to the government asking respectively that middle-income tax incentives and child tax allowances be reduced and that tax relief on mortgages be abolished to win back extra resources to finance increased cash aid to large families, they were also making a strong political attack upon middle-class privilege (13). It is the supreme paradox of politics that vested interest and privilege can only be abolished by those among the privileged and powerful with the will to do so. Rarely does that will manifest itself beyond the concession of short-term palliatives (14).

Downs takes up this point in stage three of his model - that of 'realising the cost of significant progress'. A realisation gradually dawns first upon the interest groups in the field, then later upon the general public, that the cost of eliminating a problem is extremely high. In an analysis that has relevance far beyond his own limited case study of American environmental politics he notes:

> Really moving toward a solution of the problem would not only take a great deal of money but would also require major sacrifices of power, energy and institutional advantage by large groups in the population who now enjoy these benefits. The public thus begins to realise that the evil itself results in part from arrangements that are providing significant benefits to someone - often to a great many people. (15)

The result is that effective improvements in the

welfare of groups like the poor, the homeless and the unemployed can often only come about by an unpopular 'transfer' of resources or by rapid economic growth. Successive governments since the late 1950s have failed to achieve the latter, and other groups have been generally too well organised to submit to a transfer of resources that would leave them relatively worse-off. Ultimately, as Goldthorpe notes, the 'cost of significant progress' must be measured against the power and advantage of those who must bear it (16).

By the time an issue has reached stage four of Downs' model it is subject to a 'gradual decline of intense public interest' largely resulting from the growing realisation of the size of the problem and the likely cost and energy required to alleviate or eliminate it. Three broad categories of reaction are evident at this point. First, some people become thoroughly discouraged by the immensity of the problem and experience a feeling of political debilitation. The indigenous poor, usually unorganised and unstructured in the political sense, will experience resignation, despair and reinforced alienation as yet another periodic attempt to liberate them fails; while the optimism, faith and deference of the organised poor and middle-class client groups in and towards procedural norms and values are likely to be put to a severe test. They may subsequently reject the legitimacy and inclusiveness of those norms and values and move instead towards extremes of apathy or direct action.

The second broad response comes from those who feel threatened by the dramatisation of the issue, and is a more vociferous and entrenched reaction, coming from that stratum of society immediately above the popularly-defined poverty line. To a significant extent their own limited social status and dignity is assured only so long as others are confined to a socio-economic position perceived by them as inferior. When 'democratisation of privilege and opportunity' does take place its most significant effects will be confined to the two lowest strata - those below, and those on or immediately above the poverty line. The latter group is therefore predisposed to oppose change that will make it relatively worse off vis a vis its economic (and social) subordinates. Indeed this opposition to change may be actively encouraged by a value-laden media and political system which feeds its ignorance and prejudice and which serves to deflect and distort the reality of resource allocation, fiscal policy and public expenditure (17). Instead of perceiving and questioning the very real social and economic gaps betwen itself and those publics which benefit from the status quo this poverty-line stratum is systemically encouraged and socialised to view its 'subordinates' (and they it) as its principal, unreal, economic reference point. The outcome, as Goldthorpe points out, is that 'The disruptive potential that social inequality might be thought to hold remains in fact suppressed' (18). Social conflict, criticism of the prevailing economic order and active challenge of the political process are thus conveniently confined to intra-working-class manifestations of disillusionment and alienation such as ethnic discrimination and 'scroungerphobia'.

The third response in this model comes from those who simply become bored and disenchanted by the issue and who passively await the arrival of a new stage two issue. It is likely that this group will include Ministers, MPs, civil servants, academics and journalists together with what could be termed the middle-class 'do-gooders', who hop in dilettante manner between 'fashionable' issues as the attraction takes them and just as flippantly desert them, largely unresolved.

The last stage into which an issue passes, and comes finally to rest, is the 'post-problem stage ... A prolonged limbo - a twilight world of lesser attention or spasmodic recurrences of interest' (19). By this time the issue has largely faded from political view and public memory and is unlikely to re-surface unless some event disturbs the issue status quo. The issue of family poverty was firmly suspended in just such a 'post-problem limbo' when the CPAG leadership changed. A scheme for adjusting the political status of the issue thus became an urgent priority for the new Director.

By the summer of 1968 it was apparent that CPAG's influence upon the Labour government had not been as great as the executive committee had hoped for. A thorough-going and apparently irreversible revision of social priorities had taken place; the poor were now relatively worse-off than in 1964. The Group's main 'ally', Peggy Herbison, had felt compelled to resign and a stringently 'economic' regime of Ministers had come to dominate the Cabinet. Prescription charges had been reintroduced and cuts in social services expenditure had been effected; the Group itself was acutely short of funds to finance future activities and the position was further aggravated by the need to extend rather than limit those activities. There was a sense of disillusionment and betrayal resulting from the Labour government's rejection of its socialist commitment. In the light of this CPAG was now obliged to contemplate both its future programme and the question of finding a successor to Lynes. Its Chairman commented 'The group should also explore the possibility of expanding its activities into the public relations field, in order to secure wider support from the general public' (20). A more appropriate job description for the appointment of Lynes' successor, and a more accurate synopsis of Frank Field's role as Director, could not have been made.

Frank Field's appointment as Director (21) is not so much important for a change in leadership but, rather, for a change in the style of leadership. The task of enlivening the poverty debate and dispelling popular misconceptions about the poor was an uphill one. The Group's task was not simply one of education, in some ways this was the most straightforward obstacle to be overcome. Much more difficult was the task of exposing prejudice and bias, of eroding entrenched opinion built upon ignorance and misconception, and of effectively tackling the systematic discrimination against the poor. Nor was it enough to attract sympathy for the Group's aims. Sympathy had to be translated into active, structured support capable of provoking government action. In this context, Ralph Miliband writes that:

> It is proper to be moved by television programmes on slum dwellers, or on the old or deprived children. On the other hand, such emotions do not, in practice, have much concrete consequence. More important, there are also strong contrary emotions at work. Thus there is a widespread suspicion, which affects all classes, that many people in poverty 'have only themselves to blame'; and there is a corresponding resentment that such people should be 'getting something for nothing'. Both the suspicion and the resentment are naturally much encouraged by official denunciation of 'scroungers' and 'layabouts'; and while such denunciations may be qualified by the suggestion that they only apply to small numbers of people, it may be surmised that it is the denunciation rather than the qualification that makes the impact. (22)

Inexperienced in poverty affairs and in running an interest group of any type, Field can be considered fortunate in his sense of timing in joining a group that was dissatisfied with its campaign impact and willing to entertain new ideas, a bolder strategy and the infusion of new blood. The willingness of the CPAG executive to appoint an unproved figure laid the foundation for the type of strategy necessary to meet the problems of which Miliband speaks. Much of that new strategy was to focus on public relations and a broadening of the Group's 'educational' activities. Field was neither a protege of that academic circle at the LSE to which Lynes had belonged nor was he a familiar figure on the contemporary social policy scene. Ironically, he was perhaps 'fortunate' in arriving at CPAG without the range of close connections and acquaintances that his predecessor had enjoyed within the Labour government - connections which, in retrospect may well have constrained his adoption of a more aggressively critical stance against the growing revisionism in Labour's social policy after 1964. In this sense, Field was not as sympathetic towards the Party's apologists. He had never been a member of the Party's Social Policy Sub Committee; nor had he been part of the tight caucus of academics who had contributed to the formulation of Party policy in the years in opposition; he was also much less inclined to subscribe to Fabian-style gradualism (23) favoured by leading members of the CPAG executive. Arriving at CPAG as an 'outsider' he was perhaps better placed to offer insights and observations about the 1969 impasse than those already involved.

He was also fortunate in that shortly after his arrival the chairmanship of CPAG also changed hands, with Peter Townsend moving into the Chair. Their partnership in forging a new style and role for CPAG, a determined switch from the defensive to the offensive, was crucial not only to the Group's regeneration but to its survival in the political arena. Nowhere is this watershed in the Group's political development more sharply demonstrated than in the 'Poor Get Poorer Under Labour' campaign initiated by Field and strongly supported by Townsend during the run-up to the 1970 General Election (24).

Like Lynes, Townsend was a member of the Labour Party's Social Policy Sub Committee, he had participated in the drawing-up of <u>New Frontiers of Social Security</u> when the Party was in opposition, and was a member of that group of academics who were closely identified with the upper echelons of the

Labour government. Field was therefore able to
utilise the contacts shared by both his chairman and
predecessor without having to feel constrained by too
close an association with the Party's 'old boy
network'. As a result, he was able to build upon
foundations laid by Lynes, to exploit some of the
latter's more productive channels of influence and
yet, significantly, remain free to criticise and
abandon those channels of influence when they failed
him.

Townsend had already set the tone for the new
regime in a critical speech to the 1968 Labour Party
Conference:

> Parties which are committed to greater equality
> often modify their principles in office. Vested
> interests are difficult to dislodge. Those with
> power and status have unsuspected resilience.
> Apologists of Labour's record in power would cut
> better figures if they could demonstrate that
> the Government was pursuing coherent objectives
> and, despite slow progress, had acted on crucial
> occasions in conformity with these objectives.
> The record on immigration and colour has been
> disastrous and that on unemployment almost as
> bad. Little or no serious attempt has been made
> to redistribute wealth. And the war on poverty
> has been weak and unco-ordinated. After
> devaluation the Government promised to protect
> the poor, but announced measures which left many
> of them worse off. (25)

Townsend went on to claim that not only was the
Labour government reneging on its commitments to the
poor but it was hoping, with some cynicism, that its
'allies' within the voluntary movement would step
into the breach and pick up where it had left off.
This, he felt, was neither acceptable nor remotely
realistic in tackling effectively the massive social
welfare problems confronting Britain in the late
1960s.

> We all agree that voluntary bodies can only
> exert pressure and provide chapter and verse for
> the concerted political action that only
> government and related institutions can
> provide. What is lacking is a central definition
> of objectives and strategy to meet them. The
> need for these is not being met within the
> existing political framework and is being
> recognised and expressed outside it. (26)

In the summer of 1969, in his first editorial in Poverty, Field announced that raising family allowances would remain CPAG's chief 'political target'. Commenting on the government's 'Review of Public Expenditure' which had done further serious damage to the economic position of the poor he added:

> Against this background of a worsening financial position for low income groups, and of the large numbers just excluded by the statutory definition from the numbers of the poor, CPAG intends to campaign for an increase in the Family Allowance to 35 shillings (£1.75) for each child, including the first. This inclusion makes the reform much more expensive, the gross cost is £940 millions compared to £295 millions if the first child is excluded. However, the claw-back method cuts the £940 millions to £115 millions and the £295 millions to £40 millions. The move to enlarge family allowances and benefit the first child, then becomes financially possible and therefore politically possible. (27)

In the event Field miscalculated that possibility and was forced to reflect some time later, 'Why, with such powerful allies, has the group not met with much greater success? Specifically, why was it that reforms costing only £40 million (the net cost of implementing the first stage of CPAG's January 1970 proposals) have met with such resistance?' (28).

What had gone wrong? Field, like Lynes, attributed the failure partly to the public confusion following the 1967-8 announcement of family allowance increases and the government's acceptance of claw-back only after part of the first increase had been paid to families. In addition it had also taken over three years – the duration of the review of social services – for the government to announce any increase in the first place. A difficult situation was further exacerbated by government restriction of incomes through its wage policy: 'the reforms to help poor families were made at a time when those at work felt particularly aggrieved by other government actions which penalised their efforts to earn a decent wage' (29). Field also laid a major share of the blame at the door of CPAG which, he argued:

> did not lobby anywhere near hard enough for a campaign to explain what claw-back was and why

it was being brought into operation; nor did it convince the Government of the need for a massive educational campaign on the extent of family poverty, and the importance of increases in Family Allowances to any meaningful anti-poverty strategy. With the lack of a positive lead, the welfare hawks had found it easy to drag the increased allowances into the ever-widening workshy-scroungers debate (30). The result was catastrophic, the previous political antipathy to Family Allowances was doubly re-inforced. (31)

It was against this background of failure, hostility and fundamental disillusionment with the Labour government that CPAG entered the election year of 1970 obliged and prepared to devise a new strategy to galvanise government action on poverty and, in doing so, to distance itself from the Party which it had genuinely believed took seriously its socialist commitment, because the Party had clearly 'distanced itself from the poor' (32).

NOTES

1. Butler, D. and Stokes, D., Political Change in Britain. Forces Shaping Electoral Choice (Penguin, 1971), Table 15.5, p.417.
2. MacFarlane, op.cit., p.4.
3. See Ehrmann, H., Interest Groups on Four Continents (University of Pittsburgh Press, 1967), p.247.
4. Ibid.
5. Bull, op.cit., p.150, and Field, F. Poverty and Politics (Heinemann, 1982), p.52.
6. Many small promotional groups find the costs of mass propaganda prohibitive. An obvious and infinitely cheaper alternative, therefore, is to concentrate educational and informational output upon small groups of opinion leaders and hope that ideas, opinion and discussion will gradually percolate downwards to the general public. CPAG was thus following a path followed by many other groups before it. Smokeless Air, the journal of the National Smoke Abatement Society, noted in 1957 that to get something effective done about pollution 'may well require the constant pressure of informed public opinion which can be secured not by costly mass propaganda, but rather by continued education and stimulation of the leaders of public opinion and

those who will develop and administer the measures to be taken'. Sanderson, J.B., 'The National Smoke Abatement Society and the Clean Air Act (1956)' in Kimber, R. and Richardson, J.J., Campaigning for the Environment (Routledge & Kegan Paul, 1974), p.29.

7. Downs, A., 'The Political Economy of Improving our Environment', in Downs, Kneese, Ogden and Perloff, The Political Economy of Environmental Control (Berkeley, 1972), p.64.

8. Ibid.

9. Ibid.

10. A useful example of this give-and-take approach is illustrated in comments made in the Sunday Times (5 February 1967) regarding the political repercussions which would ensue by democratising privilege. 'Government opinion is now moving in favour of a straight increase in Family Allowances. One major reason for this is the fear of political repercussions among middle-class and professional families who have been expressing strong resentment at the ·prospect of losing tax reliefs to benefit a minority of large families.'

11. He notes, 'when most people had relatively low political economic expectations, and accepted a considerable degree of hierarchy and inequality to be inevitable, political institutions attracted less criticism. With rising individual expectations, claims and assertions, the same institutions have come under increasing attack - even if, as is possibly the case, the system has become more democratic in a procedural sense'. Self, P., Econocrats and the Policy Process (Macmillan, 1975), p.120.

12. Ibid.

13. Wilson himself noted the intense pressure upon government to resist this sort of demand and proceed with tax concessions promised in the early days of his administration. He comments thus on Callaghan's pre-Budget speech on 1 March 1966: 'Although in July 1965 we had to announce, amid jibes and accusations of broken pledges, that we should have to defer our promised help to owner-occupiers, he said that in the Budget proper he would introduce the mortgage option scheme ... The calculations were such that any householder paying less than the standard rate of income tax would benefit by taking the option'. (op.cit., pp.281, 170-2).

14. Miliband has charged that it has been the nature of the Labour Party leadership in the post-war era to be neither socialist nor even 'reformist socialist': 'such reforms as these leaders may

support do not form part of any kind of coherent
strategy designed, in however long a perspective, to
achieve the socialist transformation of British
society ... The "revisionism" which dominates their
thinking does not represent an alternative but an
adaption to capitalism ... They are bourgeois
politicians with, at best, a certain bias towards
social reform. They have no intention whatsoever of
adopting, let alone carrying out, policies which
would begin in earnest the process of socialist
transformation in Britain. On the contrary, they must
be expected to resist with the upmost determination
all attempts to foist such policies upon them'.
Miliband, op.cit., p.373.

15. Downs, op.cit., pp.64-5.
16. Goldthorpe, J. 'Political Consensus,
Social Inequality and Pay Policy', New Society (10
January 1974). He notes: 'Social inequality in all
its manifestations can be thought of as involving
differences in social power and advantage; power
being defined as the capacity to mobilise resources
(human and non-human) to bring about a desired state
of affairs and advantage as the possession of or
control over, whatever in society is valued and
scarce. Power and advantage are thus closely related.
Power can be used to secure advantage, while certain
advantages consititute the resources that are used in
the exercise of power'.
17. See Golding, P. and Middleton, S., 'Why is
the Press so Obsessed with Welfare Scroungers?', New
Society (26 October 1978).
18. Goldthorpe, op.cit., and Runciman, W.G.,
Relative Deprivation and Social Justice (Routledge &
Kegan Paul, 1966), pp.285-95.
19. Downs, op.cit., p.65.
20. CPAG - Executive Committee Minutes (15
November 1968).
21. Frank Field took over as CPAG Director on 6
February 1969. Aged 26, he was Deputy Head of General
Studies at Hammersmith College of Further Education.
He had four years' experience as a local councillor
in Hounslow and had been unsuccessful Labour
Candidate for South Bucks in the 1966 General
Election. His appointment and the creation of a legal
department for the Group were both financed by a
grant from the Joseph Rowntree Charitable Trust.
22. Wedderburn, op.cit., p.188.
23. A useful analysis by Fabians of Fabian
approaches to pressure-group politics, the
dissemination of ideas and the 'permeation' of
institutions can be found in Cole, G.D.H. and

Postgate, R., <u>The Common People</u> (University Paperbacks, 1961), esp. p.423.

24. See Insight, 'Under Labour, the Poor get Poorer', <u>Sunday Times</u> (22 March 1970).

25. <u>Poverty</u>, No. 9 (Winter 1968).

26. Ibid.

27. <u>Poverty</u>, No. 11 (Summer 1969).

28. Bull, <u>op.cit.</u>, pp.150-1.

29. Ibid.

30. See Meacher, M., 'Promoting the Welfare of Scroungers', <u>Poverty</u>, No. 15 (1970).

31. Ibid.

32. Interview with Frank Field, 25 July 1977.

Chapter Six

'THE POOR GET POORER UNDER LABOUR'

> Many groups have close traditional, empirical
> and even administrative links with parties,
> which will give them added leverage when
> policies relevant to their group interests are
> being considered. The reverse side of the coin
> is that this close association may militate
> against exercise of influence on the other party
> when it is in power. (1)

Additional influence upon party policy may arise from
the fact that 'Many party members at all levels of
the party will also be members of groups, or will be
sympathetic towards interests of various kinds'.
While party discipline and party loyalty will
normally prevail in any conflict of interest for an
MP or party official, and probably for the party rank
and file also, it may be supposed that 'such group
interests will not be without influence ... (which)
may be exercised in debate, in polemics in party
organs, in voting within party meetings, and by
lobbying in the party' (2). It has also been
concluded that 'the influence of organised groups is
felt not only on but also in the political parties'
(3). Overlapping membership between groups and
political parties serves to exert an influence in
both directions and generally reinforces the
attitudes, values and opinions of the individuals
concerned (4). That some interest-groups sustain
interaction with one particular party rather than
negotiating across the political spectrum is clear
from recent political history. As Bridget Pym points
out, 'some soils are more receptive to reformist
plants than others' (5), and it is clear that in the
early 1960s and after the Labour Party had taken
office in 1964 many promotional or cause-groups had
made their mark upon it. Abortion law reform,

criminal law reform and social reform were three important areas in which a flurry of interest-group activity had been effective in persuading the Party to provide parliamentary time for debate and, eventually, legislation (although the Abortion Bill was introduced by a Liberal MP).

The values a group holds play a crucial part in determining which party the group will concentrate its efforts on. The values which underpin abortion law reform, the abolition of capital punishment, state aid for the poor and the low paid have traditionally been viewed as consistent with the social and egalitarian values of the 'collectivist' Labour Party. Alan Potter notes: 'It is, for example, difficult for a "left-wing" group to find a "sound" Conservative. If it succeeds, his "soundness" is liable to become suspect. In 1956 almost all the Labour MPs supported the Private Members' Bill to abolish capital punishment. The great majority of Conservative MPs opposed it. Conservative constit-uency committees regarded abolition as a "left-wing" cause and retention of capital punishment as an article of Conservative faith' (6). It may be argued, then, that groups will align themselves or seek to work through those parties with which they have value empathy. The belief in particular that the Labour Party is about 'equality' is a factor which initially attracts many cause-groups concerned with social reform to work through or in support of the Party. As Drucker points out, such pressure groups 'expect more of a Labour Government. Thus, we see that both those who are in favour of more equality and those who are opposed to it expect Labour to defend and extend the laws and practices which are aimed at inducing it ... Labour is about equality in that it lives in a national political environment in which others expect it to be about equality' (7). Perhaps more significantly, he adds, 'This expectation seems to transcend the lack of evidence that Labour has created a more equal Britain' (8).

We have already noted that many interest-groups have long-standing and often highly-structured links with a particular party which may well enhance their influence within that party. The corollary to this relationship, of course, is that the group's freedom to negotiate with a rival political party may well be constrained by that relationship and, indeed, the rival party itself may be reluctant to consult freely with the group because of its apparent partisanship. Perhaps the most striking recent example of this is the TUC which, in 1971, strengthened and formalised

its links with the Labour Party through the creation
of the TUC-Labour Party Liaison Committee which
presided over the formulation and implementation of
the social contract when Labour returned to power in
1974. In 1979, however, with the return to power of
the Conservatives under the leadership of Margaret
Thatcher, both TUC and individual unions were to pay
the penality of their overt partnership towards the
previous Labour Governments. Clearly, however, on
economic issues, partisanship may not only be
desirable but obligatory in the sense that the values
and principles upheld by an economic interest-group
may be unacceptable or even anathema to one of the
main political parties. The interest group will
therefore be compelled to work through the party most
favourably disposed to its views: tactically and
philosophically it will not be in a position to lobby
across party lines.

For most groups, activities directed through or
in support of a party will be only one, and probably
a secondary, channel of influence in the pursuit of
their goals. Those seeking effective and sustained
influence upon policy will more realistically direct
the greater part of their effort towards Whitehall
rather than Westminster. Liaison or association with
a party may be a useful initial or preliminary
tactic, especially in propaganda/public relations
terms. However most groups recognise fairly quickly
that 'it is important ... to develop a close
relationship with civil servants and local
government officials as they are influential in the
formulation of policy options ... for their political
masters' (9). Furthermore, there may well be a danger
in a group concentrating its efforts in the sphere of
party politics. Potter has thus concluded that:

> promotional groups in close touch with
> Government Departments avoid party politics
> because their position depends far more than
> that of the spokesman groups on the value the
> Government attaches to their advice. Spokesman
> groups are consulted in their representative
> capacity. Other promotional groups avoid party
> politics, too, even if they have a close
> affinity for a particular party. Major channels
> of communication, such as broadcasting and
> schools, are closed or very constricted for
> anything that is regarded as party political. A
> group that aligns itself openly with one party
> not only loses what support it has in the other
> but also exposes itself to the charge of being a

'splinter' group in the first. (10)

This second point, together with the recognition by many within CPAG that the Group had not achieved all it had hoped for under a Labour government, was crucial in Field's decision to distance the Group from the Party partly in the belief that Labour had distanced itself from the poor (11). It would be wrong, however, to see this decision (as some within the Labour Party appear to have done) as a product of pique or retaliation, nor should it be regarded as an isolated gesture. The decision to become less partisan should be seen as a constructive political tactic, the logical outcome of a rather unsuccessful over-identification with the Party in the preceding years. Field was supported in this decision, as will be shown, by Peter Townsend.

It could be argued with some justification that Field's initiative was rash and, perhaps, poorly judged. In retrospect, it looks much less so. The need for a new initiative, a change in policy, and perhaps a fresh orientation for the Group, was broadly acknowledged by an executive whose patience with the Labour government was exhausted. Accordingly, the decision to publish Poverty and the Labour Government does not appear to have been a particularly contentious one within CPAG and Field, supported by its principal author Peter Townsend, seems to have encountered little resistance in pushing it through. Field has commented that it had always been his function as CPAG Director to obtain the best possible deal for the poor and that, initially, he felt this could be done most effectively by lobbying across party lines, even at the risk of losing any previous good will with the Labour Party. Ultimately, of course, the decision to adopt a less partisan approach stems from a recognition that good will is no substitute for effective action by the party concerned. Such a tactic may involve some risk though, in that a group may not only lose the good will of its ally, but also fail to make a significant impression on the rival party, especially when there is a change of government. CPAG may be judged to have found itself in precisely this situation during Heath's government between 1970 and 1974. In his early inexperienced months of office, however, Field clearly felt that the risk was necessary and that it offered an opportunity for the Group 'to look for areas of agreement between parties, rather than (it) becoming a Socialist tail' (12).

Potter has suggested that the risk may appear to be exaggerated at the time of decision: 'unless the party lines are already drawn firmly, a group can usually count on what may be called the "tandem" effect. On most questions the parties are not likely to be far apart. This is characteristic of the two-party system. As long as a group does not make its cause a straight party matter, if it succeeds in moving one party, the other is likely to move too. Indeed, the parties may begin competing with each other in moving ahead' (13).

There was little evidence, however, that this new tactic could succeed where a closely partisan approach had failed. Given the furore over claw-back and raised family allowances there was even less evidence that the major parties could be manoeuvred into a situation where they would try to outdo each other in their determination to do 'something' about poverty. Indeed, the evidence pointed to the contrary. By 1969 both parties were cautious of taking the initiative because of the 1968 debacle and the much-publicised opposition of working- and middle-class employed to further welfare expend-iture. As George Brown discovered during the 1970 General Election campaign, for many middle-class people 'the most unpopular thing the Labour Government ever did was to arrange to "claw-back" family allowances from the better-off' (14). It might be argued then that the decision to opt for a strong critique of Labour's record during the election campaign and the adoption of a less partisan approach was either ill thought-out, naive or a clutching at straws.

THE LABOUR PARTY'S SOCIAL POLICY SUB-COMMITTEE

Before considering the 'Poor get Poorer under Labour' campaign, we need to examine the nature and extent of CPAG's relationship with the Labour Party. It has already been established that this relationship was not a formal one and that it relied essentially upon the shared values, opinions and political outlook of Labour politicans and leading academics, themselves Party members who had come together under the umbrella of the Party's Social Policy Sub-Committee.

Members of the Committee were appointed as individual Party members and not as representatives or delegates of important groups in the social policy field, although clearly, on occasion, individuals

117

from such groups did find their way onto it. The Committee's work tended, generally, to be uninspiring and non-controversial. Real executive power rested with the Party's research department. The Social Policy Sub-Committee essentially assumed the role of brains trust; a forum in which political realists trade interests and ideas with the 'planners' of the academic fraternity. Perhaps the key figure on the Committee in the first ten or twelve years of CPAG's existence was Brian Abel-Smith, Peter Townsend's co-author of The Poor and the Poorest. Nicholas Bosanquet, who argues that the Committee was 'heavily influenced by CPAG', nevertheless concludes that its real influence lay in 'providing inputs for the real political in-fighters like Barbara Castle in the past and in its influence with members of the NEC' (15). Bosanquet views the Committee as a valuable and influential forum in which ideas were raised, 'plugged' and steered onto the manifesto. Significantly he too, like David Piachaud and Ruth Lister, more recently, owed his place on the Committee to an old boy network dating from the mid-1950s and numbering Abel-Smith, Townsend, Titmuss and Lynes among its ranks. His assessment of CPAG influence within the Committee is shared by Townsend, who agrees that there is evidence of a relatively influential caucus or ideas group in the Committee which drew its inspiration from CPAG (16).

It is interesting, in this light, to examine the total complement of MPs, ministers, academics and trade unionists who served on the Committee after the Labour Party returned to power in 1964. At the outset, anyone wishing to analyse CPAG influence within the Social Policy Sub-Committee faces considerable difficulty. It is impossible to quantify rigorously the influence of one group within another when members of the former are not officially regarded as its representatives or delegates when taking part in meetings of the latter. Any assessment of influence is further impeded by the fact that CPAG members or supporters within the Committee did not necessarily act as a cohesive body of opinion. However, some general points can be made about the composition of the Committee in these years. First, three broad membership types are apparent: Parliamentary members such as R.H.S. Crossman, Lena Jeger, Alf Morris and Judith Hart; secondly, academic members, many of whom were concurrently ministerial policy advisers on social policy, these included Richard Titmuss, Brian Abel-Smith, Peter Townsend and, of course, Tony Lynes. The third group, described by Bosanquet as a counterbalance to academic influence within the Committee, is the trade union group. During the period in question it included Len Murray, Ray Gunter, Bill Simpson and Peter Jacques, the last being the head of the TUC's Social Insurance Committee.

Both Townsend and Bosanquet have suggested that the relationship between the academic members of the Committee and the trade unionists was not always an easy one. There had certainly been friction between the idealism and forward planning of the academic group led by Titmuss in the 1950s and the pragmatism and real politik of the trade union caucus. The tension which rose to the surface during the Committee's work on Labour's plans for reform of national superannuation in the late 1950s led Crossman to conclude that there was a 'strange new alignment gowing up in the party. On one side are the socialist intellectuals, who want to prepare blueprints ... and on the other side are the trade unionists, who are suspicious of this kind of socialist planning' (17). A similar tension emerged, as will be shown later, during the child benefits episode in 1975-7.

A second general observation to be made of the Committee is that there is evidence of a strong continuity of membership. If the correlation between the election year 1964-5, when only 7 per cent of those sitting on the 1965 Committee had served in 1964 is discounted, we find that continuity of membership exceeds 50 per cent in all subsequent years except the election year 1970-1. This point will be discussed shortly, but to understand its full implications some additional factors must first be considered.

Overall, of the 87 individuals who served in the 1965-76 period, twenty-one had formal or informal CPAG connections. The former may be identified as CPAG members or personnel, the latter, and larger, group could be broadly termed 'sympathisers' - i.e. those who advanced CPAG's viewpoint because they shared that viewpoint. Obvious examples are those MPs who regularly agreed to ask parliamentary questions and move adjournment debates on CPAG's behalf and those academics who, while not necessarily members of the Group, contributed to CPAG literature and were sympathetic to its views in debate or party polemics.

This introduces a fourth general observation. The CPAG caucus within the Committee may be further categorised occupationally, i.e. as academics and parliamentarians. During this period the academic element included Peter Townsend, Brian Abel-Smith, David Donnison, Tony Atkinson and Richard Titmuss, together with Nicholas Bosanquet, Tony Lynes and David Piachaud. Inevitably, support varied betwen individuals so that, at various times, Titmuss, Abel-Smith and Piachaud were more cautious and qualified in their support of CPAG than the others – an outcome which may be partly attributed to the constraints imposed by their tenure of advisory posts in government (18).

Many of these individuals share a further common association with government. Abel-Smith was senior policy adviser to Richard Crossman at the DHSS from 1968 to 1970 and later was special policy adviser to David Ennals (1976-8). Donnison and Titmuss respectively occupied the posts of Chairman and Deputy Chairman of the Supplementary Benefits Commission, the former sitting from 1975 to 1980, the latter from 1968 to 1973. All three were close advisers to Richard Crossman when he was Secretary of State for Social Services (19). Before becoming CPAG's first Secretary, Tony Lynes had worked in an advisory capacity at the Ministry of Pensions and National Insurance, and in 1974 became a policy adviser to David Ennals at the DHSS, working under Brian Abel-Smith David Piachaud was both a part-time and full-time member of the Prime Minister's Policy Unit from 1974, and despite his areas of disagreement with Frank Field (20) regularly contributed to CPAG's journal Poverty and co-authored with Field a series of major articles on the 'poverty trap' (21). Nicholas Bosanquet was also a contributor to Poverty, a CPAG member, and was jointly reponsible with Frank Field for a series of meetings in 1971-2 between CPAG and trade union leaders to determine areas and issues on which the two could promote a joint approach. Tony Atkinson was another contributor to Poverty and CPAG's research pamphlets.

The parliamentary element was made up of MPs who similarly, were either members of the Group or actively sympathetic to it. The intensity of their commitment varied considerably. Strong support for the group over the years ranging from parliamentary questions, moving adjournment debates, writing on behalf of CPAG, assisting it with fund raising, and so on, came from David Owen, Lena Jeger, Jack Ashley, Joan Lestor, Bruce George, Bruce Douglas-Mann, Michael Meacher, Alf Morris, Renee Short, Peggy Herbison and Frank Allaun.

Owen, Jeger, Douglas-Mann, Meacher and George

are or have been CPAG members. Meacher and Jeger have been regular contributors to CPAG literature and with the others have been leading activists within a CPAG all-party group in the Commons. Bruce Douglas-Mann, in addition to being a CPAG member, was also the Group's legal adviser from the late 1960s and through the early 1970s. In the same way that Owen was closely associated with Lynes, so Meacher was a close parliamentary ally of Field. Both, of course, have since come to hold shadow spokesman posts in the eighties and Meacher currently holds the Labour Frontbench Health and Social Services portfolio. Morris, Short, Lestor, Ashley and Allaun were all notable members of the Common's CPAG group and all asked parliamentary questions on the Group's behalf. Bruce George was the most prominent member of this group in the latter part of the period in question, asking some 105 parliamentary questions, on behalf of CPAG in the period July 1975 to July 1977 alone, when Labour members asked a total of 243 questions, Conservatives 119 and Liberals 82, of which 73 were asked by Richard Wainright (22). Peggy Herbison, apart from being a keen ministerial protagonist of many ideas associated with CPAG, the most prominent being claw-back, also assisted Field in the early 1970s in enlisting funds and support from the trade union movement for the Group.

Despite CPAG's later critique of Labour's record in office there is some evidence of common ground between the Group and the Party. Though it is difficult to prove that CPAG directly influenced much of Labour's social policy, it is clear that the Group, together with the support given by its parliamentary sympathisers and those within the Social Policy Sub-Committee, did, at the very least, help shape and contribute to a climate of debate which made much of that social policy possible. Whilst Labour Ministers might claim that they were, of their own volition, already moving in this policy direction, it is clear that CPAG helped to keep the poverty issue 'on the boil'. Indeed, it might be argued that much of the Group's role was essentially defensive. Had it not existed to pursue a role as the Party's social conscience then the weakening of the government's resolve in the field of social policy might have been greater.

A number of points are salient here. To ensure that an influence upon policy is first achieved and then sustained it is not enough for an interest group to simply have inside sympathisers. A battery of factors ultimately influence the success or failure

of groups seeking to influence or amend policy. These
include 'advance intelligence', liaison with policy-
makers and administrators, the merits and demerits of
the issue at stake, the ability of the group to argue
its case reasonably and articulately, its access to
parliamentary support, its relations with the media,
the sufficiency of its resources and, ultimately, its
ability to employ sanctions. These factors are
discussed at various points in this study. It is
appropriate at this point, however, to consider
access to sympathisers in positions of influence.

Table 6.1: Apparent CPAG support on the Labour Party
Social Policy Sub-Committee

Years	Continuity (%)*	Changes in apparent CPAG support
1965-6	70 (carried over from 1964-5)	Losses - Lynes Gains - Abel-Smith, Townsend
1966-7	60	Gains - Donnison, Jeger
1967-8	53	Losses - Titmuss Gains - Herbison, Allaun
1968-9	100	Losses - Herbison
1969-70	100	No changes
1970-1	27 (electoral distortion)	Losses - Townsend Gains - Lynes, Piachaud, Titmuss, Lestor, Morris
1971-2	74	Gains - Meacher, Townsend, Castle
1972-3	97	Losses - Titmuss Gains - Bosanquet
1973-4	70	Gains - Owen, Ashley
1974-5	55	Gains - Lister, Atkinson, George, Short, Douglas-Mann
1975-6	98	No changes

* Percentage of previous year's membership recurring
in a succeeding year.

    Reasonable access to senior ministers is
imperative, since this keeps Ministers abreast of
current developments and gives the opportunity to
present the group's own interpretation of these
events. Secondly, direct access helps offset the
dilution and modification to which a group's
proposals would be subject if they were submitted at
lower levels of the policy-making process. It was
important, then, that the Social Policy Sub-

Committee also had its fair share of senior Ministers or senior figures within the Party to make membership worthwhile. The 1964 Committee, for example, counted Harold Wilson, George Brown, Richard Crossman, James Callaghan, Margaret Herbison and Douglas Houghton among the overall membership. Changes in membership over the years show that there has invariably been a senior ministerial 'presence' and a caucus from the social service ministries, as might be expected. Finally, given that committee membership invariably changes, it is important to note that any apparent CPAG influence within the Committee has not been effectively reduced by this change. It is appropriate, therefore, that we return to the points made earlier about continuity. Discounting 1964 because of the distortion upon the Committee size and structure produced by the atypical events of a general election, and taking 1965 as the base year, a pattern of continuity between the years 1965-76 and some indication of apparent CPAG strength on the committee is revealed (Table 6.1).

Over the period in question (1964-76) some 24 per cent of all Committee members had some connection with CPAG, based on the qualification of the terms 'formal' and 'informal' cited earlier. In 1969, in the fourth year of Lynes' office, CPAG members and supporters represented a caucus of 43 per cent on the Social Policy Sub-Committee. In 1973, the fourth full year of Field's office, it was 38 per cent. It should also be noted that despite their clear disagreement with CPAG's General Election tactics in 1970 (to be discussed shortly) Titmuss, Abel-Smith and Piachaud have still been included among those generally supportive of CPAG policy. Their disagreements tended to centre more on means than ends. The individuals making up this caucus have been termed supporters on the basis of either formal membership of CPAG, as regular (sympathetic) contributors to its journal, those active in Parliament on its behalf and those who are independently identified with CPAG ideas and policy proposals. CPAG's relationship with the Labour Party has taken forms other than overlapping membership on the Social Policy Sub-Committee. Many CPAG members, workers and executive members have, over the years, been keen Labour activists and have worked indirectly on CPAG's behalf at constituency meetings and Party Conferences, presenting CPAG demands in the accepted constitutional framework of constituency resolutions. (This is a favourite tactic for a group with overlapping party membership to adopt, and is fully considered in chapter 7.)

POVERTY AND LABOUR – THE 'POOR GET POORER' CAMPAIGN

Many CPAG members and staff were genuinely elated at
Field's decision to mount a concerted attack upon
Labour's record. A decade on some continued to feel
that the criticism and distrust that was evoked was
much deserved. How then did the campaign come about,
and how did it develop against this backdrop of
apparently close Party-Group relations? Field's
comments about not wanting CPAG to become, or remain,
a 'socialist tail' have already been noted. There was
also a clear tactical factor involved in the decision
to castigate the Party in the emotionally-charged
atmosphere of a General Election campaign. If the
decision to adopt this course had ever been in doubt,
then events taking place in the last months of the
Labour government ensured that any uncertainty was
removed.

Claw-back had already produced its problems.
Many felt those problems were further accentuated by
the government's apparent lack of political will to
make a coordinated attack on poverty in general. The
problem of the disabled, for example, had been raised
continuously since 1964 but it was not until 1968
that the government embarked upon 'urgent' research
into the matter (23). Similarly, the problems faced
by fatherless families had been raised in the early
months of the first Wilson administration, but it was
not until January 1969 that a White Paper announced
the setting-up of a Committee of Inquiry into the
problem, and only in November were its members
finally appointed. For many observers, including the
Labour MP Peter Archer, it seemed that 'the steam had
really run out of the poverty issue' (24). CPAG's
immediate task, therefore, was to get poverty back
onto the political agenda.

In January 1970 Field and Townsend began the
task by outlining to the Party's Backbench Social
Security Committee the Group's controversial view
that poverty had increased under Labour governments.
As they had calculated, their analysis drew the
unanimous response that the Party could not go into
an election year facing such a charge (25). However,
it was even more important that the Group drew a
similar response from the Party leadership. A request
for a meeting with the Prime Minister on 21 October
1969 had already drawn the polite reply that Mr
Wilson was too busy. On 28 January, however, they

were successful in obtaining a 90-minute interview
with Richard Crossman, Secretary of State for Social
Services. It was not a fruitful meeting, Crossman's
response was terse and uncompromising: 'People will
simply never believe you' he warned (26). Despite his
view, the Prime Minister took their claims seriously
enough to inform the Group on 3 February that he had
arranged for them to put their case to the
Chancellor, Roy Jenkins, before the April Budget.

In the interim the government launched
something of a counter attack which clearly, and
publicly, divided its academic supporters. On 6
February Tribune had reprinted the key points of
CPAG's recent memorandum to the Chancellor, echoing
the Group's charge that 'not only has the Wilson
Government utterly failed to make inroads into the
poverty problem, but in many ways the plight of the
poor families is now worse than when the Government
took office' (27). A week later the government joined
debate, David Ennals replying on its behalf that
CPAG's conclusions could only be reached 'by the most
selective and misleading use of statistics and what
seems to be an almost total failure to appreciate the
impact of many recent achievements of the Government
in the field of Social Security' (28). Shortly after,
however, Professor A.B. Atkinson, a CPAG supporter,
addressed a Fabian Society Conference on 'Labour and
Inequality' and strongly refuted the Minister's
argument. Ennals had claimed in Tribune, and later at
CPAG's 1970 Annual General Meeting, that government
expenditure on social security had risen from £1960
million in 1964 to £3600 million in 1969. However,
Atkinson went on to show, fully endorsing CPAG's
view, that Ennals had neglected to account for the
increase in unemployment, demographic changes and
the use of claw-back, which, by switching child tax
allowances to family allowances, meant that only part
of the increase in family allowances could be
regarded as net benefit. Atkinson concluded that the
real increases between 1964/5 and 1969/70 on social
security expenditure were less than half the amount
suggested (29).

This disagreement raises once more the whole
notion of problem definition. Interested parties may
differ so widely in their assessment of a problem
that one might define it out of existence while
another might consider it so extensive and grave that
its solution demands action at the highest levels of
government. Conflicting definitions or emphases of a
problem may well keep it from the political agenda
and contribute to confusion and misunderstanding in

125

public debate. In the mid 1960s, for example, public
ignorance or misconception regarding the nature and
extent of poverty may well have been fuelled by the
conflicting definitions of the problem offered by
academics and civil servants respectively. Keith
Banting notes that:

> some officials were uncomfortable with the
> relative conception of poverty ... more
> importantly, officials were not completely
> happy with the use of supplementary benefits as
> a poverty line. They realised that every
> increase in the benefits level would increase
> the number of working families classified as
> poor; even if they took action to solve the
> problem, it would re-emerge with the next
> increase. Administrators regarded that prospect
> with distinctly less enthusiasm than did the
> academics. The Ministry never formally
> acknowledged a poverty line or used the word
> 'poverty' in their publications and in 1967 one
> of the Social Security Ministers, Patrick
> Gordon Walker, publicly criticised 'the
> continual raising of the standard and
> definition of what we mean by poverty'. (30)

The result inevitably was that the official
definition of the 'problem' identified by CPAG was
much narrower and, therefore, the numbers deemed to
be in poverty were accordingly much lower.

> Administrators rejected Abel-Smith and Towns-
> end's use of 140 per cent of supplementary
> benefit levels (as the real poverty line),
> contending that CPAG was deliberately
> overstating its case, and in the Ministry's own
> survey only the basic levels were used. The
> inevitable result was that a much smaller
> proportion of the population were deemed to be
> in low-income families; 7 per cent of all
> families with children fell below the line but
> many of these were already receiving, or were
> eligible for, supplementary benefits; only 4
> per cent of families with a father in full-time
> work fell below the Ministry's line. (31)

Politicians and civil servants may, as a result
of their narrower definitions of a problem,
deliberately seek to tackle it through the use of
what Stringer and Richardson call 'placebo
policies', in which 'as governments become

increasingly overloaded, we might expect them to pay even greater attention to the possibility of handling indicators in such a way as to define problems out of existence' (32). In the 1960s, then, Labour's narrower definition of the problem of poverty, and the introduction of 'placebo policies' such as earnings related benefit for sickness and unemployment, a refashioned National Assistance Board and the temporary use of claw-back, contributed to the popular belief that something was being done about the problem and enabled it to be hustled from the political agenda by 1968. David Ennals' selective assessment of the extent of the problem in February 1970 and his defence of Labour's record must therefore be seen as consistent with the government's definition of and approach to the problem since 1964.

However, 'the difficulty with placebo policies is that ultimately they may be seen as such. With the realisation that there has been no positive attempt to provide a long-term solution the "problem" may well return to the political agenda' (33). That, of course, was precisely the intention of CPAG during the 1970 General Election. Realistically, Atkinson's alternative assessment of Labour's 1964-70 record was accidentally or deliberately a feature of this strategy - an attempt to expose Labour policy as selective and essentially placebo in character. He concluded that the claims made for the increase in aggregate effort in the field of social security expenditure under Labour were exaggerated, with much of the expenditure increase due to demographic changes. Secondly, though Labour had increased the level of national insurance benefits in 1965, those benefits failed to keep pace with rising earnings over the next five years. Thirdly, the introduction of supplementary benefits had failed to eliminate the problem of non-take-up of benefit entitlement. Finally, the gain to low income families from the 1968 rise in family allowances had largely been offset by higher national insurance contributions and income tax rates (34).

At the beginning of March 1970 the rift between academics and politicians was further complicated. CPAG persuaded sixteen eminent social scientists to sign a letter to The Times endorsing the case for an increase in family allowances, but Titmuss, Abel-Smith and Piachaud declined (35). Abel-Smith was, at the time, a senior policy adviser to Crossman and his refusal was understood. Titmuss, however, very much the father figure of modern social administration, was not so constrained, and appears to have refused to sign on the basis of his life-long loyalty to the Labour Party and his belief that any critique of Labour's record, despite its shortcomings, was playing into the hands of a Conservative Party which otherwise looked like having little chance of winning the election. Fears that an emotional and damaging public split with Titmuss would ensue if the government persuaded him to draft an official reply to <u>The Times</u> letter were finally allayed when Douglas Houghton 'took round the lobbies a letter - drafted in Crossman's Ministry - and cajoled likely backbenchers into signing' (36). Those who did not sign, among them Michael Barnes, Chairman of the Backbench Social Security Committee, were, it was reported, subject to jibes of disloyalty and betrayal.

JENKINS' LAST BUDGET

On 3 March 1970 a deputation from CPAG met Roy Jenkins at the Treasury. Since only three other groups - the TUC, the CBI and the Scotch Whisky Association - had actually met Jenkins himself that year, it seemed clear that the Party leadership had taken CPAG's case seriously. Indeed, the Group were described as reaching Jenkins by 'an exercise in political muscle which, over the last three months, has caused controversy and bitterness inside the Labour Party and the Cabinet, has damaged at least two political careers, and may provide a bitterly contested issue for the General Election' (37).

That issue, of course, centred on the case that poverty had actually increased under a party historically and electorally identified with its diminution. The fact that 1970 was an election year and that Jenkins' April Budget offered an eleventh-hour opportunity for the government to win votes had certainly not escaped CPAG. The group's strategy was summed up by Field. 'This is an election year. Almost certainly this is Jenkins' last scheduled Budget. Very well, we shall make the Government buy us off.' (38)

In an effort to counter any public resistance to family allowance increases and to offset any 'scroungerphobia', Field also enlisted the support of a number of senior trade union leaders including Jack Jones (TGWU), Clive Jenkins (ASTMS), John Boyd (EU), Bill Anderson (NALGO) and Allan Fisher (NUPE) in co-signing a letter to Roy Jenkins on the eve of Budget urging him to reconsider an increase in family allowances (39). Whilst this may have been a welcome new initiative in enlisting union support it was, nevertheless, an unrealistic eleventh-hour appeal to a Chancellor who had almost certainly finalised his Budget weeks earlier. It proved to be a combination of straw-clutching and the firing of a warning shot across the bows of a party that had gone off course.

Field and Townsend continued to lobby Jenkins right up to the eve of the Budget. When Jenkins presented his final package of fiscal measures on 14 April CPAG clearly viewed it as a defeat for the principles on which they had fought. The Chancellor had not deemed it necessary, on the strength of CPAG's case, to 'buy the group off' in the way Field had hoped. Townsend described it as 'a totally weak Budget from a Government which chooses expediency instead of justice' (40), one designed to benefit those in the middle-income range instead of those whom CPAG regarded as the genuinely needy. In particular, its recommendations had shattered CPAG's hopes of winning increases in family allowances to the level of 35 shillings (£1.75) that Field had advocated on his appointment as Director.

There is some evidence to suggest that the government felt it could refute or at least undermine CPAG's case, thereby obviating the need to make any unprogrammed Budget concessions. On 16 April, for instance, Ennals, Crossman and Abel-Smith examined and co-revised a 'long, intricate defensive speech' (41) that Ennals was to deliver on Labour's record at CPAG's AGM later that week. Of the Budget itself Crossman noted:

> I still feel unhappy about the way I fell into a bitter argument with Peter Townsend, when he came to represent the CPAG a few weeks ago. In this respect Roy's budget is a relief to me because it does give some money to the lowest possible income groups, and to this extent we should have spiked the guns of the CPAG and of Peter Townsend and his friends. (42)

The Prime Minister had also been cautious about making concessions, fearing electoral resistance to family allowance increases that could rock his Party's election prospects. To many people family allowances were an unpopular measure and CPAG's effectiveness as a campaigning group was undermined by its inability to overcome popular prejudice. On 18 May Harold Wilson announced the dissolution of Parliament and called a General Election. In anticipation, CPAG had secured a donation of £1,000 from the Rowntree Trust to help in the production of election material and to fund an educational campaign directed at MPs detailing the material welfare of the poor after six years of Labour government. In the same month the Group released a broadsheet to the national press with a challenging first paragraph: 'The poor, worse off under Labour - with the Election Campaign about to start the Child Poverty Action Group has reaffirmed its belief that the poor are worse off as a result of the Labour Government' (43). It went on to point out that by January 1970 those on supplementary benefit were relatively poorer compared to March 1965. Even when the proposed November increases were taken into account, the gap would not close and would probably widen. The failure to announce a corresponding increase in national insurance benefits also meant that this group of claimants would continue to experience a relative decline in living standards. Finally, there was the need to consider the perilous position of the low wage earner.

> On a number of occasions you've stressed the need to increase family allowances each time adjustments are made to supplementary benefits otherwise the disincentive to work is perilously increased. Why is it then that the last two increases in supplementary benefit rates have not been accompanied with a corresponding increase in family allowances? (44)

The reaction of Labour politicans to CPAG's campaign varied from dismay and panic to outright anger. David Ennals, retiring Minister of Social Security, was one of those who fell into the former category. Speaking at the Group's AGM shortly after the Budget, he had urged that more private meetings with CPAG take place (consultation which had been rather infrequent when CPAG had adopted a moderate approach) instead of the Group resorting to what he saw a highly damaging, vituperative public exchanges with Labour politicans in the media. He also took some pains to stress that organisations like CPAG 'which hit sharply at Government will receive a strong counter-reaction' (45).
A number of points are worthy of comment here. First, the nature of his remarks to the group, indeed his chastisement of it, suggest that the Party did consider that it had a fairly strong relationship

with CPAG and that it did view it as an 'ally' of sorts (46). Secondly, his warning of a 'strong counter-reaction' against the government's critics suggests that the government did take CPAG's campaign seriously, though equally it may have misjudged the intensity of that campaign. Though a strong counter-reaction to such criticism may well be defended as a means of safeguarding political myth (i.e. the association of Labour with social justice and policies to improve the material welfare of the poor) it also carried with it some suggestion that the Party leadership felt itself beyond reproach, certainly in public. It is also interesting to note that Ennals' defence of the government's record at the AGM was prepared by Abel-Smith, historically a CPAG supporter. His involvement would seem to confirm the apparent split between Labour's academic supporters discussed earlier.

The conflict was thus already marked before CPAG launched two further blows to Labour's record. On 11 June, the group published the findings of a sample survey it had conducted in 80 parliamentary constituencies to discover the view of candidates from all parties on the issue of raising family allowances 'as the best method of reducing child poverty'. Few candidates, the Group claimed, had received any complaints against claw-back, the issue on which Labour had expected electoral resistance. No candidate polled believed that family allowances encouraged large families; indeed the only objection the Group claimed to have encountered was that some parents did not spend the money on the children. Over 70 per cent of the candidates interviewed favoured the rises suggested by CPAG, and of these only five favoured means-tested methods of recouping the increase.

The most damaging critique of Labour's record was to follow in the week of the Election, when every parliamentary candidate was sent a copy of the Group's policy manifesto, <u>Poor Families and the Election</u>. An analysis of all three party manifestos was offered, with the most severe criticism reserved for the Labour Party. Acknowledging efforts already made in the social policy field, the Group charged:

> the dimensions of poverty have not been diminished and some groups have not kept pace with the increasing affluence of others. In particular there are the following matters which justify deep concern ... national insurance and supplementary benefits have

lagged behind average industrial earnings. The wage rates of the lowest paid have not kept pace with other earnings. Since 1964 unemployment and particularly long-term unemployment, has increased and some unemployment allowances have fallen in real value. The need for a comprehensive disability scheme has not been recognised. (47)

Commenting on the Party's 1970 manifesto, Townsend's earlier arguments about coordination and a coherent approach to social policy-making rang loud. 'There is still no evidence of really coordinated planning of social policy through, say, a central department of social planning. Neither is there evidence that priority will be given to the most urgent problems of poverty. (48)' The manifesto did not contain a specific pledge to raise family allowances, only to review them. There was no commitment to a comprehensive disability pensions scheme. There was no reference to the financial problems of supporting older children at school, which the Group regarded as a 'deplorable omission' given that the government had already reneged on a 1964 manifesto commitment to do this. Nor was there any commitment to reducing means-tested schemes in favour of schemes for paying benefit as of right.

THE REACTION AND OUTCOME - THE EXPOSURE OF PARTY MYTH

The response of the Party leaders to CPAG's manifesto varied. Jeremy Thorpe sent a postcard to acknowledge he'd received it; Harold Wilson merely replied that Labour's record spoke for itself, and Edward Heath wrote to Frank Field on 1 June confirming his belief that 'the only way of tackling family poverty in the short term is to increase family allowances and operate the clawback principle' (49). It was clear, however, that a watershed had been reached in CPAG's relationship with the Labour Party.

This watershed was compounded by the Group's questioning of party myth: in effect, CPAG were undermining the spirit of Labourism, the very ethos of the Party. During the early years of the Labour government CPAG had appeared largely to accept this myth, believing that the Party had been mandated to combat poverty and deferring to it as though it took seriously its socialist commitment. In opposition and during the elections of 1959 and 1964 the Party had given a firm indication that action on poverty would be a major priority if it was elected to power. However, the u-turn in socialist policies after 1948 during Attlee's administration, the introduction of prescription charges in 1950 by Gaitskell, and the switch of emphasis to the achievement of economic growth as the prerequisite of social reform by Harold Wilson in speeches in 1963 and 1964, suggest that the poverty lobby should have been rather more cautious in its expectations of a Labour government – particularly one faced with major economic problems, and determined to manage the economy successfully. This apparent deference to myth therefore carried with it a degree of naivety, a lack of political realism, a failure to recognise that poverty was a priority not the priority, and that its alleviation, in tactical terms, depended on the tackling of what party leaders saw as more urgent priorities first.

However unrealistic some of the earlier assumptions and expectations were much of CPAG's critique remains justified, if only as a tactical means of dissociating the Group from the Party and its record. If CPAG had not attacked Labour's record then it is likely that other groups, such as Shelter or the Claimants Union would have; any untimely association of CPAG with that record would have been easily presented as an endorsement of it. Would the Group have resorted to such a critique had Field not arrived as Director in 1969 and had a General Election not been in the offing? The decision to proceed with such a campaign, though widely supported within the Group, could well have been seen by Field as a means of establishing his own imprint and authority upon the Group. A sensationalised propaganda exercise of this type could have been justified as a genuine attempt to restore povery to the forefront of political debate, but it may also be seen as a convenient means of bringing the new and unknown Director into the public spotlight. More generally, the campaign may be seen as a broad appeal to the general public, a break from the low profile style adopted by Tony Lynes.

Field has confirmed that, for him, the raison d'etre of the campaign was the attempt to expose the myths surrounding the party:

> the lynch pin of CPAG's strategy was that the rigorous questioning of Labour's poverty record would somehow lead to a shift in resources towards the least well off: surely no party would go complacently into an election year when its central myth was being so critically

examined? But we over estimated the extent to which politicans respond in a totally rational manner and under-estimated the way a party's programme becomes like an offspring: to be criticised in private but defended in public. (50)

There are some important points worth noting here. First, Field's view that Labour's central myth was its concern to do something about poverty was inaccurate. Secondly, it is clear from the comments of Wilson, Crossman and Ennals and from the provisions of Jenkins' last Budget that Labour did not regard itself as going 'complacently into an election year', and that it felt it could meet CPAG's criticisms and defend its record. Where CPAG was right was in its belief that Labour sought to 'privatise' such disputes and reconcile them 'fraternally', away from the public spotlight. Yet even here it could be argued that CPAG's overtly public campaign was impolitic given the reaction to the claw-back and the resistance to increases in family allowances that many MPs later claimed to have encountered in their constituencies (51).

Moreover, many Labour politicians felt strongly about this public exposure of party myth and some appear to have felt themselves beyond reproach. This view is partly borne out by David Piachaud who was among those academic supporters of the Labour Party who were clearly disturbed or angered at the time by what they saw as CPAG's role in 'undermining one of Labour's natural electoral advantages' (52), i.e. that it was the party most likely to deliver social reform. Piachaud adds, however, that in retrospect the tactic was probably necessary to enable CPAG to negotiate across the political spectrum during the election run-in (53).

Perhaps the most significant insight into the reaction of senior Party figures to the campaign has come from one who was very much a victim of it - Richard Crossman. Even in the early days of the campaign in January 1970, Crossman was keenly aware of the impending conflict. After a particularly heated television discussion on poverty with Peter Townsend, he wrote:

We are in trouble here because the attack is on our most sensitive point, our humanity. We ourselves are uncomfortable about the record Peter Townsend and his friends in the Child Poverty Action Group are attacking. In one way

we are terribly bureaucratic. There was another
Tory Private Member's Bill on Friday, seeking to
grant the full National Insurance Pension to the
over-80s who are excluded from the 1948 Bill.
It would have cost us practically nothing
because half of these people are on
Supplementary Benefit already but, no, we won't
do it because of the sanctity of the
contributory principle and this kind of
attitude looks meaner and meaner. (54)

By 8 February, as Crossman notes, Wilson himself had
become seriously disturbed by the aggressiveness of
CPAG's campaign and was worried that ammunition with
which to destroy the Labour government was being
readily placed in Tory hands.

It's true that if the press and the Opposition
work hard enough the Government can seem to lack
compassion and this is even more credible when
our own friends like the Child Poverty Action
Group mercilessly attack us, as they have done
in this week's New Statesman. All we have done
on pensions and benefits and National
Superannuation is dismissed as utterly hopeless
and, once we are denounced by our own side, the
Tory stuff, odious as it is, becomes effective.
These threats have seriously alarmed Harold.
(55)

The manner in which the campaign was
orchestrated firmly points to the fact that CPAG had,
and continues to have, greater expectations of the
Labour Party that it does of the Conservatives. As
Field explained:

That is why whenever we write something they say
why are you that much more bitter towards us.
These are Ministers saying this. It is unfair,
you judge us much more harshly than the Tories.
But one does expect more. It is also part of our
cover. I think at all costs the group must not
be seen as favouring the Labour Party. I think
then that we probably do judge them harder.(56)

Nor did Field agree with the view that there were
mitigating factors - such as the acute balance of
payments problems, devaluation, industrial crises
and an overwhelming programme of legislation to get
onto the statute book - in the Party's failure to
deliver the reforms called for by CPAG. He felt,

simply, that the Party wasn't trying hard enough, and was unlikely to do so unless provoked by groups like CPAG. This view was echoed by Jane Sheather, a former Assistant Director of CPAG and later Director of the National Council for One Parent Families. It was her view that groups like CPAG will always be more critical of the Labour Party simply because 'one expects more of one's own side' (57).

Peter Townsend has also taken up Field's point that Labour 'didn't try hard enough', and has concluded that Labour failed to resist civil service efforts to block radical policy initatives. Reflecting on Labour's record he commented:

> Although at the time I was a supporter of Wilson rather than Gaistkell I have to now go back and reflect that if we had had Gaistkell we'd have probably had more radical social policies than we had under the successive administrations of Wilson. I think because Gaitskell, rather like Heath in some ways, would have obstinately resisted the mandarins in the 'establishment' instead of just merely representing them as Wilson did. (58)

Field believed that the 1970 campaign also distanced CPAG from all other contemporary interest groups in terms of style. The campaign, he argued, proved that CPAG was fundamentally committed to the poor, extremely serious about the government's record, and was willing to jeopardise what relationship it did have with the Labour Party in order to improve the poor's lot. Group–Party relations and individual relationships were strained for some time after, but Field remained convinced that the Group emerged from the experience with its integrity and commitment intact and its status and credibility enhanced (59).

The fact remains, however, that the necessity for CPAG to publish <u>Poverty and the Labour Government</u> and to conduct a high-profile media campaign in the early weeks of a General Election run-in, only confirms the Group's failure to influence Labour in office and its own exclusion from the official policy community. The 'Poor Get Poorer' campaign provides a classic illustration of a cause group having to resort to a dramatic media campaign to compensate, in part, for its own inability to achieve regular and effective consultation. If nothing else, the new Group leadership demonstrated that the ground rules of Group–Party politics should be observed, but could be broken by <u>both</u> sides. As Field commented:

This party responds not through principle but by
being shown, or by thinking, that it will have
its red boxes snatched away from it. That is the
weapon we have, that we will actually cost them
votes. They will find it much more difficult to
mobilise their traditional support, and one
goes in slogging ... they have to be shocked and
shamed and bullied into doing the right things
... sometimes the Chancellor will have to agree
to see us because sometimes we say things that
will cost votes. (60)

When a group is making a case that, in paticular,
attacks the myths or image built up by a party,such
as its humanity, then, as Crossman observed, the
party's future attentiveness will be much easier to
secure.

NOTES

1. Roberts, G.K., _Political Parties and
Pressure Groups in Britain_ (Weidenfeld & Nicolson,
1970), p.99.
2. Ibid.
3. Potter, A., _Organised Groups in British
National Politics_ (Greenwood Press, Connecticut,
1975; reprinted from Faber & Faber, 1961), p.295.
4. See Harrison, M., _Trade Unions and the
Labour Party Since 1945_ (George Allen & Unwin, 1960);
Taylor, R., _The Fifth Estate_ (Pan, 1980), ch.4; and
Simpson, W., _Labour: The Unions and the Party_.
5. Pym, B., _Pressure Groups and the
Permissive Society_ (David & Charles, 1974), p.110.
6. Potter, _op.cit._, p.304.
7. Drucker, H.M., _Doctrine and Ethos in the
Labour Party_ (George Allen & Unwin, 1979), pp.57-8.
8. Ibid., p.58.
9. Richardson, J.J., 'The Environmental Issue
and the Public', in _Decision-Making in Britain, Block
V: Pollution and Environment_ (Open University Press,
Milton Keynes, 1977), p.29.
10. Potter, _op.cit._, p.305.
11. Interview with Frank Field, 25 July 1977;
and Field, _op.cit._, pp.29-43.
12. Interview with Field, _op.cit._
13. Potter, _op.cit._, pp.305-6.
14. Brown, G., _In My Way_ (Gollancz, 1971),
p.270. It should be noted, however, that the evidence
of 'opposition' often seemed contrived and confused.
In particular the media seems too easily to have

mistaken opposition to the confused arrangements of claw-back for opposition to increased welfare expenditure in general. See New Society (12 October 1967), pp.512-16, and (13 January 1967), pp.93-4. See also the Guardian, (23 March 1966 and 1 February 1967) and The Observer (16 October 1966 and 4 December 1966) and The Economist (3 December 1966).

15. Interview with Nicholas Bosanquet, 22 February 1979.

16. Interview with Peter Townsend, 18 December 1979.

17. Banting, op.cit., p.171.

18. See 'Under Labour the Poor get Poorer', Sunday Times (22 March 1970).

19. It is interesting to note that Donnison's acquaintance with Crossman appears to have begun when Richard Titmuss, a confidant of Crossman, suggested that Donnison would prove a useful adviser to the latter in his formulation of a Rent Bill. In 1969, he became Director of the Centre for Environmental Studies. Crossman, Diaries, Vol. 1, p.24. Crossman also referred to Titmuss and Abel-Smith as his 'own brains trust'. Diaries, Vol. III, p.139.

20. He disagreed with both Field's 'Poor get Poorer' campaign in 1970, which he felt had undermined the Party's electoral advantage, and as a member of the Prime Minister's Policy Unit was embarassed by Field's involvement in the controversial Child Benefits leak of 1976. Interview, 14 June 1977.

21. See Field, F. and Piachaud, D., 'The Poverty Trap', New Statesman (3 December 1971). Field and Piachaud, 'How to Bargain Away Poverty', Tribune (31 December 1971). Piachaud, 'A Profile of Family Poverty', Poverty, No. 19 (Summer 1971) and 'Fair Stages - The Effects of the Government's Pay Policy', Poverty, No. 26 (1973).

22. Author's figures - a random survey of the period July 1975 to July 1977 revealed that some 447 parliamentary questions had been asked by MPs from all parties on CPAG's behalf. The breakdown was as follows: Labour (12 MPs) - 243; Conservatives (5 MPs) - 119; Liberals (3 MPs) - 82; Plaid Cymru (1 MP) - 3. Prominent among the questioners were:
Bruce George (Lab. Walsall South) - 105
Andrew Bennett (Lab. Stockport) - 82
Richard Wainwright (Lib. Colne Valley) - 73
Neil Kinnock (Lab. Bedwelty) - 69
Lynda Chalker (Con. Wallasey) - 62
Peter Bottomley (Con. Greenwich & Woolwich West) - 43
Jo Richardson (Lab. Barking) - 27

Bryan Gould (Lab. Southampton Test) - 21.
23. Sunday Times (22 March 1970).
24. Ibid.
25. Ibid.
26. Crossman, Diaries, Vol III, pp.791-73.
27. 'Poverty in Britain and How to Overcome it', Tribune (6 February 1970).
28. Tribune (13 February 1970).
29. See Atkinson, A.B., Inequality and Social Security - Labour's Record, a paper delivered to the Fabian Conference on 'Labour and Inequality' (9-10 January 1971), esp. p.3. Reprinted in Townsend and Bosanquet, Labour and Inequality, Fabian Society (1972), pp.12-25.
30. Banting, op.cit., p.76.
31. Ibid., pp.76-7.
32. Stringer and Richardson, op.cit., p.29.
33. Ibid.
34. Atkinson, op.cit., p.24.
35. Sunday Times (20 March 1970).
36. Ibid.
37. Ibid.
38. Ibid.
39. The idea was devised in December 1969 and was influenced by the view of Sir John Whalley, former Deputy Secretary at the DHSS and briefly a CPAG committee member, that CPAG should identify its aims with those of the influential trade union movement. This enabled the Group at least briefly to boost its case and reduce its own political isolation.
40. Guardian (15 April 1970).
41. Howard, A. (ed.), The Crossman Diaries (Magnum, 1979), p.706.
42. Even as early as 1968 Crossman indicated that the Party's leaders were afraid of losing votes by appearing too radical in the social policy sphere: 'We've abolished the NAB and brought in an enormously humane system of supplementary allowances but we seem to have been almost ashamed of these tremendous social reforms partly because of the continuous criticism of CPAG on the one hand, and on the other the continual attacks of the general public that we are tolerating scroungers ... Then there are family allowances. At the by-elections we've been ashamed to claim that we have increased them because we're afraid of losing votes' (Vol. III, p.140).
43. CPAG, Press Release, Poor Worse Off Under Labour (22 May 1970).
44. Ibid.
45. Minutes of the CPAG Annual General Meeting

(19 April 1970).
    46.   See, for example, Crossman's comments on CPAG as 'our own friends', in <u>Diaries</u>, Vol. III, p.791.
    47.   CPAG (Election) Policy Manifesto, <u>A War on Poverty - Poor Families and the Election</u> (June 1970), 'The Government's Recent Record', sec. I.
    48.   Ibid., 'The Labour Manifesto', part II.
    49.   <u>Poverty</u>, Nos. 16/17 (1970).
    50.   <u>Bull, op.cit.</u>, p.15.
    51.   <u>Hansard</u>, Vol. 762, cols. 182-298.
    52.   Interview with David Piachaud, 14 June 1977.
    53.   Field has made a crucial rationalisation of the campaign here and suggests that, in effect, all the Group was doing was reminding and questioning the Party about what it had said in the past - an obvious tactic for a cause-group; 'It's a fairly delicate operation, there are no great battalions behind us, there's no clout, it's having a conviction about what one is doing and seeing the opening, that chink of political light which we take a crowbar to and, using the force of others on behalf of the campaign ... that's the process, that's what makes it very political, you trap people by their use of language, questioning what they have said'. Interview, 26 July 1977.
    54.   Crossman, <u>Diaries</u>, Vol. III. p.791.
    55.   Ibid., p.809.
    56.   Interview with Frank Field, 26 July 1977.
    57.   Interview with Jane Streather.
    58.   Interview with Peter Townsend, 18 December 1979.
    59.   It should be noted, for example, that Peter Townsend, a strong Labour supporter, was himself initially against the campaign but swung round to support Field, despite taking considerable criticism from Party colleagues. Field had threatened to resign if the campaign did not go through, and won strong support from Harriet Wilson and Walter Birmingham (whom he describes as a 'very strong Labour Man'), for his plan. He comments that the decision to proceed was extremely important because 'it indicated that CPAG was even prepared to oppose its own side, the Labour Party, if it was failing to deliver the goods'. In addition, because of it, he feels the attitude of the Conservatives immediately became more constructive and they undertook to keep the issue alive during Heath's administration. Interview, 25 July 1977.
    60.   Ibid.

Chapter Seven

DEALING WITH THE TORIES - THE HEATH YEARS

In considering the response of the Heath administration to poverty it is useful to recall the precedents established by previous Conservative governments. An appropriate starting-point for this resume is the 1950 General Election, the first to be fought after the creation of the welfare state by the Attlee administration. Conservative intentions in the social policy field were outlined more by implication than exposition during attacks on the record of the Attlee government. The party's 1950 manifesto, for example, charged that Labour had 'spread the talk that social welfare is something to be had from the state free, gratis and for nothing'. It warned the electorate that 'a vote for socialism is a vote to continue the policy which has endangered our economic and present independence both as a nation and as men and women' (1). While committing the party to supporting the welfare state, the manifesto warned that 'Britain can only enjoy the Social Services for which she is prepared to work' (2). The principle features of subsequent Conservative policy were thus quite clear. The level of benefits and services would be related to the nation's economic performance, and selectivity, not universality, would represent the key principle in determining their allocation. Andrew Gamble has noted that the Conservative vision of an affluent Britain created by the release of private initiative and enterprise, hitherto restrained by Labour's 'collectivism' and the revival of the slogan 'a property-owning democracy' 'reinforced the crusade for selective rather than universal welfare benefits that took root in the party during the 1950s' (3).

In 1959, John Boyd-Carpenter, Minister of Pensions and National Insurance, announced an important new turn in social policy. In keeping with the Party's belief that the level of services and benefits must mirror national economic performance, he introduced an increase in scale rates which broke with the Beveridge tradition of covering subsistence needs and the rise in the cost of living, and pegged them at a level where the Party could claim to have given claimants a share in the country's growing prosperity. The basis for this 'advance in standards' was, as Boyd-Carpenter pointed out, the 'consider-able measure of stability' achieved in the area of retail prices (4). The party's success in curbing price inflation was to bring with it economic stability and, for a short while, the possibility of a more flexible approach to welfare.

However, this new found 'generosity' could not be sustained. Conservative policy rested firmly on the principle that increased welfare expenditure could only come from improved economic performance. Thus, the economic crisis of 1961-2 put paid to any further extension of the principle established by Boyd-Carpenter with the result that in 1961 the Conservative government felt that the economy could only afford to adopt, in a rather limited and piecemeal form, the opposition's 1957 plans for earnings-related pensions. Rosemary Marten, former research officer on social security policy in the Conservative research department has noted that more money was lost to social services between 1964-70 by the failure of the economic growth rate in previous years than was actually gained by increased taxation. She concludes that 'had the growth rate not fallen so much from an average of 3.8 per cent per annum between 1959 and 1964 to an average of 2.2 per cent per annum from 1964 to 1969, and had the run on the £ not begun the day the 1965 pensions increases were announced, overall social service spending would have increased more than it did' (5).

It is useful at this point to consider some of the statistical evidence available for social security expenditure in the period 1951-68. Current expenditure on social security as a percentage of GNP at factor cost shows a striking constancy throughout the life of both the Conservative and Labour governments. In 1951, for example, expenditure on social security as a percentage of GNP was 0.3 per cent, in 1960 it remained at this figure, and in 1964 and 1968 it was 0.4 per cent (6). In the same period family allowances, expressed as a proportion of total personal income, figured at 0.6 per cent in 1951 and 1960, at 0.5 per cent in 1964 and 0.8 per cent in 1968, the year of Labour's increase. Perhaps the most interesting feature of social security expenditure in the period cited, as Abel-Smith notes, is that it had 'been increasing within the framework of the 1945-46 legislation quite apart from changes in policy' (7). Indeed, the evidence suggests that the importance of party policy as such had often been cosmetic and, on occasion, quite misleading. The value of family allowances seems to have been affected far more closely by the state of the economy than by apparent policy change. Furthermore, increases in social security expenditure have tended to mask the fact of demographic changes so that closer scrutiny of gross increases reveals both a growing number of welfare recipients and little change in the relative value of benefits paid. In the period 1951 to 1964, for example, the total population increased by 7.2 per cent while the population under twenty increased by 14.6 per cent (8).

By the 1964 General Election the new Conservative leader, Edward Heath, much influenced by the ideas of the Bow Group, had come to conclude that five major policy changes were necessary in 'Putting Britain Right Ahead', one of which was the establishment of 'selectivity in place of universalism in the social services' (9). At his first Conference as Party leader in 1965, Heath declared that one of the Party's three crucial avenues for the future would be 'the transformation of the Welfare State to meet "our needs" today' (10). His view, albeit one offered in opposition, constituted a firm rejection of any ideological content in welfarism and pointed, instead, to a new pragmatic and diminished role for the welfare system as a 'casuality clearing station'. This view was further outlined some years later by a Conservative spokesman on social services, John Selwyn Gummer: 'We can take refuge in the difficulty of finding an alternative as an excuse for perpetuating the present position but we cannot ignore the fact, on the simplest level, the system of social security reinforces the proper appreciation of the rights of the deprived, while often weakening the equally important realisation of the duties of the fortunate' (11). Gummer has since, as the Party's Chairman in the mid-80's, had ample platform to press such views to the Tory faithful.

The crux of the Party's plans for the transformation of the welfare state lay in the belief that welfare expenditure was already very high but so thinly spread, because of the traditional insistence upon universality, that its impact was limited. Rather than increase expenditure, which the Party felt the nation could not afford - and which it saw as a vote-loser in a General Election - it made greater sense to redefine the terms by which benefits could be claimed, thereby disqualifying some groups from receiving assistance (or reducing the level) and then to redistribute the 'savings' to the neediest. In policy terms selectivity was attractive and made sense. It enabled what the right-wing of the Party saw as a more cost-effective approach to welfare and it largely satisfied the demands of the progressive wing which sought to maintain the commitment to welfarism. Essentially, however, selectivity appealed to that tradition within the Conservative Party that emphasised self-help, independence and a spirit of individualism; where help was proved to be necessary, selectivity would ensure that some level of 'charitable' assistance was forthcoming. As one Conservative MP has since explained, 'Conservative social policy seeks to use the social services to set people up rather than to drag them down to a dependence upon welfare. Its preoccupation with help to the permanently needy is matched by a belief that it is best to ensure that as many as possible make provision for themselves rather than expect the state to undertake the task' (12).

The Conservative response to the re-emergence of poverty as an issue in the mid-1960s combined Party tradition with electoral interest. Ironically, as Frank Field has since shown, the campaign waged by CPAG and its academic supporters could readily be used to 'beat the drum of selectivity'. Despite all the expenditure on social security and the social services since 1945, CPAG had shown that serious and often large pockets of poverty still existed and that the level of benefit dispensed was inadequate for needs (13). Such a discovery served only to reinforce the Conservative's belief that the overall level of welfare expenditure should be re-ordered so that the bulk of resources was concentrated on the most needy. For all that, family poverty never became a major issue within the Conservative Party as a whole, nor was it a key element in its attack upon the Labour government in the period 1964-70. Indeed it was only during the 1970 Election campaign, in the course of CPAG's attack upon Labour's record, that the Conservatives took up the issue in any broad sense.

In May 1970, shortly before his death, Iain Macleod, the Conservative Shadow Chancellor and a

well-respected 'progressive', had met Field and
Townsend at his own request, and had committed the
Party to an increase in family allowances. Some weeks
earlier, during the debate on Jenkins' third Budget,
he had also drawn attention to what he saw as a major
omission, namely 'any relief directly aimed at child
poverty' (14). And he had pointed out that 'There are
still about 250,000 children living in poverty, if we
define that as an income below the scales of
requirements of supplementary benefits levels' (15).
As a means of bringing immediate relief to these
children Macleod advocated an increase in family
allowances with the increase being concentrated on
low-income groups by the operation of the claw-back
principle though he, like his Labour counterpart,
anticipated that it would not be 'a very popular
thing to do' (16). Macleod's view was markedly
different from that which he held in the immediate
wake of the devaluation measures of 1968 when he
complained that claw-back was a 'thoroughly bad'
principle and one which inflicted an unacceptable
burden on richer parents. Inconsistent or not,
Macleod had come to believe by mid-1970 that if
negative income tax, an essentially long-term
solution, could not be applied then there was no
alternative in the short term 'except an increase in
family allowances and, given the amount of money the
Chancellor has, that implies claw-back. Although I do
not like it, I believe it to be the right answer'
(17).
　　During the subsequent Election campaign the
Party pledged to tackle family poverty as a priority.
Its election manifesto, A Brighter Tomorrow,
promised to 'ensure that adequate family allowances
go to them that need them' (18). When Field asked
Edward Heath if this reinforced Macleod's earlier
statements he replied 'We accept that ... the only
way of tackling family poverty in the short term, is
to increase family allowances and operate the claw-
back principle' (19). CPAG were, nevertheless,
cautious, and recognised the allusion to selectivity
in the assurances that had been given. Summarising A
Brighter Tomorrow in their own election statement,
the Group noted that 'The pledge to raise family
allowances for all qualifying families, clawing back
the increase from families claiming the full child
tax allowances, has not been explicitly stated in the
manifesto. The manifesto comes dangerously near to
proposing that family allowances should be means-
tested. This would be wrong in principle and should
be specifically rejected' (20).

On taking office, it appeared at first that the Conservatives might proceed cautiously, prepared for a period of inactivity while policy options were discussed and priorities established. However, Heath had considerably overhauled the machinery of the Party while in opposition and had established the most elaborate structure of research and policy committees the Party had witnessed. He had talked at his first Party Conference after becoming Prime Minister of the need for the new government to achieve a 'quiet revolution', to be achieved largely by building upon the work done in opposition by these committees. A Conservative biographer, Patrick Cosgrove, has noted

> the Heath government was unusual in the extraordinary amount of research, argument and preparation that had gone into its five years of preparation for office: it was the proud boast of every minister that no cabinet in British history had been so well prepared for its task. Indeed it was not uncommon for the Prime Minister to ensure that there was a copy of the 1970 manifesto on the table at Cabinet meetings, so that a check could be kept on progress made in fulfilling its undertakings. Even after the about-turns in economic and industrial policy ... Heath pursued the implementation of even minor manifesto pledges with obsessive, perhaps compensatory, rigour. (21)

Any illusions that this new government would commence its term of office unsure of direction were quickly dismissed. Before the summer recess began all the new Ministers were in a position to brief their senior civil servants thoroughly on how they expected to achieve Heath's 'quiet and total revolution in the British way of life' (22). The basis for this 'revolution' was the introduction of a more rational approach to policy appraisal in place of the highly pluralist style long favoured in British central administration. The 1970 White Paper, <u>The Reorganisation of Central Government</u> (23), had provided, inter alia, for the creation of the Programme Analysis and Review (PAR).

PAR's concern with the relative value and cost-effectiveness of individual projects and policies was illustrated at an early stage, as we shall see, in the introduction of the family income supplement (FIS). Its concern with policy analysis and the extent to which resource allocation and use achieved agreed objectives made it an important contributory factor in the government's plans for the 'transformation of the welfare state to meet our needs today' (24). The White Paper had carried with it the Party leadership's firm belief that policies should fulfil definite, specifiable objectives. A major aim in the field of social policy then, aided ironically by CPAG's efforts to demonstrate the existence of serious pockets of poverty, was the rationalisation of the welfare system to meet the needs of the very poor. The White Paper also, as Richardson and Jordan point out, 'owed something to another strand of reformist thought, and advocated quantitative aids to decision-making - a "best value for money" approach in selecting between options' (25). This fitted perfectly with the belief noted earlier that the problems of welfare may have owed less to the amount of resources allocated than to the actual management of them. The result was the October 1970 Paper, New Policies for Public Spending, provided for the allocation of £92 million in 1971-2 to previous social service programmes but also for reductions in some parts of these programmes of £143 million resulting in a net loss of £51 million. Looking ahead to 1974-5 the net loss scheduled was to be £460 million. The basis for these reductions was the government's concern to 'establish more sensible priorities' (26). It also reflected the government's reluctance to finance a huge public sector borrowing requirement out of the proceeds of increased taxation - an approach many Conservatives saw as a recipe for electoral disaster. The result was that the decision to introduce FIS

> resulted from the adoption of rational criteria and analysis. The political solution would have been to honour the promise about family allowances regardless. But it could also be argued that the government was keeping a weather eye on political criteria in the future. The analysis suggested not only that the family allowance scheme would be expensive and inefficient ... but that it would antagonise voters who disliked losing from one pocket what they gained in another. (27)

THE INTRODUCTION OF FAMILY INCOME SUPPLEMENT

On 8 September 1970 Sir Keith Joseph, the new Secretary of State for Social Services, met Frank

Field and Peter Townsend to discuss his Party's plans for the poor. CPAG's aim was to remind the Conservatives of their pre-election assurances and to dissuade them from implementing a recently mooted, new means-tested family allowance 'supplement' similar to that which James Callaghan had tried, unsuccessfully, to introduce in 1967. It was argued that the introduction of the new scheme effectively amounted to a 'decision not to honour the 1970 election promise to direct more cash aid to low income families by means of increased family allowances but instead to supplement wages through Family Income Supplement' (28).

It had been CPAG's view that the best way to take families out of poverty was by raising family allowances and, in order that better-off families did not benefit from the rise, they proposed that income taxpayers should pay back their rise by forfeiting their tax-deductible child allowances. However, despite their assurances before the Election, both Heath and Macleod had voiced fears about the popularity of claw-back and both had also alluded to some possibility of more selectivity. On coming to power their reservations about the scheme were further reinforced by the findings of a study probably conducted in the Economic Adviser's branch of the DHSS. The study's conclusions were threefold:

> Firstly, that a rise in family allowances, as advocated by CPAG, would fail to help a third of poor families, since they only had one child; secondly, some of the poor families who did receive increased allowances would lose them again through income tax; finally, there was the apparent economic and administrative irrationality of a scheme which would pay out £187 million, of which 97 per cent would be recovered through income tax leaving only £6 million in the pockets of the families it was designed to benefit. (29)

The first obstacle could have been overcome, as CPAG had long advocated, by extending family allowances to the first child. However, the Group had not prepared its case as thoroughly as it might have. In particular, its own reasoning does not appear to have been sensitive to the overall framework of Conservative policy and the government's desire to contain public expenditure where possible. As Brown points out, 'further calculations showed that this would be very costly and administrative studies made it clear that it would take too long to introduce. It was therefore evident that the family allowance scheme would be relatively inefficient and the government was forced to consider alternative ways of relieving poverty among low earners' (30). This was a significant conclusion, not least because it indicated that the CPAG family allowance scheme was not rejected on the basis of policy preference but because of its apparent inefficiency and, crucially, its difficulty to administer. Furthermore, the introduction of the cheaper, means-tested FIS may have been seen by the government as an important step to fulfilling a manifesto pledge that a new Conservative government 'in coming to its decisions ... must always recognise that its responsibility is to the people and all the people' (31). Chief among these responsibilities was a concern to lessen the burden on the tax payer.

Accordingly, the alternative favoured by the government was to supplement the wages of the poorest to make up half the difference between actual earnings and an amount indexed to family size and general living standards. This scheme would cost some £8 million. Its principle drawback for CPAG was that low wage-earners would be subject to a means test to determine eligibility. Furthermore, the Group voiced its serious fears that the scheme would discourage take-up since it reinforced stigma. Brown notes that

> The final decision to adopt FIS must have been taken in Cabinet or a Cabinet committee and it is likely that agreement was reached on the principle at an early stage, before DHSS officials invested too much time in detailed planning. If so, the Cabinet probably had before it a short paper signed by the Chancellor of the Exchequer and the Secretary of State explaining the objections to family allowances and requesting authority for the Secretary of State to prepare the new scheme. Final approval would probably have been based upon a short paper from the Secretary of State alone, indicating that the financial implications had been agreed with the Chancellor and drawing attention to any aspects that might cause controversy, perhaps with particular reference to any objections that had been raised in consultations. (32)

There is little evidence to be found of CPAG taking part in such consultations on FIS other than their early meeting with Sir Keith Joseph. Furthermore the speed with which legislation was introduced suggests that preparations for such a scheme were already well advanced within the DHSS before the Conservatives took office. The apparent lack of consultation and the speed with which the scheme was executed points to the strong role played by the DHSS and seems to confirm Brown's view that 'policy-making will ... be left to those who run the service unless there are strong countervailing pressures compelling the political leadership to pay attention to wider factors' (33).

There had, of course, been the specific pledges given to CPAG by Heath and Macleod that family poverty would be tackled in the short run by an increase in family allowances. Perhaps what CPAG had not fully accepted was that pledges made in opposition, and often in ignorance of the facts of government, are frequently set aside in office when their fulfilment becomes unrealistic, impossible or politically unacceptable. Rosemary Marten points out: 'there was a specific·pledge to tackle poverty in the short-term by increasing family allowances and operating the claw-back principle. It was thought at the time that a 50p increase would cost £30 million net a year. What was not appreciated was the disastrous effect of the budget tax changes and inflation: the poverty threshold and the standard tax-rate threshold had got too close for another increase using claw-back' (34).

The selective nature of the benefit and its restricted application were unacceptable to CPAG. In total some 190,000 households, with roughly half a million children, would receive a supplement to their income but, as CPAG pointed out, 'the Family Income Supplement is aimed to help only the poorest of the poor, and it limits help to families with fathers in full-time work earning <u>less</u> than the current supplementary benefit rates' (35).

The conflicting nature of 'problem definition' that CPAG had encountered in the mid-1960s was also apparent in the rival definitions of the 'problem' given by itself and the DHSS during the FIS episode. During the Bill's second reading, for example, Keith Joseph had stated that FIS would bring 'help to over one half of the households below supplementary benefit level' (36). CPAG, however, was convinced that the Secretary of State had underestimated the number of families in poverty and offered its own estimate of 300,000 households comprising 1.3 million people, who it felt should have qualified for aid of this sort. The £8 million set aside for this purpose therefore seemed derisory to the Group. Indeed, Iain Macleod had earlier pledged some £30 million towards assisting low income families in this way and this figure had been calculated on the assumption that the Chancellor would have approximately £220 million at his disposal (37). However, Macleod's successor, Anthony Barber, returned to the taxpayer a sum of over £300 million in rebates and concessions, thus fulfilling a major election pledge to the Party's supporters.

By the autumn of 1970 it was clear that where CPAG had seen Labour as failing to act on the poor's behalf, the Conservatives seemed likely to intervene largely to control expenditure and increase selectivity. Sir Keith Joseph set the tone at the Party's Conference in September, taking great pains to elaborate the abuses inflicted upon the welfare system by those he alleged to be 'scroungers' and 'layabouts'. He also pledged to extend the number of benefits covered by selectivity, and declared his intention to impose new charges for a variety of items and services available through the National Health Service.

Such a strategy was firmly in keeping with Edward Heath's comments in 1965 concerning the 'transformation of the welfare state'. It has been said that this brand of conservatism expressed a distinct attitude towards social policy: the inevitability of the strategy had been well signposted throughout the 1960s. Though the Party's intentions may have appeared somewhat vague during the election, its traditional approach to social policy remained distinct and unchallenged.

> The social services are charged not just with the duty of relieving poverty but also with the task of enabling the recipient to move from dependence to independence. The priorities are therefore clear. First, help to those permanently in need. Secondly, the creation of an effective structure to gather up all those who, temporarily or not, need additional help. Thirdly, the extension of ways by which many of those at present condemned to dependence can begin to provide for themselves. (38)

Such views have, inevitably, found their most recent echo in the Party leadership's rationale for the 'Fowler Reviews'. Most importantly, they demonstrate that the 'Reviews' are neither new nor a break with Tory tradition but, rather, a very firm affirmation of it.

THE OCTOBER 'MINI-BUDGET'

The pattern set by Keith Joseph in September was
affirmed in the Party's October 'mini-budget'.
Income tax was substantially reduced and public
expenditure cut by £330 million in 1971/2, with cuts
of £1600 million in the year 1974/5. Cheap welfare
milk was abolished; prescription, dental, spectacles
and school meal charges were all raised. Free school
milk for children over the age of seven was
discontinued, and a substantial cut in housing
subsidies and agricultural support was effected. In
addition, the pledge to raise family allowances was
set aside and, in place of it, the means-tested FIS
formally introduced. Writing in 1974, Peter Townsend
spoke of the 'mini-budget' as marking a turning-point
in social history, a declaration of class warfare.
'It represented a return to the more authoritarian
and doctrinaire principles of Tory social
philosophy, which no Tory Administration of the post
war years had dared espouse and to which the Heath
Administration has obstinately clung. (39)'

> the management of the social services and social
> security, in particular, was to be more strongly
> infused with the principle of conditional
> welfare for the few ... through means-tested
> benefits, the prosperous working class would be
> obliged to 'fend for themselves' and 'stand on
> their own feet' and the undeserving poor, the so
> called work-shy, cohabiters and deceitful
> immigrants, would be properly vetted and
> controlled. For the small class of deserving
> poor, on the other hand, new forms of national
> charity should properly be developed and
> dispensed. The strategy reaffirmed, in short,
> the paramountcy of the values of the market.
> (40)

Townsend thus encapsulated the essence of
Conservative social policy during the Heath
administration - conditional welfare for those
identified as the 'neediest' and the cultivation of a
'spirit of independence' in less deserving cases.
This dichotomy had been made quite clear by
Conservative spokesmen, though their interpretation
of its rationale and effects would undoubtedly have
been more generous. Gummer, for example, noted that

'It sums up the two basic elements which underlie our
thought - the necessity for society to see that those
who need help can get their share of the community's
wealth and at the same time the responsibility of the
individual to help himself and contribute towards the
common good' (41).

Andrew Gamble attributes Conservative policy at
this time to what he sees as the strained priorities
of the post-war welfare consensus. Significantly, he
points to Britain's fundamental economic problems as
the determinant of what could or could not be done by
the Heath government. Stagnation and inflation had
become so intractable that 'Any government elected in
1970 would therefore have needed to rethink some of
the priorities of the post-war politics of power'
(42). This, he contends, Heath attempted to do in the
'transformation of the Welfare State'. It should also
be noted, despite the apparent divisiveness of
Conservative Budgets and selectivity in welfare,
that there had also been sympathy within the Labour
Cabinet for a similar approach in 1966/7 and that
Callaghan had only just failed in a bid to introduce
a means-tested 'family income supplement'.

There is some evidence to suggest that Heath's
adherence to the 'competition policy' outlined in the
mid-1960s was a gamble which if successful, would
have produced economic growth and enabled the Party
to include claimants in the general prosperity of the
country as it had done under Boyd-Carpenter in 1959.
There was also a strong similarity with the Wilsonian
belief that increased welfare expenditure must be
contingent upon economic growth, especially if the
economy was stagnant. 'If the economy broke out of
the vice of stagnation and inflation there would be
greater rewards for everyone. The welfare consensus
and the politics of interest group bargaining could
be established on a firm base once more. (43)'

There were two major problems, however with
which the Conservatives failed to deal. First, they
failed to explain their intentions and strategy to
the electorate. Secondly, and more importantly, that
strategy required a short-term cut in the living
standards of wage earners. The Party lacked able
communicators to get this message across in any
acceptable way. The outcome was that

> The budget deficit was allowed to grow
> astronomically. In addition, savings that were
> made in public expenditure were directed at the
> living standards of wage-earners - these
> included the rise in rents under the Housing

Finance Act and the increase in charges for
health and school milk. The result was an
enormous increase in the pressure of demand and
therefore more rapid inflation at the very time
that workers' living standards were being
squeezed. (44)

CPAG clearly felt some responsibility for this
state of affairs. Field commented in 1971:

if CPAG unintentionally played a role, however
small, in Labour's defeat, then given the move
towards inequality upon which this Government
has embarked, the Group acted against the poor's
short-term interest. Although at the time it was
difficult to say anything good about the Labour
Government, that administration has taken on an
almost Christ-like appearance in comparison
with the present government. (45)

The full extent of the dilemma in which CPAG found
itself during the 1970 election campaign is only
apparent when the terms of the 'mini-budget' are
considered. There can be little doubt that the Group
was taking a major gamble by distancing itself from
the Labour Party and by soliciting Conservative
support. There was little evidence, other than
Macleod's comments in the Commons and Heaths's
subsequent letter to the Group, to suggest that the
Conservatives were more likely to deliver reform and
increase family allowances than the Labour Party. The
wisdom of the Group's gamble must also be questioned
against the fact that both sets of promises, vague or
otherwise, had been made largely in the atmosphere of
the Election campaign. CPAG's awareness, as a result
of its experience with the Labour government, that
there was a significant credibility gap between what
a party promises in opposition (and during election
campaigns), and what it is able or willing to do when
in office might have led it to be rather more
realistic in its hopes of Conservative policy (46).
Some note of caution had been struck in the Group's
own policy manifesto, but CPAG seems to have
refrained from questioning Conservative policy more
directly, perhaps in an effort to win support in the
Party should it come to power. No doubt many within
CPAG were anticipating the sort of measures effected
by the October 'mini-budget'. What is clear is that
between January and June 1970 CPAG was in no
position, given its commitment to raise family
allowances, to do anything but set aside its

reservations and approach the Conservatives constructively and with an open mind.

Peter Townsend was to comment later that the Conservative manifesto already contained 'the ingredients for a more divisive strategy'. These included the pledges to cut income tax and surtax, reduce public expenditure, extend private and occupational pension schemes, change the housing subsidy scheme, sell council houses and take 'firm action to deal with abuse of the Social Security system ... so as to prevent the whole system from being brought into disrepute by the shirkers and scroungers' (47). Even so, he, like others in the Group, felt the ambiguity of the manifesto was such that some degree of optimism could be justified: 'in deference to the poverty lobby the harsh implications of the manifesto were tempered by unspecific promises to protect pensioner's living standards, improve benefits for the ill and disabled, give priority to community services, tackle the problem of family poverty and ensure that adequate family allowances go to those families that need them' (48). Townsend therefore felt that 'although the auguries were ominous there were therfore grounds for supposing, especially when the party failed to secure a majority of the votes of the electorate, that the inegalitarian and authoritarian predispositions of Tory social strategy might be moderated in practice' (49). However, the subsequent failure to moderate that strategy in practice resulted in an urgent re-think on the part of CPAG of its own tactics and attitudes towards the new government. Townsend had already anticipated the worst. On the morning of the 'mini-budget' CPAG released a press bulletin which quoted the Chairman as saying 'if the Government announces a different scheme it will have to be cross-examined vigorously about the history of its commitments. It will have to prove that the CPAG scheme is impracticable. And it will have to demonstrate that the alternative favoured is likely to be more effective in reducing poverty and also preferable in administrative, economic and social terms' (50).

THE OBJECTIONS TO FIS

The measures contained in the October 'mini-budget' and CPAG's reaction to them ensured that, for the immediate future at least, the Group would respond to other promises with some scepticism and to further

155

'cuts' with outright hositility. The overriding tactic was repeatedly to 'remind' party leaders what they had previously stated in public. Where promises had been broken, the Group was quick to expose the fact; where recommendations had been made, the Group continued to press for legislation. Their task was aided by Heath's own penchant for popular slogans like 'A Better Tommorrow', and a 'Quiet Revolution' affecting every aspect of British life and, most obviously, his use of themes like the 'one nation' (51). Each were ready targets for an increasingly publicity-oriented CPAG.

The chief aim now was to show that the introduction of FIS was wholly inconsistent with Heath's post-election comment that his government's aim would be 'not to divide, but to unite and, where there are differences, to bring reconciliation' (52). Neither the introduction of FIS nor the 'mini-budget' could be even loosely described as efforts to 'bring reconciliation'.

The Group's principal, non-economic objections to FIS concerned the likelihood of low take-up as a result of its means-tested nature and the limited publicity about the scheme. There was considerable evidence to show that poor or limited publicity could have a seriously depressive effect upon benefit take-up. Even after the 1966 Social Security Act, and despite considerable publicity about the avail-ability and right to benefit, Tony Atkinson had shown that there were still 600,000 old people, quite apart from additional groups of people becoming eligible for supplementary assistance for the first time since the 1966 Act, who were eligible for assistance under this means-tested programme but not receiving it. By 1970 these represented about 27 per cent of individuals eligible for assistance (53). The 1966 Ministry of Social Security Report, <u>Circumstances of Families</u>, also found evidence of individuals entitled to supplementary benefit who were not obtaining it, whether through pride or ignorance of their rights. During the Labour governments of 1964-70 the official targets for the take-up of free school dinners were never reached, and remained about 70,000 short.

Anthony Crosland, when Secretary of State for Education, admitted that 'not only in school meals but also in many other fields we still have not discovered satisfactory methods by which we can make it clear to people who are entitled to free benefits that they are so entitled and how best they can claim them' (54). Similar evidence existed on the take-up of free welfare foods. The rate rebate scheme was yet another measure where take-up had been very poor, so much so that CPAG were able to persuade Peter Walker, Secretary of State for the Environment, of the need to conduct an advertising drive to promote it (55). The Group estimated from <u>Circumstances of Families</u> that only 10 per cent of eligible low-income households were claiming the rebates, and the <u>Report of the Administration of the Wage Stop</u> (1967) showed that only 16 out the eligible 52 families surveyed claimed rate rebates.

CPAG had also estimated in the spring of 1968 that in the last year of prescription charges before they were abolished and then reintroduced (1963) less than one in five low-paid workers claimed their rights to free medicine, and a similar level of take-up was evident for optical and dental care. There was, therefore, considerable evidence to show, in the wake of broken Conservative pledges, that the alternative means-tested measures the Party had initiated were derisory in resource terms and unrealistic in terms of expected take-up.

In the following months the Group saw the Conservative government embarking on 'the most comprehensive and expensive advertising campaign ever on poor people's rights to means-tested help' in order to meet Keith Joseph's extremely high take-up target of 85 per cent for FIS (56). By the summer of 1971 CPAG could point out that even after the Secretary of State had raised the qualifying earnings level in order to keep the scheme in line with inflation, the government had still yet to achieve a 50 per cent take-up on the <u>original</u> numbers thought to be eligible. 'In the tradition that attack is the best form of defence, the Government has begun to claim success for its social policy. But in doing so it has underlined the very limited scope of the anti-poverty programme. By adding 85,000 families to the rolls for free welfare foods, 57,000 for free medicine, or only 42,000 for dental care, can the Government really claim that it has made serious inroads into poverty? (57)'. In addition, the Group reminded the Secretary of State of his earlier statements on the welfare of the poor:

> when Sir Keith outlined the Government's controversial strategy, he promised to reconsider the whole programme if it failed to reach those in need. Sir Keith's colleagues have kept their promises to the richer sections of the community. The important question is

whether the Government will keep faith with the
poor. If the Heath administration is going to
fulfil its pledge of tackling family poverty
within the lifetime of a Parliament, it needs to
change course - and quickly. (58)

The objections to FIS were further compounded by the
timing of its introduction. Although the increased
social service charges outlined in the 'mini-budget'
were to come into force in April 1971, FIS was not
scheduled for operation until September. The Group
did not expect the government to increase family
allowances and thereby make many families ineligible
for income supplements before the FIS scheme came
into effect and so it decided that its annual visit
to the Chancellor should be concerned not only with
its perennial plea for an increase in family
allowances, but with a demand to raise the tax
threshold (59).

In its March 1971 Memorandum to the Chancellor
the Group highlighted the problems of the large
numbers of workers who after doing a full week's
work, earned less than their equivalent supplementary benefit entitlement, but who continued to pay tax
at the standard rate (60). The Memorandum
demonstrated two alternative methods of introducing
a minimum earned-income relief which would lift out
of tax workers earning 'poverty wages'. The
Chancellor was to prove unsympathetic, however.
Field commented, 'Alas, our explanations must have
been inadequate, for instead of opting to take the
poor out of tax, the Chancellor effected our proposal
to the higher reaches of the tax range, so that those
at the top paid less tax' (61). This was all the more
surprising as Barber had said that he wanted to do
all he could to help the poor, but that the money
wasn't available.

In addition to these concessions, Barber's 1971
Budget redirected an enormous Budget surplus to
taxpayers. This meant that, beginning with Roy
Jenkins' final Budget, some £1200 million was to be
returned to taxpayers by the end of the financial
year. The amount allocated specifically to families
totalled £215 million, of which some £207 million in
child tax allowances benefited the largely better-
off taxpayers, while a meagre £8 milliom fell to the
very poorest families. By March 1972, Barber's
assurances that resources were not available to
assist the poor appeared hollow, if not cynical,
against his boast that his Budgets had reduced the
burden of taxation by over £3000 million (62). As

Field noted at the time, 'he has thus fulfilled an election promise, but his budgets have broken Mr Heath's pledge to create one nation' (63).

In March 1972 a further memorandum to the Chancellor, appropriately titled <u>One Nation: The Conservative's Record Since June 1970</u>, spoke of Barber's period of office as 'the age of redistribution of income to the rich'. Crucially, it commented 'our grandchildren will be at a loss to understand why this aspect of the "quiet revolution" raised almost no comment in public debate' (64). CPAG's own failure to influence the course of government policy and the remaining options open to it to do so were to come under intense scrutiny during the ensuing post mortem.

A major issue on which an internal CPAG debate now developed was its future relationship with the main political parties. While many interest groups rigidly adhered to a non-partisan style in the belief that both parties were 'almost equally open to persuasion' (65), Field sought to anticipate the question of whether this sort of approach was fitting for an issue like poverty. In other words, should CPAG continue to reaffirm its 1970 General Election tactics? The answer to the question 'which strategy?' would depend primarily on what sort of policies the Group sought from government. Measures aimed at raising the income of the poorest groups in society were favoured, albeit by different methods, by both parties. The real problem lay, however, in the possibility that 'a successful anti-poverty programme will entail a much greater equality in our society' ... 'how do we react to this when the present government has made it abundantly clear on many occasions that it is violently opposed to such a belief?' (66).

Paradoxically, despite the Group's criticisms, Field still favoured a dialogue with both parties and a subscription to the rules of the game where expedient. This was to include asking parliamentary questions, canvassing and lecturing to MP's, mailing the Group's literature and memoranda to Ministers and opposition spokesmen, and the lobbying of Common's committees. He was also in favour of taking up Tony Benn's suggestion that regular and more formal consultation should be established between Labour's National Executive Committee and groups like CPAG, DIG, Shelter and so on, though he recognised that if this ever came about, which doesn't seem to have been the case, CPAG would have to make similar overtures to the Conservatives.

Finer talks of interest groups as having one of three types of relationship with the two major parties. The strongest and more formal is 'embodiment' or affiliation (67). In 1978, for example, some 67 trade unions were formally affiliated to the Labour Party: they sponsor MPs, contribute to election funds, and their leaders occupy senior positions in joint Party-union bodies like the Liaison Committee and the NEC. In the case of the Conservative Party, Finer contends that formal affiliation as such is replaced by 'alignment'. Business, industry, commerce and farming, for example, 'must be regarded as "aligned" with the Conservatives Party'. In other words 'the link between them is not made by the organisations qua organisations but by the fact that the private individuals who compose these organisations do, as individuals, have overwhelming links with the Conservative and not the Labour Party' (68). The evidence presented in Chapter 5, however, suggests that CPAG has traditionally been 'aligned' in much the same way with the Labour Party through the close association and overlapping membership of CPAG members with the party.

The final category clearly describes the CPAG's relationship with the parties in the aftermath of both the 'poor get poorer' campaign and the October 'mini-budget'. In this case a group comes to play an 'uncommitted' or 'hard-to-get' role in its relationship with the parties. Its lobbying approach becomes either non- or bi-partisan and it seeks crossbench support for its ideas and policy proposals (69). Since Field's arrival as Director, CPAG explored both 'aligned' and 'uncommitted' approaches towards the major parties, neither of which brought lasting success. The remaining options open to the Group were thus to re-establish alignment with the Labour Party in an effort to reconstruct and make more productive their early relationship or, alternatively, to seek alignment and perhaps even 'embodiment' with some other political force with which it had a value-empathy. In the event, the Group sought to do both by rebuilding its relationship with the Labour Party at its grass-roots rather than at front-bench, level and by establishing liasion and affiliation with some parts of the increasingly influential trade union movement. It is to a discussion of this new strategy that we now turn.

NOTES

1.   Gamble, A., The Conservative Nation (Routledge & Kegan Paul, 1974), p.56.
2.   Ibid.
3.   Ibid., pp.59-60; and Eccles, D., The New Conservatism (4 August 1951), p.4.
4.   Birch, R., The Shaping of the Welfare State (Longman, 1974), p.274.
5.   Marten, R., 'The Tories: Reformers or Reactionaries?', Poverty, No. 19, p.6.
6.   Abel-Smith, B., 'Public Expenditure on the Social Services', Social Trends (CSO, 1970).
7.   Ibid., p.18.
8.   Ibid., p.14.
9.   Crossbow, No. 42.
10.   Gamble, op.cit., p.92.
11.   Gummer, J.S., 'A Conservative Approach to the Social Services', Political Quarterly (October-December 1973), pp.425-35.
12.   Ibid., p.432.
13.   See the commentary on selectivity in Poverty, No. 4 (1967); 'Towards a Policy for Family Poverty', Poverty, No. 11 (1969). See also the discussion on selectivity and negative income tax by Marten in Poverty, No. 11, pp.9-11. For a comprehensive discussion of the nature and extent of poverty, see Townsend, P., The Concept of Poverty (Heinemann, 1970).
14.   Hansard, Vol. 798, cols. 1400-1.
15.   Ibid.
16.   Ibid.
17.   Ibid., col. 1413.
18.   Nevertheless, in CPAG's own General Election policy manifesto the Group had written 'The Conservative Party shows little awareness of the extent of poverty, or of the problems of families with low incomes, and therefore of the need for a broad and co-ordinated programme of action covering fiscal, incomes and social policies'.
19.   Poverty, Nos.16/17, p.30.
20.   CPAG, A War on Poverty - Poor Families and the Election (June 1970).
21.   Cosgrave, P., Margaret Thatcher - Prime Minister (Arrow, 1979), pp.80-1.
22.   The Times (27 October 1970).
23.   Cmnd. 4506.
24.   See Spiers, M., Techniques and Public Administration (Fontana, 1975), pp.101-5.
25.   Governing Under Pressure, op.cit., p.36.
26.   Poverty, No. 19, p.6.

27. Brown, R.G.S., The Management of Welfare (Fontana, 1975), p.209.
28. Ibid., p.200.
29. Ibid.
30. Ibid.
31. Poverty, No. 19, p.5.
32. Ibid.
33. Brown, R.G.S., op.cit., p.210
34. Poverty, No. 19, p.5.
35. Poverty, Nos. 16/17, p.4.
36. Hansard, Vol. 806, col. 223.
37. Poverty, Nos 16/17, pp.3-4.
38. Gummer, op.cit., p.434.
39. Townsend, P., 'The Social Underdevelopment of Britain', New Statesman (1 March 1974).
40. Ibid.
41. Gamble, op.cit., p.434.
42. Ibid., p.220.
43. Ibid.
44. Ibid., p.224, and Field, F., One Nation - The Conservative's Record since June 1970, Poverty Pamphlet No. 12 (September 1972).
45. Bull (ed.), op.cit., pp.153-4.
46. Rarely, when in office, do parties break radically with the past. Townsend notes: 'the social policy of a government can be evaluated in different ways - in relation to long-established party objectives and principles; the expression of those objectives and principles in the party manifesto; the internal consistency of the statement of objectives and the means chosen for fulfilling these objectives; the standards and tests for policies which it perceives and accepts and more objective standards of social need or condition'. New Statesman (1 March 1974). See also Fowler, G., 'The Politics of Social Administration', Public Adminstration Bulletin (August 1977), pp.2-10.
47. New Statesman (1 March 1974).
48. Ibid.
49. Ibid.
50. Ibid.
51. The Times (20 June 1970).
52. Ibid.
53. Atkinson, A.B., Poverty in Britain and the Reform of Social Security (Cambridge University Press, 1969), p.76.
54. Hansard, Vol. 750, col. 959.
55. See Marten, in Poverty, No. 19.
56. Ibid.
57. Ibid.
58. Ibid.

59. Bull, op.cit., p.155.
60. CPAG, 'A Plan to Help Low-Paid Workers and Overcome Family Poverty', in Poverty, No. 18 (March 1971), pp.14-20.
61. Bull, op.cit., p.155.
62. Harrison, A., 'Where's the Money Gone?' Poverty, No. 23 (Summer 1972); Hansard, Vol. 833, col. 1390 (21 March 1972).
63. Bull, op.cit., p.157.
64. Field, F., One Nation: The Conservative's Record Since June 1970, Poverty Pamphlet No. 12 (September 1972), p.12.
65. See Finer, S.E., 'Interest Groups and the Political Process in Great Britain', in Ehrmann, H.W. (ed.), Interest Groups on Four Continents (Pittsburgh University Press, 1967), pp.133-5.
66. Director's Report, p.5.
67. Finer, in Ehrmann (ed.), op.cit.
68. Ibid.
69. Ibid.

Chapter Eight

TRADE UNIONS AND SOCIAL WELFARE - AN OVERVIEW

In this chapter we examine the early developments in
CPAG's strategy for liaison with the industrial wing
of the labour movement and we offer some explanation
for the increasingly influential and societal role
that the unions came to play in Labour's policy-
making structure with reference to the theory of
union 'politicisation' advanced first by Perlman and
latterly by Richter (1), and more recently by those
who see Britain moving towards a 'corporatist' style
of government (2). We consider, first, the nature and
extent of trade union interest in social policy in
this century.
      Whilst the British trade union movement has
traditionally concerned itself with securing
acceptable conditions of employment for its members
it has, on occasion, ventured beyond its sectional
role and has sought to win reform and change where
the benefits would accrue to the non-trade unionists
also. Many trade unions, in addition to their stated
economic and industrial goals, have far reaching
social and political aims incorporated in their
constitutions. These aims and interests have been
much elaborated in trade union submissions to
government.
      Perhaps the two best known examples of trade
union statements on social policy are TUC evidence to
the (Donovan) Royal Commission on Trade Unions and
Employers' Organisations in 1968 (3) and to the
(Diamond) Royal Commission on the Distribution of
Income and Wealth in 1978 (4). More recently, in
1984, a number of major trade unions made detailed
submissions on social security to the Fowler Reviews.
In its evidence to the Donovan Commision the TUC set
out ten principal objects of British trade unions.
The first two - improved terms of employment and
improved physical environment in the work place - are

164

the sort of sectional demands expected from an association established to serve the interests of its paid members. The remaining eight, however, present a rather different image of trade unions and indicate a broad concern for the welfare of the community at large. These include full employment and national prosperity; security of employment and income; improved social security; a voice in government, and improved public and social services.

A similar picture emerges from the evidence presented to the Royal Commission on the Distribution of Income and Wealth, 1978. The TUC's evidence was divided into six issues: low-paid workers; social security; family support; taxation and the 'poverty trap'; the social wage; and unemployment and multiple deprivation (5). Of its wider interests and its own 'societal role' in achieving them, the TUC submission comments

> The TUC has been active in pressing for legislation to reduce areas of discrimination; for example, the Equal Pay Act, the Sex Discrimination Act and the Employment Protection Act ... Nevertheless the TUC believes that the biggest single force in reducing low pay caused by discriminatory practices is the extension of effective collective bargaining through active trade union organisation into areas in which discrimination is practised. (6)

On the issue of social security, the TUC stated 'It has consistently been the policy of the TUC that National Insurance Benefits should provide an adequate income as of right without dependence on means-tested benefit for all those people genuinely seeking work or not in the employment field. To achieve this the gaps in the National Insurance scheme must be filled and the level of their National Insurance benefits raised substantially' (7). The TUC's evidence left the Commission in no doubt as to the unions' own solutions for the alleviation of poverty through low pay. 'The aim of the TUC therefore is to find ways in which the need for the present kind of benefits can be removed and at the same time make a substantial improvement in the financial position of low income families. The main methods must be to increase National Insurance benefits and low pay ... and relieve the tax burden on the lowest paid workers. (8)' It is useful to note the range of TUC evidence to the Diamond Commission because not only is that evidence arguably the most detailed of its type to date, it is also the most recent stage in an evolutionary process of TUC social policy which began some fifty years earlier. Thus in 1977-8 we find the TUC presenting evidence and policy initiatives on such matters as child benefits, low pay, multiple deprivation, means-tested allowances, housing support, the effectiveness of wage councils, taxation and the poverty trap and welfare provision. To understand how the TUC and individual unions have reached this broader societal concern some historical illustration is necessary.

As early as the turn of the century, trade unions had been closely involved in the campaign for the introduction of state-financed school meals and had favoured the idea of state maintenance for children. Both issues were raised at the Annual Conference of the Labour Representation Committee in 1905 and, in the same year, the TUC, the London Trades Council and the Social Democratic Federation held a conference to consider 'the state maintenance of children as a necessary corollary of universal compulsory education' (9). Significantly, Hilary Land notes that 'The "first step" towards this school meals financed by the Exchequer was supported unanimously, but a proposal for <u>full</u> maintenance was rejected as 'a revolutionary proposal' which 'would excite great prejudice and alarm' (10). Even earlier, in 1889, the Parliamentary Committee, which administered the TUC well before unions combined to produce their own party, discussed matters including old age pensions, child labour, electoral reform and public utilities. The rationale for this broader concern has perhaps only been fully understood in retrospect.

> In the more general sense, unions cannot truly improve the real wages and standards of living of their members unless they concern themselves with the economic direction of our resources and the distribution of wealth in our society. If trade unions are to be concerned with their employed members, how can they be effective without having some analysis about the cause of unemployment and the means to put it right? How can the unions be concerned with what gross wages will be for their members and remain unconcerned with what the member takes home after tax and insurance? How can a union be concerned with a member when he is well and working and yet stay inactive on his or her

behalf when he is sick or not working? (11)

The short answer, of course, is that they can't. For a trade union to perform efficiently it must operate beyond the circumscribed employer-employee relationship. Unions 'must be ever seeking to establish the kind of economic and social framework within which they can best carry out their responsibilities on behalf of their members. Looking after the whole man or woman is the only sensible way the unions can fulfil their duties to their members' (12).

It is no longer possible to isolate the trade unionist in the work place from the trade unionist at leisure. His interests, values and expections will, necessarily, carry into other spheres of his life. The trade unionist, like other individuals, is himself 'a universe of interests' (13), whose orbits intersect and whose influences vary with time and circumstance. The trade unionist may also be a single parent, a claimant of child benefits, an expectant mother, a ratepayer, a mortgagee, a council tenant, a consumer. As J.D.B. Miller notes, 'Each of these represents a potential connection with an interest, depending upon how much he is absorbed in the particular aspect of his life and what degree of organisation and selfconsciousness the interest has in the community at large' (14). Crucially, many of the trade unionists' interests are interdependent. Changes in the nature or status of one interest may well produce an outcome that can enhance or harm another. Inevitably, advances or failures in the work place may produce similar outcomes elsewhere. Goals may remain unfulfilled and benefits lost, unless some sort of initiative or intervention from a structured organisation takes place and creates a framework in which the essentials for the individuals' wider liberation and development may be established.

The outcome has been a recognition on the part of the trade unions from quite early in their development that their socio-economic security cannot be wholly achieved within the confines of the employer-employee relationship. Factors and circumstances extraneous to that relationship, such as the stability of the currency, the national balance of payments, the level and availability of state benefits to be paid in times of sickness or unemployment, the policy priorities of the government and so on, will all affect their members' life-chances. Ultimately, as we have seen at GCHQ and in the Miners Strike, they may threaten the strength and stability of trade unions themselves.

Inevitably, then, trade unions have long recognised the need to represent 'whole man' rather than 'fragmented man', and to act outside of the work place in order to sustain or preserve the achievement won within it (15).

An early illustration can be seen in the period 1934-6, when an important social struggle was waged by some unions to preserve the standards of unemployment relief. John Strachey commented; 'successive attempts were made by the National Government to depress the national standard of life by making alterations in the rules governing the receipt of unemployment relief. These attempts were resisted with a very considerable measure of success ... (and) the Government was on several occasions constrained to modify drastically their original proposals to the advantage of the unemployed' (16).

This concern for the unemployed is a crucial one and is, of course, a logical outcome of the traditional concern for those in work. Such a concern as CPAG has persistently tried to show since 1965, is consistent with the view that the welfare of those in work can only be fully established by improving the lot of those without employment. As Strachey noted in the 1930s:

> If the unemployed are driven by starvation to accept any wages and conditions of work offered to them, it will be clearly impossible for the employed workers to maintain, still less to improve, their wage rates ... the struggle for the defence of the national standard of life is, to a considerable extent, fought out over the question of the rates and conditions of unemployment benefit. (17)

His comments ring as true in 1985 as they did 50 years earlier and lend support to the view that in a time of economic uncertainty every trade unionist is a potential claimant of unemployment benefit (18). To strengthen the position of the employed the position of the unemployed must first be strengthened. Any initiative in this area has tended, therefore, to be a curious mixture of self preservation and moral responsibility. This is illustrated on the issue of family allowances.

THE TRADE UNIONS AND FAMILY ALLOWANCES

The early interest shown by the labour movement in

168

state maintenance of children was sustained throughout the first quarter of the twentieth century and resulted, in 1928, in the setting-up of a joint Labour Party-TUC committee to discuss a proposal for a national scheme of allowances financed from taxation. However, the TUC executive decided in 1930 that any decision on the matter should be postponed until the social services were more fully developed - giving some early indication of the unions' somewhat ambivalent attitude towards family support (19). Eleven years passed before family allowances were again discussed at conference. This apparent concern with social services development was little more than a 'red herring'. The real reasons for non-committal were more fundamental and show that the unions' concern with community welfare may well be important but that it is secondary to their concern to defend their work place interest. As Land notes: 'This caution towards acccepting family allowances was based primarily on the fact their introduction would interfere with wage negotiations. Moreover, many other supporters of family allowances, including Beveridge, favoured occupational or contributory schemes either of which, trade unionists argued, would penalise the childless worker' (20).

Union leaders feared that occupational family allowances would be paid for at the expense of higher wages. Such a principle was unacceptable to British trade unions and suspicion of such a scheme was further fuelled by the growing support for it in the Conservative Party in the late 1930s. The war effort, however, considerably strengthened both the trade unions' general position and their determination to resist interference in wage bargaining by government. Their success in withstanding the latter contributed to a mood of self-confidence such that, in 1941,'it was thought "opportune" to reconsider family allowances at the Labour Party and TUC Annual Conference because "we do not think that the payments of allowances during the war would materially handicap the unions in their present fight to maintain and improve standards"' (21). However, as Land points out 'at the TUC Conference a motion in favour of the introduction of family allowances was referred back for further discussion. Opinion within the trade union movement had shifted, but not far enough' (22).

The experience of the war transformed the position of the trade unions. Their co-operation had proved indispensable in a situation where manpower was the ultimate scarce resource. Yet, as Beer notes,

'Labour did not accept those heavy burdens without receiving and indeed demanding major concessions from other groups in society ... Ministers and civil servants who had found certain extensions of the social services "financially impossible" during peace time and the early part of the war now accepted them and put them into effect' (23). This influence was demonstrated most significantly on the issue on which the unions had been most cautious - family allowances.

Throughout 1942 pressure was mounted on the government for the introduction of family allowances with the result that in May it published a White Paper on the subject. In Parliament, over 200 MPs of all parties actively pressed for a debate on the issue, and in the same year William Beveridge, working closely with the head of the TUC's own social insurance department (24), gave further impetus to the call for family allowances by drawing attention to the inability of existing social policies to cope with the projected growth in young dependents. When family allowances moved to the forefront of inter-party debate, albeit temporarily, in June 1942 parliamentary opinion had shifted in their favour. It is clear, however, that the government still saw, or found it useful to present, the unions as the major obstacle to any family allowance scheme:

> The Government, however, would only act in the light of 'the report of the Beveridge Committee, the further conclusions of organised labour, and the financial position', because, the Chancellor told the House, 'it is a matter of special importance; family allowances have long been the subject of discussion in trade union circles which have been particularly apprehensive about their effects on wage negotiations.' (25)

In the event, Beveridge, in close consultation with the TUC, recommended a scheme financed by tax revenues partly, it would seem, because the government 'was not prepared to implement a scheme which was unacceptable to the trade unions'. At its 1942 Conference the TUC gave its support for the scheme, and in the following February the government committed itself to its early introduction.

The 1950s saw little development in the unions' interest in social policy. The early and cautious pragmatism of the Conservative government for a while defused the tension of industrial relations and

largely obviated the need for the unions to move into
the political arena. The relative affluence of the
early 1950s and the unions' desire to consolidate
their wartime achievements led them to confine their
initiatives to the industrial arena.

An interesting explanation of this reversion to
the traditional concerns of wage bargaining has been
offered by Richter in his reinterpretation of
Perlman's early work on trades unions and politics.
He comments of this period that

> the leaders felt they could continue to conduct
> traditional pure and simple unionism success-
> fully without significant involvement in
> national economic and political policy
> formation ... although they maintained the
> historic alliance with the Labour Party and
> indeed, beginning in the early 1950s, greatly
> expanded that commitment at the parliamentary
> party level they did <u>not</u> rely on it either for
> their conventional bargaining function or for
> broad social policy purposes. (26)

It is Richter's contention, after Perlman, that
during periods of economic and industrial stability
when, crucially, there is no significant challenge to
their legal status, trade unions will confine their
activities to the work place and eschew wider
political involvement in society. Their self-
confinement in the 1950s was further reinforced by
the fact that the Labour government of 1945-1951
failed to implement fully its election programme and,
in opting for what Attlee later spoke of as 'reformed
capitalism', largely met the aspirations of senior
union leaders. Full implementation of the manifesto
would have brought with it the demise of free
collective bargaining and the erosion of the economic
power of the major unions. Any deflection from that
course was to be welcomed. 'The predominant trade
union leaders took organisational steps within the
Labour Party to limit rather than to advance
political action in a conventional sense. They did so
because they wanted to be certain that the Labour
Party would not choose a leader who would initiate
policies that might endanger existing national
bargaining patterns. (27)'

For Perlman, a major characteristic of British
unions was the rarity and brevity of their flirtation
with politics beyond the market-place. Indeed, it was
his contention that ever since their early struggles
to win legality, a resort to political action or

initiative had become more and more remote. Any later threats to their status invariably produced real political action, but this had never been sustained long enough for effective development into a long-term socialistic programme. Indeed, as was shown in the 1934-6 struggle over unemployment benefit, union leaders have treated attempts to create a wider political programme (with the possible recent exception of the social contract) with hostility: 'the unions as a whole will finance the Labour Party with its socialistic programme and socialistic leadership, and more that half the membership will vote for its socialistic candidate ... But the heart of British unionism is still in these jealously revered organisations that stand guard over the collective economic oportunity of each group - the jobs and the working conditions that go with the jobs' (28). This is borne out by Richter's own observations of the activities of the AEU (now AUEW) and the TGWU, of which he considers the most important to be

> that since 1945 the predominant section of the British movement has not sought central planning nor social change; nor has it found it necessary to engage in political action for the economic goals of the operational requirements of the unions ... what comes through then ... is that the underlying objective of political action in the post-war years was simply the achievement, maintenance or restoration of 'free collective bargaining'. (29)

Under strong and centralised leadership the labour movement was largely content with the post-war social and economic arrangements and was prepared to resist initiatives that might interfere with the traditional bargaining process. Principally, TUC policy was designed to preserve a status quo which, during the war years, had been favourable to the movement's traditional goals. This emphasis on traditional responsibilities was to endure throughout the 1960s.

The 1960s were marked by a rationalisation in the structure of the labour movement and by a further consolidation of the TUC. The reasons for this have been documented elsewhere (30). It is appropriate to note, however, that in this decade the three largest employers' organisations came together to form the CBI, the distributive trades coalesced in 1967 to form the Retail Consortium, and the trade union sector recorded over 100 merger. More significantly, attendant upon these developments was a 'tropical growth in interest groups catering for the under-enfranchised elements in society; these included the Consumers' Association, Shelter, CPAG, the Claimants and Unemployed Workers Unions and many others seeking to influence the contents of the public agenda' (31). Of particular significance was the creation of a group of new planning agencies which served to contribute further to the developing corporate prestige of the TUC. For Trevor Smith the new agencies were 'an authoritative acknowledgement of the erstwhile de facto situation among interest groups that a two-tier system of representation existed. Membership of NEDC indicated the granting of a superior franchise: it was an exercise in elite accommodation' (32). In short, the 'franchise' confirmed for those who still held doubts that the labour movement had arrived, and was likely to remain at the highest echelons of government.

This arrival did not go unrecognised in the broader political arena, not least of all by CPAG who made a somewhat hesitant and unsuccessful approach to the TUC as early as 1967 for funds to expand its activities. This approach had undoubtedly been prompted by a resumption of trade union interest in government proposals in 1964 for wage-related social security benefits and the growing concern about the extent to which the unpopular wage-stop ruling would apply unless family allowances were increased. However, the lesson that must be drawn from the first two decades after the war is that the unions preferred to adopt their traditional role as an industrial, sectional interest-group acquiring a broader political or social outlook only on those occasions when policies or initatives emerged elsewhere which directly threatened those sectional interests. Union concern with the issue of family allowances appears to have developed as a reaction to events elsewhwere and should be seen as an extension, rather than as an abandonment, of their usual defensive role. Government proposals for family support were seen by the trade unions as a potential threat to the traditional wage-bargaining process. It was therefore politic for them to respond with alternative proposals which would broadly satisfy the needs of families and which would preserve intact the bargaining framework. This principle of wages first and allowances second was not to be readily abandoned.

Both Perlman and Richter have suggested that

when their legal status is threatened trade unions
will resort to political action to defend their
interests, and that there is a likelihood that this
'politicisation' will, at least temporarily, broaden
those interests. The events of 1964-9 do reveal a
successful, albeit limited, resort to forms of
political action, largely confined to the limited
application of direct threats of non-cooperation
with future legislation; because of their unique
relationship with the Labour Party and the latter's
reliance upon the unions' political and financial
support, resolution of the issue took place within
the consultative framework of the labour movement and
any disruption was confined to a narrow section of
the polity (33). This is important, because Perlman's
thesis suggests that wider political and social goals
are only achieved when trade union action takes the
whole economy as its chief target. This period,
however, saw the unions confine their threats and
action to an internal wrangle with their political
wing. The resolution of the issues raised by In Place
of Strife shows that the Labour Party was firmly on
the defensive, and it is clear from the comments of
both Wilson and Crossman that not only did the unions
hold the upper hand, but that the Party contemplated
a rupture in their historic alliance, in what was
widely believed to be an election year, with abject
horror (34). There was little need, therefore, for
the unions to develop what could be seen as a 'family
dispute' into a call for the fulfilment of non-
industrial goals. Their single concern in this period
was to preserve the status quo and, in doing so,
restore their sole right to resolve inter-union
disputes. This they succcessfully achieved.

Some limited intervention in the social sphere
did take place in this period. In March 1966, for
example, the TUC announced that it was to continue
its 1964 efforts to raise family allowances by once
again pressuring the government into action - this at
a time when rumours of a split over prices and
incomes' policy were rife (35). The TUC's concern
with family support was best expressed in an article
in The Times later that month.

> TUC attention has concentrated hitherto on
> anomalies in the position of family men with low
> earnings ... They adopt the Beveridge argument
> that it is irrational to provide subsistence in
> unemployment and sickness and not while a man is
> working. The TUC view is that to provide
> adequate incomes for lower paid families,

> family allowances could be substantially increased and part of the provision for children, at present made through national insurance, transferred to family allowances. Family allowances would be greatly increased therefore without additional cost if they were regarded as taking the place of income tax allowances for children, particularly as surtax and income tax payers would presumably continue to pay tax on the allowances. (36)

In February 1967, as has been noted, senior trade union leaders intervened in the wrangle over the proposed introduction of a means-tested family income supplement (37). Of considerable significance on this occasion, as CPAG was later to recognise, was the fact that the unions had successfully intervened in the course of a Cabinet debate and not, as usual, during the early stages of policy-making. It is arguable whether or not this intervention was a response to the threat to the unions' legal status posed by the Donovan Commission. What is clear is that the Labour government's attempts to maintain some sort of fragile rapport with the unions on the thorny problem of prices and incomes may well have been served by bowing to union pressure on this occasion and eliminating any further consideration of a means-tested benefit.

As a test of the Perlman-Richter thesis, trade union action during this period was a qualified failure. The unions were faced with a serious threat to their legal status and did counter with limited political action to overcome it. In this they were resoundingly successful, but their action did not develop the broader social and political concern that Perlman and Richter saw as likely by-products of the response to such a threat (38). It is possible that the latter did not develop because of the highly circumscribed nature of the dispute and the relationship between the parties involved. However, the fact that the unions quickly lapsed into their pre-Donovan insularity and failed to generate more than polite opposition to the social service cuts of 1969 confirms that their primary concern was industrial, and that they were not prepared to enlarge upon it (39). This may be because, as Hilary Land points out, family allowances have historically been isolated from the development and adminis-tration of other social security benefits, such as unemployment and earnings-related benefits, which trade unionists may see as of more direct interest to

175

them: their declining value has tended to be overlooked except in periods of economic hardship and unemployment when their importance has become more evident (40). This is best illustrated by the TUC's silence on the issue during the affluent 1950s and the contrasting concern expressed by the trade union movement during the economic crisis of the 1970s.

CPAG AND THE UNIONS - THE EARLY INITIATIVES

CPAG's efforts to stimulate trade union interest in and enlist their support for fresh initiatives to combat poverty in this period date from May 1967 when CPAG sent over 5000 copies of its wage-stop pamphlet to the Transport and General Workers Union as a means of demonstrating the realities of life on unemployment benefit. In emphasising what the Group saw as the punitive nature of the wage-stop, and stressing the need for those in employment to secure a realistic standard of living for those out of work, Tony Lynes was building on the interest shown in the ruling by the unions in 1964 and was echoing the type of argument advanced by Strachey some twenty-five years earlier. The pamphlet seems to have had little active impact upon the TGWU, though it was instrumental in the Ministry of Social Security's publication of a White Paper on the subject some months later (41).

An issue on which the TUC and CPAG could find some common ground was the intoduction of a national minimum wage. During the summer of 1967 the TUC agreed to adopt the TGWU's proposal for a minimum wage of £15 which CPAG felt was a first positive step towards reducing the role of low pay in producing family poverty. This common interest was expressed by Frank Cousins, a Cabinet Minister and former General Secretary of the TGWU, in <u>Poverty</u> some weeks later:

> the trade union campaign for a £15 national minimum wage and the work of bodies such as the Child Poverty Action Group emphasise different aspects of the attack on poverty, but their work is complementary not competitive ... trade unionists know that social benefits such as family allowances, will always have a role to play in establishing social justice. Increasing real wages will make the problem of dire poverty less urgent, but it will not remove the case for equalisation of incomes upwards, either through positive family allowances or tax

allowances. (42)

Cousins was keen to demonstrate, however, that while the labour movement was anxious to provide a degree of social justice through the collective bargaining framework, the principal responsibility for family support must remain with the state. To deviate from this traditional view would, he implied, involve the unions far too much in politics and allow the intrusion of an unacceptable artificiality into the bargaining process.

> wages in general will always be determined in the main by industrial factors, based on some concept of 'the rate for job' or 'fair wages'. Of necessity, one negotiates in the knowledge that the settlement of the minimum rate should give a worker the means to provide a good standard of living and home for the family, but taking into account the size of the family is an additional matter. This is certainly where social benefits in the form of family allowances, have a key role. (43)

In retrospect, Cousins' concern with family support seems rather superficial and the nature of his argument must be seen as a warning against optimism and high expectations. Indeed, the later part of his commentary shows clearly the traditional reluctance of trade unionists to develop a concern beyond the workplace. However, for a nascent pressure group still exploring avenues of influence, Cousins' arguments were sufficiently ambivalent to encourage further CPAG initiatives to win support.

The Group's next task was to sound out the labour movement's willingness to provide the funds required to sustain and expand its activities. In June 1967 Lynes wrote to Lord Cooper of the GMWU and to George Woodcock, TUC General Secretary, outlining the group's financial difficulties and urging support for a body sharing a 'common cause', 'I am writing to ask whether the TUC would be prepared to contribute towards the cost of continuing the work of this group ... The relevance of our campaign to the interests of the trade union movement and particularly to your unions proposals for helping lower-paid workers hardly needs stressing' (44). It is clear, however, that most individual unions and the TUC itself were reluctant or unable to furnish aid of that sort. Woodcock echoed the general sentiment: 'While we welcome your support in focusing public attention on this problem (the low paid) the General Council do not normally contribute to bodies campaigning for improved social security benefits' (45). Woodcock's statement suggests that perhaps financial assistance was not the real barrier but, rather, the TUC's own ambivalence towards the 'morality' of bringing social security benefits more and more into line with what a worker might earn in full-time employment (46). Indeed, it would have been most difficult for the General Council, or individual unions, to carry this sort of initiative beyond the prejudices and insularity of a rank and file concerned, naturally, with maintaining differentials both within and outside of the work place.

In August, Lynes spelt out the next stage of his approach to the unions and emphasised their value as intermediaries in the dialogue between government and governed. In a memorandum to the CPAG executive he wrote, 'In view of the recent unemployment figures, the probability of higher unemployment this winter and the fact that family allowances will not go up for most families until April ... I think we should urge the Government to suspend the wage-stop this winter. The obvious time to make this situation is during the TUC Conference at Brighton next week' (47). Again, however, the Group failed to make any real progress. Conference chose, instead, to address itself once more to the less controversial issue of family allowances. The subsequent resolution to ask the government to give a 10 shilling (50p) increase in allowances in addition to the extra 7 shillings (35p) due to be paid in April 1968 and the process of argument which justified it did at least bring some encouragement after the disappointment of the wage-stop. In a moment of self congratulation Lynes was moved to comment that the TUC resolution was 'precisely the policy put forward in recent months by the Child Poverty Action Group' (48).

Nevertheless, he chose not to attempt any further initiatives towards the unions largely for three reasons. Principally, CPAG lacked a network of trade union contacts to develop the sort of 'alliance' Lynes had earlier envisaged. Secondly, it was Lynes' opinion that the trade unions were simply not interested enough in family allowances and related issues to develop their concern beyond the traditional 'salutatory' resolution at Annual Conference. This was clearly demonstrated in a meeting Lynes had with Jack Jones, General Secretary of the TGWU, at which he learned that while Jones was interested in and sympathetic towards CPAG, he did not view family support as of more than peripheral trade union interest and was not willing to act upon the issue (49). Thirdly, a combination of scarce resources, early disappointments and his own belief in a low political profile discouraged Lynes from making any further attempt to win union support.

The idea of CPAG-union liason was not dead however. In April 1968 the idea was revived with a proposal from an executive member, Iain Jordan, for a more selective and structured strategy to win the support of the unions including trade union co-option to the CPAG Executive Committee. This recognised both the need to understand the mechanics of policy formulation in the trade union movement and the importance of presenting external proposals in such a way that they were readily acceptable to this machinery. Until this point CPAG had presented proposals in a rather ad hoc fashion and with little appreciation of the nuances and idiosyncracies of union policy-making.

The Group had made little effort to see issues from a union point of view when pressing for support. It might, for example, have recognised more determinedly to its own advantage that, at a given moment, the majority of trade unionists either do not have children or their families are fully grown so that their interest in family allowances will be marginal. Any strategy to win their support for an increase must therefore be sensitive to this fact and be presented in a manner which will not produce disinterest or alienation. CPAG may also have suffered because of its rather 'intellectual' image and its elitist approach to union leaders. Intellectuals have at best traditionally had an uneasy relationship with the trade union movement and CPAG's failure to adopt a grass-root strategy, at least in conjunction with the approach to senior trade unionists, can have done little to improve that relationship.

Jordan seems to have been one of the few who recognised this. He proposed, among other things, (1) that a leaflet should be prepared and directed mainly at trade unionists explaining their common interests; (2) a memorandum should be sent to all CPAG branches advising them on how to contact local trades councils and to encourage trade union branches to affiliate to CPAG; (3) a list of trade councils was to be obtained from the TUC and used to give branches the addresses of trade councils in their areas and to send literature direct from national office and invite them to affiliate to the group nationally; (4) finally, Jordan proposed that information be collected about resolutions sent to the conferences of individual unions and the TUC itself. This, he argued, would enable CPAG to use its time and resources more selectively by liaising only with those unions with a proven orientation towards social policy (50). It is significant that on the day Jordan first suggested closer links with the unions Rosemary Vear, a CPAG worker, delivered a paper to a CPAG conference in Manchester on Poverty and Social Action in which she charged that 'direct work with the trade unions and the poor are the most neglected sections of our work so far' (51). Despite this recognition within the Group for closer links with the unions the implementation of Jordan's proposals was deferred until after the appointment of Frank Field in February 1969.

Inevitably, the confusion into which the Group was thrown at the time of Lynes' resignation contributed to the delay in resuming attempts to attract union support. However, Lynes makes it clear that his own political style was inconsistent with the sort of approach required to win and retain that support (52). Furthermore, he appears to have lost the will to do so after the TUC Conference of September 1967. Lynes may not have been prepared to press too hard in the direction of the unions for fear of prejudicing his network of ministerial and civil servant contacts of whom he still had high hopes (53). Ultimately, it must be concluded that he recognised that the unions would not easily be persuaded into supporting what they saw as non-union issues and that CPAG's resources were neither adequate nor appropriate for an intensive grassroots strategy such as that proposed by Jordan in 1968 and finally launched by the Group in the early 1970s.

In the interim the idea of a trade union initiative in social policy was kept alive in a series of articles, exploring the possibilities of union action on low pay, especially in the wake of apparent government default on the issue. One of the most important of these appeared in New Society a week after the 1968 TUC Conference. Crucially, it pointed out that although Richard Crossman, Secretary of State for Social Services, realised that low pay and the failure of Labour's incomes policy were major causes of poverty he was 'politically reluctant to draw the conclusion that family allowances should go up', and he had chosen to concentrate, instead, on the low pay issue (54).

This concern, charged New Society, was spurious and evasive since the government had already shown itself intransigent on the subject of minimum wage legislation despite there being a clear case for it. More curious was the sight of a Labour government elected to promote social justice passing the buck on family poverty to a trade union movement which had repeatedly stressed that its responsibilities lay elsewhere and that family support was the concern of the state.

> Beveridge insisted on family allowances for those in work as a pre-requisite of adequate social security benefits for the non-working population. Both Mrs Hart and Crossman, however, are politically reluctant to draw the conclusion' that family allowances should go up. Instead, they emphasise the need to concentrate wage increases on the low paid. Mrs Hart has even implied that, if family poverty still exists, the responsibility is not hers but that of the unions. (55)

Judith Hart did have a point, though she was hardly likely to endear herself or her party to the trade unions by expressing it. As New Society pointed out, there was very little recent evidence that wages policy had brought about any measurable improvement in the position of the low paid. However, it concluded, 'short of minimum wage legislation of the kind that the unions are demanding (and which the government clearly has no intention of enacting), further increases in family allowances seem essential if the overlap of benefits and earnings is to be eliminated' (56).

A similar analysis was put forward by Norman Atkinson in a Tribune study of low pay (57). Atkinson showed that in 1938 the percentage of total personal income going to wages and salaries before tax was 55 per cent. In 1967, it was still only 63 per cent despite a massive 41 per cent expansion in the work force. Atkinson felt the implications were alarming: trade unions had clearly failed to take advantage of their strength and tackle the issue of wealth distribution. The argument was re-worked by John Edmonds and Giles Radice, both research officers with the GMWU, in Low Pay, February 1969 (58). In line with CPAG, they recommended that the low paid could be helped by the reform of social security and taxation policy which could then properly supplement and protect their income. Secondly, they fixed

responsibility on the unions to protect the
bargaining position of the low paid in the work place
so that they could increase their earnings.
Additionally, they argued for a statutory minimum
wage and an increase in family allowances to an
'adequate' level - the onus for achieving these
placed firmly on the trade union movement. If active
co-operation between CPAG and the unions had
temporarily failed, then at least a dialogue was
maintained in the media which helped to remind the
unions of the broader social role some felt they
should adopt. Furthermore, by keeping the issue on
the boil in the months of transition, the Group was
better placed to resume its efforts to enlist trade
union support in the autumn of 1969.

Early efforts to do this, under Field's
direction, were largely confined to fund raising.
Towards the end of March 1969 approaches were made to
Lord Balogh, Lord Sainsbury and Peggy Herbison to ask
for their assistance in a fresh fund raising bid.
This seems to have met with a rather protracted
delay, but by February 1970 the Group was ready to
launch a major appeal for funds, directed mainly at
the trade unions. Herbison's contacts and her known
sympathy for the Group's work made her an obvious
choice as the principal signatory to a covering
letter. She wrote of the Group's activities:

> Their campaign helped me when I was Minister of
> Social Security to get an important increase in
> family allowances - a move which I'm sure you
> know the TUC strongly supported. Unfortunately,
> in spite of increased family allowances, poor
> families are still in need of help and the task
> of CPAG - as well as the whole labour movement -
> remains as relevant today as it did four years
> ago ... The group ... is pioneering the
> development of welfare law in this country. This
> is a field which will grow in the near future
> and will become of vital interest to all trade
> unions. I am, therefore, writing to ask if you
> would consider seriously making a grant to CPAG
> and also consider what ways the group might be
> of use to your union, particularly on the
> research side. (59)

Her closing comments indicate a further development
of Lynes' early attempts to show the mutual nature of
the benefits that could accrue from liasion between
CPAG and the unions. CPAG was now making more
elaborate efforts to do the same. The Group's former

trade union liasion officer confirmed that, at the
time of her appointment, a 'two-way flow' strategy
was prominent in CPAG's thinking (60).

> There were three aims, deliberately kept rather
> vague to see how the work developed. First, to
> 'lobby' trade union leaders and TUC staff on the
> changes in social security policy which the
> group was currently hoping to see; secondly, to
> have a two-way educational exchange in which the
> liason officer would be available to summarise
> CPAG publications for trade union journals,
> speak to branch or shop stewards meetings and at
> the same time approach both national and branch
> officers to support CPAG branches, speak at
> meetings and supply the group with data. (61)

Meanwhile, in March 1970, Field was successful in
persuading the general secretaries of a number of
major unions, including ASTMS and the AUEFW, to co-
sign a letter to the Prime Minister demanding action
to improve low wages and increase family allowances
(62). In April 1970 Herbison's call for action also
attracted the desired support. On the eve of Jenkins'
final Budget, Harold Wilson received a joint letter
from CPAG and leading trade unionists, representing
over 3½ million workers, urging a substantial
increase in family allowances. However, such a
gesture must be seen for what it was - a protest at a
fait accompli, an admission of failure to influence
policy, and not a fresh attempt to do so. CPAG's
success, then, was in persuading some trade union
leaders that budgetary policy overlooked the
problems of poverty, but the gesture came too late to
be other than a meek eleventh-hour protest. A further
post-Budget appeal in May met similar resistance from
the Treasury.
    In June the Labour Party lost the General
Election and Edward Heath's Conservative government
came to power. Committed to a new Industrial
Relations Bill, which took much of its form from the
In Place of Strife proposals which the unions had so
strongly opposed, the Heath government embarked on a
course of action which led to confrontation with the
trade union movement.
    It was during this next phase, the period 1971-
6, that the unions developed more fully a concern
beyond that of free collective bargaining as their
legal status came under attack. Accordingly, the
unions sought to construct with the Labour Party a
formula that would return the Party to office and

compensate them for the sacrifices they had to make to help the Party realise that goal (63). It is interesting to note that it was only after the struggle over the Donovan Report and <u>In Place of Strife</u>, when victory had been achieved, that the trade unions developed a strong interest in the area of social policy, not least because their primary interest, the maintenance of free collective bargaining, was temporarily surrendered. This is important since both Perlman and Richter imply that this outcome develops during and as part of the struggle (64). Reasons for this apparent anomaly have already been suggested and the close fraternal link between the Labour Party and the unions seems to have played a major role in narrowing the focus and the effect of the struggles in the late 1960s. This was not the case, however, during the Conservative period of office (1970-4) and, as will be shown, this latter attack upon trade union power did produce developments predicted in the Perlman-Richter thesis.

Finally, there was a growing awareness on the part of the unions after their successful resistance to <u>In Place of Strife</u>, a victory achieved at the highest level of government, that they had reached a position in the polity where they could effectively challenge the executive. This awareness, combined with Labour's serious political demise after 1969 and the resulting tension between its industrial and political wings, appears to have convinced many trade union leaders, at least temporarily, that the onus of challenge to the Conservatives' industrial relations proposals and reductions in public expenditure rested with them and not the opposition party (65). Only in the early months of 1971 as the rift between party and unions began to heal did a viable joint approach to policy emerge. In the interim, the initiatives taken by CPAG and others towards the unions and their search for a new 'lead' served only to strengthen the unions' vanguard role. The essence of this development was explained by Frank Chapple of the EETPU, who charged that 'the lack of leadership by other institutions is creating a situation where a new role is being forced upon the trade unions. Accordingly, all those in the trades union movement are having to adapt to the new function in order to ensure that the vacuum is not filled by other views which could be detrimental to the interests of the country and to the trades unions' (66). A more perceptive and succinct explanation of the unions role in the polity in the 1970s, as we shall see in the next chapter, would be difficult to find.

NOTES

1.   Perlan, S.A., A Theory of the Labour
Movement (Macmillan, New York, 1928); Richter, I.,
Political Purpose in Trade Unions (George Allen &
Unwin, 1973).
2.   See for example, Brittan, S., 'Towards a
Corporate State', Encounter (June 1975); Smith, T.,
The Politics of the Corporate Economy (Martin
Robertson, 1979); Wilensky, H.L., The New
Corporatism, Centralisation and the Welfare State
(Sage, London, Beverly Hills, 1976).
3.   Lord Donovan, Royal Commission on Trade
Unions and Employers Associations. 1965-68 Report,
Cmnd. 3623 (HMSO, June 1968).
4.   See Lord Diamond, Royal Commission on the
Distribution of Income and Wealth report No. 6 'Lower
Incomes', Cmnd. 7175 (HMSO, 1978).
5.   Diamond Report, op.cit., pp.548-72.
6.   Ibid., p.550, para 9.
7.   Ibid., p.558, para 47.
8.   Ibid., p.559, para. 58.
9.   Land, H., 'Family Allowances and the Trade
Unions', Poverty (12 March 1969), p.8.
10.   Ibid.
11.   Simpson, B., Labour: The Unions and the
Party (George Allen & Unwin, 1973), pp.53-4.
12.   Ibid., p.54.
13.   Miller, J.D.B., The Nature of Politics
(Pelican, 1971), p.44.
14.   Ibid., p.42.
15.   Radice notes, for instance, that 'in order
to create a framework in which trade unionism could
function, they had to operate politically as well as
industrially. They also realised that workers were
consumers and parents, tenants and potential
householders, sometimes unemployed and sick and
certainly, in the end, all destined to be
superannuated from their unemployment'. Radice, G.,
The Industrial Democrats (George Allen & Unwin,
1978), p.88.
16.   Strachey, J., What Are We To Do? (Gollancz,
Left Book Club edn. 1938), p.186.
17.   Ibid.
18.   Crucial to this reasoning is a 1971 article
by Field and Piachaud, in which they coined the term
'poverty trap' and attempted to demonstrate to trade
unions the impact of social policy upon their

members' income and livelihood. See Field and
Piachaud, 'The Poverty Trap', New Statesman (3
December 1971); and Piachaud, 'Poverty and
Taxation', Political Quarterly, Vol. 42, No. 1
(January-March 1971), pp.31-44; and CPAG, A Social
Contract for Families, Poverty Pamphlet No. 19
(November 1974).

19. Land, op.cit., Poverty (12 March 1969).
20. Ibid.
21. Ibid.
22. Ibid.
23. Beer, S., Modern British Politics (Faber,
1971), p.212.
24. See, May, T., Trade Unions and Pressure
Group Politics (Saxon House, 1975); and Beveridge,
W., Power and Influence (1953), pp.296-317.
25. Land, op.cit. p.9; and Hall, Land, Parker
and Webb, Change, Choice and Conflict in Social
Policy (Heinemann, 1975), pp.179-96.
26. Richter, op.cit., p.17.
27. Ibid.
28. Perlman, op.cit., Ch. 4.
29. Richter, op.cit., p.218.
30. See Smith, T., The Politics of the
Corporate Economy (Martin Robertson, 1979); Taylor,
R., The Fifth Estate (Pan, 1980), ch. 1; and Currie,
R. Industrial Politics (Oxford University Press,
1979).
31. Smith, T., Trends and Tendencies in
Reordering the Representation of Interests in
Britain, paper delivered to the Political Studies
Association Conference (University of Nottingham,
1975), p.6.
32. Ibid.
33. For an account of trade union - Labour
Party relations between 1964-9, and the reaction to
Donovan and In Place of Strife proposals, see Hutt,
A., British Trade Unionism (Lawrence & Wishart,
1975), ch. 14; Taylor, op.cit., ch.3; Clutterbuck,
R., Britain in Agony: The Growth of Political
Violence (Faber, 1978); and Heffer, E., The Class
Struggle in Parliament (Gollancz, 1973).
34. Howard (ed.), Crossman Diaries, op.cit.,
pp.558-9.
35. Diaries, Vol. I, p.471.
36. The Times (28 March 1966).
37. Diaries, Vol. II, pp.251-3.
38. Richter, op.cit., ch.12.
39. Richter notes, for example, that 'one
remarkable feature of the post-1967 period was the
negligible political reaction from the Labour

movement to the increasing level of joblessness, despite certain local, and unofficial, protests in some areas' (p.226). This contrasted quite markedly with the USA where severe unemployment had been a major stimulus to political action on the part of the AFL-CIO.

40.   Hall, Land, Parker and Webb, op.cit., pp.228, 230.

41.   The Administration of the Wage-Stop - A Report by the Supplementary Benefits Commission to the Ministry of Social Security (HMSO, November 1967). The report was rather vague and evasive in its analysis of the wage-stop but it took up CPAG's suggestion that increased family allowances would be an effective and immediate means of extending help to the 27,000 families getting reduced supplementary allowances.

42.   Cousins, F., 'A Minimum Wage', Poverty, No. 3 (Summer 1967), p.6.

43.   Ibid.

44.   Tony Lynes to Lord Cooper, General Secretary of the National Union of General and Municipal Workers (13 June 1967), and to George Woodcock, General Secretary of the TUC (12 July 1967).

45.   Woodcock to Lynes (21 July 1967).

46.   Lynes had explained the dilemma himself. 'The wage-stop condemns the unemployed man and his family to live below the level of income officially recognised as adequate to meet their needs. Because the man's normal earnings, as estimated by the Ministry of Labour, would be too low to raise the family above the poverty line, they must be kept below the poverty line when he is out of work ... without the wage-stop, a small minority of unemployed men might be tempted to remain out of work, since they would be better off on supplementary benefit, so, to avoid this risk the innocent must suffer too.' Poverty, No. 2 (Spring 1967), p.4.

47.   Memorandum to the Executive Committee (30 August 1967).

48.   Poverty, No. 5, p.14.

49.   Interview with Tony Lynes, 31 May 1979.

50.   Executive Committee Minutes (28 April 1968).

51.   Vear, R., Local Action on Poverty (CPAG, 27 April 1968).

52.   Interview with Tony Lynes, 31 May 1979.

53.   Banting notes, for example, that after leaving the Ministry of Pensions 'Lynes did maintain contact with his ex-colleagues; indeed a series of

informal policy seminars attended by both academics and middle-level officials was held in his flat. These contacts proved important in co-ordinating Ministry and CPAG strategy at a critical juncture'. However, 'they did not represent a direct involvement in policy-making' (p.87).

54. 'The Morality of Idleness', New Society (12 September 1968).

55. Ibid.

56. Ibid.

57. Atkinson, N., Whatever Happened to Our Wages?, Tribune pamphlet (1969).

58. Fabian Research Series No. 270 (February 1969).

59. Executive Committee Minutes (February 1970).

60. This tactic holds some implications for the exchange theory of group politics. Garson, for example, notes that 'The exchange theory of groups portrayed group leaders as entrepreneurs selling the benefits of group affiliation for a price. Political organisations were quasi-firms, producing and exchanging legitimacy (a quasi-good) in a broader political exchange environment'. Garson, D.G., Group Theories of Politics (Sage, Vol. 61, 1978), pp.140-1. Ordinarily, group theorists have spoken of exchange theory as illuminating a relationship between a group and its members or, more classically, between groups and the state. However, it would not be unreasonable to proffer a further variation on this theme, i.e. the relationship between groups alone. In the example cited, CPAG was offering to exchange specialist information, skills and advice in return for the political support of the trade union movement. In this way, groups may combine rationally in pursuit of their overlapping interest to the higher market, i.e. that in which they must deal directly with the state. In making a rational 'exchange' at an early stage in the bargaining process they each enhance their propensity for goal achievement.

61. See Johnson, M., 'The World of the Child Poverty Action Group', Electrical Power Engineer, Vol. 56, No. 11 (November 1974).

62. Executive Committee Minutes (March 1970). In January, Field had also been successful in persuading the TUC General Council to push for higher family allowances. His lengthy memorandum on the subject was substantially quoted from during the General Council's meeting with Richard Crossman on the Labour government's new social insurance scheme and in their later representations to the Chancellor.

63. In mid-1971, Hugh Scanlon, answering a question about the involvement of unions in politics as a result of government attempts to curb their power, wrote: 'Of course, this involves us in politics. Indeed, issues such as legislation against unions and unemployment, are making unions more politically involved than ever before in the post-war period. It is inevitable that we shall see a greater involvement by trade unions in the affairs of the Labour Party, which can only be to the benefit of both the industrial and political wings of our movement'. Scanlon to Irving Richter (18 May 1971), quoted in Richter, op.cit., p.226.

64. As indeed it did do during the industrial relations struggle 1971-4, the major by-product of which was the formulation of the social contract between the TUC and the Labour Party and a pledge to repeal the Conservative Industrial Relations and Housing Finance Acts.

65. Richter comments: 'The resultant new power and confidence of the industrial wing of the movement was widely noted following the Labour government's surrender. It could be utilised for broader purposes than the repeal of the Industrial Relations Act and restoration of the status quo ante. Indeed some leaders of the industrial wing assured swifter progress towards the goal of socialism' (pp.227-8). Eric Heffer, indeed, viewed the immediate post-election period and the struggle over industrial relations as marking the ascendency of the trade union left, in contrast to the 'intellectual' Bevanite left of the 1950s. Heffer, E., 'The Left on the Left: Consensus and the Price of the Bill', Spectator (13 February 1971).

66. McGill, J., Industry, the State and the Individual (Blackie, 1976), p.96.

Chapter Nine

SOCIALISING THE UNIONS

While CPAG had initiated a number of approaches to
the trade unions in the early months of Frank Field's
office, they represented little more than a revival
of Tony Lynes' earlier attempts to involve the unions
in fund raising, letter-signing and policy
endorsement. They certainly cannot be viewed as a
coherent and long-term strategy to establish a
sustained liaison with the unions. Nor were these
efforts consistent with the sort of structural,
grass-roots approach advocated by some members in
1968, which had been rejected in favour of elite
persuasion. Essentially, Field's early initiatives
derived from the need for the Group to acquire funds
and, more significantly, from its concern for the
hostility shown to the poor by large sections of the
community, most notably the working class. In his
first major policy address to his executive Field had
analysed the tasks facing the Group, concluding that
'The ignorance of the problem (of poverty) and
hostility to poorer sections of the community is one
of the counteracting pressures against the group's
views being more willingly accepted by Government'
(1).

Field went on to assess the problem in terms of
class inequality. For him, a reduction of this
hostility and prejudice, and the elimination of
ignorance through education, would be a means of
making inroads on such inequality. He felt it
important to demonstrate to the working class, and
particularly to the labour movement, that poverty was
a product of class inequality (2), and was a problem
that could befall any worker with a large family or
one who found himself out of work for a short time.
An immediate task for the Group then was first to
demonstrate to the trade union movement the
importance of keeping abreast of social security
matters and, secondly, to encourage the movement to

lend its socioeconomic leverage to the campaign for improved benefits.

The importance of recognising the poor as simply the lowest stratum of the working class, and thereby a highly relevant target for any political activity affecting or emanating from that class, has been stated by Miliband:

> The basic fact is that the poor are an integral part of the working class - its poorest and most disadvantaged stratum. They need to be seen as such, as part of a continuum, the more so as many workers who are not 'deprived' in the official sense live in permanent danger of entering the ranks of the deprived; and that they share in any case many of the disadvantages which effect the deprived. Poverty is a class thing, closely linked to a general situation of class inequality; and ultimately remediable ... in general class terms. (3)

One of the most realistic means of achieving the remedy to which Miliband refers is to harness the influence of what has been called the 'socioeconomic leverage' (4) of the trade unions, and direct it into effective forms of action. A meeting with Peggy Herbison early in 1970 convinced Field of the unions' pontential for advancing CPAG's goals (5). Herbison had disclosed that while she was Minister of Social Security, James Callaghan had tried to introduce a means-tested family income supplement. Almost immediately she had received a strongly-worded letter from the unions urging her to frustrate its progress (6). On this occasion, trade union opposition was sufficient to persuade Callaghan to abandon his plans and it was left to the Heath government to revive them (7).

This, together with the defeat of In Place of Strife, persuaded Field that the unions were both powerful and sympathetic enough to promote the welfare of non-trade unionists also and provide him with the initiative to carry CPAG demands to Congress House (8). The outcome was a concerted attempt on the part of the Group to 'prime' the unions' social conscience. It was necessary to develop the early superficial liaison on letter-signing and fund raising into a substantive, ongoing dialogue at leadership, grass-roots and research department levels.

An impromtu discussion between Field, Nicholas Bosanquet of the LSE and Giles Radice of the GMWU research department on the usefulness of extending Group-union links produced an informal meeting between CPAG and trade unionists on 24 September 1970, the object being 'to provide regular contacts between CPAG and the unions and to talk over issues of mutual interest' (9) with representatives - mainly research staff - from the GMWU, NUT, USDAW, NUPE, TUC, ASW, TGWU and NUTEW taking part. The key issue was low pay and, specifically, how to keep this issue at the forefront of the political debate (10). Other matters discussed were the relationships between tax paid and benefits received - a concern of Bosanquet - together with the possibility of reform or abolition of tax inequities and reform of wages councils, a major interest of Field (11).

In November 1970 this co-operation extended further. A number of unions and social service organisations now embarked on a campaign to induce the government to rethink its social policy, particularly its favouring of selectivity over universality (12). Jack Jones, of the TGWU, described the campaign as marking 'a significant development in collaboration between different organisations concerned with social rights and with the interests of the low paid and the poor' (13). This was a useful development in the attack upon poverty not least because the unions were publicly stating their belief in a causal relationship between low pay and poverty and thereby were appearing to subscribe to the 'class inequality' analysis that Miliband argues is the key prerequisite for remedial political action. In practical terms it meant the unions were coming to accept the importance of social security issues to their members and were, therefore, pursuing their own rational self-interest. In a letter to the Group Vic Feather confirmed the TUC General Council's support for CPAG's efforts and restated union opposition to FIS:

> At a time when the Government is actively resisting wage claims which would enable workers to obtain decent basic rates of pay, their proposal of a family income supplement will be offensive both to the dignity and to the sense of justice of the workpeople of this country ... The Government's whole approach to social policy is a disaster. One almost gasps with incredulity that any government today in Britain, can hit at one go the sick, the injured, the old, the low-paid, the family and every wage-earner; yet at the same time can hand

out the biggest rewards to biggest surtax payer.
Only a two-faced government could talk about
'one nation' in this context and the Child
Poverty Action Group, in developing its
protest, has the best wishes of the whole trade
union movement. (14)

The earlier insularity of Frank Cousins'
analysis of wages, social security and the role of
unions now appeared diminished as Feather revealed
the implicit willingness of the unions to step beyond
the traditional parameters of free collective
bargaining to secure realistic levels of family
support. The TUC had reached the same conclusions as
CPAG that wages, taxation and social insurance issues
were closely related and that isolated consideration
of each was unrealistic (15). The fact remains,
however, that the unions have only accepted this
interrelation when it has been expedient for them to
do so.

Throughout November, CPAG and the TUC
maintained a correspondence on the Conservatives'
plans to introduce FIS. CPAG were anxious to
demonstrate the considerable support that the unions
could give to the poor: 'In moving towards a more
coherent policy for the low paid and their families
... we believe it might be very helpful in present
circumstances to investigate whether some new social
security benefits might be better administered if
they had a direct controlling interest in the shape
of union representation'. Townsend restated his
argument some weeks later: 'compared with other
countries Britain's social security benefits seem to
be flagging in recent years. One of the reasons for
this may be the lack of union involvement in their
administration' (16). This resort to 'flattery' and
deference was a new departure for CPAG. Direct union
participation in the administration and formulation
of social security benefits was seen as an effective
means of both revising and democratising them.
Townsend's latter point was a statement of CPAG'S
growing belief in the unions' developing societal
role. In addition, he was usefully exploiting the
sense of pique that British trade unions might have
felt at the thought that they, unlike their European
counterparts, were excluded from involvement in a
branch of social insurance that must be the concern
of any trade unionist.

Throughout the closing months of 1970 and into
the new year, CPAG and TUC undertook to persuade the
Heath government to initiate fiscal measures which

would raise the tax threshold and lift workers
earning 'poverty wages' out of the taxation system.
CPAG was concerned that the tax thresholds should be
lifted above the supplementary benefit scale rates. A
request to this effect was sent jointly by the Group
and the leaders of twenty major unions to Edward
Heath in March 1971. Meanwhile, in January, Field had
invited Bosanquet to address an internal CPAG
discussion on strategy with principal reference to
the question 'How far is a wages policy a necessary
part of any strategy for dealing with family
poverty?' Bosanquet's analysis was published by CPAG
a short time later (17). He warned of the dangers of
groups like CPAG remaining insular in their choice of
tactics and too single-minded in their choice of
issues:

> The pattern of debate has had clear political
> consequences in two main ways. First, the
> advocates of the poor have let themselves be
> shut off into a special lobby in which they
> appeared only to be concerned with policies for
> social security. No challenge has been made on
> the central ground of general economic policy -
> and its effects on the low-paid. Secondly, the
> debate on low pay in employment has concentrated
> on methods of raising pay - as if employment
> would be left to take care of itself. (18)

His conclusion, not altogether different from the
'growth first' strategies of Wilson and Heath, was
that there was 'a need for all those interested in
poverty to press as a matter of first priority for
general reflation of the economy. The best immediate
help to the low paid would be a growing economy with
abundant job opportunities' (19).

Of particular importance was the attention he
drew to the view that the low paid are such because
of their lack of bargaining power. This, he argued,
brought with it the need to recognise that 'the first
priority then becomes for the organised labour
movement to "shame" employers into paying better
wages' (20). Clearly, what CPAG themselves were to
draw from this was an awareness that if the labour
movement was reluctant or unable to achieve this on
its own, then it would have to approach groups
sharing broadly similar interests to lend their
support to a joint strategy. Bosanquet concluded:
'the evidence suggests a general moral for the
poverty lobby. We have to extend our attack. The
interests of the poor are vitally affected by general

economic policies. To help the poor we need changes
in these - as well as new and specific policies and
spending commitments against poverty' (21).

Support for the idea of a closer liaison between
CPAG and the unions and for a much stronger interest
in the subject of poverty on the part of the latter
had also come from Sir John Walley, Deputy Secretary
at the Ministry of Social Security during Peggy
Herbison's office. Writing in 1971, Walley argued
that, 'In a campaign for child endowment there must
clearly be the closest possible co-operation with the
TUC' (22). More specifically, he had earlier urged
CPAG to identify its own views as far as possible
with official TUC policy acknowledging, in
particular, the TUC's call for a boost to family
support in its 1969 Economic Review. Like Bosanquet,
he was concerned that CPAG should extend co-operation
as widely as possible:

> Bring out that all sorts of other people have
> the same interest ... Anyone concerned about the
> country's future is a potential ally. So are
> employers and economists bothered about wage
> inflation; common market enthusiasts; educat-
> ionists; women seeking to establish equal pay;
> income tax reformers concerned about incentives
> for the young family man; those interested in
> the unmarried or deserted mother; even those who
> complain that social security benefits are too
> lavish and are exploited by scroungers!
> Children's allowances when explained should be
> of great interest to all these. (23)

Both Walley and Bosanquet acknowledged the
importance of harnessing ideas to power. Both
identified the fact that knowledge alone was largely
worthless unless it was employed by influential or
powerful forces such as the TUC. Walley had also
urged CPAG to recognise the 'negative' power wielded
by the labour movement - the power to undermine
CPAG's plans for broad social reform simply by
serving their members' traditional work place
interests. He had warned, for example, that the
average trade unionist saw the wage-stop as 'common
sense' and that it made better tactical sense to
criticise not the ruling itself but the shortcomings
of a society which made such a ruling necessary.
Similarly, he advised the Group not to alienate
better-off families with suggestions that they
should not be entitled to child tax allowances. His
own experience at the Ministry of Social Security had

led him to conclude that 'The case for cutting these to accommodate other direct payments can be made without any such suggestions; and it will go down a lot better (and arouse interest) if it is accompanied by an expression of concern that the recognition of family responsibilities in this country's tax structure is so in adequate' (24).

An early response to this fresh call for co-operation with the unions took the form of a second meeting between CPAG and research staff from unions representing low paid workers (25), including officers from NUTGW, USDAW and the TGWU. Little was achieved, however, partly because, as Bosanquet has shown, CPAG and the unions were 'talking a different language' (26). This communication breakdown became clear in an article on the 'poverty trap' by Field and Piachaud published in December 1971 and in the subsequent reply from Jack Jones. It was Field and Piachaud's controversial view that 'for millions of low paid workers very substantial pay increases have the absurd effect of increasing only marginally their family's net income and in some cases actually make the family worse off' (27). Crucially, they argued 'We have reached the position where it is positively detrimental to many members' interests for the unions to negotiate large wage increases' (28). Responsibility for this anomalous state of affairs, they charged, lay with the government's 'polarising pursuits of selectivity and a means-test society' (29). The unfortunate result was what the authors termed 'the poverty trap'. As family income increased with wage rises so tax liability also increased and, crucially, entitlement to some state benefits could be lost as gross income exceeded entitlement thresholds. In addition, as earnings increased so a family's entitlement to free school dinners and exemptions on such things as prescriptions charges ceased. The brunt of this 'what the Lord giveth ... ' approach fell, in particular, on the poorest families, so much so, argued the authors, that a £1 wage increase could leave some families marginally worse-off than before.

For Field and Piachaud the solution to the poverty trap lay in concerted trade union action, for which they saw two clear alternatives:

> The first is to try to blast the low paid out of the means-test net. To achieve this the unions must win increases of up to 40-50 per cent for the low-paid ... Alternatively, the trade unions can insist that improvements in benefits

should be a normal and important part of the annual wage negotiations. Then, if the Government concedes adequate increases in national insurance benefits and family allowances, wage settlements may be correspond-ingly reduced. This latter strategy is in the interests of low-paid families, unions, employers and the Government. (30)

Field and Piachaud suggested that increased family allowances should remain as high a priority with the unions as increased pay; and that it was essential that benefits be enough to ensure that all working families were substantially above the poverty line. This situation would also go some way to countering the prejudices of those who complained that state support discouraged the unemployed from seeking work (31). Interestingly, Sir John Walley had advised the Group two years earlier to take just such an approach: 'Everyone believes that work should bring some reward. Make it absolutely clear that those for whom you seek a better deal are men and women in regular work who want to do the best they can for their children but just have not the means' (32).

Like Townsend before them, the authors were keen to be seen appealing to both the unions' self-interest and their wider sense of social responsibility:

For the unions it is a great and novel opportunity. By demanding – and obtaining – as part of the next wage round a return to the principles of Beveridge they would increase the net pay of family men, concentrating help on those with family responsibilities who are in greatest need, lift most working families off means tests and clear the poverty line and build a firm base from which minimum wage demands could be launched. If they seize their chance there is a real possibility that the lasting consequence of the government's means-test madness will be an extension of universal social provision achieved through union strength. (33)

The views expressed by Field and Piachaud did not win the trade union support they had hoped for. On the contrary, a number of trade unionists were clearly irritated by the directness with which Field and Piachaud appeared to be telling them how to conduct their affairs. The TUC's own press and publications officer, for example wrote that the authors were 'preaching to the converted' (34). Others objected to what they saw as an 'outside intrusion' into their affairs:

> the unions are as concerned as Messrs Field and Piachaud over implications of Government policy on real wages and they utilise as much informative research on this subject as comes to their attention. But a solution to the problem of low income families demands a more politic and comprehensive approach than that which depends on 'meetings with the Chancellor'. (35)

There is little doubt that some trade unionists were angered by what they saw as the authors' pedantic style: where arguments should have been persuasive they were interpreted as instructive. The episode showed once more the traditional unease between intellectuals and trade unionists and the fundamental tensions between prescriptive and pragmatic viewpoints. Jack Jones echoed the sense of naivety and intrusiveness that many associated with the Field-Piachaud article 'The vicious "poverty gap" that the Government's dogmatic policy of means-tested social benefits has created must be taken up as a challenge by the trade unions on the wages front ... but to talk as if concessions in the state benefits field can be used as a quid pro quo for wage restraint in some form of "annual negotiations" is to fly in the face of reality' (36). It is important to note here that the fulfilment of CPAG's demands would have required a shift in the thinking of the British trade union movement towards that of their Continental and Scandinavian counterparts. Castles and Parkin have both shown, for example, that Scandinavian trade unions have been far more flexible in their approach to any suggested interrelationship between welfare benefits - social security in particular - and wage bargaining. Castles notes that there has been 'an emphasis on the relative unity and integration of the Scandavian labour movements, the evolution of an ideology focusing on social reform rather than social ownership, and the adoption of a strategy premised on class collaboration and the use of labour movement solidarity as mechanisms providing the resource base for reform' (37). Jones was prepared to concede, however, that the unions had not been as active against poverty as they could be:

> there can be little disagreement among us that the situation that has been created requires

> stronger action by the unions – and trade
> unionists should welcome pressure from
> concerted groups to this end ... instead of
> being on the defensive for so many years the
> unions should have challenged the politicians
> themselves to treat better wages for ordinary
> families as a central feature of economic
> policy, instead of it being the fag-end of what
> was left over when the Treasury and Military men
> had pushed their priorities first. (38)

It was also his view that the attack on poverty must
be threesided – from groups like CPAG, from the
unions and from the Labour Party itself – precisely
the sort of concerted action envisaged in the early
days of the social contract. He noted, for example:

> Pressure to lift minimum wage levels helps make
> the case against the 'poverty gap' and arguments
> against means-testing reinforce the higher
> wages case. That is why we have to have close
> working from both sides – and why the Labour
> Party itself must not only be committed to the
> general principle of reversing the Government's
> policy, but have ideas ready in detail – perhaps
> based on the concept of increasing supple-
> mentary and other benefits in line with
> increased wages and prices. (39)

Nevertheless, Jones, like other trade unionists
before him, recognised the dangers to free collective
bargaining in the strategies advanced both by CPAG
and Field and Piachaud. And it was here that the
Group's reasoning was at its most unrealistic:
anything that could be even vaguely construed as
detrimental to free collective bargaining would be
unacceptable to the unions; in effect, union leaders
saw CPAG and its supporters as asking them to
regulate their members' interests in favour of a
vague appeal to a broader public, many of whom held
no allegiance to the unions. The authors had
seriously underestimated the importance of the
labour movement as a sectional interest group in
their assessment of its influence upon government,
which had been achieved and legitimised because of,
rather than in spite of, the unions' traditional
sectional role. Any suggestion of deviation from
this was, therefore, to be resisted. Furthermore,
reference to earlier issues of CPAG's own journal
Poverty would have confirmed the trade union view on
free collective bargaining, incomes policy and

199

social security. Frank Cousins had already advised
the Group in 1967 that the labour movement would
resist attempts from any quarter to confuse its
responsibilities with that of the state. Jack Jones
now re-affirmed this view:

> Government policies must not be permitted to
> create a situation where workers become
> dependent upon the good will and kindliness of
> the state for major elements of their standard
> of living - that way lies continued poverty.
> Trade unions ... have to work for a good social
> security system, without undermining the
> independent organisation of workers into
> powerful trade unions, for this is one of the
> most important ingredients of a successful
> democracy. This remains a fundamental reason
> why it would be dangerous to try to patch up the
> situation the Government has created by
> weakening the part that higher wages can play in
> raising living standards. (40)

Of particular importance here was Jones' view of the
unique nature and role of the trade union movement
and his belief that this could be seriously
diminished or modified if the collective bargaining
mechanism was tampered with. His concern was to get
wage settlements over first and then, developing
their impetus, swing round to tackle poverty on a
broader front. In this way the trade union role could
be doubly important. 'Important as a progressive
pressure group is, the trade union movement is
something more - it is a civilising factor in an
industrialised society and the basis for much wider
progress in the future. (41)'

Jones was not the only trade unionist to engage
in a public dialogue with the authors. On 10 December
Field and Piachaud had restated their case in the
columns of Tribune. Two weeks later Charles Donnet
and David Lipsey of the GMWU, one of the unions
representing the low paid with which CPAG had sought
a dialogue, offered a more direct union response,
expressing their surprise and regret that Field and
Piachaud 'should seek to put the onus on the trade
unions and particularly that they should single out
as their prime target the local authority union
negotiators' (42). One of their more striking
observations was that trade unionists were reluctant
to fall back on state benefits when their wages were
insufficient to keep families. Where CPAG and its
supporters had argued for improved benefits to

supplement wages, the unions felt that the correct
strategy was to raise wages to a realistic level.
Inevitably, however, as inflation takes hold, the
larger family, a significant minority among trade
unionists, will always suffer. Crucially, then, the
unions appear to have viewed the emphasis on the
correlation between benefits and wages as a potential
threat to the bargaining process (43). If the level
of benefits was maintained at an adequate level, they
could be used as an excuse for employers, including
the government, to keep wages at an artificially low
level. While this might assist family households, the
unions argued that it would equally penalise those
without a dependant family - the majority of the
workforce.

Donnet and Lipsey were also at pains to point
out Field and Piachaud's 'ignorance of collective
bargaining' and to emphasise the precise parameters
of union responsibility. 'As unions we do not
negotiate direct with the Government but with the
employer. We would have got the answer we deserved
had we gone along to the local authority employers
and asked not for a wage increase but for an increase
in family allowances. Only Governments can put up
family allowances, and of course there has been
constant pressure on the Government by the TUC to do
just this. (44)'

The implications of this reply were
interesting. Either the unions were already keenly
aware of and were responding to the family allowance
issue and therefore regarded Field and Piachaud's
intervention as something of an affront, or the trade
unions were not, as Field and Piachaud implied, the
active force they liked to think themselves, in which
case the latters' intervention would still be
unwelcome. Donnet and Lipsey's comments suggest the
second analysis. For example, 'union negotiators are
well aware of the problems caused by the wider range
of government means-tested benefits. But this just
makes us more determined to raise our members'
working wage above the level at which all these
apply, and in local authorities we are making a lot
of progress. As for family allowances we shall
continue to pursue improvements here through the TUC
- but not at the cost of agreeing to the continuation
of poverty wages or lower real wages for our members'
(45).

It is difficult to apportion blame for this
episode. Certainly, CPAG misjudged both the trade
union mood and the nature of unions' responsibilities. However, the trade union response had also

brought with it error of judgement and misunderstanding, not least of which was their confusion of FIS, a means-tested benefit, with the universally-available family allowance and the notion that Field and Piachaud were in some way suggesting action on family allowances as a substitute for wage increases (46). As the latter had pointed out they were 'asking trade unions to revalue the importance they put on TUC negotiations with the Government over welfare state benefits. Collective bargaining, yes, but haven't we outgrown the age when this is the only important thing the trade unions are concerned with' (47).

Field and Piachaud did, at least, gain a reaction (48) and were able to raise a number of issues for further discussion. Principal among these was the perennial question of whether the unions should remain a sectional interest group or become a quasi-promotional group concerned with broader social and economic issues affecting the community at large. In an effort to explore this issue further and establish a more constructive joint approach to poverty and low pay the Group arranged what was to be the first in a series of meetings with representatives of various unions and their research departments. Bosanquet describes this as another 'seminar-type event'. Once again though, they failed to achieve common ground. In his own account of the discussions Bosanquet reflects that CPAG were to be criticised for insularity and lack of action on some of the issues axiomatic to the debate.

> It seemed clear that the effects of the wage explosion of 1970/71, in contributing to more rapid inflation had made the lot of the poor worse rather than better. It seemed, too, that the existence of the poverty trap now made it very difficult for unions to win through collective bargaining substantial gains for their members. But CPAG ... could perhaps be criticised for having failed to concern themselves with broad issues in the distribution of income and wealth. (49)

Bernard Dix of NUPE argued that it was quite impossible for unions to bargain about family allowances - that was the role of the state and the interest-groups concerned. The principal task for the unions 'was to shift the distribution of income through vigorous collective bargaining' (50). For Bosanquet, at least, the principal outcome of these discussions was the recognition that neither CPAG nor the unions, either individually or jointly, had a clear strategy for ending poverty. Furthermore, the proposed 'series of conferences' did not develop beyond this initial meeting. Indeed, during the following two years there is very little evidence of either joint CPAG-trade union initiatives or of any unilateral efforts by the group to revive union interest in its work.

Superficially, the lack of union activity in the social policy field during these years may be attributed to trade union preoccupation with resisting the Conservatives' industrial relations policy. For much of the duration of the Heath government the labour movement found its time, interest and energies consumed by efforts to challenge the rulings of the Industrial Relations Act (51). Fundamentally, however, the extent and nature of trade union involvement in social policy must be seen as a direct function of the relationship of a particular policy to the traditional laws of free collective bargaining. Such a correlation has given the unions a very enigmatic role. They continue to represent a significant number of social service consumers and they clearly have the power to extend their influence on British social policy-making. Yet their role remains selective and cautious. This has been illustrated in their approach to the issue of wage supplementation through social policy and, particularly, in their attitude to the poverty trap. The enigma has been expressed thus:

> they have given a clear priority to their economic and wage bargaining functions and have been critical of policies which looked like attempts to buy off discontent about living standards. Where there has been an apparent clash of interests between social policy proposals and effective wage bargaining the former has been treated with suspicion; but even where this problem does not arise trade union expertise has been concentrated largely on the wages front. This choice reflects the priority accorded to earnings as a determinant of individual welfare by most trade unionists, and indeed by the whole society ... Although the unions are deeply involved in some areas of social service policy at a practical as well as an ideological level, this has not been their major preoccupation. Consequently, they have not done enough policy thinking or research in

the recent past to be really effective in those fields where wage bargaining is an incomplete response to poverty, deprivation and dis-welfare. (52)

The determination to keep free collective bargaining as sacrosanct as possible has long been a feature of British trade unionism (53). Wage control and other forms of interference with the bargaining process have more often than not been regarded as 'political' attempts to combat inflation or recession at the expense of one section of the population, the labour movement. Consequently 'increased taxation and stabilised prices, held down with the help of subsidies financed out of general taxation', have traditionally been more 'acceptable methods of combating inflation because the cost was born by the community in general' (54).

The arguments advanced variously by CPAG and by Field and Piachaud that trade unions should become far more sensitive to social security policy in the course of their wage negotiations must appear, accordingly, as an unwelcome attack on the sanctity of wage bargaining and as an inappropriate means of strenthening or encouraging union involvement in social policy. In short, the Group and is supporters were advocating a policy that was wholly unacceptable in its proposed departure from trade union tradition. After the breakdown of the Group's early dialogue with the trade unions, the urgency of establishing liaison receded as the need for an internal reappraisal of strategy grew. While CPAG embarked upon its own re-think, culminating in a reaffirmation of the need to work with the trade unions, the unions themselves took important steps to re-establish their alliance with the Labour Party in the wake of In Place of Strife and to develop a stronger interest in the welfare of the community at large. A new concept now found its way into the dialogue between unions and the Party - the 'social wage' - which was to be achieved through the formulation and implementation of a social contract. This was to have important implications for future CPAG strategy.

LABOUR'S RE-THINK - THE ORIGINS OF THE SOCIAL CONTRACT

The shock of Labour's election defeat and the alienation of many within the labour movement from the Party itself, had given impetus to a re-appraisal

of Labour's policy priorities. With this came the
inevitable post mortem and the realisation that the
Party must take the initiative in winning back the
confidence and support of its industrial wing.
Barbara Castle was among the first to attempt a
reparation, offering a tentative and somewhat
pedantic 'apology' in the course of her own
assessment as to what must now be done to heal the
rift and put Labour back into office. She suggested a
scheme in which unions could accept a flexible prices
and incomes policy together with a battery of social
and economic reforms which would act as the sugar on
the pill. In advocating this compromise on the thorny
issue of incomes policy she was perhaps sowing the
first seeds of the social contract that was
formalised four years later.

On the question of family support, for instance.
she commented, 'However politically unpopular family
allowances may be ... no one has yet found a way of
helping low income families without increasing them,
so this is just another field in which the labour
movement will have to get back to its basic
educational job' (55). On a broader front she
conceded that 'any really fundamental attacks upon
economic inequality such as wealth tax, national
minimum wage, a positive policy for the low paid,
were deferred because they were thought to endanger
our over-riding economic aim' (56). Anthony Crosland
was to echo this view three months later, claiming
that the Party's preoccupation with economic growth
and stabilisation of the balance of payments as
prerequisites of increased social services
expenditure had stultified Party thinking from
1964/1970 (57). It remained with Castle, however, to
provide the most emphatic argument for a socialist
approach to incomes policy and the call for a
resumption of co-operation between unions and party:
'the most urgent need in the next few years is to
develop a new dialogue between the trade union
movement and the political one. We must be eager to
learn from each other. Our first task is to re-
establish confidence in each other's aims and then
sit down and do some serious talking about means'
(58).

Significantly, she offered a vision of social
change in which government and unions would share
responsibility: 'unless those aims include a radical
transformation of society in which we share power as
well as responsibility, rewards as well as sacrifices
and show mutual compassion to a degree we have not
yet begun to contemplate, we cannot expect the trade

unionist to drop his traditional defences against capitalism' (59). She concluded, like Perlman and Richter, that 'industrial militancy will become self-defeating unless it is made the powerhouse for political change. For the past six years the Labour Government and the trade unions have each looked to the other to break the vicious circle. The time has come to forge a common strategy' (60).

Other leading figures in the Party were also coming round to this view. Tony Benn, for example, in calling for a new 'socialist renaissance' after the election wrote, 'it is arguable that what has really happened has amounted to such a breakdown in the social contract, upon which parliamentary democracy by universal suffrage was based, that that contract now needs to be renegotiated on a basis that shares power more widely, before it can win general assent again' (61). The basis of that renegotiation was to be the promise of some form of power sharing with the trade union movement.

In mid-1971, with the, Conservative drive on industrial relations gathering momentum, Harold Wilson took up the idea of a social contract or 'compact' between the Party and the unions offering, like Castle, a programme of social and economic reform in exchange for co-operation in establishing and maintaining an incomes policy that would check inflation. Speaking in New York about Labour's problems on prices and incomes, he said:

> for a statutory prices and incomes policy to be successful it must be based on consent: a wage freeze must be total; any statutory interference must be fair between groups, and individuals; any action of this kind must be made as far as possible tolerable by improved social services and, being universal, it could not discriminate between the public and private sector ... restraint in wages and salaries would not last long if prices and especially key prices were rising. By key prices I mean the principal elements in the expenditure of an average household, rent, bread, milk, school meals, commuter fares, shoes and clothing. In a general sense such a compact must be part of a national effort to raise living standards. (62)

Wilson was thus stating the need for a future Labour government to go much further than before in protecting the well-being of the individual. He had spoken of action on the prices of staple items in the

household budget, implied the need for travel
subsidies, clothing subsidies, a review of rent
policy and, broadly, of the need for improved social
services; but of particular concern to both CPAG and
the unions he had also spoken of the need for
fairness between groups of workers. In doing so he
appeared to echo Barbara Castle's call for action to
assist the low paid. An effective way of doing this,
a method long advocated by CPAG, would be to raise
the tax threshold, thereby taking the low-paid worker
out of tax. In emphasising the need for action on
prices and taxation, Wilson sought to spread the
burden of social reform throughout the community upon
employers, workers and consumers alike, and thus pave
the way for a more sympathetic response to incomes
policy than had been the case in the past.
Ultimately, an incomes policy was needed to create
the social wage which CPAG had long favoured, and the
social wage itself was seen as the only precondition
of such an incomes policy.

Assessing Wilson's speech, Bill Simpson,
General Secretary of the Foundry Workers Union,
wrote:

> the social compact accompanying even a
> voluntary prices and incomes policy must
> contain not only improved social benefits, but
> also policies which will lead to and maintain
> full employment. The social compact also means
> some significant shift in the redistribution of
> income and wealth in this country. This can be
> done by various taxation measures, such as
> increased capital gains and corporation taxes,
> the introduction of a wealth tax ... At the
> other end of the scale part of the increased
> income from the taxation measures mentioned
> should be used to take the low income families
> out of the income tax bracket altogether. This
> last action would be a complementary measure to
> assist the low-paid worker and this, allied with
> improvements in the social services used most by
> large families and the chronic sick, would
> create the kind of socially just conditions
> within which a prices and incomes policy could
> stand a chance of success. (63)

In effect, where Wilson had spoken of such
measures in terms of palliatives, Simpson viewed them
more substantively as part of a bargain that could
and must be struck between unions and the Party in
order that the latter might regain office. Crucially,

the historical 'electoral relationship' which existed between the Party and unions had to be replaced by another form of co-operation. Whereas in the past the Party had expected union support both at and between elections, it was now apparent that any future co-operation must be characterised by a 'spirit of mutuality' and the shaping of an intramovement consensus that would remain constantly under review (64). Secondly, as Simpson argued, both the measures put forward by Wilson and himself would benefit every working man and woman and, generally, all those in social need. His view was simply 'what is good for those groups is good for Britain' (65). Both expressed the opinion that unions must come to view their members as 'whole' rather than as 'fragmented'. The complex of interests, relationships and roles affecting or held by the trade unionist outside the work place necessitated a fresh political development in the role and remit of his representative association.

THE TUC – LABOUR PARTY LIAISON COMMITTEE

Simpson has written that even before the Party lost the election, it was accepted that a more structured form of policy liaison with the unions was essential. He notes 'the need for some additional informal machinery was realised during the last two years of office of the last government, and a small NEC liaison committee with trade union representatives was formed to meet a small cabinet committee each month. This arrangement proved valuable, but the policy liaison with the unions needs to be much stronger than that' (66). It was his view that 'At top level in our movement there is a lack of political contact which must be bridged in some way' (67). Too often in opposition, he felt, the Party had backed away from disputes or issues which it feared might divide the political and industrial wings of the movement. What was now needed was a new and powerful policy making committee of both senior party and trade union figures which could initiate a series of meetings which must develop further 'because those involved recognise the need for them if the movement is to avoid the mistakes of the past. Someone, somewhere is waiting for a lead on this. The movement's future success may well depend on the willingness of a few people to recognise the necessity of this kind of regular, pressure-free, political get-together' (68).

The 'political get-together' which did emerge fulfilled the need to draw together the senior members of the Party and the key figures on the General Council. This TUC-Labour Party Liaison Committee was to comprise members of Labour's NEC, the Parliamentary Labour Party and the TUC General Council. It therefore drew its membership and influence from the three pinnacles of the labour movement. While it was largely established to propose and coordinate changes in industrial relations legislation, it was inevitable that it would widen the scope of its work to embrace social and economic matters too. This became increasingly plausible for the trade unions because they could now claim that between 1965 and 1974 governments had sought to extend the influence of the state by politicising areas traditionally the exclusive concern of unions and employers (69). The historical reluctance of the General Council to venture beyond the parameters of industrial affairs now diminished as the unions recognised both the objective justice of reversing this trend by intervening in 'political' affairs and their growing ability to do so successfully (70).

The power factor in the TUC-Labour Party Liaison Committee equation has been noted by May and confirms the assessment of trade union power advanced by Field in his Director's Report of June 1972:

> the establishment of the Liaison Commmittee owed less to the position of the unions in the structure and financing of the Labour Party and far more to the need of the Parliamentary Labour Party to negotiate with a major interest group whose co-operation it saw as essential for the success of a future Labour Government. The historical link between the unions and the party with all its force of tradition and sentiment certainly contributed to the assessment that the difficulties that had been encountered between 1964 and 1970 were not just the difficulties of a Government and a major interest group, but of a Government and the major interest group. (71)

Perhaps the most compelling evidence of this came in the tripartite talks held by government, CBI and the TUC between July and November 1972, during which Edward Heath offered both the employers and unions the chance to 'share fully with the Government the benefits and obligations involved in running the economy' (72). The calling of the talks made it clear

that not only did the Conservative government wish to
check the growing confrontation brought about by the
Industrial Relations Act, but, more significantly,
it simply could not govern as effectively as it
wished without taking the unions into its confidence
(73). To fail to do so would be to precipitate a
clash far more destructive than that over In Place of
Strife. The wider implications of Heath's offer have
been described by May, who contends that as a result
of the bargaining overtones of this offer

> a degree of unease was expressed during the
> course of the talks by those who felt that they
> represented a pronounced shift towards a
> 'corporatist' style in British politics. While
> many of those expressing unease would admit that
> much of the contact between interest groups and
> the Government went far beyond simple
> consultation and frequently did amount to
> bargaining, it was still felt that this was
> compatible with a pluralist approach to
> politics and the ultimate supremacy of a
> Government created through majority party
> support in Parliament. (74)

May identifies three types of 'anxiety'. First,
the views held by those who feared that 'bargaining'
was taking place on major issues of economic and
social policy and not simply on the details of policy
(75). Secondly, the fear that the role of Parliament
was likely to be peripheral and of diminished
influence. Thirdly, and crucially, that these
tripartite talks implied an equality between the
parties involved. The role of government as the
'broker of interests' thus appeared to undergo a
transformation. It may be argued that government was
now brought into the competitive arena as simply one
interest among others - perphaps the 'national
interest' versus major sectional interests.

Apart from their reluctance to enter an
institutionalised pattern of bargaining with the
government, which they considered more likely to
impose responsibility than offer power, the trade
unions considered their newly-recognised strength
potent enough to secure their demands unilaterally.
Their immediate concern was to oppose the Industrial
Relations Bill and, subsequently, maintain non co-
operation with the strictures of the Act. In doing
so, far from taking up Heath's offer of a
partnership, a period of unprecedented confrontation
resulted, during which industrial action and

political posture became blurred. The essence of this confrontation has been expressed by Marsh and Locksley:

> during the passage of the Bill, the TUC was most concerned to develop and harness solidarity within the trade union movement on this issue. On the basis of this solidarity they devised a strategy which was to prove successful in severely restricting the adminstration of the Act. The General Council advised affiliated unions not to register under the Act and the few that did so were subsequently expelled. It also advised unions not to co-operate with the National Industrial Relations court and to attend its proceedings only when action was brought against them. (76)

This ensured, as the TUC had calculated, that the proceedings would acquire a confrontationist air, and the action of the unions, combined with a reluctance on the part of many large companies and employers' organisations to resort to the Act for fear of permanently damaging employer-employee relations, had severely undermined both the Court and the provisions of the Act itself by the end of 1975. As these authors have concluded, 'in this case, the trade union movement, with an almost unparalled display of unity, managed to negate a piece of legislation by refusing to co-operate with its administration' (77).

THE SOCIAL CONTRACT

Throughout this period of confrontation the rift between the unions and the Labour Party narrowed and, through the newly-established framework of the Liaison Committee, the unions secured the Party's agreement to repeal the Industrial Relations Act when it returned to power. The role of the Liaison Committee as a policy-making forum was crucial. Writing in 1976 Robert Taylor described it as 'the most vital decision-making body in the labour movement ... the architect of the social contract and the wide range of new policy initiatives that emerged in the 1970s'. The unions were to play a particularly influential role in the Committee's formulation of social and economic policy, subsequently advanced in Labour's Programme for Britain 1973 and the General Election manifestos of 1974.

Individual analysis of the 1964/70 governments by Castle, Wilson, Crosland, and others had already indicated a recognition by the Party leadership of the need for a closer liaison with the unions and a more socialist programme. In 1972 a comprehensive assessment of past errors and future needs was offered in the Party's <u>Programme for Britain</u>. The introduction is quoted below almost in its entirety since its often contradictory reasoning echoes the ambivalence of Labour's earlier period of office. In a sense it was an exercise in pure pragmatism, containing both the promises that Labour supporters were looking for <u>and</u>, implicitly, the excuses for not fulfilling them.

> No programme can meet all needs at once. Nor, for that matter, will it be possible for the next Labour Government in its first term to implement the whole programme which our members have laid down. These problems lead us to two conclusions ... First, whenever it comes to power, the next Labour Government will have a very long list of commitments - many requiring lengthy legislation and many requiring substantial amounts of money and resources. We therefore make it clear at the outset that Labour will have priorities worked out in consulation with the whole movement. (78)

The party thus made it clear that it would not be 'going it alone' in any new programme of legislation and that participation in and responsibility for new policy priorities would be more broadly based than before. Most striking however was the firmness with which the introduction sought to constrain expectations, particularly those of interest-groups like CPAG which had felt themselves poorly served by the 1964/70 governments.

> Many of the various interest groups in Britain will find a good deal in this document to encourage them. We must therefore sound a note of warning. Shelter may be right to demand top priority for housing; the Child Poverty Action Group may be justified in calling for a first call on resources for the large family; the Pensioners' Associations and MIND have their own views of top priorities, as do other groups such as the Comprehensive Schools Committee and Disablement Income Group. Everyone of those organisations can count on support from the

Labour Party, and it may be that they are right
in calling for high priority in their chosen
fields but (and here came the rub) they cannot
all be first. The problems of deciding
priorities, often a painful process of deciding
the allocation of resources between almost
equally excellent causes, is what politics is
about. (79)

Nevertheless the document must have given groups
like CPAG and Shelter some encouragement. The more
positive approach adopted by the Party and the unions
certainly gave impetus to the growing support within
CPAG for renewed liaison with the labour movement at
both Party and union level. It also resulted, as was
shown in the previous chapter, in a resumption of
CPAG activity at the Labour Party Conference in 1972.
CPAG's faith in, and expectations of,
distributive justice from the Labour Party for the
poor have seemed occasionally justified by the
Party's intermittent promises of reform. The
following year, for example, the Party expressed the
view that

The greatest scandal in Britain today is our
tolerance of poverty. Over a million people are
severely handicapped and get no statutory
benefit. Eight million retirement pensioners
get merely 1/5th of average industrial earnings
and two million are forced to resort to
supplementary benefits. Nearly half a million
children live in families where a parent is in
work but still get less in pay than
supplementary benefit would bring: 84,000
families receive FIS ... The redistribution of
income and wealth is essential if we are to
tackle poverty effectively ... Socialism is
about helping the poor and eliminating the
poverty. It is also about achieving a massive
and irreversible shift in the distribution of
wealth and income in favour of working people.
(80)

Of particular interest were the comments made on
supplementary benefit reform and a more sympathetic
approach to claimants, which were strikingly similar
to the views expressed by CPAG in the previous two
years (81). In these two years intra-movement
discussion of social policy flourished to an extent
greater than at any Conference since 1964. In 1972,
pensions, the problems of pensioners as a social

group, means-tested benefits and charges, financing of the NHS, care of the elderly and disabled, and the problems of poverty and groups in need occupied the attention of delegates (82). In 1973 it was again the often related problems of the elderly, the disabled and the poor (83). On 24 June 1974 the TUC agreed unanimously that union negotiators should, for the duration of the social contract, seek wage rises only in so far as they would keep abreast of the cost of living, taking account of both taxation and threshold agreements. Collective bargaining was to depend on the following guidelines: priority for agreements which would have beneficial effects on unit cost and efficiency and which could improve job security; a low pay minimum of £25 basic per week; the elimination of discrimination especially against women; and improvement of non-wage benefits such as pension schemes, sick pay and the duration of holiday leave. In its wake the contract was to open the door to the Sex Discrimination Act, the Employment Protection Act, the Trade Unions and Labour Relations Act, housing and prices subsidies, and initiatives on family support and pension increases. Also promised were extension of public ownership, price control via a Prices Commission, a strengthening of consumer representation, and an attack upon unemployment. Though much of this failed to materialise, and indeed many felt the situation later deteriorated in some of the fields under review (84), at the time it was the promise and consensus for reform and innovation that mattered most to groups like CPAG and, indeed, the unions themselves (85).

The mood, hopeful for the first time since 1964, was summed up by Michael Foot: 'The Labour Party and the unions, united as never before in the way they believe they can serve the nation, offer a combination of cures for the immense problems which certainly face us. They are designed to produce a new industrial climate, a much wider sense of social justice, a new confidence that the Government will keep faith with the people and that the people as a whole will therefore respond to the national need' (86).

CPAG now sought to develop this impetus and direct the attention of unions and the Party towards the groups it identified as particularly hard hit by inflation. Its proposals, in a document appropriately titled A Social Contract for Families, included reforms to relate benefits and taxation to earnings, a call for a higher basic rate of family allowance, a lower rate of income tax, free school meals for all children, a one-parent family allowance in accordance with the recommendations of the Finer Committee, a new disablement allowance, and a housing allowance to help poorer tenants cope with increased rents (87). In advancing these proposals the Group was restating a strategy pursued for more than five years. Significantly, it was also acting in the spirit of Labour's Programme for Britain 1973, the 1974 White Paper on the chronically sick and disabled and the social contract itself. Nevertheless, CPAG saw its proposals as the tip of the iceberg, the first thrust in a series of attacks upon social and economic injustice. Labour's 1973 programme had already set a firm, gradualist tone and it would clearly have been unwise to eschew a selective strategy while the new Labour government of February 1974 and the unions were still picking up the threads of their former relationship.

As CPAG's 1974 Memorandum to the Chancellor stated:

> A concerted attack upon poverty would involve other measures – including a review of eligibility for unemployment insurance benefit; the introduction or improvement of earnings-related benefits, including pensions; the introduction of a minimum wage; reviews of urban aid programmes, the regional employment premium, rate support grants and local rating ... we have sought to concentrate on those matters of closest relevance to the responsibilities of the Chancellor in his preparation of the Budget bearing also in mind the desperate need to take a number of major steps to create a just society and thus ensure a reduction of inflationary and selfish pressures upon the economy. (88)

In retrospect, the Memorandum, like most of those before it, seems to have had little bearing on the Chancellor's policies. At the time, however, it was an integral part of CPAG's attempt to galvanise the labour movement into action both to bring about social reform and to restore its own flagging morale. The Group felt it imperative to influence the policy recommendations of the unions in their dialogue with government. Their role as co-architects of the social contract and the continuation of their influence upon the Labour leadership after the election through the machinery of the Liaison Committee, confirmed the trade union movement's status as an insider group.

This status had not gone unrecognised by CPAG which, during this next period of Labour office, redoubled its efforts to work with and through the unions to achieve its own goals. Its ability to achieve them, however, rested to a considerable extent on how the unions viewed the prospect of liaison with CPAG – quite clearly, to date, an outsider group. The unions' role in the social contract and their partnership with the new Labour government carried with it the need for a 'strategy of responsibility'. The contract firmly embodied the principal of 'power with responsibility'. CPAG, of course, was neither bound in this way nor a party to the terms of the contract.

The Labour Party leadership had already alluded to the need for a patient and responsible approach to the establishment of priorities in the introduction to its 1972 Programme for Britain. In doing so it had raised the spectre of policy overcrowding that had dogged its 1964–70 period of office and which had led to tension and hositility among its supporters. The following chapter examines the view that the social contract and the establishmemnt of the Liaison Committee, by conferring upon the unions a social and economic, as well as an industrial, role, may have contributed significantly to a process of rationalisation within interest group politics in Britain in that it now became imperative for small groups like CPAG to channel their voice through the TUC – fast developing as a key spokesman group on social issues. We go on, therefore, to examine the growing involvement of the TUC and individual unions in social issues and how an outsider group like CPAG amongst others, sought to harness that interest for its own ends.

NOTES

1. Director's Report to the CPAG Executive (21 March 1969).
2. A comprehensive analysis of poverty in class terms has been offered by Bill Jordan in Paupers – The Making of the New Claiming Class (Routledge & Kegan Paul, 1973). See also Field, F. (ed.), The Conscript Army (Routledge & Kegan Paul, 1977) chs. 2 and 3. For a comparative study in the field of education, see Byrne, D., Williamson, B. and Fletcher, B., The Poverty of Education (Martin Robertson, 1975).
3. Miliband, R., 'Politics and Poverty', in

216

Wedderburn, D. (ed.), <u>Poverty, Inequality and Class Culture</u> (Cambridge University Press, 1974), ch. 9, p.185.

4.   Finer, S.E., 'The Political Power of Organised Labour', <u>Government and Opposition</u> (1974), pp.391-406. Miliband notes that 'In terms of pressure group politics, the most important of all such voices (i.e. on the poor's behalf) is - or could be - that of the trade union movement; and both individual unions and the TUC have, in the last few years, shown much greater concern for low-paid workers and for the deprived generally than in earlier periods. Given the fragmentation of organised labour, its sectional divisions and its usually low level of solidarity this must be reckoned as progress indeed' p.191.

5.   Interview with Frank Field, 25 July 1977. See also Field, F., <u>Poverty and Politics</u>, <u>op.cit.</u>, p.18.

6.   Even here it should be noted that Peggy Herbison herself had orchestrated the trade union reaction after 'leaking' the Callaghan proposal to them in the first place. See Banting, <u>op.cit.</u>, p.152, and Crossman, <u>Diaries</u>, Vol. II, pp.251-3.

7.   See Poverty Pamphlet No. 19, <u>A Social Contract for Families</u> (November 1974), <u>p.3</u>; and <u>Poverty</u>, Nos. 16/17, pp.8-16.

8.   Reflecting on Herbison's disclosures, Field says that 'it was at that point that a strategy did evolve of not so much being concerned with rank-and-file trade unionists because we do not have the skills or expertise to do that, or the resources, but channelling in heavily to the trade union leadership'. Interview, 22 February 1979.

9.   CPAG Executive Committee Minutes (September 1970).

10.   The key figure in setting up this dialogue was Nicholas Bosanquet, whose contacts with these trade unions derived from his earlier work with the Prices and Incomes Board for which he had co-authored a report on low pay. He says of the original meeting, 'at that time I was fairly well informed on the subject and I convened a meeting: I think it was the National Union of Tailors and Garment Workers Research Officer, USDAW, some GMWU Research Officers and Norman Willis of the TGWU, who was probably the most prominent trade unionist in his area, and we had a general discussion about low pay and a subsequent meeting on ways that CPAG would work in with the trade union movement'. He also speculates that the meetings encouraged Field to set up the Low Pay Unit later. Interview with Nicholas Bosanquet, 22

February 1979.
    11. It is interesting to note here that CPAG
was attempting to explore possible areas of mutual
concern between itself and the trade unions by
sounding out and appealing to the latter's self-
interest. This is a tactic which has been
successfully employed by groups in the USA which lack
socioeconomic leverage. Environment groups have, for
example, combined with labour unions and, in some
cases, business corporations wielding substantial
political influence to strengthen their cause. See
Roos, L.J. Jr, The Politics of Ecosuicide (Holt,
Rinehart & Winston, Illinois, 1971), chs. 1,2, 4 and
16; and Crenson, M., The Unpolitics of Air Pollution
(Baltimore University Press, 1971).
    12. This included representatives of NUPE,
TGWU, USDAW, Family Service Units, East London
Settlement, BASW, NCCL, National Society for the
Unmarried Mother and her Child, National Institute of
Social Work Training, The Albany Settlement,
Shelter, Mothers in Action, NUS, Quest, Task Force
and the Claimants Unions.
    13. Ibid.
    14. Feather argued that child poverty could
not be abolished by wage increases alone. Instead,
'The solution lies in using a battery of means which
can be concentrated in the area of most need. The
income tax and social benefit systems must take
account of the needs of different sized families in a
way that the wages system cannot'. Vic Feather, 'Low
Pay and Poverty', Poverty, Nos. 16/17, pp.29-30.
    15. Feather commented, for example, 'At the
TUC we are suggesting that in respect of those who
pay tax the introduction of a minimum earned income
allowance, coupled with an increase in family
allowances, including an extension of the clawback,
would bear directly on the problem of family
poverty'. Ibid.
    16. Townsend to Feather (19 November 1970).
    17. Bosanquet, N., 'Jobs and the Low-Paid
Workers', Poverty, No. 18 (Spring 1971). Reprinted in
Butterworth, E. and Weir, D. (eds.), Social Problems
of Modern Britain (Fontana, 1973).
    18. Poverty, No. 18, p.2.
    19. Ibid.
    20. Ibid.
    21. Ibid., p.6.
    22. Walley, J. 'Children's Allowances: An
Economic and Social Necessity', in Bull, D. (ed.)
Family Poverty (Duckworth, 1972), p.117.
    23. 'A New Deal for the Family', Poverty, No.

10 (Spring 1969).
    24. Ibid., p.12.
    25. Bosanquet to author (3 April 1979). The meeting took place on 22 September 1971 and Bosanquet describes it as 'an exploratory discussion which had no very immediate result'.
    26. Bosanquet, N., 'Trade Unions and the Poor', Poverty, No. 22 (Spring 1972).
    27. Field, F. and Piachaud, D., 'The Poverty Trap', New Statesman (3 December 1971). The arguments advanced largely stemmed from an earlier article by Piachaud, 'Poverty and Taxation', Political Quarterly, Vol. 42, No. 1 (January–March 1971), pp.31–44. This has since been developed further by Bradhsaw, J. and Wakeman, I., 'The Poverty Trap Updated', Political Quarterly, Vol. 43, (1972).
    28. 'The Poverty Trap', New Statesman (3 December 1971).
    29. Ibid.
    30. Ibid.
    31. See Marquand, D., '... And That Great Fat Pig', New Statesman (18 September 1970).
    32. Poverty, No. 10.
    33. New Statesman (3 December 1971).
    34. 'Correspondence', New Statesman (17 December 1971).
    35. Ibid.
    36. Jones, J., 'Wages and Social Security', New Statesman (7 January 1972).
    37. Castles, F., The Social Democratic Image Society (Routledge & Kegan Paul, 1978), p.46. See also Parkin, F., Class Inequality and Political Order (MacGibbon & Kee, 1971).
    38. New Statesman (7 January 1972).
    39. Ibid.
    40. Ibid.
    41. Ibid.
    42. Donnet, C. and Lipsey, D., 'How to Bargain Away Poverty' (Reply), Tribune (24 December 1971).
    43. See Bradshaw and Wakeman, op.cit., pp.464–5 and correspondence in the New Statesman (17 December 1971).
    44. Tribune (24 December 1971).
    45. Ibid.
    46. Field & Piachaud, 'How to bargain away Poverty' (Reply) Tribune (31 December 1971).
    47. Ibid.
    48. Ibid. Commenting on the impact of the 'Poverty Trap' article some years later Field attempted to explain its reasoning: 'There were efforts to forge a trade union link up from the early

70s onward and important in that was, really, the "poverty trap" article, in that up to that point trade unions kept saying well we really must be concerned about these issues, but didn't really do much about it. The point of the article was that it summed up, in very ordinary language, the whole state of welfare for very many people, the overlap of taxation and benefits, and that trade unions had to be concerned because they couldn't win real wage increases for their members but it could actually make them worse off'. Interview (28 April 1979).

49. Poverty, No. 22 (Spring 1972).
50. Ibid.
51. See Taylor, R., The Fifth Estate (Pan, 1978), ch. 4; and Heffer, E., The Class Struggle in Parliament (Gollancz, 1973).
52. Hall, Land, Parker and Webb, op.cit., pp.90-1.
53. See Dorfman, G.A., Wage Politics in Britain 1945-67 (Charles Knight, 1974).
54. Hall et al., p.185.
55. Castle, B., 'A Socialist Incomes Policy', New Statesman (25 September 1970).
56. Ibid.
57. Crosland, A., A Social Democratic Britain, Fabian Tract No. 404 (January 1971).
58. New Statesman (25 September 1970).
59. Ibid.
60. Ibid.
61. Benn, A., The New Politics: A Socialist Renaissance (Fabian Society, 1970).
62. 4 May 1971, quoted in Simpson, op.cit., pp.221-2.
63. Ibid., pp.222-3.
64. This was summed up most forcefully by Jack Jones in an address to a Fabian Society fringe meeting at the 1971 Party Conference. 'There is no reason at all why a joint policy cannot be worked out. But let us have the closest possible liaison. This is not just a matter of brainstorming in the back rooms of Congress House and Transport House just before the next election. In the past we have not had the dialogue necessary. The unions and the party leadership perhaps have both been unsure of their own ground but we can make this policy into a great campaign to open up the approach to genuine industrial democracy based on the unions.' In Taylor, op.cit., p.130.
65. Simpson, op.cit., p.223.
66. Ibid., p.236.
67. Ibid.

68. Ibid., p.237.

69. John Gollan has noted that 'with state intervention in industrial relations and the state itself emerging as the other side in many disputes, strikes and industrial unrest are compelled to assume a political significance and the old reactionary efforts to compartmentalise industrial and political action are rapidly disappearing. Workers are no longer inhibited from taking industrial action because it has a political connotation; this shedding of such inhibitions has great political significance for the future'. Hutt, A., British Trade Unionism (Lawrence & Wishart, 1975), p.258.

70. Gollan notes 'all the actions against the Industrial Relations Act or in defiance of the counter-inflation Act were obviously in part political and had to be so as the government was acting politically against the unions. But this tendency has gone even further. There has been official industrial action in support of pensioners and the NUPE strike, superimposing upon a wage claim the further demand for a rapid phasing out of private beds in NHS hospitals. These are matters which go beyond immediate industrial aims'. Ibid., p.258.

71. May, op.cit., p.43.

72. Skidelsky, R., 'The State - Why it Will Grow', New Society (2 October 1975); and Cawson, A., 'Pluralism, Corporatism and the Role of the State', Government and Opposition, Vol. 13, No. 2 (Spring 1978).

73. See Behrens, R., '"Blinkers for the Carthorse" - The Conservative Party and Trade Unions 1974-79', Political Quarterly (October-December 1978), pp.457-66.

74. May, op.cit., p.75.

75. This development is fully discussed in three recent books: Smith, T. Politics of the Corporate Economy (Martin Robertson, 1979); Richardson, J.J. and Jordan, A.G., Governing Under Pressure (Martin Robertson, 1979), esp. chs. 3 and 6; and Barnes, D. and Reid, E., Government and Trade Unions (Heinemann, 1980), part IV.

76. Marsh and Locksley, op.cit., p.29.

77. Ibid. See also Finer, S.E., 'The Political Power of Organised Labour', Government and Opposition (1974), pp.391-406.

78. Labour's Programme for Britain 1972, p.6.

79. Ibid.

80. Labour's Programme for Britain 1973, p.8, and Derrick, P., 'People's Capitalism', New Statesman (7 June 1974).

81. 'More emphasis must be given to encouraging the sick and unemployed to claim supplementary benefits and the SBC must adopt the positive approach with these two groups of claimants that it has used with pensioners ... The present appeals tribunal machinery must be overhauled in order to ensure a consistent approach between one local tribunal and another. Better treatment must be given to claimants living as members of another person's household.' Labour's Programme for Britain 1973, p.72.

82. See Composite 21 (state benefits), pp. 305, 309, Report of the 71st Annual Conference of the Labour Party (1972).

83. Report of the 72nd Annual Conference of the Labour Party (1973), esp. POEU motion of composite 28, pp.227-30; and 'The Appendix of Resolutions and Decisions of Conference', p.362.

84. 'The Strange Death of a Social Contract', New Statesman (26 January 1979); and The Guardian (3 September 1975).

85. May notes that in this period the unions gained 'The opportunity to take the initiative and not simply to react to policies initiated elsewhere. Thus the defensive and negative aspects of trade union political action which have necessarily dominated its approach to the legal position of the unions are less in evidence and the unions have the opportunity to propose policies which they are anxious to see given legislative enactment'. And he concludes that 'this enables the unions, at least in principle, to make more headway with some of their policies which are less directly related to the traditional union areas of wages, working conditions and the legal framework governing their activities. Thus the demands for a substantial increase in the old age pension which have been particularly pressed by the TGWU and adopted as TUC policy have been accepted by the Labour Party as a top priority, down to the precise monetary amount asked for by the TUC', (op.cit., p.19).

86. 'Annual Financial and Economic Review', The Times (26 September 1974).

87. Field, F., and Townsend, P., A Social Contract for Families - Memorandum to the Chancellor, Poverty Pamphlet 19 (November 1974).

88. Ibid.

Chapter Ten

LIAISON WITH THE LABOUR MOVEMENT, 1972-5

The re-emergence of industrial relations issues in
the first two years of the Heath government clearly
disrupted CPAG's brief dialogue with the trade union
movement, and minor progress only was made with one
or two unions. Frank Field claimed in June 1972, for
example, that a useful relationship had been
established with a variety of unions which could be
activated 'as issues arise which affect their sphere
of influence' (1). Union representatives in the gas
and electricity industries had, for example,
provided CPAG with information on the number of
families who had been unable to pay bills and had had
their electricity and gas supplies cut off. This was
seen as a particularly useful area of co-operation
with the unions given the failure of the DHSS's own
Memorandum of Guidance: Fuel Debts Among Low Income
Groups (2) (1972) to reduce significantly the
hardship caused by disconnection.
    In a similar vein, Field reported that 'some
local fire brigade workers have expressed concern at
the greatly increased fire risk which results from
these families cooking on calor gas and lighting
their homes with candles' and talked of meeting the
Fire Brigade's Union in July 1972 'to see what
pressure they can exert to stop this practise and we
are exploring why the SBC and local welfare
departments are not meeting the bills of families who
fall behind in their payment of gas or electricity
bills' (3).
    That these examples constituted an effective
dialogue, however, is arguable. There seems to have
been a tendency on Field's part to confuse general
trade union sympathy for CPAG's fuel campaign with
effective and substantive offers of assistance and

223

support. Moreover, far from winning union co-operation on the issue of disconnections, some CPAG members encountered strong resistance to the idea. In the course of discussions between the Department of Energy and the national executive of the Electricity Consumer Council, for example, one leading CPAG member sought to persuade the participants that the categories covered by the code of practice on disconnections should be extended to cover all families with children, the disabled and a variety of low income groups, but was rebuffed - on some occasions quite vociferously - by the electrical industry unions. Far from helping to alleviate the problems of the poor, he was forced to conclude that this was one among a number of examples 'where the interests of low income families and the power of the unions has actually been used to resist improvements and bring about changes which cause a deterioration in the quality of life for low income families' (4).

One of the most interesting initiatives undertaken by the Group in 1972 centered on an effort to establish a dialogue with the unions administering social security benefits in order to reach an agreement 'on a programme of reform for both workers in the social security section and the claimants' (5). The value of this joint approach had been stated by Hilary Rose in a CPAG pamphlet. In many situations the victim of what she saw as the dehumanising system of state welfare was not always the claimant but often the dispenser of benefit. It was her view that 'The low paid bureaucrat behind the desk of the Social Security office or the Housing Department, stands at the abyss of the poverty he confronts daily, held back only by his respectability' (6). Any campaign to improve the lot of the claimant while the bureacrat's economic situation remained static would only serve to aggrevate the tension in their relationship. For Rose, it rested with the poverty lobby to recognise that 'Too often the bureaucrat and the client are trapped within their own labels and we have to look for methods of opening the trap' (7).

Her view carried with it an allusion to the sensitivity of DHSS staff to criticism by poverty groups. There was a tendency for roles to become stereotyped with the local officer too frequently cast in the role of villain. Unconstructive criticism had the unfortunate result of adding to the tensions in the officer-claimant relationship. It was important, therefore, that groups like CPAG made efforts in future to consider the effects of their campaigns on both sides of this relationship. This initiative was an effort to do just that.

It was Jonathan Bradshaw's view that 'Supplementary Benefit officials have always been extremely sensitive to the criticism of CPAG and Field was becoming increasingly aware of the antipathy between Social Security officials and CPAG, and what he was trying to do was really to get them to mobilise behind the campaign and see themselves as part of the problem they were talking about, instead of as the enemy all the time' (8). The initiative was an admission on CPAG's part that its campaigns had 'perhaps focused too much on the "appalling way social security officials treated claimants"' (9). Even so, such campaigning was only a very small part of the group's total activity and it is important to note, for balance, that equal blame was accorded the poor offices and facilities provided for social security staff.

TRADE UNIONS AND LOW PAY

The decision to continue efforts to liaise with trade unions had been closely guided by Field during an internal reappraisal of strategy in July 1972 (10). An immediate outcome was the attendance of the Group at the 1972 and 1973 Labour Party Conferences. The 'reality' of CPAG-union relations was best summed up by Jane Streather and Stuart Weir after their attendance at the 1972 Conference:

> we were encouraged by the warm reception the group received, but we felt that we are a long way from having any real influence upon the labour movement. The group has already discussed the need for a trade union liaison officer and union attitudes at conference have shown how necessary such an appointment is. In the meantime we need to seek to begin a dialogue now by building upon existing contacts. It is also necessary to begin a policy of education within the labour movement and to make more contacts at the local level, and of members of the NEC and in Transport House. Any attempt to influence policy-making should be by means of the democratic process within the party and not by a reliance on having a few mates on Transport House Policy Committees although, of course, we should continue to use them too. (11)

This latter jibe was almost certainly directed at

Field who seems to have relied quite heavily for his trade union strategy on his relationship with David Basnett of the GMWU (12) and Terry Parry of the FBU. Both men were known to be sympathetic to CPAG and were prominent in Conference debates, fringe meetings and TUC discussions on poverty. However, Field's personal friendship with them was no substitute for a systematic and properly-executed strategy to influence the trade unions at all levels, particularly at the grass roots. More striking is the fact Field seems to have monopolised this area of CPAG's work until the appointment of the Group's trade union liaison officer - also his initiative. Though the issue of CPAG-trade union liaison had been aired during a review of strategy in 1972, it is clear that the issue was introduced and stage-managed by the Director. It is also clear from discussions with CPAG staff and members of the executive that no real group discussion of the liaison proposal took place until after Field had established the pattern of contact with Basnett, Parry and others, and had made the appointment of a trade union liaison officer a fait accompli.

An important outcome of the Group's attendance at the 1972 Conference was the reaffirmation of its belief in the establishment of a national minimum wage and the need for an effective trade union strategy to combat low pay. Once more, as with family allowances, the Group was on uncertain grounds. Its early 1970-1 dialogue with trade union research officers on the subject of low pay had been selective, confining the discussion to representatives of unions with large numbers of low-paid members. The Group had not really tested general trade union opinion on a policy for the low paid and had perhaps underestimated the strong opposition to such a policy voiced by some unions. For the larger and stronger unions such a policy implied a national minimum wage which, in turn, would necessitate statutory involvement in wage bargaining by government (13). This was unacceptable to them.

The lack of concerted trade union action on low pay in the early 1970s proved a serious barrier to CPAG's efforts to assist low-income groups. The maintenance of differentials and the pursuit of maximum self interest by many of the more powerful unions remained paramount. This led the Prices and Incomes Board to comment in April 1971:

> The unions have not, by and large, been
> particularly effective in improving the

relative position of lower-paid workers. Any attempt to increase the earnings of the low paid solely by raising general levels of pay substantially will, in the absence of greater productivity, serve merely to increase the rate of cost inflation. A concerted trade union policy towards the low paid must involve a recognition that a relative improvement of the position of some must mean a relative worsening of the position of others. (14)

Matters had not been helped by taxation policy. In 1955 the average wage-earner, married with two children, paid a mere 3.3 per cent of his gross income in tax and national insurance contributions. By 1975 this had risen to 25 per cent, and by 1977 had reached 32 per cent. The tax burden of the average family increased almost tenfold. The taxation factor in pay bargaining was summed up in a 1976 study by the Low Pay Unit which concluded that 'Between 1970 and 1975 trade unions more than doubled gross pay for the male worker on the lowest decile ... The Inland Revenue, at the same time, more than trebled the tax bill of a worker in this position' (15). According to Robert Taylor

attacks on welfare state scroungers have been most vociferous among the low paid, some of whom would be better off for short periods on the dole than in active work. This is a low pay not a high benefit problem, but union failure to improve the wages of low paid workers makes it difficult to apply effective resistance to those who want to tax social benefits or lengthen the periods of time between their up-valuations. The unions have been far better organised in defending Government attacks on public sector jobs than in crusading for those on low wages. Indeed, a major failure of the unions has been over achieving a better deal for the low paid. (16)

The Group's strategy for influencing the unions was accordingly seriously limited in the area of low pay by these factors and by the two-tier nature of the trade union movement. The strategy has, however, taken other forms and other issues as its target. One of the most interesting ventures of the Group was its initiative in 1973 to combine with other central London charities and voluntary associations to form a branch of the TGWU as a means of unionising its own

staff and establishing a useful vehicle for sending
resolutions to Conference. One of the earliest aims
of the branch's social policy committee, consisting
of representatives from Shelter, CPAG, SHAC and the
North Lewisham Project, was to press the TGWU to
establish its own central social policy committee on
the lines of that created by the GMWU.

In a submission to the Committee on Voluntary
Organisations some time later, the Group explained
the raison d'etre of the branch and outlined the
nature of its liaison with the labour movement:

> CPAG operates on two levels. In the first
> instance its staff are active trade unionists.
> The Group was responsible for bringing into
> being a branch of the Transport and General
> Workers Union which caters for other similar
> voluntary bodies. The Group is also concerned in
> lobbying all trade unions ... The trade unions
> are in a position to exert pressure on
> Government on many issues. CPAG hope to
> influence trade union policies from within. At
> the present time the trade unions are very
> anxious to improve their public image; to let it
> be seen that they are taking an overall view of
> issues beyond just that of salaries. CPAG want
> to be able to take advantage of this. They try
> to achieve results by discussion and by giving
> information to the unions. (17)

It is perhaps only since 1974 that CPAG'S efforts
have had any measurable effect. The key to success in
1974 was to rest primarily in keeping liaison at a
low key and testing any radical demands initially
upon 'friendly activists' who had been of some
assistance in the past. Essentially, the idea was to
keep the mood of the labour movement continuously
under review, thereby reducing the risk of untimely
comments or intervention and, positively, enhancing
the Group's ability to exploit rapid changes in
policy and attitude. The principal theme was
educative - a demonstration of the importance of
social security matters, particularly with regard to
redundancy, sickness benefits, strikes, accidents
and retirement to active trade unionist (18). The
Group had been much influenced in its thinking by its
attendance at the Labour Party Conferences in 1972
and 1973, both of which had seemed to offer an
opportunity to assess and shape the mood of grass-
roots opinion, unions and the Party, on the subject
of a social contract. Attendance also offered a

chance to reconstruct old relationships.

CPAG AND THE LABOUR PARTY CONFERENCE

Strong criticism of the continued breakdown in CPAG's relations with the Labour Party after 'Poor get Poorer' had come from two relatively new figures in the Group, Stuart Weir, later to become Director of the group's Citizens Rights Office, and Jane Streather, Assistant Director with responsibility for branches. Both were uneasy about the Group's relationship with the Conservative government, and firm in their belief that CPAG was not being critical enough. The muted tone of CPAG's criticism until late 1972 seems largely to have stemmed from the fact that the Group's Director was working behind the scenes on an individual basis in the hope that concessions could be won. These did not materialise, however, and Streather and Weir were reluctant to neglect the Group's disrupted relationship with the Labour Party any longer. Even so, regardless of the Group's belief in the misdirection of Conservative policy, CPAG-Conservative relations could not have been helped by the overtly pro-Labour make-up of the group's executive or by the reluctance of many within it to work with the Conservatives. Streather and Weir, for example, were committed to a realignment with the Labour Party as a matter of some urgency and both saw an exercise in political education at grass-roots level as an important new initiative in forcing poverty back onto the political agenda. The first stage of this exercise was to take place at the 1972 Labour Party Conference. In the event, any further thoughts of neutrality were abandoned.

They were initially aided in their efforts to stimulate delegate interest in poverty and in the work of CPAG by Weir's own personal contacts. The latter had worked as a diarist for The Times, and had made a number of useful contacts whose influence proved valuable at the Conference. Chief among these was Frances Morell, unofficially Tony Benn's press officer. Through Morell, they were able to buttonhole both Benn and another sympathetic MP, Frank Allaun, who used their influence at Conference to generate some initial interest in both the CPAG delegation and its fringe meeting.

However, CPAG's attendance was 'avowedly exploratory' and was not helped by the exclusion of poverty from the Conference agenda. Nevertheless, Weir was confident that the experience had been

useful and could be built upon to achieve a more
lasting impact at the next Conference. He wrote at
the time:

> our attendance at the Conference gives us the
> opportunity of informally reviewing contacts
> and extending them. We would also wish to put to
> use our knowledge of the policy-making
> processes of the Labour Conference and organise
> contacts with local parties to influence the
> resolutions and amendments to resolutions
> submitted for the next conference. We suggest
> that we begin by contacting those parties which
> submitted resolutions and amendments this year
> and by asking CPAG members who are active in
> local CLPs to put forward resolutions and
> amendments. We would also have to be prepared
> for the compositing process (i.e. the business
> of deciding the form of resolutions for debate).
> As this year's Conference debated only a few
> social policy resolutions ... it is likely that
> the 1973 Conference will devote more time to
> social policy. (19)

This was a logical strategy for a group which
considered it was rapidly exhausting its avenues of
influence. Despite the fact that conferences have not
always been the most effective vehicles for
influencing the party leadership they remain a useful
base upon which to build grass-roots political
education and the Conference strategy appears
popular with groups having overlapping party
memberships (20).

Weir's post-1972 Conference comments were a
recognition of the receptiveness of the Labour Party
to this sort of strategy. Lewis Minkin notes that
over the last twenty years or so constituency parties
have been 'subject to organised attempts to instigate
and mobilise resolutions and amendments for the
Annual Conference. This was never carried out
directly by the NEC or the parlimentary leadership
... The activity was always carried on by groups
independent of the official institutions of the
party' (21).

Some of this instigation took place via an open
appeal circulated directly to constituency parties.
He notes: 'Normally the organisations indulging in
this open form of appeal were those whose purposes
are widely shared within the party. The Campaign for
the Young, the Chronic Sick and the CPAG were among
those who attempted this exercise' (22). Further,

'perhaps the most successful operation was mounted by
the CPAG in the early seventies using specimen
resolutions sent out direct to the constituency
parties and to their local action groups' (23).
Streather and Weir were in contact with Minkin during
the 1972 and 1973 Conferences when he was completing
his study of the Labour Party Conference, and they
were able to draw upon some valuable advice as to the
mechanics of resolution-making (24). Accordingly,
Minkin was able to conclude that 'The most successful
organisation in stimulating resolutions was the
CPAG. In 1973, working through sympathisers and
through direct circulation of the CLPs, it produced
24 resolutions and 5 amendments which could be traced
to its circulation. This was an unusually high
figure. In general the preliminary agenda of the
Party Conference with its approximately 500
resolutions and amendments was remarkable for its
spontaneous character' (25). How then did CPAG come
to be so apparently sucessful in 1973?
      The Group approached the formulation of its
Conference strategy with three main objectives –
first, to ensure that issues such as family
allowances, a minimum wage, reform of social
security, and abandonment of the wage-stop were
debated at Conferences by persuading CLPs to put
forward differing resolutions on these issues;
secondly, the Group sought to widen the debate on
such issues within the labour movement by introducing
the 'home responsibility payment' and a minimum wage
fixed at a percentage of average earnings. Finally,
the Group sought 'to add to the Labour Party's
Programme for Britain, a document more given to good
intentions than commitments, more specific pledges
on family allowances, reform of the social security
system, the abolition of means-tests etc.' (26).
      The Group made some initial errors of judgement
in its objectives. It subsequently noted, for
example, that 'by proposing that the minimum wage
should be set at 80 per cent of average earnings we
inevitably forced the platform into opposition'.
However, the Group could still claim some success.
'CPAG certainly did make an acknowledged impact; the
issue of poverty was brought to the forefront; and 3½
out of 5½ resolutions inspired by the group were
passed and will be added to the Party's programme'
(27).
      Resolutions on major issues for the Group, such
as a minimum wage, family allowances, taxation,
supplementary benefits, housing and educational
benefits, were sent by CPAG to all constituency

231

parties in Britain with a covering request that each consider submitting one for the conference. The aim was twofold - to get resolutions submitted and for parties to debate the issues at branch level. This attempt to develop a grass-roots exercise in political education was reinforced and given further impetus by the follow-up correspondence and visits to the constituencies prior to Conference to confirm that the issues had at least been seriously discussed, if not taken up. When the list of Conference resolutions was published in July 1973 the Group could claim that 'our suggestions were well represented. Some resolutions were worded exactly as we suggested and signed by three or four parties' (28).

This success in getting resolutions on the conference agenda is born out in cross-comparisons with the 1972 list of resolutions. In 1972, for example, there were six resolutions on the issue of a minimum wage. In July 1973 this had risen to fourteen, eight of which had originated with CPAG. On family allowances there had only been one resolution in 1972 but seven in 1973, all of which were CPAG's. A similar pattern could be found in the case of supplementary benefits; seven resolutions in 1972 but thirteen in 1973, seven of which CPAG claimed, 'were comprehensive ones of ours' (29). In addition to canvassing, the CPAG also asked a small number of constituencies to submit amendments 'so that there would be cross-reference of resolutions (e.g. to amend family allowances to include reference to tax credits, and to amend social services and welfare to include family allowances) and to enable more of "our" delegates to be present at the crucial compositing meeting' (30). Table 10.1 (31) povides a summary of the final agenda of resolutions for the 1973 Conference.

Perhaps the most frustrating feature of the Conference debates for CPAG was that the arrangements committee had split the resolutions into sections - education, social security, family allowances - which corresponded both with the sectionalised format of the Party's programme and the manner in which social policy in general had been broken down since Beveridge. This meant, of course, that there would be no comprehensive debate on poverty. Indeed, the debate on the elimination of poverty came at the end of the agenda - which CPAG saw as an indication of low priority. Subsequent protests about the arbitrary categorisation by CPAG delegates from Bury St Edmunds and Salisbury constituency parties led to

Table 10.1: CPAG influence upon social policy
resolutions submitted to the 1973 Labour Party
Conference

Influence	Issue	Constituency Party
	Minimum wage paras 116-37	
	116	Upminster
	117	Aberdeen South
*	118	Wolverhampton South West
	119	Sidcup
*+	119	Newcastle upon Tyne – amendment
*	120	Bermondsey
+	121	NUPE
	121	Coventry South East – amendment
	122	Bedford
	122	Glasgow
	123	Brecon and Radnor
	124	Torbay
*	125	Birkenhead
**	125	Paddington
*	125	Merthyr Tydfil
*	126	Folkestone and Hythe – amendment
*+	126	Bury St Edmunds – amendment
*	127	Mitcham and Morden
	Social Security paras 231-41	
	231	Devizes
	232	Hitchen
	232	Eton and Slough – amendment
	233	Portsmouth South
	233	Havant and Waterloo – amendment
*+	234	Oxford
	235	Nantwich
*	236	Howden
*	236	Bradford
*	237	Lambeth Central
*	238	Beaconsfield
*+	239	Cambridge
*	240	Penrith and Border
	241	Post Office Engineering Union

Taxation
paras 242-54

	242	Stepney and Poplar
	243	Eastleigh
	244	Oldham East
	245	Hemsworth
	246	Luton
	247	Dartford
	247	Maidstone - amendment
	248	Carlton
	248	Yarmouth - amendment
	249	Harlow West
	250	Northwich
	251	Wood Green
	252	Birmingham, Perry Barr
*+	253	Chelmsford - tax credits
*	254	Welwyn and Hartfield - tax credits
*	254	Brent North - tax credits
*+	254	Harlow - tax credits, amendment

Family allowances
paras 255-60

*	255	Liverpool Toxteth
*	256	Ormskirk
*+	257	Norwich North
*	258	Saffron Waldon
*	259	Chesham and Amersham
*+	259	Bury St Edmunds
*	259	Leicester - amendment
*+	259	Chelmsford - amendment
*+	260	Salisbury
*+	260	Blackpool South - amendment

Elimination of
poverty
para 424

*	424	Swansea Borough, and Crewe

Housing
paras 157-94

*	161	Battersea North, and National Union of Agricultural and Allied Workers - amendment
*	162	Newbury

```
           Education
           paras 270-89
*          272                Bath, Newcastle upon Tyne,
                              and    Aberdeen    South   -
                              amendment
*          273                Ravensbourne
```

* Resolution written by CPAG.
+ CLP known to have CPAG contacts, i.e. members or supporters.

a discussion by the NEC and, after the matter was again raised on the first morning of Conference, to a comment by the Conference Chairman, Barbara Castle, in which she regretted 'that we have not had one comprehensive debate on poverty at this conference' (32).
    The submission of resolutions for debate constituted only the first stage of the Conference strategy. The second stage involved securing publicity for the Group's activities, at Conference itself and in the national media, organising leafleting, fringe meetings and individual lobbying of delegates. The major breakthrough in stimulating interest in poverty came with the publication by CPAG of a set of briefing notes for delegates, Unequal Britain. Interest was also stimulated by holding a fringe meeting on 'Poverty and the Redistribution of Wealth' which was designed both to introduce the work of the Group and present its Conference theme. Some 500 people attended to hear addresses by Tony Benn, Joan Lestor, Jack Jones, Frank Field and Peter Burns of War on Want. The meeting produced reports on two BBC news programmes and led to a call by Benn for 'a new antipoverty alliance of Trade Unions, the Labour Party and radical pressure groups pledged to fight together for the elimination of poverty in Britain' (33).
    Perversely, the most interesting outcome of CPAG's attendance stemmed from one of its failures. All the issues noted earlier, bar one, were either accepted by the NEC or remitted for further discussion. The exception was family allowances: 'the NEC (in collaboration with the Big Unions) opposed the Family Allowance resolution and there had been no real opportunity to relate the issues. The Family Allowance resolution was opposed because "the drafters have included a home responsibility payment which we have not yet thought through and above all because it wants to commit us to a specific figure on

the tax threshold" (B. Castle)' (34). The rejection of the family allowance resolution and the role played in that rejection by some major unions led Streather and Weir to conclude that the Group should build upon its Conference strategy by taking up Field's 1972 proposals for liaison with the trade union movement:

> When we knew that the NEC were opposing the Family Allowance resolution, we made a point of 'talking to as many union delegations as possible to ask for support. Although the support was not forthcoming, we are now in a position to follow up some of our contacts. Perhaps one of the most encouraging things said by a union leader was that they were proposing a resolution because they wanted to show that they were concerned with those out of work as well as those within work. A precedent has of course been set by the TGWU in relation to pensions and possibly one of the most important tasks for CPAG is to encourage this trend. (35)

That trend was to be encouraged throughout the remaining part of 1973 and into the early weeks of 1974. With the return of a Labour government under Harold Wilson in February of that year CPAG's efforts were given a further impetus and a new sense of urgency. A broader-based and more structured approach to the labour movement, and the trade unions in particular, was now warranted.

The raising of family allowances provided most common ground with the labour movement in 1974: Lord Allen, Chairman of the TUC, had already stated earlier in the year that the attack on family poverty was to be one of the TUC's top priorities. The Group's chief task, therefore, was to develop ways of sustaining trade union interest in the issue and translating promise into action. An important initiative was taken in September by one of the group's branches, Haringey, which submitted a paper outlining a possible strategy. Haringey argued that for the Group to make any real impact on the movement there must be some overall policy. This, they suggested, could be divided into four main areas (1) national and CPAG activity, (2) local trade union branch, trade council and CPAG branch activity, (3) research into low pay, wage negotiations and wage structure, and (4) rights guides and welfare rights stalls advising trade unionists of their rights: 'not only should CPAG lobby and pressure the TUC and its

conference, and union leaders, but it also needs to
lobby individual union conferences where contact can
be made with local officials and elected lay
delegates. This should also be carried through Trade
Council and union branch level where contact can be
made with the rank and file movement' (36).

Liaison at grass-roots level was seen as
particularly important because of a credibility gap
between union leaders and their rank and file. At
national level, trades councils were largely
ineffective but, at the local level, they could prove
useful vehicles for getting CPAG's views across.
Additionally, local trade union branches could be
viewed as potential recruiting grounds for CPAG
members. Liaison could expand in other directions
also. Where CPAG branches were undertaking projects,
the assistance of the relevant union could be
enlisted. Haringey, for example, had formed a sub-
committee to take a critical look at educational
welfare benefits and had enlisted the active guidance
of the local branch of the National Union of Teachers
(37). Haringey also advocated more CPAG research into
union-related matters like low pay, wage
negotiations and wage structures, the poverty trap,
overtime working and various related state and local
authority benefits. Liaison with trade union
branches and local trades councils has since become
an important feature of CPAG branch activity,
although the closer one examines CPAG - union liaison
in the 1970s, the clearer it is that it has been more
substantive and sustained at the local level. Liaison
at national level has, with a few exceptions, been
ephemeral and more productive of verbal assurances of
support than firm evidence of it.

THE APPOINTMENT OF A TRADE UNION LIAISON OFFICER

In September 1974 CPAG held one of the first fringe
meetings to be organised by a non-trade union body at
the TUC conference. Echoing the sentiments expressed
by Lord Allen earlier, Field remarked:

> if the trade union movement wishes to continue
> its role of championing Britain's poor and
> hardpressed it will go away from this week's
> conference determined to see the two twin evils
> of our time - inflation and family poverty -
> brought under control. Earlier this year Lord
> Allen, TUC Chairman, made the abolition of
> family poverty the number one priority of the

unions when they seek to influence the Chancellor's Autumn budget. From now on CPAG will put all its energies to supporting Lord Allen and his colleagues on the General Council on the need to increase family allowances and extend the scheme to the first child. (38)

Oddly, Field underplayed the inconsistency of this appeal, noted earlier, that wage increases to improve the lot of the low paid were likely to prove inflationary and that the alternative, increases in social security and family allowance benefits, was not widely supported within the trade union movement.

In a press release immediately after Conference, the Group revealed its intention to 'institutionalise' its liaison with the labour movement:

> Recognising that the movement, and especially USDAW, has become increasingly concerned about the problems of poverty and that the wage-earner, as part of the family unit, must participate in government decision-making on social reforms, CPAG decided this summer to appoint a Trade Union Liaison Officer, the first such officer in a charity pressure group of this kind. (39)

The appointment of Marigold Johnson, a part-time worker with CPAG, in July 1974, confirmed both CPAG's strong belief in the growing influence of the trade union movement upon social policy and the failure of the Group's earlier and rather piecemeal efforts at liaison. She noted of her appointment: 'Probably the strongest argument to influence the decision to appoint a member of CPAG staff to act as liaison officer with the unions was the realisation that the Government of the day was clearly intending to take the TUC into its confidence in decision-making, and that the unions were therefore likely to be in a position to influence social policy' (40). Her appointment centred on three aims of the Group which were initially kept flexible until her role developed. Principally, it was the liaison officer's task to lobby union leaders and TUC staff on the changes in social security policy favoured by the Group. This was to be augmented by a conventional two-way educational exchange in which the liaison officer would summarise CPAG publications for trade union journals, speak to branch or shop steward meetings, and approach both national and branch officers to support CPAG branches, speak at meetings and supply the group with data.

Johnson's appointment was very much inspired by Frank Field and met with some scepticism from other staff and members who favoured a more orthodox choice. While Johnson had been active for some years in Labour Party politics and enjoyed a reputation within the London 'voluntary' scene, she perhaps was not the most ideal choice for this role. She had, by her own admission, few contacts within the trade union movement and was a little-known figure in trade union circles. Her upper middle-class background could also have done little to enhance her prospects of liaising with trade union officials who had largely worked their way up through the ranks, and were traditionally suspicious of 'outsiders'. The Group's Chairman appears to have been remarkably deferential to Field's presentation of her appointment as a fait accompli, and did little to support the counter-arguments of members of staff and the executive who favoured the appointment of a Ruskin college-type candidate, or of a trade union research officer with a feeling for and knowledge of trade union politics. Field's view, that trade unionists would welcome and be flattered by the opportunity to liaise with such an urbane and clearly articulate member of his staff, seems flippant and poorly judged against the backcloth of trade union politics and his group's previous inability to establish an effective dialogue.

Much of the liaison officer's work took the form of contributions to the group's work in various trade union journals and bulletins (41). Writing in <u>Social Services</u> Johnson sought to explain CPAG's concern with propaganda: 'It has always been CPAG's belief that any voluntary organisation or pressure group achieves more by disseminating information than by any other means ... if more people are made aware of their rights as citizens, if more facts are known about the widespread poverty and deprivation that exists in this country, then a small organisation can bring about change' (42). This view seemed to ignore the fact that for the previous ten years CPAG had released a deluge of information and data on poverty and deprivation to opinion leaders in government, Whitehall, the parties, the media and within the trade union movement itself, but had failed to make any significant impact. Such a view also carried with it the erroneous assumption, as had been proved repeatedly, that trade unionists would readily acquire an interest in the welfare of non-trade unionists or recognise a responsibility on their part to achieve social reform. The growing interest of the TGWU in the welfare of old age pensioners remained, at this point, the exception that proved the rule despite the sympathetic implications of the social contract.

CPAG were, perhaps, too presumptuous in their interpretation of the TGWU initiative as the beginning of a positive new trend in union thinking that would encourage the development of a concern for the welfare of the community at large. The pensions campaign had been seen by the Group as reflecting a shift in union thinking towards general social responsibility, and a radio broadcast by Len Murray, TUC General Secretary, in June 1974 had given further impetus to their interpretation. Murray's statement that 'the TUC has now got to be exposed to much more pressure from activists, from a much wider range of representatives' which meant for him 'the enlargement of politics and the involvement of a lot more people in the process of political decision-making' (41) was seized upon by the Group as further indication of the trade union movement's willingness to act 'societally'. While Murray's comments may well have seemed encouraging, it is important to remember that in the case of the trade unions 'It is the power to withhold a function that constitutes their strength; not their power to coerce' (42).

The traditional socio-economic strength of the unions rests in their ability to withdraw labour. But it was - and still is - unthinkable that they would withdraw labour in support of social security reform. In other words, in the economic sphere, in their role as 'producer groups', the unions can state an intention and be able to carry it through if necessary in the final resort by sanctions. In the case of social policy this facility did not obtain. Those interest groups who pinned hopes of social reform on trade union action were confusing the very real <u>influence</u> of the unions on economic and industrial issues with moral persuasion on social policy issues, which was not sanction-based.

Assessing the mood of trade union leaders, the Group's liaison officer had spoken of the immediate task of the group as 'building on the growing willingness of union leaders to concern themselves with aspects of welfare and social security outside wage bargaining'; 'if it can be harnessed to the campaigns of the poverty lobby it could exert great pressure' (43). Yet the principal evidence of this willingness, the TGWU's pensions campaign, was

atypical. Retirement pensions are one of the few
subjects in which all trade unionists share a common
interest, because, unlike other welfare payments,
they may be seen as an extension of the wage system
in that trade unionists can associate the weekly
national insurance deductions from their pay as a
means of financing their upkeep in retirement: a
clear continuum is thus established. In the case of
other welfare benefits, however, trade unionists may
see themselves 'burdened' by the unemployed, the sick
or those with families. The connection may be no less
clear, but the implication may be far less
acceptable.

This can be illustrated in the case of the wage-
stop. The Group had, with good intention, sent copies
of its Unemployed Workers' and Strikers' Guide to
Social Security and its Wage-Stop pamphlet to all
members of the TUC's Economic Committee and most of
the major unions in the belief that 'further trade
union support will considerably strengthen pressure
on the Government to announce the early abolition of
this outdated and unjust rule and thereby implement
the resolution passed at the 1973 Labour Party
Conference' (44). The TUC had itself expressed its
concern about the hardship caused by the ruling as
early as 1964 in talks with the Ministry of Pensions
and National Insurance and had raised the possibility
of introducing earnings related unemployment
benefits (45). Yet the ruling had continued
throughout the life of the Wilson governments with
little moderation and had led Sir John Walley to
conclude in 1969 that 'the ordinary citizen sees the
wage-stop as common sense' (46). For many trade
unionists, abolishing the wage-stop meant that their
less well-paid colleagues were able to receive more
when unemployed than in normal full-time employment,
so that life on the dole was more attractive
financially than full-time work. There was little
reason to suppose, therefore, despite the Party
Conference resolution in 1973, that trade union
leaders would go out on a limb to campaign vigorously
for an end to the ruling.

CPAG had similarly unrealistic expectations of
early union action on family allowances. Discussions
betweeen the Prime Minister and the Secretary of
State for Social Services made it clear by the autumn
of 1974 that action on family allowances would be
limited and delayed. This produced the rather odd
conclusion at a subsequent CPAG executive committee
meeting that 'this underlined the importance of the
group's growing work with the trade unions as they

241

were proving the one body to which the Government sometimes listened' (47), despite the earlier statements on the trade unions' role in family allowance campaigning made by Jack Jones, Frank Cousins, and Donnet and Lipsey amongst others in the 1960s and early 1970s (48).

One of the few substantive gestures of support received by CPAG at this time came from USDAW - a union with a significant proportion of women and low-paid workers within its ranks - which for this reason had been more sympathetic than most to CPAG's efforts in the fields of low pay and family support. In the July issue of its journal <u>Dawn</u>, the union submitted two propositions, agreed in discussions with CPAG, for consideration by the TUC at its autumn Conference, and one for the Labour Party Conference. From the TUC it urged action on poverty and low pay and support for the social contract. Of the Party it demanded the eradication of poverty, focusing especially on the need for an increase in family allowances, an investigation of the effects of taxation, and a reduction in the range of means-tested benefits.

The success of the Group's subsequent attendance at the TUC Conference is uncertain. Throughout the autumn, USDAW had continued actively to support the Group's family allowance campaign and during Conference Lord Allen chaired a fringe meeting on poverty convened by CPAG. Assessing the impact of the poverty debate upon the delegates, Marigold Johnson later wrote, 'the day as a whole was extremely useful to CPAG. I established a lot of union contacts, but above all there cannot be a single delegate who remained unaware that CPAG existed as an active body keen to co-operate in the social policy of the movement' (49). Lord Allen was equally convinced that the Group's presence had been beneficial both to itself and to union delegates. He declared himself pleased that CPAG were now moving towards closer contact with the TUC, if not in an official capacity, certainly through personalities involved with trade union work. 'This I think essential and nothing but good ... will accrue from activity of this kind to the CPAG. (50)'

The usefulness of this type of approach was tenuous, however, and the idea of holding further fringe meetings at the TUC Conference was abandoned after this initial attempt. The meeting was neither successful as a means of influencing policy nor a profitable use of resources. An audience of 60 or 80 was, to CPAG, less useful than getting resolutions passed.

In 1974, at least, CPAG attracted more publicity for their appointment of a trade union liaison officer and for their attendance at the Conference than for their positive achievements through either. Their failure to make an impact upon the resolution-making process and to draw nothing more than a polite acknowledgement of their efforts from the TUC and the vast majority of trade unions confirmed their status as an outsider group and obliged them increasingly to exaggerate both their influence and their progress through the media.

Whilst failing to achieve the consultative relationship it had sought with the trade unions, CPAG had attempted, nevertheless, to associate itself with the growing influence of the trade union movement by being seen to attend the latter's functions, by supplying it with information and research findings, by encouraging the issue of joint statements on poverty, and by actively promoting liaison. In reality the relationship was superficial. To make the illusion more substantive and enduring so that the unions themselves would help transform the illusion into reality was the next step. This can be seen in the group's subsequent approach to the TUC.

LIAISON WITH THE TUC

Some weeks after Conference Marigold Johnson began a short correspondence with the TUC. In a letter to all members of the Economic Committee she issued a polite reminder about earlier TUC promises of action. In July she asked the Committee to endorse CPAG proposals for an increase in family allowances in its submission to the Chancellor, remarking that, 'The TUC Economic Committee agreed on that occasion to include a recommendation that one means of reflation would be to increase Family Allowances' (51). Since nothing had emerged from this she now asked whether the Committee would be prepared to raise the issue again. Careful to stress a benefit exchange she added 'if the TUC Economic Committee is prepared to include discussion of a family allowance increase on its agenda, we would be very pleased to supply copies of the complete (CPAG) memorandum to the Chancellor. We would also like to suggest drawing the attention of your union members to the considerable amount of up-to-date information contained in the memorandum' (52).

The Group continued its efforts to 'persuade by correspondence' throughout October and November. Writing to Len Murray in October, Johnson commented

> we are hoping very much that when your Economic Committee meets to present recommendations to the Chancellor for his autumn Budget the TUC will feel able to include some mention of those measures on its agenda. You will remember that the recommendation on family allowances was included in the proposals the TUC made to Mr Healy in July, and we feel more strongly now that the Chancellor cannot afford to wait until next year to make some further provision. (53)

Two weeks later she wrote again, asking for 'this vital aspect of the social contract' (54) to be included on forthcoming agenda. The response from trade union leaders amounted to little more than polite gestures of verbal support.

Once again the Group appears to have confused sympathy with offers of outright support. In October, for example, it claimed as a success a discussion of its family allowance proposals at at least two meetings of the TUC's Economic Committee and declared that 'replies supporting our objectives have so far been received from 8 out of the 14 members ... A similar letter went to a further group of Trade Union leaders (thirteen non-members of the TUC Economic Committee) asking for a public commitment to support our proposals. Encouraging replies have so far been received, so we now have a total of twelve top TUC leaders already on record as willing to give support to our proposals' (55). This 'support' can have held little more than propaganda value for CPAG's efforts, since it was not translated into action. The response was only to be expected from a trade union movement preoccupied with other issues. While the sympathy of trade union leaders to the problems of the poor and the low paid was never in dispute, at real issue was their willingness and freedom to act in the interests of these groups. In looking too hard for signs of encouragement and support CPAG had, perhaps, confused the former with the latter.

Similarly, on those occasions when TUC policy or policy statements appeared to resemble those advocated by the Group, CPAG was quick to attribute this to its own influence, despite the strong possibility, given the broad conditions of the social contract, that social security reform was already under close consideration by the TUC's own research

department. Writing to David Lea, Secretary of the
TUC's Economic Department on 8 November, Johnson
remarked 'we were very pleased to see from press
reports that the Economic Committee's recommendations to the Chancellor included in some measure at
least those which we had submitted for your
consideration'. Had there existed an effective
dialogue between the two on low pay, child poverty
and family support, then CPAG would have known
precisely trade union thinking on these issues and
might have been much better placed to establish the
extent of its influence. In the event, any dialogue
had been superficial and fragmented: and any positive
claim to influence was therefore unfounded.

The opportunity to exchange views with the TUC's
Economic Committee finally came on 5 December. The
TUC confirmed its support for the independence of
each union in negotiating separate arrangements on
pay and therefore felt it must reject CPAG proposals
for either a Low Pay Board or a national minimum
wage. Its rejection of their proposals was entirely
consistent with the views consistently expressed by
union leaders and their research staff since CPAG's
inception. On CPAG's hopes of sending regular
'programmes for action', documents and proposals to
the Economic Committee, Lea made it clear that this
would not be possible as the Committee could not
constitutionally consult with other groups. Its
principal responsibility lay in looking after the
interests of its members and any interest in broadly
non-union issues, like family allowances, arose
largely because they were seen as having some effect
on union membership. The Committee's view that union
leaders and research staff would probably welcome the
opportunity to read CPAG material but that formal
consideration of consultative documents and
proposals produced by outside pressure groups was
precluded amounted, in effect, to a brush-off (56).

This is of crucial importance in understanding
both the TUC's role in policy-making and its
relationship with outside interest groups. As the
'peak association' of the trade union movement the
TUC has developed clear lines along which interests
are channelled and policies formulated. Each year,
the delegates' conferences, both of the full TUC, and
of individual unions, produce a number of
resolutions, many of which are concerned with social
policy. The General Council has two key roles - to
act upon resolutions passed and to act independently
as matters arise between these conferences, for
example, as a result of government proposals. Its

principal role, therefore, is 'to represent its own members, there are no structures which are essentially designed for the advancement of pressure-group interests' (57).

The General Council meets every month and is serviced in the area under discussion here by two key committees - the Social Insurance Committee and the Economic Committee. Groups like CPAG may send documents and literature to these committees but a formal relationship is impossible. Matters cannot be raised or submitted for agenda by non-affiliated bodies, although an affiliated organisation can ask General Council to consider submissions made by it. The only way an interest group can get submissions discussed or issues raised is to persuade an affiliated union to do so on its behalf. CPAG continuously sought to do this, without much success, from 1973 both through its staff's membership of a Central London branch of the TGWU and through resolutions put forward by sympathetic trade union branches throughout the country. Part of CPAG's failure to get its resolutions on Conference agenda stems from the fact that such resolutions are either inappropriate for trade union discussion or, more significantly, they are superfluous in the sense that the TUC is invariably kept up-to-date on the issues concerned by its own servicing committees. Indeed, it is probable, as the child benefits campaign shows, that CPAG may be seen as treading on the toes of such committees. Whilst its research findings are usually received with interest, its attempts to galvanise trade union action may be seen as intrusive and unwelcome.

The TUC has rejected any change in procedure to accommodate outside interests because it sees its prime responsibility to its own members most of whom are neither poor, nor have large dependent families. Such political insularity may no longer befit a major corporate interest that is widely viewed as a key 'estate' in the sociopolitical order. Given the views expressed by senior trade unionists that the unions should increasingly move into politics in the same way that the state has chosen to politicise industrial relations, then it is reasonable to expect the labour movement to expose its own views and policies to criticism and discussion by groups who also have an interest in these areas. Not to do so seriously undermines Len Murray's view that the unions have come to recognise and welcome the 'enlargement of politics'.

If the trade union movement is to concern itself

with issues which affect its members outside of the
work place (e.g. unemployment, sickness, the health
service, pensions, single parenthood, sex and race
discrimination, family poverty) then a case can be
made for enlarging the scope of its politics by
lending political muscle to interest groups, long
active in these areas, which often lack the necessary
resources to achieve sustained attention for the
problems of their clients. However, the TUC has
clearly adopted the view that if it allows one such
group to achieve regular consultative status then the
dam is effectively breached for a deluge of others to
follow. As a result, CPAG has not developed a
sustained consultation with the Social Insurance or
Economic Committees. Consultation has been
irregular, ad hoc and superficial, though it is
likely that the Group has been more successful in
getting its views across to the trade union movement
than most other groups (58).

In so far as CPAG had any influence on the TUC
in this period it was generated through contacts with
individual unions and sympathetic union leaders. In
some cases when dealings had taken place with
individual unions it was clear that CPAG had briefed
them beforehand. This had particularly been the case
with the GMWU, NUPE, NALGO, USDAW and, more recently,
CPSA and ASTMS which played useful roles in the child
benefits campaign (1975-7). In addition, there was,
and continues to be in the 1980s, an informal network
of contacts within the trade union movement that has
been useful in disseminating the Group's ideas and in
lobbying on its behalf. There was in this period the
seeds of a more structured relationship with the
trade union movement that has matured particularly
under Ruth Lister's stewardship in the eighties and
which has been accompanied by significant
representation of trade union officers on the CPAG
Executive, joint campaigning and publishing. CPAG
courses for trade unions and the modelling of trade
union internal work on social security and taxation
issues on established CPAG practice.

It is the white-collar unions like SCPS, CPSA,
ASTMS, NALGO, NUPE, ACCT, AUT and the NUT, together
with the GMWU (GMBATU), USDAW and the Garment Workers
that have proved most receptive to CPAG advances.
Probably the reason for this is their greater
expectation of servicing. They expect more
literature and more discussion of policy, place a
greater emphasis on the research side of trade
unionism than do the strictly manual unions (59).
Allied to this - indeed probably its determinant - is

the fact that such unions have better-paid and better-educated workers and higher subscription incomes. Not only is there a greater awareness of social and economic issues, but these unions can afford to research them further. The additional findings of groups like CPAG are therefore welcome and perhaps less subject to prejudice in their interpretation. Accordingly, resistance to new ideas and policy change is less in evidence in this sector.

CPAG quote David Lea who said that the Group 'had considerable influence and effectiveness as a pressure group ... (and) was in line with TUC policy on Family Allowances, wages councils and probably on employment protection ... (he) was anxious to ensure ... (CPAG) had all useful TUC documents and would be pleased to help by supporting them. CPAG reports etc., were valuable and should, where possible, be sent to all his officials at the TUC' (60). Yet the evidence suggests that he was simply showing the usual courtesies. Indeed, his comments also led the Group to conclude: 'In general, we must not be surprised to find TUC documents and policy more sympathetic than CPAG to Government - this was because we were concentrating on particular areas, whereas the TUC must have regard to the whole economy' (61). This points quite clearly to the 'strategy of responsibility' the TUC had been obliged to adopt as part of the terms of the social contract and its dialogue with Labour leaders through the Liaison Committee. It also implied that the TUC would remain very cautious in its dealings with groups not party to that dialogue. The TUC's own insider status depended upon its assumption of a 'strategy of responsibility' and it may well have considered that it was inappropriate and unethical for it to be seen to associate itself or its views too closely with those of CPAG.

Furthermore, it may be that the TUC viewed pressure groups like CPAG as constantly requiring the filip of favourable publicity to draw attention to themselves and their work. The TUC had no such requirement; it had a well-defined role to play in society in general and the economy in particular, and this was recognised and largely accepted by government and public alike. Indeed, as the Parliamentary Under-Secretary for Social Security at the DHSS in 1974 has explained, contact between his Department and the TUC on matters of common interest often bordered on the systematic.

Right through the period I was there Bryan

O'Malley and I spent a lot of time with Peter
Jacques and Terry Parry, representatives of the
TUC Social Insurance Committee. I think that
it's right and proper that if the TUC have a
Committee which is more or less handling the
ground that you as a Minister are handling you
would be foolish not to liaise closely with
them. After all, 11 million people are organised
trade unionists and they are a force to be
reckoned with in the country, they have a
powerful voice and I think it is right that we
ought to listen to the point of view of the TUC
on social questions as, indeed, on every other.
(62)

It may be argued, therefore, that the TUC did
not and does not have to justify its existence or its
activities to quite the same extent as a small
pressure group which only maintains its pressure by
remaining newsworthy. Inevitably, criticism of
government is more likely to attract the attention of
the media and the group's membership (who like to see
their leaders 'doing something') than passive
support of official policy. In contrast, it is
argued, the TUC stands very much on its own and
enjoys institutionalised access to government by
virtue of its well-defined representativity. It does
not need to make waves to attract public or
government attention, and it may be compromised by
its association with those who do.

THE GROUP'S LOBBYING ACTIVITIES

In a review of the Group's lobbying activities in
1974, Frank Field claimed that efforts centred on the
trade union movement had already 'begun to pay
dividends'. In particular, he concluded 'the group
has a right to take some credit for the increase in
family allowances announced in the last Budget.
However inadequate the increase is the group's
lobbying activities have helped to net over £200
million for families in the coming year' (63). While
CPAG had certainly contributed to the climate of
debate in which an increase in family allowances
became acceptable, and remained the only group in
British politics actively campaigning for so long on
this particular issue, the certainty of its claim
could not, of course, be substantiated.

The Group had taken a three-pronged approach to
lobbying. The first centred on the relationship

established by Field (and to a lesser extent Johnson) with individual trade union leaders. The second concerned the dialogue between CPAG staff and full-time officials of the unions and the TUC. The third, was the Group's grass-roots approach to union rank-and-file members conducted, most successfully, by its branches. It was the Director's view that future co-operation with the unions rested on its ability to demonstrate their shared interests. 'Trade union leaders are in business to further the interests of their members as they conceive them, and it is important for us to show, wherever we can, the link in interests between the poor and the rest of the working community. (64)' He also noted the particular role he believed the unions expected CPAG to play: 'none of the trade unions expects us to become an appendage of the labour movement. They think we are far more valuable as an independent organisation even though this gives us the right to criticise the trade union movement' (65).

In explaining the rationale of the Group's recent correspondence and meetings with the Economic and Social Policy Secretariat of the TUC, Field added that he and Johnson had 'been attempting to find out how decisions are made and priorities arrived at, at Congress House'. This initiative was, quite clearly, long overdue and it is surprising that greater efforts were not made in the period 1970-1 to discover that 'although individual trade union groups can get particular issues raised on the agenda of relevant committees at the TUC, not surprisingly most of the power lies in the hands of full-time officials' (66). Although his own observations bore out the TUC's reluctance to allow direct lobbying, Field remained convinced that 'they are influenced by our published material and the coverage we get in the media' (67).

If the information, knowledge and contacts acquired in this period were to be of any use in furthering the Group's aims, Field felt they must be employed within the framework of a fresh strategy to enlist more permanent union support. He identified a number of issues where this might be done. They included increasing national insurance and means-tested benefits; the extension of the family allowance to the first child; inequality at work; discrimination against the non-industrially injured; and public expenditure cuts. The key factor in enlisting union support lay in demonstrating the manner in which these issues affected both trade unionists, and non-trade unionists. Given the

unions' frequent insistence that their first duty was
to their members, Field felt that it would be
difficult for them not to act. The additional value
of that action would lie in CPAG's selection of
issues where union support would also bring about
benefits to non-trade unionists. Publics that were
largely unorganised or poorly organised, such as the
poor, single parents, the handicapped and the
consumer would now benefit, he hoped, from the
efforts of the unions because union members could
also be found among the underprivileged groups
identified.

The case of the long-term unemployed
illustrated this. Field claimed:

> we will be able to show that trade union members
> who remain unemployed for any length of time
> become disenfranchised in respect of National
> Insurance benefits. Hopefully this will allow
> us to mobilise trade union support not only for
> the extension of insurance benefits for the
> unemployed, but to those other groups who are at
> present excluded. We must also attempt to get
> the trade unions to campaign for an abolition of
> the discrimination against the unemployed in
> our Social Security System, such as the wage-
> stop, as well as the need of higher national
> insurance benefits. (68)

It was politic, as Sir John Walley had advised
earlier, for the Group, where possible, to adapt its
demands to previously stated union policy. (This may
also have provided the opportunity for the Group, on
occasion, to claim subsequently to have influenced
union policy.) In the past, for example, CPAG had
been in favour of the extension of legal aid to
Supplementary Benefit Appeals Tribunals so that
claimants could be assisted in the defence or
articulation of their case. However, subsequent
research by the Group revealed that the vast majority
of unions were opposed to this overtly 'legal'
approach and favoured, instead, the proper training
of trade union representatives as the best means of
ensuring that the interests of those appealing were
properly considered. As Bosanquet noted 'people
don't understand that the unions have a very definite
business, a very definite set of issues to do with
wages, earning levels, relativities, composition of
pay etc. and this is a tremendously absorbing thing
for them. If somehow you can't gear in what you do to
their consuming interest you are going to be treated

a bit like an outside maverick, an optional extra'
(69).

Thus, on the issue of discrimination against the
non-industrially injured, Field commented: 'At
present, the trade unions favour discriminating in
favour of those claimants who have been industrially
injured at work. It is very important for us to be
able to show that many people's disability results
from accidents at work, but are not officially
recorded as such' (70).

In early January 1975 the opportunity arose
again for CPAG to meet with staff of the TUC's Social
Insurance and Industrial Welfare Committee,
including Peter Jacques the Secretary and his
assistant, Trevor Mawer. The occasion provided the
opportunity for discussion on some of the issues
Field had identified as priorities for the Group. On
national insurance benefits, for example, there was
TUC support for the CPAG view that reform and
extension of the principle were necessary (71). The
TUC recognised the attractions of occupational
pension schemes, but agreed with CPAG that in the
long term these had been responsible for the low
level of the state pension scheme. On the issue of
support for the non-industrially injured the TUC
recommended that the terms of reference for
industrial injuries benefits should be revised and
that provision be made to include, as CPAG had
favoured, diseases resulting from industrial
processes.

Jacques saw reform 'as widening the
possibilities of collective bargaining over wage
rates to sick and disabled with Government support,
rather than a special hardship allowance' (72). In
doing so he was breaking with the traditional
compartmentalisation of social policy and collective
bargaining and advocating the use of unions'
bargaining power to achieve social reform - a
mellowing in approach since the debates on the
'poverty trap'. More broadly, it set the tone for a
more overtly political role for the trade union
movement in the period 1975-8, when both the union
movement and CPAG channelled their energies into the
child benefit campaign. This campaign brought full
circle ten years of CPAG efforts in the family
allowance field and brought it once more into
conflict with a Labour government procrastinating on
an issue for which it had already stated its firm
support.

By the mid-70s CPAG could point to a well
established informal relationship with individual

trade unions and the TUC cemented by the participation and involvement of its own leaders in the policy-making structures of the Labour Party and through frequent visits to Congress House where the 'potentialities' of CPAG initiatives were talked through and assessed. There had been instances, too, of speeches by trade union leaders being drafted by Peter Townsend and other senior CPAG figures. In Townsend's own view ... "It would be a mistake to suppose that these continuous, if mainly indirect, contacts had less influence than the more formal public overtures of later years".

The Child Benefit Campaign, to which we now move, illustrates both how these informal relationships were valuable in the groups work and how the basis for a more structured involvement with the trade union movement was futher developed.

NOTES

1. Director's Report (June 1972), p.9.
2. See Johnson, M. and Rowland M., Fuel Debts and the Poor, Poverty Pamphlet No. 24 (1976) p.18
3. Director's Report (June 1972).
4. Interview with Jonathan Bradshaw, 2 November 1978.
5. Director's Report (June 1972).
6. Rose, H. Rights, Participation and Conflict, Poverty Pamphlet No. 4.
7. Ibid.
8. Interview with Jonathan Bradshaw, 2 November 1978.
9. Ibid.
10. Field had been under considerable pressure to raise the Group's strategy in the wake of two critical papers, Future CPAG Policy and Strategy and Poverty and Unemployment, produced by Malcolm Wicks and Adrian Sinfield respectively. Both felt that CPAG had, thus far, been much too selective in its choice of which issues to control and had unnecessarily narrowed the poverty debate to a small number of publics which made up the 'very poorest' rather than the 'broad poor'. Both argued that this had caused an under-utilisation of resources (i.e. media coverage, money, manpower) and that narrow concentration on the very poorest inevitably isolated them from the broader issues of poverty where they shared problems with much larger publics. Sinfield cited unemployment as an issue on which the Group should do more work. In a rejoinder Field had persuaded the

executive that CPAG's resources and structure
necessitated a narrow approach; that a single-issue
campaign was ideal for a group of CPAG's type, had so
far proved relatively successful and that he was to
take up the issue of broader co-operation with other
publics anyway in his proposals for trade union
liaison.

11. Report to the Executive on the CPAG/CRO
Attendance at the Policital Party Conferences
(1972).

12. It is interesting to note that Basnett has
traditionally placed great emphasis on trade union
research and the wider education of his members. His
own roots lay in trade union research and he welcomed
the flow of information from CPAG on social security
matters as a valuable contribution to his union's
strong research orientation. Innis MacBeath notes
that one of Mr Basnett's jobs was as NUGMW Education
Officer, when he not only pushed ahead with a large
programme of membership education but had a leading
share in giving the NUGMW the best funded and most
professional research department in the movement.
MacBeath, I. Cloth Cap and After (George, Allen &
Unwin, 1973), p.190.

13. See Taylor, op.cit., pp.244-6.

14. Quoted ibid., p.245.

15. Low Pay Unit, Trade Unions and Taxation
(1976).

16. Taylor, op.cit., p.245. For a lengthy
discussion of this topic, see Dorfman, G., Wage
Politics in Britain 1945-67 (Charles Knight, 1974).

17. Summary of Oral Evidence Given by CPAG to
the Committee on Voluntary Organisations (9 December
1975) p.3. Similarly, Frank Field wrote to Len Murray
of the TUC on 22 January 1974: 'over recent years the
CPAG have tried to strengthen its links with the
trade union movement. We have tried to do this by
providing information which trade unions could find
useful in wage negotiations and also supplying
individual members with data when they are going on
official delegations'.

18. Nowhere had the importance of these issues
been better demonstrated than in the Conservative's
Social Security Bill, an adjunct to the Industrial
Relations Bill, introduced by Keith Joseph in
June/July 1971. The Bill abolished the traditional
first three days of benefit for those unemployed, ill
or injured for two weeks or more. In doing so the
government saved a miserly £19 million which
contrasted rather starkly with the massive handouts
returned to surtax-payers at this time. The Act also

included provisions which cut social security to the
wives and families of those on strike. The government
also abolished unemployment pay for the first six
days if workers were on short-time working. In all,
the Act constituted one of the most serious attacks
to date on social insurance and gave considerable
substance to the arguments advanced by CPAG for trade
union involvement and education in social benefits
and welfare rights. In this light one of the Group's
trade union liaison officer's first tasks was to send
copies of CPAG's pamphlet, The Unemployed Workers and
Strikers Guide to Social Securities, to all unions.
    19. Streather and Weir, Report to the
Executive on the CPAG/CRO Attendance at the Political
Party Conferences (1972).
    20. See Potter, op.cit., p.308; Duff, P.,
Left, Left, Left (Allison & Busby, 1971), p.185.
    21. Minkin, L., The Labour Party Conference
(Allen Lane, 1978), pp.41-2.
    22. Ibid., p.42.
    23. Ibid., p.370.
    24. Interview with Jane Streather, 25 January
1980.
    25. Minkin, op.cit., p.406.
    26. CPAG and the Labour Party Conference 1973,
p.1.
    27. Ibid.
    28. Ibid., p.2.
    29. Ibid.
    30. Ibid.
    31. Tables adapted from CPAG and the Labour
Party Conference 1973, pp.2-4.
    32. Ibid.
    33. Ibid.
    34. Haringey Poverty Action Group, untitled, 2
September 1974.
    35. It is interesting to note a similar
development in the autumn of 1979. Early in September
the NUT published a pamphlet, The Case Against the
Cuts which argued that Conservative cuts in education
had failed to yield the benefits claimed and that the
education system, having sustained cuts of £1.5
billion over the previous six years, could not cope
with further cash withdrawals. The pamphlet
signalled the start of a campaign which was joined by
CPAG and the Advisory Centre for Education. Together
they were described as 'taking on the issue of the
proposed end of statutory services such as school
meals, milk and transport; providing information on
how the cuts are hurting and how to fight them at
local level'. 'Wasting the Talents of 30,000 Young

People', New Statesman (31 August 1979).

36. CPAG press release, Poverty Lobby at the TUC (4 September 1974). Earlier in the year the Group had announced: 'CPAG, along with other concerned groups, is mounting a big campaign this Autumn to press for Family Allowances for the first child as a Budget 1975 measure and an interim increase in existing family allowance to a minimum of £250. As part of this campaign, it will be urging the 70-odd CPAG branches to get together with local union branches, seeking support for resolutions at the political party conferences, and the TUC. If unions are ready to act in support of wider social policy issues such as abolishing the 44 means-tested benefits in favour of universal measures such as FAM they will make good the hopes implicit in the Social Contract - and with the example of the TGWU's splendid stand on the pensions issue, CPAG feels confident of national support for a benefit just as closely linked to the long-term solution of the problem of poverty'. Child Poverty Looks to the Unions (July 1974).

37. Ibid.

38. Marigold Johnson to author (26 July 1977).

39. See for example, 'The Work of CPAG', Electrical Power Engineer, Vol. 56, No. 11 (November 1974) and 'CPAG Strengthens Ties with Trade Union Movement', Social Services (6 July 1974).

40. 6 July 1974.

41. What Are We Here for Brothers? transcript of Radio 4 Analysis (13 June 1974), p.14.

42. Finer, S.E., 'The Political Power of Organised Labour', Government & Opposition.

43. Marigold Johnson to author (26 July 1977).

44. Executive Committee Minutes (5 July 1974).

45. Report of the 90th Annual TUC Conference (1964), pp.164-6.

46. Poverty No. 10 (Spring 1969), p.12.

47. Executive Committee Minutes (5 July 1974).

48. Support for increases in family support had been forthcoming from the TUC, but the problem of verbal assurances of support and good intent being transformed into sustained political action remained. See TUC, Economic Review (1970), p.59.

49. Johnson to Tyler (5 September 1974).

50. Lord Allen to Johnson (16 September 1974). An interesting observation on this personalised approach to winning union support has been made by Bradshaw, who notes, 'It wasn't working with the unions as a mass body but working with key union leaders and getting them to attach their names to

memoranda and getting (later) the TUC Economic Committee to sponsor child benefits in their reports. It was never trying to mobilise the trade union movement. It was a very tacit type of support.' Interview, 2 November 1978.

51. Johnson to TUC, 23 September 1974.
52. Ibid.
53. Johnson to Len Murray, 17 October 1974.
54. Ibid., 29 October 1974.
55. Executive Committee Minutes (25 October 1974).
56. Minutes of the CPAG-TUC Economic Committee Meeting (6 December 1974).
57. Interview with Trevor Mawer, Assistant Secretary to the TUC's Social Insurance Department, 31 May 1979.
58. Bosanquet comments of CPAG, 'they never won the affection nor, I think, the confidence of the trade union movement, but on the other hand they didn't get seen as a totally hostile force by the trade union movement and that is important'. Interview, 22 February 1979.
59. See Lapping and Radice, op.cit., pp. 46-54.
60. Minutes of CPAG-TUC Economic Committee Meeting (6 December 1974).
61. Ibid.
62. Interview with Bob Brown, former Minister of Social Security, 20 February 1979.
63. Field, F. The Group's Lobbying Activities (December 1974). He added: 'For the last 4 years we have witnessed a major shift in power from the Executive to the Trade Union movement and the group's various lobbying activities reflect this change'.
64. Ibid.
65. Ibid.
66. Ibid.
67. Ibid.
68. Ibid., p.3.
69. Interview, 22 February 1979.
70. The Group's Lobbying Activities, p.4.
71. It was agreed by CPAG and staff of the TUC Social Insurance Committee that three major reforms were essential in this area: (a) to review disability allowances so that fewer depend on supplementary benefits and take-up is up to the rate suggested by, for example, attendance allowance, claims; (b) to review the earnings-related principle - it was 'repulsive' to insist on a six monthly renewal of assessment. Earnings-related benefits 'perpetuate inequalities' in the view of the TUC; and (c)

sickness benefits - the TUC would support extension to those now excluded. Memorandum of Meeting at Congress House (10 January 1975).
    72. Ibid.

Chapter Eleven

CPAG AND THE LABOUR MOVEMENT
1974-9 - THE CASE OF CHILD BENEFITS

The child benefit scheme, which figured so
prominently in discussion of British social policy
between 1974 and 1978, rested on the need for a
merger of child tax relief and the family allowance
and the transfer of that relief from the wage-earning
father to the mother in the form of an over-the-
counter payment. In a 1969 pamphlet, Labour's Social
Strategy, the Labour Party had set out proposals for
what later became its child endowment scheme. In 1972
the Conservatives developed the theme in a Green
Paper advocating the idea of a child credit within
the framework of its overall tax credit scheme (1).
The trade union movement, too, had registered its
support for the introduction of a child benefit
payable to the mother in evidence to the Select
Committee on Tax Credits set up by the Conservatives.
This position was endorsed further in the TUC's
Economic Review of 1974 and, in May of the same year,
the final seal of approval was given by the
TUC-Labour Party Liaison Committee in a statement on
family poverty which read 'It is of the utmost
importance that the new Child Benefit Scheme to be
introduced next year provides benefits generous
enough to represent a determined and concerted attack
on the problem'. This concern was echoed in the
Labour Party manifesto of October 1974 which promised
'The Labour Government will attack family poverty by
increasing family allowances and extending them to
the first child through a new scheme of child credits
payable to the mother'.
    The Conservative Party, too, was committed to
its introduction as a first stage in its own proposal
for a tax credit scheme. By October 1974, then, there
appeared to exist a positive and encouraging
consensus between CPAG, the political parties, the
trade union movement and what might be broadly termed

the 'family lobby' in favour of early action on family allowance reform.

THE FAMILY ALLOWANCE MOVEMENT

An early initiative was not to materialise, however. The Labour government announced that it could not introduce the new scheme until April 1976 because of administrative and legislative difficulties. The response of the family lobby was to cohere briefly and ineffectually under the coordination of an umbrella body, the Family Allowance Movement, launched by a study group convened by the British Union of Family Organisations, whose participants included CPAG, Gingerbread, the National Council for Social Services, the National Council for One Parent Families, the Confederation of Parent-Teacher Associations and the Mothers Union.

While action on family allowances for the first child remained the key goal of FAM, their broader complaint was that 'no Government has accepted the urgency for direct action to help families during a period of rapid increases in the cost of living' (2). On 16 July 1974 a delegation visited Barbara Castle, Secretary of State for Health and Social Security, with the aim of securing a commitment to an immediate extension of family allowance to the first child: their target date was April 1975. However, Castle reiterated that while the newly-elected government did regard action on this issue as a priority, legislative and administrative problems still precluded any extension of existing provision before April 1976.

From FAM's viewpoint the case for an early, improved family allowance system was threefold. Family allowances had not been increased since 1968 and since then inflation had seriously undermined the subsistence character of family support. In addition, the frustration and sense of deprivation felt by those with families was further fuelled by changes in fiscal and taxation policy which had increasingly transferred spending power towards the single and the childless. Secondly, a rise in the level of food prices in 1974 over 1973 had caused a decline in nutritional standards resulting from this failure to keep family allowances at a realistic level. These developments were now further compounded by Labour's procrastination over 'administrative problems' and the likely serious effects upon the 7 million first or only children in

Britain. Few within the family lobby could forget that Labour had made similar promises about early action on family support in 1964 and had then delayed for four more years.

CPAG, embarking on the tenth year of its own campaign for improved family support, and very much the central force in the child benefits episode, drew attention to the perils of delay and stressed the importance of early action:

> There are fourteen million children in this country. The responsibility for the welfare of those fourteen million falls on a minority of the population. At the present time 81 per cent of children are to be found in a quarter of all households. The child benefit scheme would help to spread more fairly over the whole population the burden of rearing children. Child Benefit would simplify and unify the system of income support for children. (3)

Clearly, CPAG saw FAM as a useful, broadly-based vehicle for harnessing the type of massive grass-roots support for extension that it could not have achieved alone. FAM was not, however, destined to play a critical or long-term role, and broke up shortly after its inception with each of its constituent organisations choosing to tackle the issue in its own way. In addition to proving a rather unmanageable body, participation in FAM was not consistent with CPAG's traditional and highly individual approach to family support. CPAG had long considered itself the best equipped and most experienced campaigning group of its type, and its overriding concern with the issue of family allowances may have been at variance with the goals of other less experienced and less political participants for whom the issue of family allowances or child benefits was, more usually, of secondary importance. Participation in umbrella bodies invariably requires a trade-off or compromise in the views of the participants in order that an agreed policy can emerge. It is not clear that CPAG felt it necessary, or was prepared, to make such a compromise. Ultimately, the Group seems to have concluded that it could best serve the cause for higher benefits by acting independently.

The break-up of FAM, one of the relatively few attempts to bring together the disparate strands of the family lobby, was all the more discouraging because CPAG's own campaign to force union leaders to take action on the issue of family support was waning and, although both party manifestos referred to the scheme in the October General Election, the Group failed to make it a platform issue for candidates. Indeed, it may well have seemed by the end of 1974 that interest in the issue had subsided. Unknown to the child benefit campaigners Barbara Castle had, for example, already failed on two occasions in 1974 to persuade her senior Cabinet colleagues to establish an Anti-Poverty Strategy Committee. We now learn from the 6th January 1975 entry in her diaries that Castle had already agreed to a postponement of the full child allowance scheme until 1977. With the prospect of a deferred scheme there was also a muted attempt at the meeting of the Cabinet's Legislation Committee on 14 January to exclude Castle's Child Benefit Bill from the programme for the new parliamentary session. By early March, however, the commitment to a scheme of some sort had stabilised, but only on the proviso that April 1977 would be the agreed starting-point, with an undertaking to extend family allowances to the first child in one-parent families in 1976. A week later the Bill had received the final nod of approval from the Legislation Committee. On 28 April Castle called a press conference to explain the delay in commencement of the child benefit scheme and to elaborate the Cabinet's proposals. She was to comment later that the conference had gone off 'remarkably smoothly' and agreed that she had been let off lightly by the lobby. A year later, as we shall see, even this compromise scheme was under threat of abandonment.

REACHING THE STATUTE BOOK

In the meantime, to assure its critics that its commitment to the scheme was firm, the Labour government moved quickly to submit the Child Benefits Bill for its second reading on 13 May 1975. Opening the debate, Castle described the Bill as achieving

> a long overdue merger between child tax allowances and family allowances into a new universal, non-means-tested, tax-free cash benefit for all children, including the first, payable to the mother. In this way it ensures that the national provision for family support is concentrated first and foremost where it is needed most - on the poorest families; and that it goes to the person responsible for caring for

the children and managing the budget for their food, clothing and other necessities. (4)

The introduction of the Bill at this point amid controversy about the timing of the scheme took many within the family lobby, including CPAG, by surprise and shows the difficulties pressure groups which lack advance intelligence may have in both accurately perceiving political or administrative developments and subsequently responding to them effectively. CPAG were now obliged to put together a hurried briefing note for MPs involved in the Committee stage and a belated set of proposed amendments. The Group's efforts at self-assurance (5) did little to mask the fact that all their amendments were unsuccessful. The passage of the Bill became all the more curious for the fact that Labour backbenchers were themselves reluctant to vote against the government even on the amendments they themselves had put down. The most important amendment suggested by CPAG was for the inclusion of specific target dates for commencement of the scheme. This the government refused to do.

The Child Benefit Act of August 1975 proposed the replacement of the existing system of family allowances and child tax allowances with a single child benefit payable for each child, including the first. The government had hoped to introduce the scheme by 1976 after stating that administrative and legislative problems would preclude action in 1975. The government now sought to use a similar excuse for postponing the scheme's introduction until April 1977. For the interim, Ministers offered a stop-gap measure to aid single parents by the introduction of a Child Interim Benefit of £1.50 a week for their first child (6). Observers could have been forgiven for viewing this as a prelude to total abandonment of the scheme. Between August 1975 and May 1976 CPAG continued to press the case for improved family allowances and child tax allowances prior to introduction of the new scheme (7). In May 1976, however, the Labour government confirmed the growing suspicion that the scheme was to be axed and offered only the vaguest of hopes for any future introduction.

THE ABANDONMENT OF CHILD BENEFITS

For CPAG the implications of abandonment were clear. Not only had a key family support scheme fallen by the wayside but so too had a scheme which was paramount to Labour's overall social policy strategy. CPAG voiced the general concern: 'In deciding to shelve the Child Benefit Scheme the Cabinet have abandoned the kernel of their policy for family support and a reform which stood beside the new pension as the principal social reform of the present Parliament' (8). This apparent correlation between the pension scheme and family support was to prove an important factor in mobilising support for the scheme's restoration.

The fierce reaction of the family lobby to what was seen once more as a cynical sacrificing of the poor and those with dependent families upon the altar of national interest was shared by Barbara Castle who described it as 'the eruption of a growing anger at the stubborn masculine bias of British politics. It is an expression of despair at the failure of the Government's political will to create a more equal society' (9). Charges of 'stubborn masculine bias' may well have been accurate, though members of the Labour government were keen to shift responsibility for it to the trade unions, the co-architects of the much-vaunted social contract. Joel Barnett, for example, a central figure in the Cabinet discussions on child benefits, has since taken particular pains to lay the blame for procrastination and phased delivery elsewhere. Of the Cabinet wrangles he recalls that

> To our surprise when we first discussed our disagreement of the cost in Cabinet, we found that it had just not been appreciated that our child benefit policy meant a reduction in child tax allowances. Neither Jim Callaghan ... nor Dennis Healey, had fully taken the point on board. When they did they became nervous and suggested that we had better talk to the union leaders in the TUC. They too (or some of them) had not appreciated the consequences of the policy they nominally supported. On reflection, the TUC exhibited its male chauvinist bias by drawing back. Instead of an immediate transfer from the father, it now favoured a phasing over three annual stages. When this was eventually announced, we could not blame it on the TUC and they would not accept responsiblity openly. (10)

What the former Chief Secretary to the Cabinet does not establish is the extent, if any, to which the government, and his Department in particular, manoeuvred trade union leaders into fearing the consequences of the policy and accepting the need for a phased introduction of the scheme. We consider such a view shortly. In the meantime it is also worth noting Barnett's view of Barbara Castle's reaction:

> The consequence was that Barbara Castle ... blamed the Government in general, and David Ennals and me in particular. Some time later, at a joint meeting, Terry Parry, the TUC spokesman on child benefits, conceded what I had been telling Barbara for some time, but she still found it hard to accept that the blame lay anywhere other than with the Government. In a sense it was true, for we could have made the immediate transfer from 'wallet to purse', but in her heart I am sure Barbara knew we could not practically have gone ahead against the outright opposition of the TUC. (11)

Castle's own frustration, like that of CPAG, was further fuelled by the trade union factor - the knowledge that the scheme had been abandoned in the wake of a long, painful but ultimately successful process of persuading the trade unions of the importance of social policy to their members and of the need for them to act in the political arena to secure social justice. 'The tragedy of the Government's retreat from the legislation on child benefit ... is that it comes at the moment when the trade union movement has been converted to the understanding that old style collective bargaining will not change society. It must comprise social, as well as economic aims. (12)'

There was some evidence to support this view. Already in the early 1970s Jack Jones had taken an important initiative on state retirement pensions and had been successful in extending his union's bargaining remit to include consideration of the economic well-being of pensioners. In doing so he had created a precedent upon which other unions and the TUC could build. The potential of the trade union movement in infuencing social policy had not simply caught the imagination of those like Castle anxious to harness political muscle to the claims of the weak client groups served by her Department or those union leaders increasingly aware of the need to develop a 'strategy of responsibility' - a societal policy that would shift trade union interests from the purely defensive and reactive representation of the 'fragmented man' to a concern for the well-being of the 'whole man' (13). This theme and the importance of developing it had also been recognised by CPAG.

In this light, it is interesting that as late as April 1976, a matter of weeks before the government's abandonment of the original child benefit scheme, Jack Jones still felt confident enough to write:

> The Government has promised the new Child Benefit will become payable for all families next April. Very shortly, therefore, it will be putting the final touches to this scheme. One of the most important remaining decisions is the level at which child benefit will be set ... Government is about to decide on the living standards of the nations 14 million children, and the trade union movement will be watching the outcome with considerable interest. (14)

Jones' comments raise once more the importance of advance intelligence. Here was a leading figure in the trade union movement and a senior member of the Liaison Committee under the firm impression, on the eve of the policy reversal, that the child benefit scheme was proceeding unimpeded. Clearly the government was either not prepared to take the trade union movement into its confidence on this decision (which has interesting implications for the validity of the social contract and for the TUC's status as an insider group) or its decision to abandon the scheme was a last-minute one.

The other obvious explanation for this apparent snub, and it seems in retrospect the more realistc one, is that the government intended to introduce another and more demanding phase of wage restraint and the implications of a transfer from wallet to purse at this stage were too much to bear for both Treasury ministers and 'spending ministers', who saw in the scheme a threat to their own claims for resources. For the government to have announced its true intention at an earlier date might have aroused trade union suspicion of the severity of the next stage of pay policy and allowed time for the mobilisation of strong, sustained opposition. Even so, it would seem from Castle's comments and from trade union pledges of support for the family, that the government seriously misjudged the unions' mood on this issue.

THE ROLE OF JAMES CALLAGHAN

The personality of the new Prime Minister must also be seen as a major factor in the decision to abandon, at least temporarily, the child benefit scheme. There is some case for arguing that Harold Wilson deliberately passed the buck on child benefits to his successor, James Callaghan, rather than risk a delay in his resignation as Prime Minister. The very nature of the switch from child tax allowances to child benefits ran against the grain of orthodox Treasury thinking and was thus likely to make the issue both complex and antagonistic. A central obstacle then was

> the ruling Treasury convention that cash payments like child benefits counted as public expenditure while the loss of revenue from child tax allowances did not. This meant that some of the public expenditure 'cost' of the scheme, which was to come from the contingency reserve, represented the conversion of tax reliefs into child benefit, so it seemed greater than it was. (15)

This detracts, however, from the major role played by Callaghan himself. Callaghan's reputation on social policy was not likely to instil confidence in those pressing for reform. His attitude to increases in family support while Chancellor in the 1960s had been grudging. He had even attempted to go against the grain of Party policy in 1967 with a proposal for a means-tested family benefit.

Keith Banting has noted that in the 1960s social scientists and interest-groups, in the course of advancing new ideas and policies ... 'had far greater influence with the intellectual politicans in the Labour Cabinet, such as Crossman, Crosland and Jenkins, than with others such as Callaghan' (16). As Prime Minister, Callaghan seems to have assumed, as he had in the 1960s, that increases in family support were still unpopular, particularly during a period when wage-earners were being asked to restrain their wage demands. Banting's view that 'Callaghan had shrewd political instincts, and by 1967-68 he was increasingly convinced of one overriding point: as Labour's problems continued to grow, and their popular support to decline, they could not go on antagonising their political base, the manual working class' (17) seems to have held as true between 1976-8 as it did ten years earlier.

More significantly, as Chancellor, Callaghan

had aimed at a regeneration of industrial investment to counter low growth and poor export performance. To do this, he had favoured a restriction in private consumption or public expenditure. His view was that those without dependent families, those in full-time employment, and especially the skilled-manual and middle-income groups 'were unwilling to sacrifice their standard of living so that social security could be improved' (18). Callaghan, Healey and a majority of the Labour Cabinet appear to have sustained this view throughout 1976-9, particularly in their subscription to the view that public expenditure had impeded prospects for economic growth. Child benefits, inevitably, became part of the Callaghan government's 'programme of restraint' (19), and was borne out in the government's economic reasoning.

Before the April 1975 Budget the child tax allowance for a child under the age of eleven, the only child eligible, was £240 per annum – the equivalent of £2.35 a week net of the tax on family allowance. According to Castle, the rate of child benefit needed to ensure that subsequent children received as much help as they did then through tax relief and family allowance was £2.24 per week. In the two-child family the mother would therefore receive £4.48 (her family allowance was £1.50). The father would lose £2.34 from his pay but, overall, the family would gain a moderate increase in support through the extension of the benefit to the first child. This 'bonus' was, however, hardly sufficient to encourage the trade unions to give the scheme their wholehearted support, so Castle had attempted to improve it beyond its apparent break-even level. In doing so she met, as her predecessor Peggy Herbison had done in the 1960s, with concerted political opposition from Cabinet colleagues who sought to utilise the resources of the government's contingency fund, from which the scheme was to be funded, for their own ends. She comments, 'obviously a higher rate than the break-even one was desirable in order to make the whole process more palatable. It was about this that I was arguing with the Treasury when I was removed from office' (20).

Immediately prior to this, the Chancellor, Dennis Healey had announced his plan to increase the child tax allowance to £300, at a cost of some £300 million. Castle's initial reaction was favourable: 'It seemed good news at first. A higher tax allowance automatically jacked up the level of child benefit. But it also jacked up the cost in public expenditure.

In my innocence I did not see how the argument was developing' (21). The break-even rate now rose to £2.64. In a two-child family the father would lose £3.16 from his pay and the mother's cash over the counter would raise to £5.28. The overall rise in income would be 62p and the overall cost about £110 million. This provided the room for manoeuvre that both Callaghan and Healey had been seeking: 'at that price, the argument now ran ... the gain to the family - the sweetener for the switch - was not big enough to enable us to sell the loss of take-home pay to the wage-earner. And no doubt, spending Ministers ... were only too ready to listen to the argument that a figure of £110 million was too high and that cheaper solutions could be found' (22). Of additional significance was the treatment meted out by the government to the unions. If little else, the manner in which abandonment took place, without apparent consultation, did at least guarantee trade union reaction to restore pride and purge embarrassment. Castle invited them to react firmly: 'All we are left with is David Ennals' vague statement that the government intends to bring the scheme in "in time". And there are some red faces in the TUC. Perhaps the trade unions will not take their discomfiture lying down' (23).

THE CABINET LEAK

The speculation which surrounded the reasons for the government's decision to abandon child benefits and the extent of union involvement in that decision was to end, somewhat dramatically, only two weeks after Castle had offered her own analysis of the debacle. On 17 June 1976 New Society, in an article perhaps unprecedented in the recent history of social policy, published a detailed account of the Cabinet's volte-face on child benefits based upon classified information, including secret Cabinet minutes, leaked to Frank Field, by an undisclosed source.

The disclosure began on 8 April 1976, a few days after Callaghan succeded Wilson as Prime Minister. On that day, David Ennals took over from Barbara Castle at the DHSS and promptly informed his Cabinet colleagues that family support was now below the level of provision under both the Heath government of 1970-2 and even that of the Wilson government in the late 1960s. The increase in child tax allowances in the Budget two days earlier had only restored support to its 1974 level, and was still markedly below that of 1971. Ennals advised the Cabinet that to restore the support for a three-child family to the level it had been under the Conservatives in 1971 would require a child benefit of £2.90. The Chancellor's counter-proposal, however, amounted to only £2.50 per week plus a 50p premium payable only to the children of single parents and to those families with larger numbers of children. The Treasury scheme was rejected by Ennals in a second memorandum to the Cabinet on 4 May 1976. He argued that the Treasury scheme would mean that almost all two-parent families with more than one child would be worse off in real terms by April 1977 than they were in April 1976, and repeated that to reduce expenditure in real terms on family support would be seen by many as a confidence trick.

By 29 April the role of the TUC had also become clear. Field revealed that the Cabinet minutes of 29 April recorded Ennals as saying that failure to increase the real level of support for families would add to the difficulties in negotiating pay policy with the TUC and would be likely to stiffen their opposition to the phasing-out of food subsidies - part of the programme of restraint described earlier. He went on to note: 'It was at this Cabinet meeting that members began to discuss the effects of withdrawing child tax allowances on the negotiations for stage 3 of incomes policy. The Cabinet concluded that it might be best to postpone the child benefit if the funds were not available to pay an acceptable rate' (24).

Concerned that the government would be accused of bad faith (and perhaps that the morale of his own Department would suffer at the hands of the Treasury once again) Ennals now presented new administrative and financial arguments why the scheme should not be abandoned. The DHSS, he recalled, had already argued that £2.70 child benefit was the lowest desirable rate and that £2.65 was the lowest flat rate which would ensure that no family was made worse off in cash terms. The cost of the latter was estimated at £160 million a year plus a further £45 million for overseas dependants.

At the same meeting memoranda were also presented by the Chancellor and his Chief Secretary, Joel Barnett. Both restated the view that a basic rate of £2.45 plus a 50p premium would give a cash filip to all families and a real gain to families with one child, to one-parent families with one child, and to one-parent families generally. Significantly Healey pointed out that there was no

commitment to maintain child benefits in line with
inflation, as Ennals had assumed in his previous
memorandum. Moreover, since he believed that only 7
per cent of families drawing family allowances were
poor, the Chancellor argued that the use of premium
payments was a more cost-effective means of reducing
poverty.

Field charged that after this Cabinet meeting of
4 May the Prime Minister 'began working behind the
scenes' (25). At the next Cabinet meeting 6 May,
Callaghan claimed to have received an 'excellent
report' from the Party's Whips that had caused him to
re-think the political wisdom of introducing the
child benefit scheme. The Chief Whip, Michael Cocks,
reported that after sounding out opinion he had
concluded that the introduction of child benefits in
April 1977 would have what Field termed 'grave
political consequences which had not been foreseen
when the Bill went through the House of Commons'
(26). Field revealed that in the ensuing discussion
Ministers believed that the distribution effects of
child benefit could not be 'sold' to the public
before the scheme was introduced in April 1977. 'In
summing up, the Prime Minister commented that to
defer the scheme would also require careful public
presentation. The two Cabinet meetings of the 4th and
6th of May had scuttled the child benefit policy.
(27)'

It was after this second meeting that the trade
union factor in the child benefit equation came to
dominate Cabinet thinking. A major consideration was
how best to prepare the public for abandonment of the
scheme, a subject all the more sensitive because of
the prominence of family support in Labour's last two
manifestos, and because a commitment to improvement
was already on the Statute Book. The subsequent
discussions and the Cabinet's room for manoeuvre were
now undermined by a series of 'leaks' to the press.
These leaks produced what the source presumably hoped
for - the intervention of those trade union leaders
who had earlier stated their commitment to the
scheme. On 24 May they successfully forced the
government's hand at a meeting of the TUC-Labour
Party Liaison Committee. The government's position
was tenuous enough to oblige it to endorse a
statement which read 'It is of the utmost importance
that the new child benefit, to be introduced next
year, provides benefit generous enough to represent a
determined and concerted attack on the problem (of
poverty)' (28).

However, perhaps the most interesting of

Field's disclosures was that the full trade union delegation at that meeting were not aware that a small group within their ranks, the trade union caucus on the NEDC, were to meet with senior Ministers, including the Chancellor, later in the day. At the Cabinet meeting next day the Chancellor reported that the TUC had been asked, at this private session, to agree to a postponement of the child benefit scheme for three years because of the effect the loss of child tax allowances would have on take-home pay. Field quoted the Cabinet minutes directly: 'On being informed of the reduction in take-home pay, which the child benefits scheme would involve, the TUC representatives had reacted immediately and violently against its implementation, irrespective of the level of benefits which would accompany the reduction in take-home pay' (29). TUC leaders and Ministers both resisted any cut in child tax allowances, since this would look like a reversal of the Budget strategy governing stage 2 of the incomes policy. Later that day, Ennals was instructed to announce in the Commons the effective postponement of the child benefit scheme.

The New Society leak provides a striking similarity to the wrangles and splits over family support that characterised the Wilson Cabinets of the 1960s. Where they differ most is in the influence accorded to trade union responses to increases in family support. This produced a good deal of confusion in 1976. The Prime Minister and Chancellor presented the effect on take-home pay as the key factor in the Liaison Committee and Cabinet discussions. Moreover, they also presented it as if it had been suddenly discovered at a later stage - a claim apparently given substance by Michael Cocks' 'survey' of the Parliamentary Labour Party, a survey that looked all the more spurious given the signature of some 111 Labour MPs to an early Day Motion urging the government to fulfil its manifesto commitment. As Field rightly pointed out, 'the effect on take-home pay had always been the point'. It seemed more than probable that the pay argument had been contrived in a moment of pure political expedience by the government to justify somehow the demise of a policy on which it could not agree and for which it lacked political will. However, in the light of the Prime Minister's and Chancellor's reasoning, the role and response of the trade union movement bears further examination.

THE REACTION TO ABANDONMENT

The sensitivity of the child benefits issue, the effects of the disclosures, and the public embarrassment of an apparently divided trade union leadership, conspired to produce a swift reaction to David Ennals' announcement. Four days after the New Society leak, the TUC-Labour Party Liaison Committee met in what might be generously described as a spirit of compromise. Ostensibly the Committee met to approve the final draft of the new three-year social contract but union leaders made it clear that they required assurances that any future contract would carry a clear affirmation by government that it would revise and execute the scheme within the next year or so. Barbara Castle and Ian Mikardo were now successful in galvanising considerable trade union support for the introduction of the scheme by demonstrating that Healey had put union leaders over a barrel and had made them look foolish by encouraging their support for the abandonment of a scheme which was quite contrary to their earlier public commitment.

By 24 June, Callaghan had virtually transformed the barrage of criticism his government faced over postponement into an issue of confidence in his administration with a warning to Labour backbenchers that they must choose between instant implementation of the scheme and the continuation of Labour in office (30). He also made it quite clear that there could be no question of a Cabinet reversal on the issue and that the postponement applied not only to 1977 but to 1978 also.

By mid-July, with new modifications to the scheme proposed by CPAG and The Times, the TUC-Labour Party Liaison Committee's Working Party on Child Benefits now agreed, at its first meeting, to the idea of a phased programme to introduce the benefits scheme authorising, in the process, the preparation of a joint paper from the DHSS and Treasury outlining how this could be achieved. The meeting also went some way in explaining the apparent ambivalence of the TUC on the transfer of cash from wallet to purse. It now transpired that the TUC's own Social Insurance Committee had not swerved from its early commitment to the scheme but that confusion had arisen when individual members of the General Council had expressed their opposition to it. There was thus a clear split in both camps - government and trade union - on the issue.

'CHILD BENEFITS NOW' - THE CAMPAIGN

While the issue had clearly caught the imagination of both Parliament and the media it also provided a focal point around which the family lobby and the women's movement could unit - some two years after the demise of FAM. On this occasion CPAG itself was to act as principal convenor and the very fact that it saw some usefulness in a broad-based approach perhaps demonstrates the increasingly peripheral role CPAG saw itself playing in the affair. Just as in the late 1960s the issue of family support had become a private wrangle within Cabinet and the immediate policy community, so too in 1976, any sustained influence upon the issue seemed out of CPAG's reach. The issue had passed to a new tier where CPAG lacked the leverage or resources to compete. Some influence had, of course, been effected through the leaking of Cabinet minutes to the media by the Group's Director. Yet even then CPAG was unable to develop its influence further and the issue was drawn into the sphere of the Liaison Working Party. Any remaining hope of influencing the outcome thus lay in winning broad public support - something which had been noticeably lacking over the years.

This curious resort to a public campaign when all else had failed meant CPAG and the 'Child Benefits Now' campaign were seeking the support and goodwill of those whom Labour politicians and trade union leaders had described in the past as the chief obstacles to reform. Improved family benefits had consistently been upheld to be electorally unpopular by Labour leaders. The affair took a further twist with the campaign's determination to persuade unions, to incorporate family support considerations in their wage bargaining with government. That, in itself, could have doomed the campaign from the start.

The effort to win public support was generally unsuccessful. The highlight, a petition aimed at attracting 1 million signatures, barely attracted 23,000; a rally and public meeting at the House of Commons attracted only 200 people, most of them activists; the mobilisation of mass support floundered. More successful, however, and perhaps more realistic, was a parallel campaign to mobilise the support of rank-and-file trade unionists, and women members in particular. Trade unions such as ASTMS and CPSA, with strong women's sections, were active in their efforts to speed through an early introduction of the full child benefit. No trade

union, however, chose to become a constituent member
of the campaign itself.

Union independence was perhaps best illustrated
in the initiative taken by ASTMS and, notably, by its
Women's National Advisory Committee which persuaded
the National Executive to press its sponsored MPs
into active support for the scheme. The union
explained its involvement partly in terms of its
interest in social policy but more specifically
because it 'now had a substantial number of women in
membership and some of these were single parents who
had to meet the cost of having children looked after
while they were at work. After tax deductions there
only remained 62½p out of £1.50 child interim
benefit' (31). This suggests that CPAG may have been
on the right track in its efforts to demonstrate a
common interest with trade unionists on some aspects
of social policy. It may also confirm the change CPAG
had earlier claimed to have detected in the
philosophy of some trade unions - a consideration for
the 'whole man' rather than the 'fragmented man'.
ASTMS was still, however, one of only a small handful
of unions actively lobbying in support of child
benefits at this time. The overwhelming majority of
trade unions remained uninterested or inactive
partly because, as Jack Jones had pointed out in the
early seventies, most trade unionists either do not
have families or their families have grown up.

In the interim the Liaison Working Party on
child benefits broadened involvement in the issue,
albeit superficially, by inviting evidence on the
matter from the child benefits 'lobby'. By the end of
July the Working Party announced that a revival of
the scheme was imminent with a full phasing in by
1979 and a modified scheme in 1977. However, while
the commitment to a revival of the scheme in some
form or another had been secured it left little doubt
that the Government would choose the cheapest and
least elaborate option available. This new
compromise amounted to a weak palliative in place of
what had been an important and long-awaited election
pledge. It also ensured that the campaign to secure
the original, full scheme would continue.

Vigorous lobbying of union leaders, research
departments and branches began to produce results at
last in the July and August of 1976 - the trade union
conference season. Unions such as NUPE, the CPSA,
COHSE, the FBU and GMWU now added their weight to the
campaign for the full scheme. Constituency Labour
Parties and trade union branches accepted and
submitted conference resolutions on the issue; in

some cases, like the CPSA, actually raising a resolution at the TUC's own conference. Other unions, such as NUPE, pressed home the need to defend the scheme as part of a wider campaign to halt public expenditure cuts in general.

On 23rd September David Ennals closed the gap between the Government and the 'lobby' a little further with an announcement that the Cabinet had decided that day to phase in the full child benefit scheme by 1979. Crucially, however, he also confirmed that the possibility of extra resources being allocated to the scheme was remote.

STRENGTHENING THE COMPROMISE

For CPAG and the Child Benefits Now Campaign the Government had still not gone far enough in meeting its promises of 1974. The compromise scheme was still viewed as a poor deal for those seven million families who had expected a more generous scheme to be introduced in 1975-76. CPAG's response was to take the issue to the Labour Party Conference in October, in an effort to maintain the impetus created at the TUC conference. The group had worked for some time to win constituency support for the issue and must take much of the credit for the successful debate on a composited motion containing no less than 17 constituency resolutions on child benefits most of which it had largely engineered (32). The Government, however, remained unmoved.

On 1st April 1977 David Ennals, Secretary of State for Social Services and Stanley Orme, Minister of Social Security made elaborate gestures of enthusiasm towards a scheme which they praised as 'universal' and 'generous'. As if oblivious to the Government's early volte-face, to trade union ambivalence on the issue and to the highly controversial 'leak' episode Mr Orme still felt able to praise: 'the good sense of the Government, the TUC and the Labour Party - through their joint-working party - which overcame the phasing-in difficulties and made the start of this scheme this April possible' (33). His comments were of further significance for the exclusion of any reference to the efforts of CPAG or the Child Benefits Now Campaign on the issue. In speaking of Government-Party-TUC co-operation the Minister had defined the precise frontiers within which the issue had been resolved. The implication was that other efforts had largely been incidental or peripheral to the decision reached by the 'offical' policy community.

The reaction of those outside this policy community to the compromise scheme was critical. On the day it commenced CPAG showed that its universality was misleading and had failed to account for husbands drawing invalidity benefit who had transferred their tax allowances to their working wives. Perhaps the most damaging challenge to the Government's optimism came from <u>The Financial Times</u>. The scheme which Mr Orme had so enthusiastically described as having 'enormous potential' was peremptorily dismissed as 'an immense money recirculating operation with a pathetic result' (34). Perhaps the only consolation to be drawn was that the principle of transferring money from the father to the mother had been finally established.

The introduction of the scheme in April 1977 did not signal a halt in the Child Benefits Now Campaign. CPAG, the Campaign itself and a number of unions continued to lobby for a more generous scheme. ASTMS, for example, together with COHSE and the Society of Civil and Public Servants led a motion at the 1977 Women's TUC Conference which condemned 'the shameful vacillation of the Government on this question' and which went on to demand: 'the immediate introduction of the full scheme as originally planned but index-linked to keep pace with cost of living increases and age related' (35). This demand for index-linked benefits was taken up by CPAG also but with the new scheme's introduction accomplished the Government could remain more assured than ever of its immunity to change. It was the lobby's hope that the Government would agree to allocate some part of the £2¼ billion earmarked for tax rebates in November, to the child benefit scheme. However, attempts to persuade the Government to adopt this course of action and switch resources from an electorally profitable tax scheme to rather less popular benefit claimants, were ill met.

The Government's position was summed up by Stanley Orme in a letter to CPAG on 5th May 1977:

I am afraid a November increase is quite out of the question. We have already provided £90 million for families with the introduction last month of a benefit for the first child ... The rate of child benefit must go up in April 1978 because of the next phase of the transfer from child tax allowances. As a member of the joint Labour Party/TUC Working Party I am of course very well aware of the call of the TUC and

Labour Party members for additional resources for child benefit during this phasing in period. (36)

What Orme did not, or could not, reveal was that the government, in consultation with the Liaison Committee; was already examining the possibilities of further financial support for families from April 1978 over and above the level of provision already announced. On 15 July, Ennals announced an increase in provision of the order of £300 million which seemed, at least briefly, to pre-empt the demands of the campaign, and indicated once more the 'blind lobbying' of groups lacking advance intelligence. The Secretary of State now felt able to claim that

> The Government has stuck to its Manifesto commitment to bring in this new benefit, a major social advance. We agreed, with the Labour party and the TUC, that it should be phased in over three years and we have put in a substantial sum of extra money for this second stage. 1979 will see the third phase, when the remaining child tax allowances for children under 11 will disappear and almost all family support will come to the mother through child benefit. (37)

CONCLUSION

The advancement of the extra support raises a number of points. While CPAG and the 'Child Benefits Now' campaign may well have created the climate of demand in which payment of an extra £300 million from April 1978 became irresistible, their roles throughout remained those of outsider groups and, therefore, of secondary importance. The event which gave CPAG most, albeit brief, influence during the affair was the New Society leak which played a prominent part in reviving the issue by enlarging the political debate. It contributed, in particular, to a more determined effort on the part of some trade unions to get the scheme off the ground and counter the criticisms of ambivalence that the leak inevitably sparked.

Furthermore, it was CPAG and the campaign, together with those unions such as ASTMS and NUPE which had parliamentary committees, which largely galvanised backbench opinion, supplied material for parliamentary questions and debates, and which generally ensured that the government would find its parliamentary reception as hostile as that of the media. It was also largely CPAG which maintained a lengthy dialogue with the Treasury and the DHSS on the issue, and it was from CPAG, as the most active interest group in the field, that much of the evidence and informed opinion, required by campaigners, the media and, to some extent, the Liaison Working Party itself, came.

In the final analysis, however, CPAG and its supporters relied on the influence and good will of the trade union movement to carry the day. The public campaign as such had little influence upon the course of events. Perhaps the most realistic assessment of CPAG's influence was that it 'primed' a number of trade unions and their leaders for the later, decisive stages of the affair when the final terms of the scheme were agreed within the confines of a policy community comprising government, party and the unions. CPAG was never a part of this policy elite. The manner in which the issue was confined to these three interests was borne out in a TUC broadsheet shortly after the July announcement of additional resources which noted:

> The detailed views of the TUC/Labour Party Liaison Committee Working Party on the phasing in of the child benefit scheme were put to Ministers prior to the Governments announcement of changes in this system of benefit ... They concluded that child benefits should be increased, firstly to cover reduction in child tax allowances, secondly to protect the level of benefit against inflation and thirdly to secure a real increase in the amount of benefit. (38)

Each of these measures had been strenuously lobbied for in a stream of broadsheets, articles and memoranda released by CPAG. Indeed, despite the prior raising of these issues by CPAG in both its letter to Stanley Orme on 1 April and in a memorandum to the Chancellor in June, the supreme irony of the child benefit episode was that much of the 'dialogue' had not been published. When the government finally announced the provision of extra support in July, it could be construed that the government had met its manifesto commitments in a roundabout way and had pre-empted much of the lobby's argument.

As for the TUC, it saw itself as acting largely independently of the groups that made up the family lobby. Some TUC staff were implicitly critical of what they saw as CPAG attempts to present itelf as the instigator and leader of the campaign. Yet the reality of the child benefits saga is that had CPAG not taken up this issue it seems unlikely that the unions would have taken the initiative. Their own record on family support, admittedly not a primary concern, has been one of ambivalence and prevarication. If some unions had not been embarrassed and angered by the New Society leak then the 'giant' may well have slept on.

The child benefits episode also shows the limits of conventional influence for a pressure group, notably the oportunity to participate only at the periphery of this management process. The episode demonstrates something that all such groups should recognise from the outset - that simply getting an issue onto the political agenda is no guarantee that it will remain there, or that it will bring the required legislative action. The dangers of an issue drifting into obscurity are further heightened when both the campaigning group and the Minister most sympathetic to it are excluded from the decisive stages of politcial choice and discussion. But for the leak, James Callaghan might have pulled off a master-stroke in removing Barbara Castle from the Cabinet.

Castle's removal from office and her sympathetic attitude towards the family lobby also raises the subject of client groups in politics. While the leaking of Cabinet minutes to Frank Field (39) achieved what both he and the 'source' presumably hoped for - the positive intervention of the trade union movement in the struggle to introduce child benefits - the unions are perhaps not usually seen as obvious 'clients' of the DHSS. More usually 'clients' are seen as the various welfare groups with claims upon DHSS resources. Typically, such groups are neither well-resourced nor possessed of socio-economic leverage. Indeed, their influence as such may stem more directly from the moral aspect of their 'case'. The client groups of other Departments whose interests are threatened or challenged by the claims of those such as CPAG look remarkably strong by comparison. Indeed, the electoral influence of middle-income groups in the 1960s, and of the trade unions in the 1970s, seems to have been so great that for both Harold Wilson and James Callaghan the mere anticipation of their disagreement to further expenditure on family support was sufficient to ensure that high-level attempts would be made to restrain such expenditure. It is not surprising, therefore, to find the Chief Secretary of the Cabinet commenting thus on DHSS Ministers' attempts to jack up the level of family support in 1976: 'Thus when they were arguing for Dennis to announce in his Budget something more than the minimum increase, the ground had already been dug from under them. I was able to argue in Cabinet that any more for them would be less for someone else (40).

The resulting irony is twofold. On the one hand, as Frank Field pointed out, this argument was based on the premise that changes in family support would affect take-home pay at a time when the Treasury was pressing for a further round of pay restraint. An argument was thus being advanced towards the unions as _sectional_ interests. However, leaking of Cabinet minutes and exposing the Prime Minister's plan to abandon the child benefit scheme resulted in an extraordinary boomerang effect that obliged the unions to become _promotional_ interests - clients of the DHSS, as it were - for a brief but decisive moment. While it would be unwise to make too much of this, the whole episode may hold some useful lessons for welfare groups eyeing the coat-tails of their more resourceful colleagues.

NOTES

1. Proposals for a Tax Credit System, C. 5116.
2. CPAG, Family Allowance Movement (July-August 1974).
3. CPAG, Do Not Abandon Child Benefits: A Briefing Note (June 1976).
4. Hansard, col. 330 (13 May 1975).
5. See Hansard, cols 339-40, 340-1; and for references to the CPAG campaign by Kenneth Clarke cols. 330,387-8; and by Norman Fowler col.343.
6. Do Not Abandon Child Benefits, op.cit., and Castle, B., 'The Death of Child Benefit', New Statesman (4 June 1976). See also Lister, R., 'Family Policy', in Bosanquet, N. and Townsend, P. (eds), Labour and Equality (Heinemann, 1980), p.188.
7. See CPAG, Poverty, No. 32 (Autumn 1975), pp.38-40; Poverty, No. 33 (Winter 1975/6), p.29; and Poverty, No. 34 (Summer 1976), pp.20-5.
8. Do Not Abandon Child Benefits.
9. New Statesman (4 June 1976).
10. Barnett, J., Inside the Treasury (Andre Deutsch, 1982), pp.54-5.
11. Ibid., p.55.
12. New Statesman (4 June 1976).
13. See McCarthy, M.A., Group Representation in the Plural Society: The Case of the Poverty Lobby,

PhD thesis (CNAA, Trent Polytechnic, 1981), chs.7-10.

14. The Times (28 April 1976).

15. Castle, B., The Castle Diaries 1974-76 (Weidenfeld & Nicholson, 1980), p.380.

16. Banting, op.cit.

17. Ibid., p.94.

18. Ibid., p.97.

19. For a broader discussion of this, see Bosanquet, N. 'Labour and Public Expenditure: An Overall View', in Bosanquet and Townsend, op.cit., ch.2.

20. New Statesman, (4 June 1976).

21. Ibid.

22. Ibid.

23. Ibid.

24. Field, F., 'Killing a Commitment: The Cabinet vs. the Children', New Society (17 June 1976).

25. Ibid.

26. Ibid. See also The Guardian (21 June 1976); and CPAG, The Great Child Benefits Robbery (April 1977), pp.4-5.

27. New Society (17 June 1976).

28. Statement of TUC-Labour Party Liaison Committee Working Group on Child Benefits (24 May 1976).

29. Field, 'Killing a Commitment'.

30. Guardian (25 June 1976).

31. Minutes of the Second Meeting of the Women's National Advisory Committee: ASTMS (26 June 1976).

32. Report on the 75th Annual Conference of the Labour Party 1976, pp.259-61, 266-9.

33. New Child Benefit: A Social Revolution, DHSS Press Release Nos.77/865 (1 April 1977).

34. 'A Mountain That Brought Forth a Mouse', Financial Times (5 April 1977).

35. WNAC (ASTMS) Minutes (30 April 1977).

36. Stanley Orme to Ruth Lister (5 May 1977), (MIN:SS) 17545.

37. Child Benefit - Government gives £300 Million Extra for Children, DHSS press release No. 77/215 (15 July 1977).

38. Labour - TUC Information Broadsheet (1 September 1977).

39. Field, Poverty and Politics, pp.157-8.

40. Barnett, op.cit., p.53.

Chapter Twelve

RE-UNITING ... "A DIVIDED AND DISILLUSIONED PEOPLE":
THATCHERISM 1979-1983

The 1979 General Election: A Watershed

The General Election of May 1979 was to prove a
significant watershed in the affairs of CPAG. Three
factors were paramount. Firstly, the new Government
was to bring with it a determined economic regime and
a hard-nosed reaffirmation of principles of self-
help and value for money. This was suffused with an
aggressive economic and social morality that had only
spluttered at the margins of Tory fashion in recent
years. The Conservatives were now led in an abrasive
and determined style that would have been denounced
in the Heath years as unfeeling, arrogant, and
bullying. Under Margaret Thatcher, however,
arrogance and abrasion, combined with a readiness to
chastise all-comers, including the remnants of
Heath's old guard who had come to form a significant
element in her first Cabinet, were soon hailed as the
requirements for the visionary and single-minded
leadership that the Prime Minister's image-builders
claimed were necessary to haul Britain up by its
bootstraps. In Party terms the discrediting of Edward
Heath was perversely complete ...

> In the nine years that Heath had been Leader, he
> had completed the transformation of the Party's
> image from one which appeared, above all, to
> protect the interests of the wealthy, the land-
> owning, the titled and the businessman, to that
> of a meritocratic Party which encouraged market
> forces so long as they did not radically change
> the balance of the mixed economy or the welfare
> state: in short, the post-war consensus. (1)

In stark contrast, the new Leader saw herself as
precisely the sort of radical she believed Edward
Heath had failed to be and, like many of her

colleagues - embittered by what they saw as an unnecessary and demeaning return to the back-benches in 1974 - she squarely blamed Heath's interventionist style of politics after the autumn of 1972 and the vagaries of the so-called 'post war consensus' as the reasons for her Party's loss of office and standing with the British electorate. Margaret Thatcher had no such qualms regarding the impingement of the 'market' on economy or welfare state nor, in the aftermath of the 'Winter of Discontent' which had finally brought the Callaghan Government to its knees, did she perceive the social contract and consensus politics as anything other than the bankruptcy of responsible and decisive government.

For the new Prime Minister the social and political consensus which forged the mainstream Butskellite tradition was the cause of, and not the solution to, Britain's social and economic ills. Her perceptions of the recent history and fortunes of her Party were critical to her Government's policy outlook and she was fixed with transforming both ...

> On winning the General Election, Thatcher was acutely aware of the experience of the previous Conservative administration. Like most political leaders, she was guided in her actions by a need to break away from the quality and tone of her immediate predecessor ... Thatcher was intimidated by the memory of Edward Heath's 1970-74 Government, which she had so eagerly damned as soon as it came to an end. It was economic policy which was to bring about the change in Britain she wished for ... Although she was happy to support Heath's interventionist policies until the election defeat in 1974, her instincts were toward a set of policies which confounded the postwar Tory tradition and she found that the economic alternative offered in monetarism ... matched those political needs. (2)

For Margaret Thatcher the overall failure of the Heath Government was readily condensed into that Government's singular inability to bring the unions to heel. For Thatcher the insatiable pay demands and workplace malpractices of the trade unions were at the heart of Britain's malaise. They were, in short, the 'British disease' and she meant to cauterise them. Her resolve was hardened by the events of the previous winter as the Callaghan Government succumbed to a wave of discontent that had rumbled louder and louder as the reality of the much-vaunted social contract fell miserably short of the ideal. From the ashes of that discontent now rose the spark for Thatcher's political and moral crusade against the unions. The Prime Minister's intentions were, thus, clearly signposted in the run-up to the election itself ...

> During the industrial strife of last winter, confidence, self-respect and even our sense of common humanity were shaken. At times this society seemed on the brink of disintegration ... by heaving privilege without responsibility on the trade unions, Labour have given a minority of extremists the power to abuse individual liberties and to thwart Britain's chances of success. One result is that the trade union movement ... is today more distrusted and feared than ever before. (3)

For the Conservatives in 1979 the trade union movement, central focus of CPAG's activities for much of the seventies, remained no more than a selfish, arbitrary and powerful interest group which had not only damaged the economy and undermined Britain's growth but had had the audacity to challenge and perhaps dispossess the very authority of Government itself. It had done it in 1974 with Heath and it had given a repeat performance with Callaghan in 1979. Enough was enough. The first job of the new Government would now be ... "To rebuild our economy and re-unite a divided and disillusioned people ..." And, beyond that, ... "To restore the health of our economic and social life by controlling inflation and striking a fair balance between the rights and duties of the trade union movement" (4).

The very movement in which CPAG had seen a growing and substantive promise for advancing the position of the poor was now itself lined up in the sights of a Government bent on trammelling its role in the workplace and positively removing it in the broader political sphere.

The third factor in this watershed was unique to CPAG itself and was to produce a necessary and, perhaps overdue, rethink of strategy, priorities and action. In December 1978 Frank Field had indicated his intention to resign his position as Director to fight Birkenhead in Labour's colours. It was an ambition he had long held and one which, as he later revealed, his position and platform at CPAG had enabled him to nurture (5). Writing in the wake of his own election and the arrival at No 10 of Margaret Thatcher he, too, had a firm presentiment of the difficulties CPAG would confront in the Thatcher era and warned the Group's supporters that ... "Over the next decade CPAG will have its work cut out to fight a rearguard action, let alone take the struggle into the enemy's camp" (6).

Those presentiments were to be well borne out in the next six years, a period of bewildering legislative activity which was to see the demise of the Supplementary Benefits Commission; the abolition of earnings-related supplement; the introduction of two punitive and divisive Social Security Acts in 1980 and another in 1981; an Education Act in the same year that cut back drastically on the provision of free school meals and transport to school children; the introduction of a Social Security and Housing Benefits Act in 1982; a Health and Social Services and Social Security Act in 1983; cuts in the real value of unemployment benefit; a slashing of social security support to the families of strikers and, ultimately, the Tory piece de resistance of June 1985 - Norman Fowler's Reform of Social Security.

Even allowing for the traditional non-committal nature of Conservative manifestos and the need for the new Leader to edge forward cautiously, the signposts for a bleak era in welfare were firmly marked out in the election ritual of 1979. The themes of 'value for money' and 'better use of existing resources' - classic precursors of Fowler's 'nil-cost remit' in 1985 - together with the favourite Tory cry of redistributing resources to those in 'greatest' need or the more politically emotive 'genuine' need were clearly evident behind the thin veil of the 1979 manifesto ... "The lack of money to improve our social services and assist those in need can only be overcome by restoring the nation's economic prosperity" (7).

Such thinking had firm echoes of Wilson's belief in welfare contingent on growth and in Heath's own 'competition policy', but the follow-through was entirely Thatcherite and smacked loudly of good housekeeping and the New Right's predeliction for 'commonsense' in Government. Thus, if economic growth was the longterm basis for improvements in welfare then in the short-term ... "Some improvements can be made now by spending what we do have more sensibly" (8).

Good housekeeping was calculated to attract and hold firm that growing middle-class who saw in an expanding welfare state, and in the burgeoning social

security system in particular, a pull on global tax
revenue and a drain on their own spending power that
was conceived as, at once, politically, economically
and morally unacceptable. Good housekeeping might
not simply keep the welfare state in check but would
also provide a springboard for the all-important tax
cuts the Government had boasted it would introduce to
free spending and enterprise. The manifesto was to
raise another theme which has, since, also been fixed
firmly at the centre of Tory thinking on welfare and
one which CPAG had seen as politically inimical to
the broad interests of the poor since the days of the
wage-stop - this was the disincentive to work. The
manifesto warned ...

> Income tax starts at such a low level that many
> poor people are being taxed to pay for their own
> benefits. All too often they are little or no
> better off at work than they are on social
> security ... We shall do all we can to find
> other ways to simplify the system, restore the
> incentive to work, reduce the poverty trap and
> bring more effective help to those in greatest
> need. Restoring the will to work means, above
> all, cutting income tax. It also means bringing
> unemployment and short-term sickness benefit
> within the tax system ... The rules about the
> unemployed accepting available jobs will be
> reinforced and we shall act more vigorously
> against fraud and abuse. (9)

The stage was thus firmly set for an
unprecedented erosion and in some instances total
reversal of many principles and much practice central
to the raison d'etre of the welfare state. Moreover,
this was set in train at that moment in CPAG's
history when a new order was ushered in.

A NEW ORDER

Frank Field's imminent departure for the House of
Commons brought with it the opportunity for a rethink
of the Group's activity and strategy, not unlike that
initiated in the early 1970s. With it came the
appointment as his successor of Ruth Lister, the
Group's Deputy Director. Lister had been with CPAG
six years already and was a well-established and much
respected figure on the welfare scene and was a
natural and well received choice to lead the Group.
Her leading role in the organisation of the Child

Benefits Campaign and her work in bringing together the disparate strands of the so-called 'poverty lobby' under the aegis of that Campaign and in cementing links with local groups, trade union activists and the increasingly important 'womens movement' convinced many that she had added organisational and political skills to her proven ability as a researcher and writer.

While Field had been seen as an impressive publicist and lobbyist for the Group, much of that lobbying had been reserved for the confined circles of Westminster and the senior echelons of a small number of sympathetic trade unions. It was here that Field believed the key to mobilising influential opinion lay and while there is some evidence that he may have been right, the Group's energies were only superficially directed towards public opinion at large. It was here, however, that the new Director saw both CPAG's principal weakness and what could become with the necessary effort and 'education' the Group's strength for the future. For Lister, there were particular lessons to be drawn from the Group's experience with the Labour Government 1974-79 that had clear implications for CPAG's broader impacts. Key among these was the protracted struggle over the long-term rate of supplementary benefit for the unemployed. It had transpired during the final demise of the Callaghan Government that both David Ennals and Stan Orme had wanted to introduce the rate but believed they could not steer it through Cabinet because of the hostility towards the unemployed perceived by Cabinet Ministers among their constituents (10).

This wariness of prejudice and the exploitation of it to avoid policy commitments had strong parallels with the perceptions of Wilson, Brown and Callaghan in the sixties. Lister herself felt that by the mid to late seventies public opinion on social security in general had reached a nadir (11). The Group's trade union strategy which had been very Labour-oriented in these years now seemed much less appropriate with the arrival in office of a Government which had promised the electorate it would bring the unions to heel. Worse still, the electorate itself was bitterly divided over the social contract and the impact and images of recent industrial action. Though now residualised, the value of CPAG's trade union liaison strategy was not to be written off, rather it was to be redefined.

Frank Field had himself indicated that the unions would need to remain paramount in the Group's

strategy. Commenting on the rise under Labour in the
real value of pensions and other long-term national
insurance benefits, he explained that ...

> The impetus for this achievement came from the
> trade union movement. Such interest was not
> shown by the movement in other areas of social
> policy and the lesson is clear for reformers
> wishing to see the next Labour Government
> committed to a radical attack on poverty. (12)

Where Field had drawn heavily on the baronial
influence of a very small group of senior trade
unions leaders and had set a pattern for 'leader-led'
change and action in the trade union response to
social security issues, Lister believed the future
lay in 'rank and file-led' strategies and it was
here, in the grass roots of the unions, that CPAG was
to devote its energies in the years to come.
Moreover, a rank and file approach was deemed
necessary as part of the Group's general attempt to
defeat scroungerphobia ... "Trade unions offer and
still offer a fairly wide audience to the Group
notably through their rank and file members and
access to them is a useful way of countering the non-
sympathetic position of the media" (13).

There was, of course, to be considerable
continuity in Frank Field's work much of which was
recognised as having been of key value to the Group's
development. However, there has been a much greater
thrust during the term of Ruth Lister's office in
giving attention to public opinion in general,
although this has been restricted by limited
resources. In turn, that limitation has necessitated
closer work with and through other groups in the
poverty lobby and the womens movement, especially at
local level. There has continued to develop since
1979 a conscious policy to decentralise strategies.
The highly selective use of key opinion leaders
during, first, Tony Lynes secretaryship and then,
more assiduously and more politically under Frank
Field, has given way to a recognition that the
campaign to improve the lot of the poor - whether the
characteristic of poverty be a large family,
unemployment, sickness, disabilty or single
parenthood - must, perforce, recognise the role that
can be played with and through a range of interests.
It must also be more popularly based than the odd eve
of budget meeting with the Chancellor or the sort of
reliance that had sometimes been placed on deference
by politicians to the collective weight of written

academic protest. On a typical occasion Field notes
...

> CPAG's membership was never much above 2,000
> during the 1970s, but amongst this group were
> some of the country's most respected academics.
> The main points of the Group's demands -
> reiterating the results of the Hotel Rembrandt
> conference on the priority to increase child
> benefit - were drafted as a letter to The Times
> and almost all the professors of social policy
> were invited to sign, which they promptly did.
> It's surprising how susceptible left-wing
> politicians are to the views of the academic
> community in this field. (14)

By contrast, in the mid-eighties CPAG has become
far more of a membership organisation numbering in
early 1985 some 5,000 or more members. As membership
has risen so that membership has become more diverse
and senior academics no longer predominate - not
least in their traditional preserve of the Group's
Executive Committee which now comprises social
workers, trade union officials and welfare rights
activists. One of the more interesting developments
since Lister became Director is that the general
changes in CPAG's outlook and remit, notably an
emphatic move towards public opinion and a more
pronounced welfare rights commitment - not least
through an extremely active Citizens Rights Office -
have also been expressed in the composition of the
Executive Committee. The result is an Executive in
which academics are now to be found very much in the
minority and in which those from the trade union and
welfare rights sectors dominate. Indeed, there has
been occasion of late to deliberately draft in an
academic representative merely to give the Committee
more balance.
    The Executive remains, as ever, involved,
participative and critical where necessary,
sometimes to the point of rejecting the preferred
policy objectives of the Group's fulltime staff.
However, in general, tradition and practice soldier
on and it is to Lister, her deputy Fran Bennett, and
the CPAG/CRO staff that the task of agenda-setting
and subsequent policy direction invariably falls.

AN EARLY AGENDA

Throughout the period of transition in 1979 CPAG saw

its priority as support for families with children and the need to extend its normal educational and campaigning work. This was achieved in two ways, on the one hand through active involvement as a Committee Member in the work of the International Year of the Child and through the production of ..'more varied publications which we hope will inform a wider public audience about the needs of children' (15).

A barrage of such work marked the year, beginning with Lister's own The No-Cost No-Benefit Review in January; through Field's Capitalising on Success in March; Lister's A Budget for the Year of the Child in May; Jo Tunnard's Uniform Blues aimed for the new school term in September and David Piachaud's pointed Cost of a Child two months later in November. In December, three members of the Group, Alan Walker, Paul Ormerod and Larry Whitty, the Head of Research at the GMWU and destined six years later to become the General Secretary of the Labour Party, powerfully argued in Abandoning Social Priorities that the new Government was not only cutting the living standards of very poor families but were doing so to free public expenditure for redistribution to the rich in the form of tax cuts. The general theme was rounded off appositely by Ruth Lister in the Group's February 1980 publication The Great Child Benefit U-Turn?

The publications accompanied other, traditional, forms of CPAG activity with unemployment joining child benefits as the chief priority. The renewed interest in unemployment, following an apparent lull in the Group's active interest after the publication of Wasted Labour by Field and Lister in 1978, was to prove particularly timely as the Government quickly made clear the control of inflation and not the creation of jobs was their overriding concern. Prophetically, the Group warned its members ...

> Our major concerns are the poverty and stigma of unemployment. We are increasingly aware that the unemployed are under attack as scroungers and skivers. With unemployment expected to rise during the next four years, we are increasingly concerned that the unemployed will go without rather than claim the already inadequate social security benefits to which they are entitled. (16)

Taking a clear lead from the Conservative manifesto the Group made clear that one of its principal concerns would be to ...

> Particularly look at the question of the
> unemployed being 'better-off' than those in
> work and show that this is a very small problem
> compared to the very serious problem of poverty.
> Despite evidence of particular hardship among
> unemployed families with children and the long-
> term unemployed, the unemployed are still
> discriminated against in the social security
> system. (17)

The growing costs of education to poor families
were also to figure prominently in CPAG's work in
1979 as was work on social security which now took on
..."a new sense of urgency with the Review of the
Supplementary Benefits Scheme and the forthcoming
Social Security Bill" (18). Central to the latter was
an inevitable pre-occupation with the inadequacy of
social security scale rates for children which even
after the November 1979 uprating still foundered at
the miserable daily level of 74p for a child under
five and 89p for those aged between five and ten
years. Work on both fronts recognised the imminence
of a further undermining of the position of poor
families as the Government's Social Security and
Education Bills were driven towards the statute book.
Prospects were bleak ...

> With the proposed and anticipated cuts in public
> expenditure, the cost of education, already too
> high for many poor families, seems bound to
> increase substantially. Our campaign for
> improvement in the provision of travel to
> school, school meals and milk are all likely to
> be set back by cuts in public expenditure and in
> all three we may lose what free provision there
> is now. (19)

Six months later the Group's worst fears were
confirmed. From the moment the Education Bill
received the Royal Assent in April 1980 CPAG ...
'Were receiving telephone calls and letters from
parents horrified to find that they had lost the
right to free school meals for their children' (20).
Even a firm reminder to the Secretary of State
for Education of his assurances to the Group the
previous year that the provision that the Government
was asking local authorities to make ...'in fact
assumes that they will continue to provide free meals
at a level of family income somewhere between the

present level and the supplementary benefit/FIS
levels ...' (21) drew only the most negative and
complacent of responses.

IS CPAG'S POLICY RIGHT?

As the extent of the Government's programme gradually
unfolded in the early months of 1980 so, too, the re-
appraisal of CPAG's own strategy and priorities
gathered impetus. The Executive was already engaged
in a major review of the Group's position when an
article in The Guardian on January 30th by the social
policy leader writer Malcolm Dean set out the
challenge posed by the Thatcher Government to the
thinking of the poverty lobby and to what he saw as
its 'sacred cow' - universal child benefit. It fell
to Jonathan Bradshaw, writing in the April issue of
Poverty, to expound and explain the Executive's own
thinking.

He began by reminding CPAG supporters that the
objective of the Group was to focus attention on the
plight of poor families with children and to advance
and lobby for policies to assist them. He explained
in detail the tightrope that CPAG must walk ...

> There is always a difficult choice to be made
> between working for policies there is little
> hope of attaining in the short-term and pressing
> for policies which may be less than perfect but
> which are more 'realistic'. (22)

The Executive had concluded that the Group must
do both. It must

> Raise issues which enhance the level of
> aspiration for the political agenda in the late
> 1980s, while at the same time pressing for
> changes during the period of this Government. So
> a policy is needed which it is realistic to
> campaign for during the period of this
> Government but does not let a different
> administration 'off the hook'. (23)

The Group's work had paid dividends in the past
so why abandon direction now? After all, according to
Bradshaw, the increases in child benefits in 1967/68,
the Group's successful critique of FIS, the womens
campaign on child tax credit, acceptance of
integrating FAM and tax allowances in child benefits
and the increases in 1977, 1978 and 1979 could all in

no small part be attributed to CPAG lobbying. However, there had been failures too - the introduction of FIS; the debilitating effects of the protracted introduction of child benefits; the failure to secure subsequent index-linking of child benefits before the May 79 election. On balance, then, the Group had no cause for self congratulation. Indeed the evidence suggested that CPAG successes lay less with positive achievement and rather more with limiting adverse change through principled rearguard action. Many observers might actually look to the period 1974-79 as one of failure and

> Families are now reaping the consequences of these failures. Depite the Group's efforts there has been a decline in the value of child support since the war and our level of child support is one of the lowest in Europe. So what should the Group do now? (24)

One thing was certain, the cost of improving child benefit was likely to prove substantial and, for a Government committed to cutting public expenditure, probably prohibitive. Bradshaw calculated that in 1980/81 alone it would cost £952 million to increase it to the short-term insurance child addition level. More simply, every 1p increase in child benefit would cost £5.6 million in a full year. The knock-on effect of a failure to secure an improving real level of child benefits in the next few years could prove calamitous

> Child benefits could well decline in value absolutely in the next few years and the net disposable resources of families with children would then decline further in comparison with the childless as the latter benefited from increases in personal tax allowances. At the same time the shift to indirect taxation and cuts in public expenditure, particularly in education benefits, will hit families hardest. If the Group pursues its present policy it could be argued that it will not even succeed in maintaining the value of benefit. (25)

The Executive had conducted a 'searching examination of the Group's policy on child benefits' and had reviewed all the principal arguments and alternatives to a universal scheme. These included the possibility of age-related child benefits; the introduction of higher child benefits for the second,

294

third and subsequent child; an increase in the child benefit addition to ease the burden of single parent families; a re-introduction of child tax allowances; the pros and cons of making child benefits taxable; the usefulness of tax credits; the introduction or enhancement of other means of family support; the restructuring of child benefits on an income-related basis and, finally, the prospects for the introduction of a minimum wage.

While each clearly held an attraction and enjoyed some degree of support within the Group, the Executive had found nothing to persuade it that the Group's central preference for universal child benefit should be abandoned

> The CPAG Executive has considered all the options and resolved to continue to pursue its existing policy. None of the other options is as satisfactory as a universal child benefit ... There is very widespread understanding of the importance of a universal child benefit and there is still hope that the 'party of the family' will recognise the case for a substantial increase in child benefit now. (26)

SOCIAL SECURITY SLASHED

Only a year after winning the election the Government had pinned two Social Security Acts to the Statute Book. They had progressed almost untouched; there had been little public outcry. If the Fowler Reviews in 1985 were to explode the myth of the Thatcher Government's adherence to the central principles of the welfare state, then the Social Security Acts of 1980 were the means of laying the charge. There could be no doubt that the Acts were unpopular and divisive. Even the Secretary of State admitted as much as he introduced the No 2 Bill to the Commons ...'It must be one of the most uncomfortable and unpalatable Bills that any Minister has had to bring before the House of Commons in a long time ...' It was, he added 'A Bill to amend the law relating to social security for the purpose of reducing or abolishing certain benefits and of relaxing or abolishing certain duties to increase sums' (27).

CPAG could do little other than lobby, petition and lament

> Clearly we have failed so far in our efforts to get across the damage that this legislation will

do to the living standards of millions of claimants. That does not mean that we must stop trying. If the Government is not made to realise that there are people who do care very strongly about what it is doing then social security could be the first in line when the Treasury cap next goes round for expenditure cuts. (28)

The Government's obsession in cutting public expenditure was central to both pieces of legislation. The first Act had sought to break the link between pensions and earnings or prices, whichever was greater. Now pensions would connect with prices only. Claims that the No 1 Act would produce a thorough review and overhaul of the supplementary benefits system proved unfounded. It failed visibly to even address, let alone tackle, the huge and increasing dependence on supplementary benefit among claimants. In a clear precursor of 'Fowler' the Act's neutral cost remit became 'A polite smokescreen for cuts in many claimants living standards' (29).

Writing in the August 1980 issue of <u>Poverty</u>, John Douglas of the Group's Citizens Rights Office concluded that the package was 'designed so that the total number of losers would be two million and the total number of gainers would be roughly half a million' (30). The so-called 'neutral cost' of the package was, however, to be destroyed by the No 2 Act since the cut in the short-term national insurance benefit rates introduced by the latter meant that there would no longer be any increase in the real value of the ordinary rate of supplementary benefit.

The unemployed and school-leavers were to be discriminated against. Although the long-term rate of supplementary benefit was now to be paid after one, rather than two, years, the new arrangements did not extend to the unemployed. School-leavers found themselves unable to claim benefit until the end of the holidays following their final term. Those with capital over £2,000 were now debarred from receipt of supplementary benefit and only those in actual receipt of supplementary benefit would now be eligible for exceptional needs payments.

Objectivity in assessment, such as it was, and accountability were also to be casualties. Officers administering supplementary benefit would now be able to take decisions on individual cases in their own right. Recourse to the Secretary of State or Parliament was unnecessary. As John Douglas pointed out ... 'Benefit Officers will have their own code compiled by the Chief Benefit Officer, which will remain secret and which will tell them how to exercise the substantial amount of discretion they will retain under the regulations, and this means that many of the guidelines which are very important in ascertaining how much a claimant gets will continue to remain out of public view' (31). In the event, however, the S Manual, the Code to which Douglas referred, was subsequently published.

The second Act was much less coy about its aims. It did not employ the 'neutral cost' smokescreen. The commitment to index link short-term national insurance benefit and invalidity benefit was now set aside, ostensibly for three years in the first instance, although in practice the abatement was only applied in the first of the three years. The real issue was that it was justified as an interim measure in lieu of taxation but was not lifted when unempoyment benefit was brought into tax. In the event it took a backbench revolt, briefed by CPAG both directly and through the Unemployment Alliance, to persuade the Government to restore it. Earnings related supplement was to disappear in 1982; pensioners and the unemployed were once again hit; true to form the state's responsibilities to strikers and their families were now to be slashed and the Government's attack on the unions was now pursued through the infrastructure of the welfare state. Supplementary benefit support was cut by £12. Urgent needs payments to strikers or their dependents were to be very strictly defined and the disregard of £4 of any tax payable to a claimant involved in a trade dispute was abolished.

Tony Lynes noted that the full extent of the cuts brought on stream by the 1980 legislation was only partly understood and that 'for the majority ... since nobody's going to tell them what they would have got under the old rules, the cuts will be concealed' (32). Many of the biggest losses inflicted by the Government were to come through abolition of the earnings related supplement – a measure which caught widows and women drawing maternity allowance in its wake as well as impacting most directly and most punitively on the sick and the unemployed.

1980 was to prove a particularly debilitating year for the unemployed as the Prime Minister herself confirmed that sentiments expressed in the Manifesto were not simply the passing rhetoric of an election campaign. Speaking in May, Mrs Thatcher was quite clear, '... that this year was right to cut the increase in unemployment benefit by some 5% below the

level that it would otherwise have been, because I
believe that it is right to have a larger difference
between those in work and those out of work' (33).
    This 'difference' and, for the Government, the
political need to maintain and even widen it was to
become a key element in the New Right's continuing
critique of a profligate welfare state. The second
Social Security Act was, of course, to erode the
position of the unemployed even further in 1981 and
1982 also, notably in the abolition of the Earnings
Related Supplement. 5 years on from the Prime
Minister's statement, the 1985 Green Paper Reform of
Social Security was to re-affirm that a central
concern of the Government's intentions in the field
of social security was 'To ensure fairness between
the position of claimants on the benefit and those
with similar levels of income in work' (34).
    Ultimately, as Lynes was to point out, this very
terse approach to welfare raised three key issues.

> The first is whether the present cuts represent
> a temporary setback or a permanent diminution of
> the role of social security in Britain ... The
> second question is whether the distinction
> between means-tested and contributory benefits
> will become less clear-cut ... (and) ... An
> equally serious risk is that making means-
> testing apparently more acceptable will
> strengthen the hand of those who argue that the
> proper role of the State is to provide no more
> than a basic minimum income for those unable to
> support themselves. (35)

CO-OPERATION AND COALITION: CPAG, THE UNIONS AND THE WELFARE LOBBY

The attack on the unemployed and the Government's
expressed intent to trammel the activities of the
trade unions through discriminatory cuts in support
to the families of strikers, once more pointed up the
common ground between the Group and the Labour
Movement. An early joint initiative was the
establishment of the Trade Union Forum in late 1979 -
a small informal grouping of CPAG staff and research
officers from a number of key public sector unions.
This met initially every two months but since August
1984 has opted to convene as and when major issues of
common interest arise. Intellectually, at least, the
Forum carries some echo of the CPAG - trade union
'seminars' launched by Nick Bosanquet some ten years

earlier. However this later initiative has succeeded where its 'predecessor' failed in two key respects. First and foremost it has, quite simply, endured, and it continues to provide an unusual and valuable means whereby CPAG and trade union staff keep each other informed and explore grounds for harnessing the strengths of their respective organisations. Secondly, the Forum and CPAG itself have come in recent years to act as a sort of 'broker' between the various trade union reserach departments and it has helped to inform debate and shape policy particularly, for example, on taxation issues. One result has been that a number of key unions, including NALGO, GMBATU, NUPE and TGWU, have come out in favour of using the married man's tax allowance for financing child allowance. Unemployment has proved a continuing catalyst. CPAG initially had the idea for the Benefit Charter for the Unemployed in February 1981 and the Trade Union Forum worked on this with the TUC, latterly, adopting the idea officially.

One of the more interesting general observations to be made of CPAG since 1979 is that it has acquired a much more 'feminist feel' about its work. There has, clearly, been an increased emphasis on issues which affect women and their family roles, for example, discrimination against women in the social security rules and regulations. Some of the changing emphasis has come about through the work of the Trade Union Forum. Its broad-sheet <u>Family Policy is a Trade Union Issue</u> was subsequently published by a number of unions involved and interest in CPAG's own work and policy has been further stimulated and developed by the increase in womens officers and welfare rights specialists among the staff of many of the larger trade unions. It is perhaps the combined efforts of all three - CPAG, the Forum and individual trade union leaders and officers, which have produced the sort of trade union view on social security expressed by Moss Evans in the wake of the 1980 legislation

> The Government's proposal to reduce supplement-ary benefit to strikers families by £12 is an obvious and vindictive part of the Government's attack on trade union organisation. However, the other elements of the two social security Bills are also matters which directly concern trade unions. In addition, child benefit is not being raised to meet inflation, a move which did not need legislation. Any member of the union

may become unemployed, sick, suffer injury,
become a parent or be bereaved. All union
members hope they will eventually draw a
pension. The attack on these benefits is a trade
union issue ... The Social Security Bills are an
attack on the welfare state itself ... The trade
union movement is very much aware of the worth
of the social security system. We have fought
strongly for the national insurance system and
against the means-test. It is no coincidence
that the Government should attack trade unions
specifically and social security recipients in
the same legislation. (37)

The attack on social security by the Thatcher
Government in 1980 proved, as Moss Evans indicated, a
further area for common cause. The early eighties saw
the development of a close relationship between CPAG
and the two key Civil Service unions, the CPSA and
the SCPS, producing in 1980 an anti-social security
cuts co-ordinating committee in which the Group came
to play no small part and later, in 1982, joint
publication of a 'cuts leaflet' with the two unions.
In the same year the Group, this time with NACAB
also, joined forces with the CPSA and the SCPS once
again to tackle the problems arising on the
introduction of a postal claim form for unemployed
supplementary benefit claimants.

Unemployment, and a growing concern among
unions that little was being done either to arrest it
or alleviate its effects, remained paramount and
brought with it opportunities for CPAG and the CRO to
demonstrate the practical dimension to their work
with the trade unions. The Group noted in 1981 that

the continuing rise in unemployment with its
attendant problems of people needing to claim
benefit and cope with the social security system
has given rise to a closer and more practical
working relationship this year between CPAG and
the Labour movement. (38)

In a year that saw trade union affiliations to
the Group rise to three hundred, CPAG's publications
took on a distinctive 'consumerist' feel with <u>On
Strike, Have You Lost Your Job?</u> and <u>Pay More Get Less</u>
dominating the welfare rights bookstalls and the TUC
fringe. More significant, perhaps, was the
increasing use of CRO resources and skills by
individual trade unionists and by trade union
branches fighting redundancy notices. One notable

incident came in the printing trade

> Senior NATSOPA stewards in London, faced with
> two thousand redundancies approached us for
> information on how redundancy pay affects tax
> and social security entitlements. The CRO
> responded by running an advice session at the
> workplace and producing a special fact sheet for
> them. (39)

Elsewhere the CRO also became closely involved
in providing information, advice and advocacy back-
up to trade unionists who established the Unemployed
Centre in Pontypool. Branches, too, reported a major
upsurge in work with trade unionists and the
unemployed throughout the early eighties. The taxing
of unemployment benefit from July 1982 and the non-
restoration of the five per cent cut in value added
further to the impetus for such liaison.

The revival of liaison and co-operative work
with the trade union movement has been only one facet
of the Group's campaigning strategy in recent years.
Another important element has been the forging of
closer ties with the Group's colleagues in the
welfare lobby. We noted earlier that the Group's work
has, inevitably, been restricted by limited
resources and that such limitations had necessitated
close work with and through other groups, especially
at local level.

That there has been more localised work is clear
from both the increased activity and sophistication
of some of the larger CPAG branches. Certainly, under
Lister, it has been hoped that branches would play a
much greater part in the direction and workload of
the Group, though there has not been any extra
emphasis in terms of staff support to branches from
Macklin Street. Even so, branches are better serviced
and they themselves have become inextricably bound up
with other groups. The result has been much valuable
cross-fertilisation of ideas, resources and
activities at local level. This in turn has given a
much firmer reality to the grassroots welfare
movement.

It is difficult, as Ruth Lister readily admits,
to pinpoint positive achievements since 1979 as much
of the Group's work, even in harness with other
organisations, has been about 'principled rearguard
action' rather than strident policy advance (40). In
a sense, then, the achievement of CPAG has been in
the field of prevention rather than cure. The halting
or, at least, the modifying of damaging Government

policy has been the order of the day. The Group has won much support in the process from a growing body of Conservative MPs and party activists that it has done much to inform and cultivate in the period since Mrs Thatcher first took office. CPAG moved quickly in the Prime Minister's first term to inform and consolidate the views and work of an influential group of Tory backbenchers, including two current junior ministers Chris Patten and William Waldegrave, who declared themselves increasingly uneasy with the direction of Conservative social policy. Their individual and collective efforts, supported regularly by CPAG briefings, have contributed significantly in smoothing many of the rougher edges of Government policy and in delaying, blocking or, more commonly, reducing the impact of social security cuts.

In the autumn of 1980, for example, it had been widely expected that a further round of cuts would be announced in the Chancellor's Economic Statement. It was feared in particular that the Treasury would press home a repetition of the five per cent abatement and that legislation to remove the duty to uprate pensions and other long term benefits in line with inflation was now in the offing. In the event, after pointed questions from her backbenches and a confrontation in Cabinet during which Mrs Thatcher was allegedly reminded of her pledge to maintain the real value of the pension on the <u>Weekend World</u> television programme during the election campaign, no further cuts were announced. Instead, the Government decided to claw back the one per cent by which the 1980 uprating exceeded inflation.

Similarly, during the Budget of 1981 the decision to uprate child benefit in line with inflation whilst personal tax allowances were frozen was attributed, at least in part, to the influence of CPAG supporters and the 'child benefit lobby' on the Tory backbenches.

Again, in the Autumn of 1981, there were renewed reports of Treasury pressure to slash social security expenditure and strong fears of a cut in unemployment benefit. Once more the Chancellor failed to steer further cuts through Cabinet. It was decided instead to make good the two per cent shortfall for pensions and long-term benefits (excluding the long term SB rate for those below pension age) only. However, once again, the reaction of the Tory backbenches was so hostile that the Chancellor was obliged in the Budget to make it good for all benefits. There were to be similar successes in the Autumn of 1983 in blocking

Treasury attempts to re-index-link a range of benefits for the unemployed and young people and, later still, many leading Conservatives as well as Tory backwoodsmen were able to draw closely on CPAGs counter-arguments to Norman Fowler's <u>Reform of Social Security</u>.

Elsewhere, the Group has assured its continuing party political independence in its profitable use of 'breakfast meetings' with senior Conservatives at the party's annual conference - a 'working session' that usually draws senior DHSS and Treasury Ministers, leading backbenchers and the Chair of the Conservative Women's National Committee in which the Group has found a valuable, if unusual, ally since 1979. During Mrs Thatcher's second administration backbench opposition to social security cuts has, perhaps, been rather more fragmented and less 'organised' not least because of a highly individualistic intake after the 1983 Election. Even so, as the debates on the Social Security Reviews were to demonstrate in 1985 there were still and continue to be many Conservative allies for the Group to cultivate.

However, we remain concerned for the present with CPAG's liaison with other groups in the child benefits and social security 'lobbies'. A notable achievement here, and one which reflects the sort of co-operative work referred to above was the successful lobbying by CPAG, FSU and the National Council for One Parent Families for an amendment to the Employment Bill (1980) to allow pregnant women paid time off work to attend ante-natal clinics. Rather more impressive, however, were the joint efforts of CPAG and NCOPF in pressing, successfully, for the abolition of the contribution tests for the maternity grant - a campaign which led also to the establishment of the Maternity Alliance.

There is clearly a useful and semi-regularised relationship of sorts, with NCOPF which itself has become far more of a pressure group in the last few years. CPAG's December 1980 paper, <u>Swings and Roundabouts</u>, a response to the Government's Consultative Document on Maternity Benefits, had rejected each of the three key proposals for change which, for the group 'amounted to no more than a variety of ways of re-allocating the existing money spent on the Maternity Grant, allowance and pay in each case making some women better off at the expense of a far larger number of losers' (41). The group called instead for the Maternity Grant to be increased to £100, thereby restoring its value to that of ten years earlier.

CPAG's involvement in the issue had brought with it an additional impetus that found expression in the establishment of the Maternity Alliance with NCOPF and FSU in the November. The Alliance would become 'an umbrella organisation under which lay people - especially individual mothers - professionals and groups such as trade unions and women's organisations can come together ... a forum of what needs to be done in the legal, social and financial fields as well as to press for improvement in medical services' (42).

By the time of the Alliance's response to the Fowler Reviews in June 1985, which we shall come to later, its membership exceeded some fifty organisations, including the Health Education Council, Brook Advisory Centres, COHSE, the Health Visitors Association, the Royal College of Midwives, the Royal College of Nursing, SENSE, the Spastic Society and fifteen Community Health Councils.

Towards the end of 1980 CPAG jointly published with the Family Service Unit <u>Living From Hand to Mouth</u>, a survey of the living standards of 65 families on supplementary benefit. It was the sort of work the DHSS itself would have to take clear notice of. It was, in the group's own words, designed to present

> ... a graphic picture using the words of the families themselves of just how dismal life on supplementary benefit is for families who are long-term claimants. It found that families were not even able to enjoy the minimum standard of living that according to the Supplementary Benefit Regulations they should be able to receive. (43)

The Report was presented to DHSS Ministers amid renewed Treasury pressure for further social security cuts. One favoured target was the supplementary benefit scale rates. This was to provoke a further flurry of joint campaigning, this time with CPAG and the Disability Alliance heading a consortium of eight voluntary organisations covering the main client groups. The cuts were, as we have stated, subsequently averted other than for a decision to claw back a one per cent overshoot. It was a significant concession since much greater cuts had been widely predicted.

Further joint activity has been undertaken through an informal grouping of welfare organisations known informally to the participants themselves as the 'anti-social security cuts group' established in the early 1980s. This was and continues to be a very loose coalition set up to oppose the 'divide and rule' approach of the present Government which is so threatening to the already highly fragmented nature of British social policy and which seeks to exploit the brittle pluralism of. an impoverished welfare lobby.

This informal 'anti-cuts group' has thus far proved a determined venture in resisting Government's attempts to play one welfare organisation off against another in the bid for resources and attention. As the leaks from the DHSS and other departments, notably the Treasury, begin to spring in the autumn of each year, so a co-ordinated response from the anti-cuts group begins to crystallise. A coalition which has, as occasion demands, numbered CPAG, NCOPF, the Low-Pay Unit, the Family Service Units, the FWA, Age Concern, Disability Alliance, RADAR, Youth Aid, CHAR and SHAC among its ranks is inevitably fluid, but it remains the case that as particular issues arise some groups will emerge as 'key worker' or 'spokesman' by virtue of function, their own position largely bolstered by the support of the 'pack' (44). SHAC, for example, which came to join the 'group' only in the latter part of 1984 has been at the forefront of the anti-cuts group's work and statements on the housing benefits issue since that time. On taxation and low pay the coalition has inevitably looked to the Low-Pay Unit for particular direction. Even so, it is CPAG which is seen as overall leader of the pack.

The existence of such an informal grouping has been particularly important in a period when Government has viewed social policy very much in nil cost or zero growth terms. The financing of initiatives in welfare and social security thus substantially assumes a zero-sum character. If the cake remains static then the only means of gaining a bigger slice is through redistribution and playing one client public against another. Clearly, the view of the anti-cuts group is that this has to be withstood. Ironically, the very sophistication and diversity of the welfare lobby have contributed to precisely the sort of conditions in which Government might divide and rule. Greater sophistication among a multiplicity of groups has made it increasingly difficult for each to attract and then sustain resources and publicity for their activities. Welfare rights, social security and the human tragedy of individual cases have far less headline value in the mid eighties than they did in the mid seventies and mid sixties. In a very real sense the welfare lobby has itself become overloaded with a range of groups preoccupied with and involved in 'rights' issues. CPAG is no longer out on its own, as perhaps it was in the sixties and perhaps even as late as the mid seventies. In its second decade the Group has had to cede its quasi-monopolistic position in the field to an extensively populated welfare lobby whose development, paradoxically, it is partially responsible for setting in train.

It may appear, then, that the active presence of other specialised groups has reduced the importance with which CPAG is perceived and rather more narrowly confined its traditional role as 'champion of the poor'. Yet the evidence suggests that while CPAG is no longer a lone voice in the wilderness, it may well have become the choir leader and nowhere is this more clearly illustrated than in the work of the Group's Citizens Rights Office and the use of and deference to it by other bodies.

THE CITIZENS RIGHTS OFFICE

In the 1975 report, <u>Which Way Welfare Rights</u>, the Welfare Rights Working Party, comprising CPAG and a range of other welfare rights organisations, spoke of the creation of a CPAG Legal Department in 1968 and a Citizens Rights Office in 1970 as enabling the Group ... "To embrace a commitment to protecting and extending poor people's rights". It went on to note also that ... "As CPAG's activities have broadened, so it no longer has a monopoly of the field. Other national and local organisations such as SHELTER, Claimants Unions, DIG, Mothers in Action, Legal Action Group, tenants associations, community development projects, are equally concerned with the rights of poor people to an adequate income, decent housing, protection from eviction etc and more generally, to protection from the sometimes arbitrary decisons of private and public bureaucracies" (45).

The Working Party went on to observe that as more organisations have become concerned with and involved in welfare rights work so definitions of welfare rights had changed and that this had led to CPAG and a number of other rights organisations coming together to "... discuss their common problems and talk about the implications of their separate strategies and tactics and the desirability of working each in their different ways towards a common set of aims and objectives" (46).

To some extent, clearly, work between CPAG and individual groups directly, together with that with trade union research deparments, the Trade Union Forum, with the Unemployment Alliance, with the Family Allowance Movement, and, more recently, with the Anti-Social Security Cuts Group have each become the practical demonstration of those sentiments. Yet it is the work of the CRO over the last 15 or 16 years which has become the most enduring touchstone for other groups in their liaison with CPAG.

Unique from the outset, and very much influenced by the thinking of Tony Lynes during his own leadership of CPAG, the Citizens Rights Office was seen as ... "A pioneer among advice centres ... The CRO broke away both from the Citizens Advice Bureau tradition, as well as from the ideas for neighbourhood law centres that were being aired at the time, by employing one lawyer to whom cases requiring his expertise would be filtered through trained lay staff competent to deal with the majority of cases" (47).

By the mid seventies at least, the work and experience of the CRO had well proved the value of lay advocates working alongside a qualified lawyer. More importantly for the Group, it could be claimed that ... "As part of CPAG, the CRO has been able to move beyond the simple enforcement of individual poor people's rights to the extension of these rights through a variety of advocacy techniques and through the courts and Parliament" (48).

The work of the CRO has continued to demonstrate a major belief of the 1975 Report that welfare rights activities have added a new dimension to pressure group activity. By 1980, CPAG could justifiably claim that as the numbers of poor families living below the poverty line and those dependent on supplementary benefit had increased, as had, consequently, the need for help in claiming benefits then ... "So has the workload of the CRO as more claimants need help with the exceedingly complex social security system on which they are dependent" (49).

The rationale of the CRO was distilled succinctly by CPAG in its 1979 Annual Report thus ..."The case work of the CRO shows very clearly where reforms are needed in the social security system and our proposals for policy changes are very dependent on the lessons learned from this work" (50). That rationale was to be well demonstrated throughout the

next five years and, notably, during the passage of
the 1980 Social Security Acts. The outcome for the
CRO was to be ... '... more work on all fronts',
whether it took the form of direct provision of
advice and advocacy skills to claimants and welfare
rights advisers, specialist briefing notes to MP's
for Parliamentary debate or the running of study days
and training courses on the legislation for welfare
rights officers and social workers.

The impact of this legislation on the work of
the CRO is usefully illustrated in its receipt of
over 5,500 enquiries in the year, around half of
which came from claimants or those looking to advise
them. More than half of those enquiries concerned
supplementary benefit with a further 10% raising
national insurance issues. The resulting casework
contributed, as usual, to the educational work of the
office. In the last quarter of 1980 alone, the CRO
held twelve courses across the country largely on the
implications of the new laws for supplementary
benefits. Moreover, these were in addition to the
week-long courses and half-day working seminars it
had traditionally run four times a year on particular
aspects of social security law and welfare rights
work. 1980 was to see the launch of a new training
initiative ... 'the beginning of special one-day
conferences on aspects of social security
appropriate for particular groups'. Significantly
... 'the first of these was held in December for
trade unionists' (51). The year closed, with some
irony, with the award to the CRO of a DHSS grant to
monitor the new supplementary benefit scheme which
had done so much to increase and complicate its
workload.

The following year, 1981, the CRO was confronted
in its own words with conflicting demands on its time
...

> Not only did there continue to be a stream of
> new legislation for which help with briefings
> was given, but the monitoring of the post 1980
> supplementary benefit scheme and the continued
> demand from welfare rights advisers and social
> workers for training, meant that it has been a
> struggle to achieve a happy balance between
> responding to these demands and doing a
> sufficient quantity of case-work to ensure that
> our experience of the problems confronted was
> maintained. The demands of cases sent to us for
> advice on possible appeals to the Social
> Security Commissioners on supplementary benefit

matters have at times threatened to dominate our work at the expense of other areas. (52)

The level of enquiries received by the Office in 1980 was exceeded with over six thousand telephone enquiries and a further one thousand written queries. Once again the central concern from claimants, welfare rights advisers, and social workers alike was supplementary benefit and, particularly, the treatment of resources. Tribunal work, inevitably, was given a fresh impetus by the events of 1980. Even so, the CRO staff were to note that the pressures upon the Office had, however, shifted the emphasis more towards advocacy work before the Social Security Commission rather than at tribunals ...

... This perhaps reflects a more general movement of the Rights Office away from being a 'primary' agency taking cases at an initial level to more of a secondary agency assisting other agencies and taking difficult cases and those subject to further appeal from them. This has been one of the ways by which we have had to ration and rationalise our work. (53)

This growing 'specialisation' was to bring with it some notable early successes, not the least of which was the CRO's successful lobbying for the establishment of entitlement to attendance allowance for epileptics and mobility allowance for mentally handicapped people. Alongside the case-work and advocacy, education and training continued to flourish with interesting co-initiatives developing with the Joint Council for the Welfare of Immigrants on issues of immigration and benefit entitlement and with the Kensington and Chelsea Area Health Authority in providing a series of study days on health and social security issues. As if to prove the value of casework and 'working at the coal face' the CRO spent some effort also in ... 'underlining the importance we attach to rights work within social work departments and the value of at least a general knowledge of welfare rights by social workers ...' in its evidence to the Barclay Commission (54).

Social workers and welfare rights advisers were drawing increasingly upon the work of the CRO throughout 1982 also. The role of the Office as a 'secondary' advice agency was to give further substance as local authorities, trade unions and other voluntary organisations gave renewed effort to welfare rights work.

The establishment of welfare rights officers around the Country together with the greater complexity of supplementary benefit has meant that we are increasingly servicing other organisations and workers although individuals are still the largest group of people writing to the Office for advice or ringing us up. (55)

Around seventy per cent of all written queries and fifty per cent of telephone enquiries once again concerned supplementary benefit, with national insurance, disability and housing benefit issues trailing quite a way behind. Overall, the year saw some eight thousand enquiries to the Office. In an analysis of enquiry-source the CRO revealed that social services departments and voluntary organisations closely followed individuals as the key users. Between April 1982 and April 1983 the Office opened 81 new files, most concerned with supplementary benefit and most of them requiring appeal to the Social Security Commissioners.

In a particularly demanding year the CRO was also to publish the Welfare Rights Bulletin every other month; produce the Parliamentary briefing for the Health and Social Security and Social Security (Adjudication) Bills for both the House of Lords and the House of Commons and put together submissions to the Social Security Advisory Committee on time limits, board and lodgings ceiling and on a range of draft social security regulations. In 1983 individual claimants, voluntary organisations and social services departments once again proved the key sources of enquiries to the Office with, in telephone terms at least, the percentage working out at forty two per cent, twenty three per cent and fourteen per cent respectively with Citizens Advice Bureaux the fourth key user group at thirteen per cent. A major area of work in the year inevitably stemmed from the full scale introduction of housing benefit in the April.

... This in turn set off a demand from some local authorities for teaching on the supplementary benefit system aimed at their housing benefits staff. Courses were organised for individual authorities such as Camden, Portsmouth and Milton Keynes ... Additionally a series of day-long teaching sessions will run for the Institute of Housing in London, Birmingham, Glasgow, Bradford and Bristol ... The joint CPAG/SHAC Rights Guide For Home Owners

was re-written and published in the autumn.
Publication was followed by a series of joint
day courses with SHAC on its contents. (56)

The joint CPAG/SHAC guide was only one element
however in a range of published work pouring forth
from the CRO in 1983. Alongside there came also the
National Welfare Benefits Handbook and the Rights
Guide to Non Means-Tested Social Security Benefits,
both published in time for the annual up-rating of
benefits in November. In December there followed
Supplementary Benefit Legislation Annotated in which
the CRO also had a hand.
    Elsewhere, the CRO had met with the Social
Security Advisory Committee (SSAC) and with Judge
Byrt, incoming President of the Appeal Tribunals; the
Office had participated in CPAG's evidence to the
Race Relations and Immigrations Sub-committee of the
Commons Home Affairs Committee and had itself echoed
CPAG's developing liaison with other groups through
its own involvement in the various sub-committees of
NACAB, RADAR, the GLC's Welfare Rights Computer
Group, Right to Fuel and the Lord Chancellor's
Advisory Committee's Legal Services Conferences.
    By the close of the first Thatcher
administration, and partly as a result of that
Government's burdensome legislative programme, the
CRO had come to acquire a clear secondary role. It
was now rather less involved in, though not entirely
free of, the more mundane and run of the mill social
security work and able to operate, as well as being
looked to, as the principal specialist group in the
field advising and to some extent servicing the other
welfare rights agencies and groups which had come to
replace it at the 'coal-face'. Ironically, the CRO
has since increasingly found itself having to draw on
the general case-work provided by other groups in
order to give its parent body, CPAG, that 'nuts and
bolts' backup that Tony Lynes spoke of in the sixties
as so vital in informing the pressure group activity
of the Group (57).

COUNTING THE COST

It is no mere coincidence nor simply a testament to a
growing sophistication in their operations that the
work of both CPAG and the CRO increased substantially
in the three and a half years of Mrs Thatcher's first
administration; so much so in the CRO's case that it
underwent an important role change as a direct

consequence of having to ration and rationalise its work-load. There were, of course, a multiplicity of factors. Take, for example, the case of unemployment. In May 1979 there were just over half a million unemployed people receiving supplementary benefit, yet within three years the figure had rocketted to 1.5 million. There were two chief causes - a massive and sustained rise in the numbers of unemployed and, perhaps more disturbingly, a deliberate cut in the real value of State support through the national insurance scheme to those out of work. Mrs Thatcher's pre-occupation with 'skivers' and 'scroungers', so shabbily illustrated in the extraordinary DHSS 'snoop squad' adventure, Operation Major in Oxford in 1982, found a vindictive chord in a range of Government policy throughout the period.

Moreover, this occurred in parallel with a deliberate boost to the position of those in the high income bracket. CPAG supporters were to write as much in the run-up to the 1983 General Election ...

> This widening of pay inequalities over the period 1979-1982 is remarkable when set against the long term stability in the distribution of earnings. It is also clear that it is the intended consequence of Government decisions. A policy of selective wage control has been operated which has pressed most heavily on the low paid ... Unemployment does not fall evenly on the working population; low wage earners are far more vulnerable to redundancy. This has meant that the Government's 'incomes policy, in the form of more than four million unemployed, has hit the low paid hardest'. (58)

The Group was to conclude abruptly that the social costs of monetarism had been borne directly by the unemployed and, in particular the great legion of long term unemployed people. They were, quite simply ... 'the conscripts in the battle against inflation and the casualties of economic restructuring' (59).

In her first three years of office and with an election still six months away Mrs Thatcher's instinct 'towards a set of policies which confounded the post war Tory tradition' took unemployment from 1.3 million to over three million. The figures, however, only told part of the story. The exclusion of some groups from the equation and a wholly immoral shift in favour of 'massaging' statistics and 'problem' re-definition, led to an official under estimation of the extent of unemployment by at least a further one million people, notably the disabled, large numbers of married women and those unemployed for short periods. Small wonder that the CRO was to express bewilderment at the sheer volume of supplementary benefit work pouring in between 1980 and 1983. The position was further complicated and exacerbated by an increased dependancy on supplementary benefit as a result of Government cuts in national insurance benefits. Writing in Thatcherism and the Poor Geoff Fimister explained the impact of the Government's intrusion into this hitherto shaded corner of the Welfare State ...

> where previous regimes had neglected the levels of national insurance benefits, the present Government has deliberately aimed to reduce the value of many of them. This has contributed substantially to the 'mass role' for supplementary benefit. Some cuts have been made in a rather brazen fashion ... on the other hand others have entailed extreme deviousness (national insurance children's additions). Cuts in national insurance benefits have undermined the credibility of the 'insurance principle'. (60)

The mass role for SB to which Fimister refers is even more disturbing given that the Government was manifestly aware, on coming to Office in 1979, of the serious limitations of and flaws in the supplementary benefit scheme. Indeed the Supplementary Benefits Commission, before its own demise at the hands of Patrick Jenkin, had already shown it to be barely adequate to meet needs and CPAG's own views were particularly well documented. Abuse, mis-use and non-use of the scheme by successive Governments, as CPAG had persistently and strenuously shown, merely opened the door for the Thatcher Government to erode further the weakened fabric of social security provision. Writing in the same publication Carole Walker concluded that the Government had ...

> added to these past failures its own much less tolerant and much less sensitive attitude towards recipients of State benefits. First, senior ministers have themselves led a well orchestrated campaign on the issue of fraud and abuse and, in particular, on the 'work shy syndrome' ... Second, this Government has been the first to insist that the social security budget takes its share of public expenditure

cuts. Whilst the most severe cuts have fallen on other benefits, their impact has been deliberately to increase dependence on supplementary benefit and to concentrate help ... on those dependent on means-tested benefits alone - to the detriment of the many other low income families. However, even the safety net has not survived unscathed. (61)

If the reform of supplementary benefit was carried through with relish and with particular emphasis on its 'nil cost' or 'neutrality' similar features were evident in the Government's approach to housing support which produced, as Norman Fowler's own Review Team was to admit in 1985, arguably the most unsatisfactory and complicated measure of State support ever introduced under the banner of the Welfare State and which amounted to a classic device by which Mrs Thatcher's Government could, as Ruth Lister and Paul Wilding described it, 'export' its own responsibilites to local government, to charities and to the voluntary sector.

The role of local government proved controversial in other areas of welfare provision also, notably in the case of free school meals. Here was an area where the discriminatry and stigmatising effects of Government policy and ideology were particularly in evidence. Under a Tory Government appropriately led by a Prime Minister dubbed 'the snatcher' in 1971 for her abolition of free school milk when Education Minister, the reality of universal provision and a common standard was punctured with the burden of cost shifting towards parents once more. With the terse and engineered move towards local autonomy in provision came declining standards and a further opportunity for Central Government to demean the poor by subjecting them to the means-test. In its wake there followed ... 'enormous local variations in prices, quality and standards of meals, ineligibility for free school meals and, indeed, whether a service is provided beyond the bare statutory minimum' (62).

Worse still children moving from one local education authority to another could now find themselves ... 'suddenly ineligible for free meals, faced with higher charges for poorer quality meals, or even without a meal at all'.

Reflecting on Britain's first dose of Thatcherism and the prospect of a more determined second term as the Tories cashed in on the emctional swell of the 'Falklands factor', Ruth Lister and Paul

314

Wilding were in no doubt that it was the poor who would suffer the brunt of Thatcher's Britain.

> ... it is the poor who suffer most from the ideological parts of Thatcherism, branding them as feckless and fraudulent, poor because of charcteristics rather than because of circumstances ... it is the poor who suffer most from the <u>reduction of statutory responsibility</u> which has been one of the Government's central concerns ... it is the poor who suffer most from the re-definition of the role and purposes of social services, which can aptly be described as <u>residualism</u> - a limitation of provision to the poorest. (63)

In three and a half years the Thatcher Government had increased stigmatisation, discrimination, dependancy and anxiety. It had sown the seeds of a deep uncertainty for the future, not least with a second term looming, and given an impetus to privatisation and to declining standards in its relentless concern to reduce public expenditure and narrow the frontiers of State responsibility. In these three and a half years it presided over a near tripling of unemployment and a massive increase in the numbers of people and families dependant on an increasingly ramshackle and thread-bare supplementary benefit system. At the same time it had plundered some £2,000 million annually from the social security system. At the centre of this onslaught on the poor and the unemployed there remained, as ever for CPAG, the issue of Child Benefit and the broader question of Britain's advancement towards an imaginative, fair and progressive family policy. The latter, especially, was to achieve particular prominence in the six months preceding the 1983 General Election as CPAG and others set out the alternatives to a radical and regressive strain in Tory thinking which, during yet another episode of leaked Cabinet papers, came to offer a disquieting preview of Mrs Thatcher's second term of office.

NOTES

1. Wapshott, N. & Brock G. <u>Thatcher</u>, MacDonald & Co., 1983, p.106.
2. Ibid., pp.183-84.
3. <u>The Conservative Manifesto 1979</u>, p.6.
4. Ibid., p.7.

5.   "In the Autumn of 1969 CPAG advertised for a Director. Working for the Group held out a number of attractions for me. In the first place it would provide a direct opportunity to campaign for poor families. As I had aleady fought a Parliamentary seat, working for CPAG had the additional advantage of building up a range of technical information and political skills which would be useful for a member of the House of Commons." Field, F. Poverty & Politics. (HEB.) 1982, p.29.

6.   Poverty, No. 42, April 1979, p.2.

7.   The Conservative Manifesto, 1979, p.26.

8.   Ibid.

9.   Ibid., p.27.

10.   Interview with Ruth Lister, May 9th 1985.

11.   Ibid.

12.   Field, F. 'How the Poor Fared' in Coates, K. (Ed.) What Went Wrong Spokesman, 1979, p.160.

13.   Interview with Ruth Lister, May 9th, 1985.

14.   Field, F. Poverty & Politics, pp.46-47.

15.   Report of the Child Poverty Action Group for 1979 (to October) p.1.

16.   Ibid., p.3.

17.   Ibid., p.4.

18.   Ibid.

19.   Ibid., p.5.

20.   Poverty, No. 46. August 1980, p.34.

21.   Ibid., p.35.

22.   Bradshaw, J. 'Child Benefit: Is CPAG's Policy Right?', Poverty No. 45, April 1980, p.15.

23.   Ibid.

24.   Ibid., p.16.

25.   Ibid.

26.   Ibid., p.20.

27.   Poverty No. 46, August 1980, p.3.

28.   Ibid., p.4.

29.   Ibid., p.5.

30.   Ibid.

31.   Ibid., p.6.

32.   Ibid., p.10.

33.   Ibid., p.11.

34.   Reform of Social Security, Cmnd. No. 9518, June 1985, p.23, para. 2.70.

35.   Poverty, No.46, p.12.

36.   Interview with Ruth Lister, May 9th 1985.

37.   Evans, M. 'Trade Unions & Social Security Acts', Poverty, No.46, p.28.

38.   Report of the Work of the CPAG 1981, p.5.

39.   Ibid.

40.   Report of the Work of the CPAG, 1980, p.5.

41.   Ibid.

42.   Ibid.
43.   Ibid., p.4.
44.   Interview with Ruth Lister, May 9th, 1985.
45.   <u>Welfare in Action</u> - A CPAG Report, November 1975, p.1.
46.   Ibid.
47.   Ibid., p.8.
48.   Ibid., pp.8-9.
49.   <u>Report of the CPAG 1979 (to October)</u>, p.6.
50.   Ibid., p.7.
51.   <u>Report of the CPAG, 1980</u>, p.1.
52.   <u>Report of the CPAG, 1981</u>, p.1.
53.   Ibid.
54.   Ibid., p.2.
55.   <u>Report of the CPAG</u>, 1982, p.1.
56.   <u>CPAG Annual Report</u>, 1983, p.4.
57.   Interview with Ruth Lister, May 9th, 1985.
58.   Walker, A; Winyard, S; Pond, C, 'Conservative Economic Policy: The Social Consequences' in Bull, D. and Wilding, P. <u>Thatcherism & the Poor</u>, April, 1983, p.17. (CPAG).
59.   Ibid.
60.   Fimister, G. 'Social Securty: Extending the Mass Role', ibid., pp.34-35.
61.   Ibid., p.36.
62.   Walker, C. 'Supplementary Benefit: The Sinking Saftey Net', Ibid., p.50.
63.   Lister, R. and Wilding, P. 'The Verdict on Thatcherism', Ibid., pp.75-76.

Chapter Thirteen

FREEDOM AND RESPONSIBILITY: FROM FAMILY POLICY GROUP
TO FOWLER

In its 1983 General Election Manifesto the Government
assured the Electorate that ... 'Freedom and
responsibilty go together' ... and that ... 'The
Conservative Party believes in encouraging people to
take responsibility for their own decisions. We shall
continue to return more choice to individuals and
their families. That is the way to increase personal
freedom. It is also the way to improve standards in
the State services' (1). Just two years later in June
1985, the Government enshrined those principles in
Reform of Social Security. More pointedly, the
Manifesto asserted that ... 'Conservatives believe
equally strongly in the duty of Government to help
those who are least able to help themselves...' and
that the Government's record so far... 'Rebuts the
totally unfounded charge that we want to "dismantle"
the Welfare State ...' (2). Those sentiments, too,
were to find their expression in the 1985 Green
Paper, described by Norman Fowler as ... 'The most
substantial examination of the social security
system since the Beveridge Report' (3).
        For CPAG the next two years were to be spent in
comprehensive preparation for that 'substantial
examination' and in advancing counter arguments to
the dismantlement of Beveridge. An icy wind of change
had already blown in the leaks emerging from the CPRS
in September 1982 and from the Family Policy Group in
February 1983. One leading CPAG member, Malcolm
Wicks, was certain that in the wake of the huge
majority of June 1983 a second dose of Tory social
policy would now complete the move towards 'two
nations'.

        ... The leaked papers from both the 'Think
    Tank', the CPRS and the Ministerial Family
    Policy Group show that more radical options are

now being actively considered. The Tory years of
1979-83 were a trial run from which the
Government has learnt some important lessons.
The extreme Right is now poised to mount a
successful assault on the Welfare State ... (4)

For Wicks, the second Thatcher administration would
have far reaching implications for social security
and would herald the de-indexing of pensions from
prices; the restructuring of the State Earnings-
Related Pension Scheme (SERPS); the Tories would hold
down unemployment benefit and supplementary benefit;
and they would attempt to means-test Child Benefit.

The move away from collective provision,
combined with rampant individualism - far from
allowing more choice and liberty - would be
associated with increasing greed, disregard of
human suffering and social division. (5)

There was abundant evidence in both the leaked
deliberations of the CPRS and in the evidence that
had emerged from the Family Policy Group to suggest
that those fears were well justified.

THE THINK TANK REPORT

The thinking of the CPRS had been revealed in an
authoritative leak to The Economist in September
1982, in which it became clear that its brief had
amounted to a search for ...'options for radical cuts
in public spending, many involving the dismantling of
huge chunks of the Welfare state' (6). Although Ruth
Lister was able to reflect some months later that
divisions within Cabinet had ensured that the report
became a 'dead duck' by the Conservative Conference
in October 1982 there was no question of the content
of the report being buried for good. As David Lipsey
was to point out in The Times the following February
...'in the Departments, in Departmental planning
units and the recesses of the Treasury, work on the
report's proposals to slash the welfare state goes on
... the mandarins know full well that once the
election hurdle is cleared, the Government's
ideological determination to curb the public sector
will put them back in the real cuts business' (7).
The basis of such cuts was, moreover, political
rather than economic as Lister herself pointed out
...'underpinning the Think Tank report is the premise
that, without radical cuts of the kind outlined,

public spending on welfare will rise to such a large
proportion of total resources that a massive increase
in taxation would be required to fund it ...' and
that ...'this is less an economic assumption than a
political prejudice' (8).

Worse still, the prospect of further cuts and a
deeply moralistic approach to family policy were
being advertised, as CPAG protested, in the immediate
wake of a DHSS-sponsored study into deprivation that
had remarked forcefully ...

> it is impossible to resist a re-iteration of the
> general conclusion from much of the work that
> benefit rates, particularly of supplementary
> benefit and child benefit, are simply too low at
> present for some families to avoid real hardship
> and damaging consequences to health and other
> life chances of their children. (9)

In a special issue of Poverty devoted to an
analysis of the CPRS report, Francis Williams of The
Times was certain that it had sprung from two sets of
economic assumptions of dubious merit ...

> the first ... was that without rapid economic
> growth, public spending as a proportion of
> national output will grow inexorably to the end
> of the decade, requiring a massive increase in
> taxation to pay for it. The second was that an
> increase in the proportion of GDP taken by
> public spending is inherently undesirable. (10)

It was, of course, a reiteration of that
recurring governmental view that the level and
sophistication of social services, health services
and education should be a direct function of 'what
the economy can afford'. The Prime Minister was to
say as much in her introduction to the 1983
manifesto. She did not doubt that ... 'we have a duty
to protect the most vulnerable members of our society
...' but, and here came the predictable rub, ...'only
if we create wealth can we continue to do justice to
the old and the sick and the disabled. It is economic
success which will provide the surest guarantee of
help for those who need it most'. It was this brand
of thinking and its emphasis less on the crisis in
public expenditure and rather more on making
deliberate choices between welfare or tax cuts that
was to find its strongest echo in the 1983 Green
Paper 'The Next Ten Years'.

If much of the hue and cry that surrounded the

Report had concerned its radical thoughts on the future of the NHS and state education and its elaboration of the relative merits and de-merits of public versus private provision, the implications for social security had taken a back seat. As Fran Bennett, then Research Officer with GMBATU and later Deputy Director of CPAG, pointed out ...'no such root and branch reform of the structure of finance was suggested for the social security system; the Report merely pointed to the large savings which could be made if benefits were not index-linked year by year' (11). But that, of course, was the quiet revolution proposed by the Report - a revolution that would affect millions of the most vulnerable and the poorest in society and a revolution that would build on a savage reduction in the social security budget of some £2 billion a year already. The Government's 'supporters' were already carrying the idea forward. Bennett cited a servile editorial in The Times on December 1st which stated flatly that ...'no modern Government can afford to be hooked on a commitment constantly to revalue social benefits upwards'.

The point had, however, been missed ...'this Government could not be hoist by its own petard by abandoning a commitment to index-linked benefits, for the simple reason that it made no such promise in its pre-election manifesto ... whilst not openly abandoning some link with inflation as the normal measure for benefit upratings, the Government has, nonetheless, made massive inroads into claimants standards of living' (12).

Thus far, the Government had not come out into the open on what it saw as the vexed issue of index-linking social security benefits and had, in effect, sought to head-off resistance, especially on its own damp flanks, by allowing the value of benefits to decline as a consequence of institutional 'inertia' rather than by openly prosecuting a case for non-index linked payments. Many benefits, of course, were not covered by a legal obligation to uprating anyway. Child Benefit itself had not been maintained at its April 1979 level in real terms and as Bennett observed ...'the Government was able to exploit a legal loophole in the loosely drafted rules for linking rises in child benefit with upgrading in the child additions paid with contributory benefits, in order to reduce significantly in real terms the total amount received for children by claimants of contributory benefit' (13).

For the Government's part, if money could be saved by quietly overlooking, delaying or actually reducing benefit payments, then that was an acceptable way of avoiding a loud and unedifying joust with the poverty lobby and the opposition parties. That, asserted Bennett, had now all changed ...'the significance of the Think Tank proposals to de-index social security benefits lies in its heralding the end of the shadow-boxing to which we have become accustomed over the past few years' (14).

That strategy of cuts by stealth could now be jettisoned from a position of extraordinary strength in the opinion polls in the wake of the Falklands war. Yet, paradoxically, the huge expenditure on the South Atlantic campaign had also exposed the sheer cynicism of Government claims that the country simply could not afford even basic levels of service provision and subsistence benefits. That claim was driven hard in a Think Tank, report that was manifestly uninterested in social principles or in arguments for a properly resourced social security system and which was wholly motivated instead by a belief that the welfare state was a burden on the tax payer that must be reduced at every opportunity. That was the way to release initiative and enterprise, to foster responsibility and to enhance freedom. In tactical terms it constituted yet one more example of the Government willfully embarking on an offensive against the poor. There was, in Bennett's view, a very clear lesson here for the poverty lobby:

> ... in our desire to defend claimants against yet further cuts in benefit levels, we often ignore ... positive arguments in favour of expanded versions of 'they've suffered enough already'. We plead for mercy - or even a stay of execution - rather than challenge the principles by which 'justice' is meted out. (15)

FREEDOM AND RESPONSIBILITY: THE FAMILY POLICY GROUP

The notions of 'freedom' and 'responsibility' spelt out in the 1983 manifesto had earlier underpinned the thinking and proposals of the Family Policy Group also, as might be expected of a caucus of Cabinet Ministers given a firm brief by the Prime Minister to add meat to the bones of her arguments for the restoration of Victorian values and principles. It was all the more likely given that they were guided in their discussions by a right-wing journalist, Ferdinand Mount, who had now entered the stratosphere of 10 Downing Street as the Prime Minister's policy adviser, having coming to her attention as the author of a book <u>The Subversive Family</u>. It was inevitable, then, that some members of the Family Policy Group should arrive at the view that families should be encouraged ...'to reassume responsibilities taken on by the state, for example, responsibility for the disabled, the elderly ...' (16). Here was the exporting of state responsibilities that CPAG were to refer to in the run up to the election and the seeds also of Norman Fowler's Buxton speech of September 1984 to the Association of Directors of Social Services in which he was to reaffirm the Tory view of welfare as resting on the "twin pillars" of the individual and the state. Here, too, was a signpost for the Government's proposals for community care and social security as set out in the Green Paper of the following year.

But there was a good deal more in the FPG deliberations as Hilary Land pointed out ...'of course, one of the FPGs major objectives is to cut public spending on welfare. That this should be presented as 'family policy' and as a means of strengthening 'the family' is significant but not new ... alongside it sits the myth that the unemployed, at least unemployed men, are work-shy scroungers who must be 'encouraged' to be self reliant. Implicit in this is the belief that unemployment is voluntary and therefore the fault of the individual ...' (17).

She was certainly right that there was nothing new in this. After all the 1979 manifesto had spoken provocatively of 'restoring the will to work', of acting ...'more vigorously against fraud and abuse' and of tightening up ...'rules about the unemployed accepting available jobs'. Indeed, the 1979 manifesto and now the proposals of the FPG raised two themes that were to be seen as central to the Social Security Reviews of 1985. These were attempts to equate the incomes of the poorest in work with those of the poor out of work and, a vigorous reduction in public expenditure in order to facilitate tax cuts for a third Conservative election victory. The Governments of Mrs Thatcher have proved nothing if not consistent. The concern to isolate the unemployed poor was and continues to be a determinedly political ploy. Moreover, that ploy was to be executed against a backdrop of scrounger-phobia and an obsession with skivers decidedly more sophisticated and pervasive in its presentation than the disdain shown for the feckless and the work shy in Mrs Thatcher's first term of office.

The sentiments and goals expressed in May 1979

continued to develop throughout the Social Security
legislation of 1980 and 1982; through the discussions
of the CPRS and FPG in the early weeks of 1983; in
the section of the June manifesto that spoke of
'responsibility and the family' and in the Reviews of
the welfare state through 1984 and 1985. Yet as the
Government's thinking has entrenched so the
circumstances it seeks to address have changed
considerably. Consequently, the principles that
guide it have come to run even harder against the
grain of social disadvantage. The sheer growth in the
legion of unemployed; the misuse of the supplementary
benefits system to paper over the cracks; the
entrenchment of long term unemployment and the total
unwillingness of the Government to confront the
realities of the labour market have merely served to
exacerbate the highly precarious position of most
claimants out of work. What we see, therefore, in the
FPG proposals according to Land ..."is a re-assertion
which is always made more forcefully at times of high
male unemployment and rapid social change, that men
and women have, or ought to have very different
responsibilities within the family. Or at least
within marriage; note that one-parent families, the
majority of whom are mothers and children, must be
encouraged to be 'responsible and self reliant'
whereas mothers with husbands should be encouraged to
stay at home" (18).

Few could have been surprised, therefore, when
in Reform of Social Security a couple of years later
the Government spoke of the unemployed and single
parents as the 'undeserving poor' and built in as a
central theme of the Reviews a so called incentive to
work by further distancing the unemployed from the
mainstream of society.

In pursuing policies that would promote self
respect and a sense of individual responsibility the
Family Policy Group had clearly set out, in Malcolm
Wick's view, the "ideological trinity" at the heart
of the New Rights thinking - that of family, private
market and voluntary sector. Responsibilities
undertaken by the state were to be exported in the
direction of all three as one means of
...'encouraging the private provision of social
needs' (19); Individuals were to be given a firm push
towards self reliance and an impetus would come from
paring social assistance to bare safety net levels;
that, Ministers believed, would develop the will to
work. Elsewhere the Tory talisman of 'consumer
choice' and 'competition' were also prominent; the
state would no longer just work in harness with the

voluntary and private sectors, it would now find itself in active and direct competition with them.

Though the 1983 manifesto did later back away from detailing the proposals any further, the sheer generality of its content could not obscure the fact that there was every intention to give reality to this ideological trinity. For the poverty lobby the issue was not so much if but when. In the interim, an alternative case had to be stated and the debate on family policy had to be won.

> ... it remains to be seen how the Government will translate these aspirations into policies. In the meantime, we need to sieze the opportunity provided by The Guardian leaks to encourage a wide public debate about the principles upon which a forward rather than backward looking family policy should be based. (20)

There was, as Fran Bennett had made clear at the time of the CPRS leaks and now Ruth Lister and Malcolm Wicks demonstrated in the light of the Family Policy Group proposals, a clear opportunity to galvanise the debate on the future of family policy. Regardless of the content of those proposals, the Government had put family policy back on the agenda and here was an occasion for CPAG to set out its stall. It fell to Lister to restate and re-present ... 'our principles for the development of a positive family policy'.

The first of these was that ...'family policy should be built on genuine freedom of choice and a recognition of the diversity of family patterns' ... (21) at the heart of which was the group's concern that family policy should concentrate on issues of care and financial support for children rather than upon moral or ideological judgements about the nature and structure of family life. The group sought also to draw particular attention to the economic impact of child-rearing and to demonstrate that the income of those with children fails frequently to reflect the needs and responsibilities attendant in raising a family. The concern was, then, that ...'family policy should reflect the needs of families at different stages of the life cycle ...' and ...'should recognise the additional financial pressures on families with dependent children and that everyone has an obligation towards children, our most precious resource, whether parents themselves or not' (22). Here was a central plank in CPAGs policy since 1965,

the necessity for society at large to recognise
children as an investment for the future and one that
must be properly funded by all since all would share
in the return on that investment. The resources
required in such 'funding' were not wholly economic
nor were they simply to do with rising levels of
benefit. Rather, in CPAGs view ...'family policy
should be based on maintaining and expanding the
social wage ...' (23) and would require better social
services, more resources for education, improved
child care facilities and a fully developed range of
community support services.

The group was also concerned to challenge
assumptions that the total income of a family is an
accurate guide to the living standards of all of its
members. Such assumptions were, as it had repeatedly
explained, inaccurate and misleading and gave no
indication of the existence of 'hidden poverty' among
some members of a family, notably women and children.
The assumption that the breadwinner automatically
makes over all earnings for equitable distribution
within the family was, in CAPGs view, not only an
economic myth but also an obstacle to the achievement
of ...'the rights and needs of individuals within
families as well as those of the family as a unit'
(24).

The recognition of individual rights within the
family, especially in terms of perceived
responsibilities for child-rearing or broader
societal expectations about the role or gender of the
breadwinner, was especially important to the group,
not least because of the FPGs own regressive
observations on self reliance and family
responsibilities. These had also drawn the critical
attention of Hilary Land:

> ... self reliance, meaning individualism, in
> the context of the FPGs ideas is a creed to be
> adopted by men, upon whom women must depend
> while they care for their children, sick and
> elderly relatives - and, of course, their
> husbands. (25)

It was CPAGs strongly-held view that family policy
must not be conceived as an instrument for enforcing
patterns of reliance, responsibility or earnings. In
short, it ...'should not reinforce the artificial
division of labour between women and men'. As Ruth
Lister pointed out, the relatively low earning power
of women remains an essential factor in family
poverty, especially in one-parent families. A

progressive, imaginative and, above all, an
equitable family policy ...'will need to embrace
employment policies to ensure that parents of either
sex have the same opportunities to combine parenthood
with paid employment. Neither wages nor the tax or
social security systems should assume or reinforce
the economic dependence of one sex upon the other'
(26).
     This was an important truth to grapple with
since the distortion or abuse of rights and
responsibilities within families was not simply the
outcome of decisions or actions taken by members of
the family alone. Rather, such decisions had to be
seen in a broader context of the flawed and
discriminatory social, fiscal and economic policies
pursued by Government and state. Even in the most
progressive families, where individual rights were
upheld and responsibilities and earning roles were
shared, the distorting mechanisms of the tax and
social security systems and the sexual prejudices
inherent in economic activity had to be understood
and challenged if the pathway to a progressive family
policy was to be cleared. As Hilary Land notes ...'in
any society there is inevitably a tension between the
family and the state, in part because each is a
system for allocating rights, responsibilities,
rewards and resources. There are also important
questions to address about the impact which a highly
centralised, bureaucratised and undemocratic state
machinery has on its citizens. At least the FPG
recognise these as issues ...' (27).

THE 1983 GENERAL ELECTION

The pace of social policy was to move swiftly
throughout 1983 and into 1984. In the wake of a March
budget that had contained "some scraps of good news
for the poor", notably the restoration of the cuts in
child benefit and the adult rates of unemployment
benefit - both a testament to campaigns energetically
sustained by CPAG - there followed yet another leak,
this time demonstrating the Chancellor's implacable
opposition to any proposal to use savings from the
abolition of the married man's tax allowance to
improve child benefit. With it came an
acknowledgement that CPAG had been among those
'setting the pace' on the issue. Two days later, on
23 March, it became clear that the Chancellor was not
alone in opposing such a proposal, with reports that
the Labour Leadership were re-considering a 1982

327

party commitment to phase-out the married man's tax allowance as a means of financing a much-enhanced child benefit, and that Labour's Treasury team favoured the introduction of partially-transferable tax allowances. A swift response by CPAG and others, warning the Shadow Cabinet and Labour's NEC that the opposition of the 'family lobby' would be vehement, produced a further report two days later that the Shadow Chancellor, Peter Shore, had failed to win support among his colleagues for transferable allowances ... 'on the grounds that it would be maintaining the married man's tax allowance by another name' (28).

There were further leaks the following month, this time directly to CPAG, of proposals for an experimental scheme to send some contributory benefit giro cheques by second-class post. A written protest to the DHSS and a well placed parliamentary question by a sympathetic Tory back-bencher, produced a statement in the Commons from the Minister, Tony Newton, that his Department had abandoned the plan, at least in its proposed form and for the present. April was to prove an especially important period in both the run-up to the election itself and in consolidating CPAG's increasing effort to present, explain and confirm 'poverty' as an issue of major public, and not simply parliamentary or academic, interest. The chief landmark proved to be the launching of the first in a series of 'mega-conferences'. This began on April 16th 1983 with the highly successful "Poverty of Politics" Conference at the University of London Union and reached its most recent peak in the massive 1,200 strong event of June 1985 on the social security reviews held jointly with Action for Benefits. With the 1983 General Election only five weeks away "Poverty of Politics" was to prove a significant and imaginative new development in the Groups campaign to galvanise and broaden the debate on the future of family policy. It was to address, in particular, the question of whether or not the first four years of Thatcherism had brought about ..."a seachange in economic, political and social policies towards the poor". At the heart of a series of debates and workshops attended by over 500 people ..."from a galaxy of local and national voluntary organisations, trade unions, churches, political parties, women's groups, unemployed centres, universities and local authorities ..." there stood precisely those issues raised by the CPRS and FPG reports and in CPAGs riposte to them. On a practical level here was a major political exercise in examining ways in which the experiences of participants from a wide range of pressure groups, welfare agencies, local authorities and trade unions could be drawn together and re-shaped as the basis of an effective anti-poverty programme for the future. It offered, in particular, the most useful forum yet for the development of a strategy that would harness the skills and resources of activists in the civil service unions with the needs of claimants themselves and those working directly with them in the Unemployed Centres and the front-line welfare rights agencies.

In May there were to be yet more disclosures from a government rapidly resembling a sieve. One indicated that the DHSS was exploring a possible shift from universality to means-testing in the payment of child benefit as one means of financing the introduction of a £3 billion disability income scheme; and as if to prove that the work of the FPG lived on, one-parent benefit would be frozen under such a proposal because, in the words of The Guardian, '...some Ministers believe that the state would be subsidising immorality and illegitimacy by extending support' (29). A prompt denial of the proposal by the Social Security Minister, Hugh Rossi, failed to satisfy either The Guardian itself or CPAG and it drew from the Prime Minister, in a letter to Mr Rossi's Labour counterpart, Brynmor John, on the 20th May a firm assurance that ...'there are no plans to make any change to the basis on which the benefit is paid or calculated'.

In the final run-in to the 1983 General Election, CPAG put forward its own analysis of the party manifestos. It warned especially that the Conservative Manifesto held nothing for the poor and that '...it could conceal future plans to cut benefits for children and others below pensionable age'. If there were any remaining doubts about the course of action a second Thatcher Government, buoyed up by jingoism at the polls, would take they were brutally vanquished with, first, a leak in Time Out setting out secret Cabinet plans for the privatisation of national insurance, prompting a swift denial once more from ministers, and confirmation by the Prime Minister herself at the end of May that cuts in the real value of unemployment benefit would be a firm possibility in her second term as one way of countering the so called 'why work syndrome'. Both issues were to gain in profile as the government moved forward on its plans to reform social security.

'A GREAT DEBATE ON THE WELFARE STATE'

Those plans were given an early and clear advertisement in October with Norman Fowler's statement in a <u>New Society</u> interview that the time was now right for ...'a great debate on the welfare state'. In November, only six months after ministers had denied the <u>Time-Out</u> leak, the Secretary of State announced his intention to establish an inquiry under his own chairmanship ...'into provision for retirement, concentrating initially on the issue of portable occupational pensions and then expanding to a wider consideration of the whole basis and financing of state pensions' (30). On 6 February 1984 he announced a further inquiry into Housing Benefit and on 2 April two further reviews of particular interest to CPAG - a Review of Benefits for Children and Young People and a Review of Supplementary Benefit. In May a further review of maternity provision was also announced. The rationale for these reviews was explained by the Social Security Advisory Committee:

> ...since the Beveridge Report, published in 1942, there has been no major attempt to reassess the principles underlying social security provision in this country, despite the fact that in the intervening period there have been major economic changes, attitudes to social security have shifted and the balance and nature of the provision have altered - sometimes quite significantly ... there has thus been for some time a need to take a general look at the manner, form and scope of assistance offered to disadvantaged groups within the community ... This (the Review) provides an opportunity for useful strategic thinking and goes some way to address the difficulties consequent upon a process of a piecemeal development. (31)

Mr Fowler clearly shared this view. The complete Review package, together with a major survey of people with disabilities, would constitute the ...'most substantial examination of the social security system since the Beveridge Report' (32). There was, however, a cruel deception here. Beveridge was nothing if not a monument to those who understood the 'giant evils' of poverty, need, disease and squalor and the despair that flowed from them. Over the decades since, the Beveridge Report has come to be regarded as an enduring testament to society's ability to respond with compassion and humanity through the mechanisms of the state to those evils. The durability of this response had been closely tested in the past but never so severely or with such hostility as was now contemplated by some sections of the Government and the Conservative Party. While, at the moment of announcement, the Secretary of State's own views and aims may have been rather more to do with a desire for a simplification of welfare, the motives of the Prime Minister, and the Treasury 'hawks' were unequivocally political, and were fired by an ideological obsession for slashing public expenditure, transferring resources and appeasing the sirens on her immediate right. No amount of presentation on the efficacy of 'streamlining', 'value for money' and 're-distributing resources to those in greatest need' could hide the unpalatable fact that the welfare state was stalked by a wolf which was so brazen in its intent that it had freely dispensed with the sheep's clothing.

There is considerable evidence to support this view. It requires only a cursory stock-take of the Governments action, inertia, and thinking on the welfare state since 1979 to concur with it; the social security packages of 1980, 1982 and 1983; the cuts in unemployment benefit; the fall in the value of child benefit; the strident moral haranguing of the unemployed and single parents; the betrayed confidences of the Think Tank and the FPG; the restraint of a pre-election budget; the meaningless call for 'public debate' that never transpired in the publication of the March 1984 Green Paper <u>The Next Ten Years; Public Expenditure and Taxation into the 90's</u>; and, now, the cynical attempt to curb debate once more by allowing for only the most desparately short of consultation periods on the social security reviews themselves. The Reviews were announced, moreover, at a time when CPAG were once more setting out the impact of recent Government policy on those with families, on the unemployed, and upon those invalided. They were aided, moreover, by the publication of the DHSS's own Low Income Family Tables which drew out the ...'undesirable social consequences' of an economic policy which had prioritised the control of inflation and a sharp cut in the PSBR at the expense of rising unemployment and cuts in welfare.

The Group had noted in it's 1984 pre-Budget Memorandum to the Chancellor that ..."the real challenge facing the Chancellor in this, his first budget, is not whether he can find room for tax cuts (and the threat of possible tax increases has been met by almost universal disbelief in the City) but whether he will do something to translate the Government's concern 'to help the needy' into concrete action" (33).

CPAG's recommendations were spelt out; a fifty pence increase in child benefit to £7 to bring it in line with the tax allowance increases effected by the 1983 Budget; the extension of the long term rate of supplementary benefit to the unemployed starting, if necessary, with those with children; and end to the Government's highly discriminatory non-payment of Invalid Care Allowance to married women; the restoration of the five per cent abatement in the invalidity pension and an inquiry into the operation of the Housing Benefit scheme. Together, this package of reforms would do much to alleviate poverty and address discrimination in three or four key areas of social assistance. CPAG's case for improved child benefits, for example, rested ...'on the cost effectiveness of child benefit as a means of improving incentives and on its key role in reversing the long term financial trend against families with children generally ...' (34).

The most expensive of the Group's recommend- ations and the one most likely to draw resistance from the Treasury and key sections of the Conservative Party was that for the extension of the long term supplementary benefit rate to be paid to the long term unemployed ... 'This long overdue reform is becoming ever more urgent as the numbers of the long term unemployed continue to mount. It has the weight of both the SSAC and the Social Services Select Committee behind it, as well as all party support'. More pointedly, the Group asked... 'How much longer can the Government ignore the overwhelming case for ending this discrimination against one of the poorest groups in the community?' In the Group's view, then, such measures would amount to ...

> ... A modest programme of action which is much less ambitious than that which we would want to see fulfilled in the longer term to meet the needs of the fifteen million people living in poverty or on its margins ... The more limited measures which are the subject of this Memorandum would, nevertheless, make an important contribution to easing the difficult- ies of many poor and hard pressed families and

would fall within the philosophy of a Conservative Party which has played its part in establishing the existing institutions of the Welfare State. (35)

THE SOCIAL SECURITY REVIEWS – A FLAWED APPROACH

Although CPAG was to submit formal evidence to the Reviews of Housing Benefit, Supplementary Benefit and Benefits for Children and Young People, it was concerned at the outset by both the claims made for the scope of the Review by Ministers and by the timetable for consultation. It warned that if the Reviews were to offer 'genuine opportunities for public debate and consultation' they could not be conducted at the sort of break neck speed which the Government's timetable for submission of evidence clearly demanded. It was therefore ... 'Rather concerned to note that the consultation documents were not issued until six weeks after the Secretary of State's announcement, in the House of Commons on April 2nd 1984, of the two most recent Reviews; and that the deadline for submission of written evidence was a mere ten weeks after the publication of the consultation documents'.

Yet the concern for an extended period of consultation was only the hors d'oeuvre for a far more serious and substantial critique of the Government's proposals, which were fragmented, ill conceived and ill-thought through ...

> We are also anxious about the piecemeal and confused nature of the agenda for debate. The Secretary of State claimed ... That the Reviews amounted ... 'To the most substantial examination of the social security system, since the Beveridge report.' Yet, on the surface at least, the Review teams will not even be examining the whole of the social security system, not to mention the structure of personal taxation which has now become an important mechanism of income maintenance and distribution for the majority of the population. (36)

Elsewhere, the Group pointed out that it was clear that national insurance benefits would only be considered in the Reviews of pensions policy and maternity provision and that ...'There seems to us to be an undue emphasis (in the remainder of the Reviews) on means tested benefits considered in isolation from the non-means tested elements of social security provision' (37). Perhaps of even greater concern, was the 'hidden agenda' of the Reviews. There had, of course, been very recent speculation that the Government was contemplating the integration of income tax and national insurance contributions; there had been firm evidence, strenuously denied, that Ministers would examine a switch to means testing of child benefit to fund a disability income scheme; there had been talk of further cuts in the value of unemployment benefit and, ultimately, there was the very real prospect of the Reviews simply being used as a smoke screen for massive tax handouts to the Government's supporters. After all, as The Times was to point out in June the cumulative total of social security cuts since the Government came to power in 1979 was now £6.5 billion (38). In the first three years of Mrs Thatcher's Government the richest one per cent of the population had increased their income while that of the poorest ten per cent actually fell (39). In 1984 alone, the year of the Reviews, some £4.17 billion was handed back to tax payers over and above normal indexation as a result of tax changes brought about in both Mrs Thatcher's terms of office. The richest one per cent of tax payers was scheduled to receive forty four per cent of this largesse while the poorest twenty five per cent would receive crumbs from the table to the derisory value of a mere three per cent. Moreover, as CPAG pointed out ... 'These figures do not include the £860 million pounds accruing largely to the better off through changes in capital taxes over and above indexation in the same period' (40). By the beginning of 1984 some 4.5 million families were dependent on supplementary benefit. The economic position of the unemployed had deterioriated sharply vis a vis average male earnings. In 1972 unemployment benefit had stood at seventy five per cent of average male earnings but had plummeted to forty seven per cent by 1982. In contrast, most other EEC Countries had improved on their 1972 position. In West Germany, for example, unemployment benefit was up from seventy to seventy five per cent of earnings and in France it had risen from eighty five to ninety per cent.

It was not surprising, therefore, that CPAG pointed to reports in the press which ...'suggested that the issues under consideration are much wider, and the proposals for reform much more sweeping, than the consultation documents indicate'. While the group ... 'Welcomed an open debate which considered radical and wide ranging proposals for change, such a process should not happen behind closed doors. If such issues as the integration of income tax and national insurance contributions ... Are being examined the public should be given an opportunity to comment on them ... We therefore urge the Government to give a <u>clear and definitive list of the issues under consideration</u>' (41).

Of further concern was what the group referred to as the ...'Imposition of an arbitrary financial ceiling'... a direct reference to the DHSS description of the Reviews as ... 'A substantial re-examination of the social security system to see if better use can be made of resources and staff withir the present overall level of social security expenditure'. It was the clearest indication yet, indeed re-affirmation, of the Government's preoccupation with 'value for money', 'targetting' and a firm signal that the 'most substantial examination of the social security system since Beveridge' would have the financial and policy drag-weight of Mr Fowler's 'nil-cost remit'. Targetting was, of course, a double-edged sword. CPAG had itself shown in supplementary comments to the Review teams that in 1981-82 some £900m at least of social security benefits had not gone to those entitled to them; the danger now lay in a nil-cost remit which would merely and wholly unacceptably re-distribute static resources among the poor themselves. The clear prospect was one of large numbers of poor people substaining cuts in income to boost the income of <u>very</u> poor people.

It was grotesquely unjust. The overwhelming part of this was unclaimed benefit arising from stigma, difficulties in making a claim or complete ignorance of its existence. Despite the fact that these resources had been voted by Parliament to social security beneficiaries and that they should be regarded as part of the total monies available to the social security budget in any such Review, those 'un-claimed resources' were not considered as such at present. With the Group's call for an examination of the structure and scope of social security benefits there came also an urgent plea for an examination of existing methods for financing social security. If the government was genuinely interested in efficient and equitable distribution of resources then that would be one way forward. One option, for example, would be the removal of the 'ceiling' on liability for national insurance contributions which in CPAG's view would be ...'both an overdue reform in itself and a source of considerable revenue for improvements within the social security system, raising an estimated additional £1,270 million in this tax year' (42).

The Reviews were partial and selective in other important ways also. Noticeably absent, for clear political reasons, was any regard to ...'the hidden welfare state of tax reliefs and privileges, which have the same impact on the total of public expenditure as increases in the social security budget, but by a public accounting convention are treated as foregone revenue and are not included in the public spending totals'.

If the Reviews were really about meeting real need and channelling resources most effectively then ...'the resources available in ... mortgage interest tax relief and the married man's tax allowance should be included within any debate on the availability and re-direction of resources'.

Ultimately, and given such criticism and reservation, the Reviews looked set to rake over old ground and to repeat the same mistakes that had occurred with previous grand attempts to simplify social security and target resources which had, in the case of the supplementary benefit reforms of 1980 and the introduction of the housing benefit scheme in 1982/3, left millions of poor claimants even poorer and produced little if any progress in simplifying the bureaucracy of welfare. The Group was to point out finally in its critique of the Review strategy and its claims for change, that ...'the "crisis" of welfare expenditure predicted in the Think Tank Report in 1982 appears to have been exaggerated'.

The debate which the Reviews should presage would involve difficult political choices between levels of public expenditure and taxation and would have, as CPAG's Pre-Budget Memorandum to the Chancellor had pointed out, to address the central problem that ...'the welfare state has failed in one of its prime purposes - to abolish want'. The "right issues" would have to be clarified and the way forward in tackling poverty was clear ...

> higher child benefits are an essential starting point for any more rational and equitable system of income distribution. A programme to tackle low gross pay levels, for which the social security and taxation systems cannot compensate adequately, and a more progressive income tax scheme, are also essential elements of a coherent anti-poverty strategy. (43)

CHANGED PRIORITIES AHEAD – EVIDENCE AND EDUCATION

The Group was to submit evidence to the three Reviews in which it had the closest interest; these were, respectively, the Reviews of Benefits for Children and Young People, of Supplementary Benefit and of Housing Benefit. It responded also, separately, to the Review of Maternity Benefits. 1984 was indeed a year of "changed priorities", not simply in regard to government policy but also in the direction and character of CPAG's own activity which saw further emphasis to and development of 'public education work'. With it there came a raising of public awareness of poverty and social injustice through increased branch work, conference initiatives, the exploring and forging of contacts with potential 'allies' and through the production of new educational material to "get the message across to a broader public". While the Reviews presented CPAG with the occasion to get its own campaign message across they were to provide also a further and unprecedented opportunity to confirm its increasing role as a 'resource-bank' for other groups. In 1984, therefore, CPAG found itself in the driving seat once more ... 'providing other groups with the detailed facts and figures necessary to tackle the often complex and technical issues at stake ...' and it declared itself ...'convinced that the two functions of 'getting the message across' and acting as a resource group for those with an interest in the detail are crucial and will continue to develop its work on both fronts during the coming year (44).

It was not, however, simply a matter of posting hundreds of photocopied briefings to any individual or group who simply required them. There was the vital task of assuring that requirement in the first place. That was to be done by detailing the course of government policy and explaining the alternatives in such a way that a 'great debate on the welfare state' could truly take place and government would be forced to listen to a well informed and broad section of opinion. 1984 was to be a year in which briefings to MPs and the media were despatched on everything from the Government's decision to remove child benefit from the annual Budget process, to the need to match the rise in personal tax allowances with attendant increases in child benefit and saw also the provision of detailed back-up information for the committee stages of the Finance Bill. Alongside came a renewed effort to stimulate Parliamentary interest in the longer term questions of poverty and inequality which culminated in the provision of detailed briefings for debates in both Houses on an Opposition motion drawing attention to the 'widening gulf between rich and poor'.

It was a year, too, of important publications, each with a clear message for the Review teams. The introduction of cuts in housing benefit and their impact on young people in particular provided a valuable opportunity for a joint study with Youthaid, resulting in Families Rent Apart which set out the punitive increases that young people would now have to contribute from their wages to their parents housing costs. The Group's interest in the housing field extended also to the controversial issue of board and lodging arrangements and to the submission of evidence to the Inquiry into British Housing. There was written evidence also to the Archbishop of Canterbury's Commission on Inner-City Areas and the publication of a leaflet on children and poverty for the 'Mission Alongside the Poor' project.

In the traditional mainstream of Poverty Pamphlets the Group set out two critical reports on the administration of the social security system notably, We Don't Give Clothing Grants Any More which revealed wide-spread confusion and maladministration and ...'the continuing problems resulting from complicated or unclear provisions' in the new supplementary benefit scheme introduced in 1980. There followed Nobody's Benefit which presented ...'a clear picture of local housing authorities struggling to cope with a scheme introduced with inadequate preparation and guidance from central government and of claimants confused and often left without benefit for weeks as a result of mistakes or delays'.

In the broader realm of family policy a joint venture with the Family Welfare Association produced Carrying the Can: Charities in the Welfare State which demonstrated ...'that charities in the 1980's were having to meet basic needs which should rightfully be met by the wages and social security systems'. Elsewhere, the burden of parenthood at about £15 billion per year, or £150 per week, for a family with a child under five, virtually ignored by the state, was set out by David Piachaud in Round About Fifty Hours Per Week. In the twelve months from the announcement of the Reviews in April 1984 a flurry of material on the prospects for the family and the future of child benefit, much of it in a fact-sheet form for broadest possible circulation and impact included Child Benefit Under Threat, Child

Benefit: Going, Going, Gone, Benefits Take-Up, and the 1985 pre-Budget memorandum: A Tax on Children?. At the heart of this work there was, of course, the Social Security Reviews Fact Pack and 1984: Changed Priorities Ahead.

Cooperative work was to acquire particular prominence in the year of the Reviews. Much of it was taken up with ongoing issues such as education where, through its involvement in the Education Alliance, CPAG continued to draw attention to education cuts affecting low-income families; similarly, in the tenth year of its membership of the Disability Alliance, the Group took up once more the urgent case for reform in the scope of invalid care allowance and disability benefits for women; 1984 proved to be a year for further work with the Royal College of Nursing, the Maternity Alliance, and the various health associations. As ever, as a long-time member of the Unemployment Alliance, there remained the task of pursuing the case for an extension of the long-term supplementary benefit rate to the long-term unemployed. With a keen eye on the possibility of a review of personal social services also, CPAG was in 1984 to join VOPSS - Voluntary Organisations and Personal Social Services ...'a grouping of various major voluntary bodies concerned with the impact of restrictions on local authorities' abilities both to fund voluntary organisations and to provide services for groups in their communities'. It was a year in which the group also took the significant step of helping to establish Action For Benefits with the civil service unions and in which the more public face of its work was presented in an Open Space television programme.

Changed priorities required new initiatives in public education and these centred on a major poster competition, first launched in 1983, which sought entries that would challenge conventional images of poverty and which gave the Group's work an interesting new publicity dimension - not least in the mounting of an exhibition of successful designs at the Royal Festival Hall in April, before moving onto a national tour that came to rest at York Minster for Christmas. The competition was also to give birth to the theme of the 1984 AGM - 'Beyond Poor Images' - attended by over four hundred people. Nearer home, and following the succesful launch of its 'public education project' the previous year, which had taken as its aim an even-wider dissemination of facts and arguments on family policy, the Group's membership soared in 1984 to well

339

over 5,000.

Education was the key to CPAGs annual presentation at the political party and trade union conference 'fringe'. Attendance at the Conservative Party conference proved doubly valuable with both an opportunity to confirm 'the message' with many established supporters and to get it across for the first time to a growing body of independent back-benchers who might hold doubts as to the true course of government social policy. There was an additional bonus, too, in that the fringe meeting - "Women and Children First: A Look at the Social Security Reviews" - would reach a far wider public with its recording by a BBC Television crew for a Panorama programme on the future of social security. There was for the first time, and with the knock-on effect of social security reforms on personal social services uppermost, a CPAG fringe at the annual conference of the Assocation of Directors of Social Services.

This welter of activity and initiative provided both the public back-drop and a much expanded communication network for the evidence the Group provided to the Review teams, no more so than in its submission on benefits for children and young people in which it talked of ...'a significant increase in child poverty in recent years, marking a shift in the burden of poverty to the young ...' with a result that ...'growing numbers of families are having to resort to means-tested benefits to try to help their incomes up to the poverty line'. The Group's concern was that successive governments had failed to devote sufficient resources to tackle child poverty, opting instead for the political compromise of special means-tested provision for the poor. Effectiveness of those means-tested benefits, however, had been undermined by chronic low take-up especially among the poorest families and had actually contributed to the vexed problem of the poverty trap. They had proved complex to administer and had stigmatised the poor and isolated them increasingly from the mainstream of society. Worse still, the burden of taxation in the welfare state had shifted increasingly towards the low paid and had fallen upon families with children at all income levels. In the Group's view, the Thatcher Governments had deepened this "anti-family taxation trend".

It was vital to drive home once more that child benefit was ...'now the major means of achieving fiscal equity between those with and without children and of re-distributing resources over the life cycle ...'. So much so that there was ...'A good case for a

greater re-distribution to all families with
children in this country; at the very least there
should be no further deterioration in their position
relative to the childless' (45).
    The Review must, therefore, lay the foundations
of an adequate and rational system for child support
and that would require a raising of the supplementary
benefit scale rates for children and an extension of
the long term supplementary benefit rate to the long
term unemployed, beginning with those with children.
The Group restated also its view that child benefits
must be increased in line with personal tax
allowances and that a single and adequate benefit,
paid without regard to the parents employment status,
would take large numbers of families out of the
poverty trap and also provide a more cost-effective
support to that minority of families in the
'unemployment trap' than would increases in tax
allowances. Those views would take a more structured
form a few months later, at the turn of 1985, when
CPAG were to call together nearly forty
organisations, many not previously involved in such
campaigns, to explore ways of countering the rumoured
threat to Child Benefits. That early meeting would
eventually pave the way for the formal launch of Save
Child Benefit in November 1985.
    CPAG was concerned also that much had yet to be
done to ease the position of young people who had
been the target for recent cuts in supplementary
benefit; further moves to increase the dependence of
the young unemployed on their parents were especially
unacceptable. Rather, the Group charged, there were
clear arguments for increasing benefits to young
unemployed people. One option was the establishment
of a national scheme of educational maintenance
allowances ...'to create a real choice for young
people above the minimum school leaving age' with the
net cost being seen as an investment in the future
workforce in much the same way that the Government
justified expenditure on YTS. CPAG's work with
Youthaid on the impact of the increased contributions
expected of young people towards their families
housing costs and the tensions this caused was also
drawn out. The Group was certain that families should
be left to sort out their own affairs without
interference from the Government and that
...'Ideally, there should be no such deductions from
housing benefit in respect of expected contributions
to housing cost' (46).
    In its evidence to the Supplementary Benefit
Review the Group was equally forthright, concluding

that the current role and use of supplementary benefit had undergone a sea-change for which it was badly designed, ill fitted and administratively unprepared. In particular ...'the transformation of supplementary benefit from a small residual element in the social security scheme to the main means of support for people not in work, is the root cause of the problems which currently beset the scheme'. The proper role of supplementary benefit, in CPAG's view, remained ...'as a residual scheme, underpinning a comprehensive system of adequate, non-means tested, non-contributory benefits, which genuinely meet the needs of those unable to support themselves through paid employment' (47).

Furthermore, current levels of supplementary benefit were much too low, failing especially to meet the needs of the long term unemployed and families with children. An immediate way forward would be the raising of the children's scale rates as a matter of priority. Of concern also, if of secondary importance, was the Group's recommendation that all claimants with children should be treated as householders, with the abolition of the 'Non-householder rate' as a longer term goal.

There was a firm recommendation that equal rates of supplementary benefit for each spouse would go some way in recognising married people as individuals with individual needs provided that the introduction of a single rate (doubled for a couple) was not made at the expense of single parents.

CPAG were certain that the nil-cost basis of the Reviews would impact adversely on some vulnerable groups, noting that ...'In a system of last resort, the introduction of a 'group entitlement' on a nil-cost basis can only lead to unacceptable losses'. The proposal that special payments could be absorbed into basic benefit rates would have ... 'a paradoxical effect of reducing payments to the most vulnerable groups, whilst increasing the benefit levels of those without special expenses'. If the Reviews were to make positive advances in the distribution and administration of social security resources, two other avenues would be the raising of 'earnings disregards' to at least the prevailing rate of inflation and the introduction of a disregard on training allowances in respect of child care costs. More broadly, the moment was long overdue for a comprehensive review of earnings disregards throughout the whole social security system.

At the heart of CPAG's evidence to the Housing Benefit Review was a call for preliminary work ...'to be undertaken on a non-means tested approach to housing assistance, which would replace tax relief on mortgage interest, housing requirement for supplementary benefit and housing benefit'. The Review would also have to address what the Group charged to be the 'gross imbalance between assistance to all owner-occupiers with mortgages and low income families with rents to pay' (48). Put simply, the highly political issue of tax relief on mortgage interest and the possibilities its abolition would hold for an equitable re-distribution of resources, would have to be met squarely and courageously by any government making claims for an effective chanelling of resources to those most in need.

The increase in the numbers of those claiming Housing Benefit had, CPAG concluded, come about by a combination of three factors - the massive increase in unemployment, large rises in rent and rates and the growing numbers of low paid workers. A way out of the morass would be the introduction of the new unified Housing Benefit scheme covering all housing costs for low income individuals. It added that ...'such a scheme should be designed so as to 'buy out' Housing Benefit Supplement with no losses and to remove non-dependent deductions from Housing Benefit entirely'. However, such a scheme could not be carried out under Mr Fowler's nil-cost strictures without significant and unacceptable losses to claimants.

The debacle of housing benefit administration had also provoked the Group and it made clear that any new reformed scheme should be run by the DHSS centrally and not by local authorities which had ...'unfortunately proved themselves unable to administer housing benefit to an acceptable standard of efficiency and effectiveness'. A number of important initiatives could now be taken whilst Government planned the transfer of all housing benefit administration to the DHSS. For example, private tenants in receipt of supplementary benefit and certificated housing benefit should become a DHSS responsibility as priority; housing benefit claimants should be given access forthwith to the independent system of Social Security Appeals Tribunals like other social security claimants. In the final analysis ...'the DHSS cannot be allowed to abdicate responsibility for the operation of housing benefit'.

COUNTDOWN TO THE GREEN PAPER

In the weeks leading up to the publication of the Green Paper <u>Reform of Social Security</u> in June 1985, CPAG sustained its campaigning work with a host of groups and agencies having a direct interest in its outcome and it continued to press home the case for a comprehensive reform of social security that would truly bring about a simplification of welfare and the channelling of resources to those who needed them. It was in no doubt, however, as to the task ahead given a growing indication of the Government's likely course. The year of the Green Paper ...'could prove to be the most significant time for the future direction of social security policy since the 1940's; CPAG's contribution to the debate will be as thorough as possible and will reach out to as many people as possible' (49).

In <u>Social Security</u> Reviews: Countdown, published in April, eight weeks before the Green Paper was released the Group set out once more its concerns that Mr Fowler's grand reform of the Welfare State would be nothing of the sort, not least because of the flawed approach he had adopted from the outset. With much of the evidence submitted to the Reviews now freely available, it was clear that many groups and individuals shared a fundamental concern that the Government's nil-cost remit would have the effect of redistributing resources away from many of those desperately in need of a boost to their incomes. In the shadows was the ever present spectre of a Treasury bent on curtailing social security expenditure and determined to achieve cuts by one route or another to facilitate a tax bonanza that the Chancellor saw as the pre-requisite for a hat-trick of election victories. The fact that many submissions of evidence had made clear that options and scope for increased social security expenditure clearly did exist, led the Group to conclude that the early signs pointed to ...'damaging decisions about the overall level of social security spending ... being determined not by economic imperatives, but by political choices'.

Nowhere was this better illustrated than in the pressures exerted by the Chancellor, Nigel Lawson, upon his opposite number at the DHSS. The issue would turn, argued CPAG, on the fact that ...'Norman Fowler wants to use any savings to restructure the social security system and claim the Beveridge mantle. Nigel Lawson wants cuts of two billion to four billion pounds to finance tax cuts before the next Election'.

It was, moreover, an analysis broadly endorsed in the City and the well-informed financial press. As the <u>Financial Times</u> pointed out ...'Treasury Ministers have privately made little secret of the fact that they agreed to the Social Security Reviews only because they were determined to obtain cuts'. The result was that on the eve of the Green Paper ...'the prospect for benefit cuts appears to be increasing as the likelihood of radical reform recedes' (50).

Those prospects were made clear in a number of kite-flying exercises in March and April in which Norman Fowler set out what would, in June prove to be the key points of the Green Paper. These were targetting resources to more effectively meet need; a pronounced exporting of responsibility to the individual; the so-called simplification of welfare; and measures which would, recalling the Prime Minister's own ferocity towards the unemployed at the time of the 1983 Election, demolish the 'why work' syndrome. Each of these, CPAG saw as part and parcel of an 'ideology' of welfare. The Government's recommendations could not be dismissed as mere pragmatism alone. They constituted, rather, a clear political and philosophical view about the role of the Welfare State in British society in the mid-1980's. Targetting was especially ideological in its concept; it brought in its wake political and moral judgements about the deserving versus the undeserving poor and found its most effective banner in the repeated use of the slogan 'redistribution to those in <u>genuine</u> need'. CPAG made its own views quite clear:

> ... in elevating targetting to a central pillar in its social security policy, this Government is now going further and is challenging the basic Beveridge principle of 'security against want without a means-test.' In doing so, it is raising fundamental questions about the role of the social security system in a modern Welfare State. (51)

Targetting also betrayed a philosophy that viewed the relief of poverty as the single aim of the social security system. For CPAG, this was "an extraordinary narrow goal for a modern industrial-ised society". It was, moreover, a major retreat from the wider aims and provision of Beveridge which were as much concerned with prevention of poverty as with its relief. At the core of the Beveridge plan stood the premise that the Welfare State was for everyone,

345

it was universal. Now, as CPAG explained, the Government had presented the prospect of "a social security scheme which is designed simply to relieve poverty by means of targetting" and the net result would be the ghettoising of the poor.

Strong candidates for the expenditure axe were already emerging at this time. Prime among them was Child Benefit for which there was every indication of a freeze and perhaps even a real cut in value. Alongside was the prospect of a re-vamped FIS scheme – a 'family credit.' There was some indication also that the Maternity Grant would be means-tested as a basis for increasing it from twenty five pounds to seventy five pounds. Supplementary Benefit, meanwhile, was in the frontline for 'simplific- ation'. The weekly additions and lump sum single payments that many hard pressed families required to keep their heads above water were in line for abolition, probably as the basis for financing an increase in the basic scale rates. Benefits for the unemployed were also, in CPAG's judgement, to be the target of cuts; the removal of rights to Supplementary Benefit for sixteen to seventeen year olds was gaining currency; a cut in Unemployment Benefit after six months or a higher benefit lasting six months only had also been floated; so, too, had the removal of assistance with mortgage interest payments for those on Supplementary Benefit.

Housing Benefit looked increasingly likely to draw cuts as great as fifty per cent and the State Earnings Related Pension Scheme, according to a lead article in the <u>Daily Telegraph</u> in mid-April, faced abolition with the Government keen to push people into a hazy myriad of occupational and private pension schemes.

The publication by CPAG of <u>Countdown</u> proved of far more consequence than a mere timely resume of what the Government had or had not been saying about the future of the Welfare State. Its chief importance lay in its pre-emptive strike against the Government in a propaganada war that the latter was clearly intending to wage unilaterally in the weeks directly preceding the Green Paper as the chief means for easing its public passage. <u>Countdown</u> now opened up and extended the debate on the Reviews, some two months before publication of <u>Reform of Social Security</u>, and took the edge of any Government offensive. Indeed, the Government was to find itself increasingly placed on the defensive as it was forced prematurely to contemplate publication of the Green Paper amid the glare of hostile and well informed critical opinion. The kites flown by the DHSS had now come down to earth with a resounding thump. The value of <u>Countdown</u> in extending the lead-time for public debate was, in due course, illustrated in the Secretary of State's announcement in June that the period for the submission of responses would be a peremptory nine weeks – pointing up once more CPAG's doubts of the previous June of the Government's willingness ...'to provide genuine opportunities for public debate and consultation'. The content and timetable for <u>Reform of Social Security</u> now made it manifestly clear that the great debate on the Welfare State was indeed, as CPAG had feared, "being conducted in a hurry".

REFORM OF SOCIAL SECURITY

Announcing publication of the four volume Green Paper to a packed House of Commons on June 3rd 1985, the Secretary of State Norman Fowler set out what for many was to be the unhappy and the unacceptable quid pro quo of Thatcherism's guardianship of the Welfare State ...

> ...The Government also believe that our tradition of State support for those in need is one which should be maintained and developed. But social security is not a function of the State alone. It should be a partnership between the individual and the State – a system built on twin pillars. (52)

There followed the expected revelation that ...'The Review has shown that there are several major causes for concern'. The Secretary of State went on to spell these out as the complexity and antiquity of the social security system; the burgeoning cost of social security which had increased five fold since Beveridge and which now stood at £40 billion a year and thirty per cent of all public expenditure; Mr Fowler confided his fears for the ability of SERPS to cope with the surge of four million extra pensioners in the early part of the next century – fears fuelled by the apparent prospect of a trebling in expenditure on pensions; and his calculations and anxieties had provoked in him the unerring conclusion that ...'we must ensure now that we have a soundly based social security system which the Country can afford'.
        The Secretary of State's concerns were most closely directed at his own Party's favourite cry of

the heart, when belt-tightening is the political order of the day, that ...'The social security system does not always help those most in need'. Here, as CPAG had so accurately set out first in its evidence Changed Priorities Ahead and then Countdown, was the drum beat of selectivity and the forward march of targetting. They were to be attended, moreover, by a predictable jibe at the unemployed which, no doubt, Treasury Ministers and perhaps the Prime Minister herself saw as a useful political ploy in persuading the increasing legion of the low paid that something was finally being done about the scroungers and the skivers. Thus Mr Fowler could assure his colleagues that ...

> ...Under the present system low income working families can face both the difficulty of escaping the poverty trap - where they may get no increase in total income when their earnings rise - and also the unacceptable position that they can be better off out of work. That position must be changed. (53)

The Tory drive on welfare to all intents and purposes, then, appeared to be bound-up with winning the political hearts and minds of poor working families with children who, Mr Fowler acknowledged, had been ...'a major priority of the Review'. The task now was to make better provision for this important group and that would be done by abolishing FIS and introducing a new benefit Family Credit - as Countdown had predicted. The new Credit would be paid on the same basis as help to unemployed families in that it would relate to the age of the children, and it would break with the FIS tradition by relating to take home pay rather than gross earnings. Most controversially, it would be paid by employers through the pay packet. The new Family Credit would be paid in addition to Child Benefit for which the Secretary of State also had some transient words of assurance

> ...the Government believe that the extra responsibilities carried by all those bringing up children should be recognised. Child Benefit will, therefore, continue to be paid for all children irrespective of the means of the family. (54)

The new Family Credit would form, in the Government's view, part of ...'a coherent system of income related benefits ... covering basic income support, assistance with housing costs and help for low income families'. These were to be on a common income test and a common structure. In this way the Government believed it could combine the political goal of equity with its administrative goal of simplification. However, the real issue at stake was that ...'it will provide the same level of help at the same level of income for those in and out of work ...' and that would fulfil a major promise of the 1983 Manifesto.

In one of the other major areas of review, Supplementary Benefit was to be replaced with a new Income Support scheme, the central concept of which would be ...'that the regular extra payments now made on the basis of detailed individual assessment should be absorbed into the main rates of benefit'. The quid pro quo, as CPAG had also pointed out during the course of the Reviews, was that their absorption into the main scale rates would allow those rates to increase for certain groups, identified by the Secretary of State as pensioners, single parents and the long term sick and disabled. There was in Mr Fowler's view a clear filip here for the family lobby in that ... 'families with children will not only receive assistance for each child but also a premium to reflect the extra pressures they have to cope with'. There was also to be a welcome easing of the earnings rule for the long term unemployed and the disabled.

At the heart of the new Income Support scheme was a proposal that would prove, subsequently, the most controversial of all - a cash limited Social Fund, operated on a discretionary basis by specially trained staff at local DHSS offices. Whilst the Income Support scheme was designed to meet the needs of almost all claimants, the Social fund was presented as recognition ...'that the system must be ready to cope flexibly and quickly with particular problems ... it will provide emerging help when needed and help those who face particular difficulties' (55). In time, it was expected that the Social Fund would also provide ...'a better basis for contributing cash help to enable people to be cared for in the community rather than in institutions'. The Social Fund would also be the means through which the increased Maternity Grant - up from twenty five pounds to seventy five pounds - would now be paid to mothers in order to ...'concentrate help where and when it is most needed instead of providing a token contribution to everybody when it may be of little practical use'.

Housing Benefit, meanwhile, was deemed by the
Secretary of State to be 'excessively complicated ...
expensive and poorly targetted with over one third of
all households - some with incomes up to average
earnings - receiving benefit'. The intention now,
then, would be to move towards a much simpler system
...'based on the same net income assessment basis as
the Income Support and Family Credit systems ...' and
to ...'provide help on the basis of rent and rates
together rather than separately as at present'.

Henceforth, Housing Benefit would meet one
hundred per cent of the rent for the poorest families
and would now apply equally to those in and out of
work. However, there was a clear price to pay for
this apparent beneficence. That "large proportion of
people" living in households in which no rates were
paid and in which ...'there is no effective link
between payment for and use of local services' would
now find themselves on the giving end of the
Government's proposals to ensure that such a link was
made. The Government had in mind a contribution of
around twenty per cent from these households to their
rates. Significantly, within three days of the
announcement, figures leaked to Gordon Brown MP
suggested that seven million out of the 7.5 million
housing benefit recipients would suffer losses under
the Green Paper proposals (56). These new details
were to prove an important aid in illuminating
proposals the Government had sought to keep
deliberately vague and shadowy by not citing figures
in the Green Paper in the first place.

There were to be administrative concerns also.
If the periods for consultation and reply were short
then the timetable for enactment of the proposals
looked positively breakneck. The Secretary of State
announced bluntly, with little apparent regard
either for the controversy or complexity of the
proposals, that ...'the change in the benefit year
will be brought in at the time of implementation of
the major structural reforms. We expect this to be in
April 1987'.

FIGHTING BACK - ACTION FOR BENEFITS

The Reviews proved right the sentiments expressed in
the Group's 1984/5 Annual Report that 1985 would be
...'the most significant time for the future
direction of social security policy since the 1940's'
and that its own contribution to the debate would

have to be as thorough going as possible. First out of the frame was <u>What Future for Social Security</u>, a preliminary commentary on the Green Paper. It was short, direct and to the point and it provided a valuable and early response that Parliamentarians and the media, in particular, could draw upon as the political debate was winched upwards. It restated the Group's charge that the Reviews had been hamstrung from the outset by their nil-cost remit and their exclusion of the 'hidden Welfare State'. Ideologically, it warned, the Green Paper ...'moves the centre of gravity of social security policy towards private and means-tested provision, behind the facade of empty commitments to the collectivist principles central to the Beveridge scheme'. The reforms were neither comprehensive nor coherent and fell far short of the extravagant claims made for them by Mr Fowler in 1984. In so far as they approached anything like a clear strategy for social security ...'it is one of retreat from the principles underlying the Beveridge plan of "security against want without a means-test"' (57).

A firm public edge was given to the Group's response with its extraordinary joint conference with Action for Benefits on June 17th which attracted over twelve hundred people. The public face of the Group's work, which had begun so spectacularly with the 'Poverty of Politics' conference in 1983, through 'Beyond Poor Images' in 1984 to the massive 'Poor Britain' event in March of 1985, now reached an appropriate and well-planned peak in the immediate post-Green Paper debate with this ultimate of 'mega-conferences' and the simultaneous publication of <u>What Future for Social Security</u>. If the urgency of mobilisation of opinion against the Reviews was the point then the point was well, if unhappily, made by the Government's announcement the following day that Child Benefit was to be cut in real terms by thirty-five pence as part of the benefit uprating process. The Government abandoned the commitment given to the House of Commons in July 1980 to maintain the real value of Child Benefit by keeping it in line with inflation. Inflation at June 1985 would have dictated a rounded-up increase of fifty pence; in the event Child Benefit rose by only fifteen pence and the Government could look forward to a saving of £150 million per year, given improvements to FIS and Housing Benefit, at the very moment it was re-asserting its claims to be the party of the family. The erosion of Child Benefit, and the paving of the way for its demise, as CPAG had so vigorously warned, had been confirmed. It provoked publication of a further Save Child Benefit leaflet in July which made no bones of the Group's view that children were being penalised to finance the Government's plans for tax cuts and that the Government's new schemes for family support were discriminatory, marginal in impact and highly unlikely to make any significant in-road against child poverty (58).

The main thrust of the Group's riposte to the Green Paper came, however, in its formal response Burying Beveridge - a very substantial and comprehensive reply over two hundred pages long and, once again, very much a resource bank for those concerned with both the broad canvas of the social security system and the minutiae of data. From the outset the response challenged the notion, pervasive throughout the Reviews, that the cost of social security was somehow a 'burden' and 'millstone' and it offered international comparisons to substantiate the Group's persistent argument that the UK's social security expenditure was and is below average. The burgeoning expenditure to which Mr Fowler had referred and his expressions of anxiety in regard to its factor as a proportion of GDP were explained and dismissed as substantially the outcome of rising unemployment and the Government's own convoluted housing policies.

Moreover, the Group were certain that ..."there is no evidence to show that social security expenditure has adverse effects on the economy" as Conservative manifestos and Ministers alike had claimed. The counter arguments to the Government's ideology of welfare, to its 'ideological trinity of family, private market and voluntary sector; to its concept of the 'twin pillars' of individual and state; to its predilection for targetting and self-reliance and to its usurpation of the Beveridge mantle were each, once more, rehearsed and sharpened. It was, however, in the finer detail of the proposals and in the differences between their claimed and probable impact on families and children that CPAG was on strongest ground and the proposals were made to look precisely what they were - piecemeal, ill-conceived and divisive.

In its general critique of the proposals for family support the group was forced to conclude that ..."The gains for even poor working families will be modest or non-existent and many will be worse off than now. The proposals build on the worst aspects of the present child support system. A structure of family support which gives pride of place to means-testing is inefficient, ineffective and divisive and will not solve the problem of child poverty" (59).

At the heart of its concern was the growing uncertainty over the future of child benefit, which it firmly re-stated was a reliable source of income for poor families, a valuable weapon in tackling the poverty trap and the only independent source of income for many women. While the public campaign to save child benefit, including publication of <u>Mothers Lifeline</u>, quickly gathered pace, drawing some fifty organisations representing women, children, families, the trade union movement and health and social services together, CPAG itself targetted the groups who would be most affected by its erosion or demise. These were: those not taking up entitlement; those on low incomes but just above the qualifying income level; families where income was unevenly or unfairly distributed; immigrant mothers afraid to claim for fear of jeopardising their rights of residency in the UK; and, now, those who would receive less money under the family credit scheme than they did from FIS. The overwhelming evidence supporting the value of child benefit to mothers, not least in a recent public survey conducted by CPAG itself, had been cast aside.

The outlook for family credit was no less encouraging and brought with it a highly retrograde and discriminatory manoeuvre in its payment through the wage packet. The Secretary of State had made no secret of the fact that he expected the new scheme to be seen as related to, if not actually part of, wages since it would be paid through the payslip on application to the DHSS. Its payment in this way would not only introduce what for many claimants would be the demeaning intrusion of the employer into their personal circumstances, but it would mean that in most two-parent families the money would go to the wage-earning father and not to the mother. It was a blatantly sexist and wholly backward step and it completely ignored the evidence that benefits paid in this manner fail frequently to find their way to the members of the family for whom they are destined. The move would do much also to undermine the hard-fought-for independence of many women with children not themselves in paid employment.

A central intention of the new family credit was to reduce expectations in both the workplace and in the social security system and that could be achieved in the Government's mind by giving a misleading boost to take-home pay through the inclusion of social assistance in the wage packet. After all, the Green

Paper had made this quite explicit in its quite patronising observation that family credit ..."should offer significant advantages for employers in ensuring that employees perceive more clearly the total net remuneration they receive" (60).

Any pretence on the part of the claimant to dignity and privacy, together with the prospects for many mothers of maintaining an independent source of income, had been effectively bull-dozed. Worse still, the role of the employer in facilitating disbursement of the new credit was likely to reduce take-up even further. CPAG had already pointed out that FIS, which family credit was to replace, was characterised by miserably low take-up. That would now diminish further. The ultimate irony of the piece, however, must have been the prospects of an increased administrative burden for those small businesses already protesting at their current onus. The Government had, indeed, overlooked, ignored and chosen not to listen with astounding insensitivity and poor judgement.

One of the isolated bright spots was the provision of enhanced support for older children but even this was off-set by current trends in the payout of FIS, which went largely to parents with younger off-spring. Arguments for targetting looked increasingly tenuous with the growing recognition that the new scheme would still only reach less than 50% of the 'low income families' identified in the Green Paper. Summarily, CPAG rejected ..."the structure of child support proposed in the Green Paper with its increased reliance on means-tested benefits"... and added that it believed that ..."FIS should have been replaced by an adequate child benefit - not by family credit, which in many respects will be worse than FIS" (61).

The aims of the Green Paper had been ruthlessly exposed. Reflecting some weeks later in <u>Poverty</u> Paul Ormerod and Gerard O'Neill concluded that while the Government had made much of two objectives, meeting genuine need and simplifying welfare, it was a third objective that was paramount ..."that of making the social security system more 'consistent with the Government's overall objectives for the economy'". It was their view that the main justification for the Reviews turned on the Government's idiosyncratic concerns with the supply side of the economy. One outcome, then, was that

... the reform of social security is meant to

provide further inducements to the unemployed to take jobs. This is achieved by concentrating means-tested benefits on the 'working poor' particularly those with children. Indeed, the proposed reform ultimately provides for a re-distribution of social security spending from the 'old poor' to the 'young poor' and from the non-working poor to the working poor. (62)

Concerns for the growing army of 'young poor' also featured strongly in CPAG's response. Young people would now lose out under the lower income support rate for the under twenty-fives, students would be deprived of housing benefit and income support and calls for an education maintenance allowance had been ignored. The Government approach to maternity provision was substantially self defeating. There was, on the one hand, support for the principle of provision for all families with children yet, on the other, there was the proposal to abolish the universal maternity grant. A new means-tested grant of £75 would now be available to families on income support or family credit from a social fund which, CPAG protested, would put off many mothers from claiming given its image as a helping hand for 'bad managers'. Those failing to claim income support or family credit would be deprived of help with maternity costs. Moreover, the £75 grant would mean less help for many of those on income support anyway. Even where support with costs over £75 was given it looked likely to be in loan form. While the period over which maternity allowance could be paid now acquired a welcome flexibility, eligibility for the allowance was to be more rigidly defined with as many as 85,000 mothers losing out altogether. Overall, the proposals were disappoint-ing. In the Group's view the allowance should be paid over a longer period and at a more adequate level with the first step being taken by restoring the 5% 'abatement' imposed in 1980. On maternity pay, the Green Paper was virtually silent ..."dismissing all suggestions for improvements as they would add to public spending and increase employer's administrat-ive burdens". Yet, the Maternity Pay Fund had, in fact, been in surplus and there was, therefore, in CPAG's view every reason why ..."maternity pay should be raised from 90% to 100% of earnings, since this was promised in 1981 in exchange for the abolition of earnings-related supplement" (63).

Free milk and vitamins were also to be in less ready supply and would now be available only to those on income support. Young mothers under sixteen would be obvious losers under the new proposals unless their own parents were on Income support. Here, too, the Government had discriminated against the mother. The new family credit rates would include 'compensation' for the loss of free milk and vitamins but it would go to the father and not to the mother.

Supplementary benefit was the second front in CPAG's critique of the Government's proposals. Most damning was its observation that the Green Paper repeated precisely those mistakes made by the Government in 1980 when it had extended dependence on supplementary benefit and implemented its reforms within a similar context of neutral cost remit. Five years on, CPAG concluded wearily

> ...the proposals in the Green Paper repeat these two critical mistakes, and for that reason are also likely to fail. No proposals are made to reduce the numbers dependent on supplementary benefit by improvements to non means-tested benefits; so the complexities of means-testing millions of people will continue. No additional resources will be put into the housing benefit scheme. Instead, the Government merely proposes to change the name and nature of the supplementary benefit scheme yet again. (64)

Simplification of supplementary benefit looked remote in the extreme; there were no proposals to improve take-up; the inadequacy of the scale rates had not been addressed; and rights to some benefits were to be abolished as a result of absorption of single payments and additional requirements into the discretionary, cash-limited Social Fund.

There were multiple concerns about the Fund itself, not least in regard to its vagueness. In common with most of the other Green Paper proposals, the amount of funding had not been made clear. The prospect, moreover, of recoverable payments to claimants together with what looked likely to be a substantial cut in the amount of resources currently invested in the schemes and benefits it was to replace, were matters of extreme concern to the Group. One set of DHSS papers leaked to CPAG and passed on in turn to the Labour MP Gordon Brown, suggested that only £100 million would now be available to replace schemes currently costing over £230 million. It provoked in him the view that

> ...the detailed operation of the Social Fund

will subject those already poor to even greater
suffering and hardship. For a leaked set of
documents which discloses the Government's
first thoughts on the operation of the fund has
now become available. It shows how the DHSS
local office will be transformed from a poverty
relief to a debt-collection agency and
demonstrates how the experimental theories of
the New Right are to be put into practice. (65)

Elsewhere, the fund generated controversy among
social workers and welfare agencies who, the Green
Paper made clear, would be expected to help 'police'
the new arrangements and collaborate in a scheme that
many saw as undermining the hard-won trust between
social services departments and their clients. For
many, the Social Fund was ..."reminiscent of a
nationally administered Poor Law with its moralistic
overtones, fear of stigma and potential degredation
for claimants who are obliged to apply to it" (66).
Mr Fowler's call for a ..."more varied response to
inescapable individual need ..." smacked loudly of
segregation and the marginalising of some groups of
claimants and it heralded an extraordinary shift in
favour of loans and means-testing. Community care,
funeral expenses, maternity support, financial
crises, and budgetting arrangements were each
kaleidescoped into the under-resourced purview of
the new proposals and a panoply of groups would be
adversely affected - single parents, informal
carers, widows, babies and young children, expectant
mothers, those given assistance with heating costs
including pensioners, young people under twenty-six,
those on job creation schemes and the unemployed. For
CPAG

...the proposals for the Social Fund are
unacceptable. The imposition of cash limits
belies the Government's claim that the Fund will
respond 'flexibly' to claimants' needs. The
return to discretion is likely to mean a return
to discrimination, particularly against the
unemployed, black claimants and those who
persist in pursing their case. It will also mean
more friction between claimants and DHSS staff.
If the central guidelines are gradually
introduced, the wheel will have turned full
circle to the pre-1980 situation - except that
claimants will not be able to appeal against any
decisions. (67)

The group's other chief area of concern was housing benefit - a major target for cuts which the Government was later to admit would be of the order of some £500 million affecting between five to seven million households. Some 1.8 million faced losing entitlement to housing benefit altogether. While the proposals for housing benefit might well unify and simplify the scheme, they were ..."not desirable at any price". There was concern from the Group that injustices inherent in the new Income Support Scheme would knock-on into housing benefit also and that single parents and families with young children would probably lose out. The taper for assistance with rent and rates, amounting to 70% of net income, would deepen the poverty trap and would hit those getting assistance with rates only especially hard. The administrative prospects of local authorities collecting the proposed 20% contribution to rates looked horrendously chaotic and were likely to repeat the events of 1982-83. They would almost certainly aggravate the current problems local authorities faced in dealing with rate arrears. The Group was additionally concerned by the proposal that housing benefit review boards be given an extended period of trial since ..."a review which has equity as its objective cannot countenance the present structure which results in unfair variations in treatment". If housing benefit claimants were denied appeal to the Social Security Appeals Tribunals then the only favourable alternative had to be an independent system of housing benefit appeals.

TOWARDS A WHITE PAPER

The Group responded also to a range of issues which might not have, six or seven years ago, been so readily associated with its work and which illustrate well the sheer range of interests above and beyond child poverty that CPAG is now involved in. They included provision for retirement, for death and for widowhood and amounted also to something of a trial run for the Green Paper on personal taxation due later in the autumn. They were set out, moreover, in campaigning style in the joint CPAG-GLC publication <u>Past Caring</u>. In the midst of this extraordinary level of activity, however, the Government was already bull-dozing a path to an end of year White Paper, confirming for many observers in the process that the Green Paper itself had had white edges and was rather more a statement of intent than an invitation to

meaningful debate. Furthermore, the Government had
already begun to enact its proposals in advance of
any such White Paper. The annual round of benefit
upratings in November proved a significant launch-
pad for a number of changes in provision and began
the process of slippage that, in CPAG's view, would
herald the demise of child benefit, certainly in its
present form. A budget geared directly to huge tax
cuts the following spring could then pave the way for
the legislative 'tour de force' scheduled for April
1987.

It was not an entirely easy path however. The
submission of 7,200 proofs of evidence and the
climate of debate generated by those such as CPAG and
NCOPF on the proposals for family policy, or by the
trade unions and the CBI on the highly controversial
plan to abolish SERPS or perhaps, in the efforts by
those such as Shelter, SHAC and a host of other
voluntary organisations in opposing the massively
punitive impact of the proposals to reform housing
benefits, each brought a range of hurdles into which
the Government blundered with some disorder and
embarassment. Between August and November alone, the
DHSS was set back on its heels by a combination of
administration oversight, faux pas and sheer over-
ambition - adding to the humiliating reversals
already suffered on Invalid Care Allowance and Board
and Lodging in which CPAG had been closely involved.
It was obliged, miserably, to rethink its position on
SERPS, on widowhood, on some aspects of maternity
provision, on housing benefit and to re-assess the
level of resources it had originally set aside for
its much-vaunted and, subsequently, much-criticised
Social Fund.

Even the Government's own Social Security
Advisory Committee, found much to concern and disturb
it. It accepted, for example, the need for
simplification but was adamant that ..."this cannot
be at the expense of adequate help for vulnerable
groups". It was certain, too, that within the context
of a nil-cost reform ..."only a limited degree of
simplification is possible without causing undue
hardship to groups at present receiving help in
recognition of special needs". It had similar fears
for the role and adequacy of the Social Fund
concluding that ..."it would be unacceptable if a
fixed budget did indeed mean that the Fund was unable
to respond to need ...". It was, moreover, ..."a
radical move in a demand-led service and has led to
much doubt about the ability of the Fund to cope with
disasters and with end-of-year demands which cannot

be denied but which are outside the budget". In the final analysis, it had continuing and deep-seated doubts about the proposals noting that ..."many of the proposed changes are highly controversial and most are complex. It will not help either the recipients of benefits or the Government's desire for smooth and cost-effective administration if the reforms are not fully thought-through or introduced within sufficient time for staff and the public to become accustomed to them" (68).

Exactly twenty years on from The Poor and the Poorest the two assumptions that Abel-Smith and Townsend had spoken of as governing much of Britain's economic thinking since the war - that poverty had been 'abolished' and that we are 'a much more equal society' with the differences between the living standards of rich and poor much smaller than before - had been given their strongest rebuff to date by Reform of Social Security. Writing on the eve of CPAG's second generation Peter Townsend, the group's Chair for the overwhelming part of those two decades, reflected that ..."the Fowler Reviews are in fact a late example of the measures that have been taken or proposed since 1979 by a Government determined to break the post-war consensus of the Welfare State" (69). Successive Governments had, he argued, since 1945 spent proportionately more on social security and social services if only because the numbers needing help, including a burgeoning middle-class of 'beneficiaries', had increased. Througout its first thirty or so years leading Conservatives had played their part in this expansion of the Welfare State. 1979, however, had indeed proved to be the historical watershed.

THE DECEMBER WHITE PAPER - A DIVIDED BRITAIN?

Norman Fowler's promise to the House of Commons on December 16th that the early new year would bring "comprehensive legislation" to enact the terms of the White Paper Reform of Social Security will no doubt further concentrate the debate on the future of the Welfare State, not least because a new Social Security Act will coincide with CPAG's own 21st anniversary themes of "Divided Britain" and "A Fairer Future for Our Children?".

For over four million people the changes proposed will bring cuts in the levels of support they receive through the social security system. Only half this number are likely to benefit, and marginally at that, from the White Paper. Pensioners and the unemployed are among those who bear the brunt of the Government's single-minded obsession with curbing what it sees as the burgeoning Welfare State. The unemployed without a family will suffer significantly. Some 860,000 such people will be worse off under Mr Fowler's revised system, a quarter losing as much as £5 per week. Over 2 million pensioners will be especially hard hit as a result of their becoming a target for both rent and rate cuts (70). On the latter front everyone now, whether disabled, aged or unemployed will have to find a 20 per cent contribution to rates and that means finding it from benefit levels threatened by other planned cuts in the system.

At the heart of the White Paper lies the highly controversial Social Fund — overwhelmingly criticised in the seven and a half thousand responses to the June Green Paper. It is here, perhaps, that the strains on the system will really tell. Many of the uses to which it will be selectively and thinly put are currently met by a system of single payments costing £241 million in 1984-85 and already under severe pressure. The Social Fund, however, intends to meet need by effectively ignoring a great chunk of it. It seems unlikely, for example, that the Fund will finance even 60 per cent of the needs currently met by single payments and those that are met will largely be through discretionary payments and recoverable loans. The principle of universality so central to Beveridge is to be bundled aside in favour of a pronounced and essentially political lurch towards selectivity. At the time of writing the Institute of Fiscal Studies calculates that the White Paper brings in its wake £750m of cuts in social security. That does not include the 'savings' already in process as a result of slippage in the November 1985 benefit upratings — the £150 million net cut in Child Benefit being a clear case in point.

The vast level of benefit entitlement not claimed last year, thought to be in excess of £900 million, is understood to have not been carried over in Mr Fowler's plans. It is a grotesque irony that the White Paper cuts together with savings in Child Benefit broadly equate with this sum. It is disturbing that such a high figure of non take-up, and it is believed to be a conservative estimate, exists alongside some of the most virulent episodes in scroungerphobia, much of it Government-led.

The assault by the Governments of Margaret Thatcher on the poor has been unedifying in the extreme. Since coming to power in 1979 the Conservatives have plundered some £2000 million a year on average from the social security budget, with their unswerving insistence that the poor must bear their share of the general cuts in public expenditure.

In truth, however, the poor and the poorest have borne a wholly disproportionate share of the cuts. Indeed, in the key debate on the Welfare State back in April 1985, the House of Commons Library furnished Members with the evidence to show that real cuts in social security between 1979-84 amounted to £8,200 million with a further £2,700m of cuts effected by taxing unemployment benefit since 1982 (71). At the present time it is likely that those cuts now exceed £13,000 million, and this in a period when unemployment has tripled; the number of single parents has risen by a fifth; when the number of pensioners has increased without recent precedent; when over 400,000 unemployed claimants remain neither in receipt of unemployment benefit or supplementary benefit; when requests for free clothing for poor families have swamped the charities; when the Government persists in claiming it can find other priorities for the £85m it would cost to pay Invalid Care Allowance to married women carers and when the number of children in poverty approaches the 4 million mark.

In this same period, successive budgets have disproportionately raised the tax bands for the rich and the well-off and they have benefitted further from a relaxing of capital gains tax, capital transfer tax and the abolition of the investment surcharge. While the social security budget has been trussed and carved the 'hidden Welfare State' of tax cuts, allowances, fringe benefits and interest on unearned income truly burgeons. So much so that one calculation puts the cumulative value of tax handouts almost exclusively served up to the richest 5 per cent of the population, at £12.9 Billion – virtually identical to the sum plundered from the social security system (72).

As the Government now proceeds with "comprehensive legislation" in the Spring of 1986 it will reflect, however, that it has not had it all its own way. White Paper there may be but it is one distinctly frayed at the edges and a good deal lighter than the magnus opus Mr Fowler first hoped for. Indeed, in many ways the omissions, the back tracking and a series of significant policy reversals that have forced the Secretary of State to contemplate the enactment of many of his key proposals only after the magic hat-trick of election victories has been secured in 1987 or early 1988, are each testaments to the mobilisation of argument, opposition and counter-proposals by groups such as CPAG. Certainly, the clear disruption to the timetable for enacting the White Paper and the continuing disarray in much of its substance means that chinks of light remain for a group like CPAG to force wider as it has so successfully done in the past.

Throughout its twenty years CPAG has remained a group concerned to question and change prevailing attitudes to the nature of poverty, its definition, its measurement and its remedies and, of course, it has been the concern to change or modify attitudes which has proved the major stumbling block to a wider and more sustained influence. The need to overcome attitudinal barriers and to counter 'scrounger-phobia', not least on the part of Government itself, has been a major feature of the Groups greatly enhanced efforts to educate the general public and to extend alliances with like-minded bodies, including trade unions and womens groups in recent years. The mobilisation of a very broad-based but well-informed body of opinion against the social security reviews is only the most recent case in point.

The sheer complexity and ongoing nature of the issue has been daunting. Poverty was in 1965 and continues to be in 1986 a problem fraught with conflicting definitions and methods of measurement and it affects a section of the public many see as substantially outside of the mainstream of society. Increasingly, 'solutions' to poverty have acquired an all or nothing decisiveness with which policy makers have found it impossible to come to terms. Even where governments have apparently committed themselves at the hustings to 'do something about poverty' the constraints of office and party calculations of exact electoral advantage have invariably militated against it.

The decision to concentrate at the outset on child or family poverty and to adopt an emotive and readily identifiable name have proved impressive and shrewd tactical judgements. Above all it enabled campaigns to be built around a single mechanism - family allowances and later Child Benefits. The considerable influence the group has brought to bear as a result may be seen in one strand of orthodox "attitude group" behaviour at least ..."that of ideas and sentiments brought to bear with political skill and organisation" (73).

Its political skills have been in evidence throughout the tenure of each of its directors, in the wisdom and continuity given to the group by Peter Townsend in over 20 years involvement with it and in the activities of an impressive and committed staff which has gone from strength to strength over the two decades; we need only recall the sheer energy and grasp of fine detail shown by Tony Lynes in a period of office that laid the foundations for CPAG's early and prickly Fabian style - a period when the group almost single handedly pursued the alleviation of child poverty through increased family allowances and the abolition of the wage-stop. It was a time when a frequently evasive and rudderless Labour Government was forced back on course by those such as Lynes and Townsend who pointedly acted as its social conscience.

Later, in the first of two major watersheds for the group - the 1970 and 1979 General Elections - the arrival of Frank Field and Peter Townsend as director and chair respectively ushered in an era in which CPAG became more self assured, more publicity conscious and more uncompromising. The courageous decision to confront and attack the Labour Government's record on poverty in the heat of the 1970 General Election served notice that CPAG would remain fiercely independent and uncompromising in its determination to get the best deal possible for the poor, regardless of who was in power. More recently, under Ruth Lister, the group has perhaps truly consolidated its position as a non-partisan campaigning organisation that enjoys close and fruitful relationships with <u>all</u> the parties and a much improved relationship with the damper flanks of the Conservative Party in particular. It is perhaps in the years since 1979 that CPAG has comprehensively 'gone public'. These have been and continue to be years characterised by a raising of public awareness of poverty and social injustice through increased CPAG branch work, conference initiatives, alliances with trade unions, womens groups and within the voluntary lobby itself and through the most vigorous campaigns for public education yet. It has certainly played a lead role in ensuring that Norman Fowler's "great debate on the Welfare State" has actually taken place even if the Government has remained selective in what it admits to hear.

The Social Security Reviews of 1985 have perhaps confirmed what many people knew already, as no doubt will the campaigns planned for its celebratory 21st year, that CPAG is still in the driving seat of the family lobby after two decades of campaigning that would have exhausted the energy, skills and resources of lesser groups (74).

NOTES

1.   The Conservative Manifesto 1983, p.24.
2.   Ibid.
3.   'Norman Fowler's Agenda', New Society, 27 October 1983.
4.   Wicks, M. 'Back to the Poor Law' New Socialist, No. 12, July/August 1983.
5.   Ibid.
6.   The Economist, 18 September 1982.
7.   Sunday Times Business News, 6 February 1983
8.   Poverty, Spring 1983, p.3.
9.   Ibid., p.4.
10. Ibid., p.7.
11. Ibid., p.11.
12. Ibid.
13. Ibid., p.12.
14. Ibid.
15. Ibid., p.13.
16. Land, H. 'Family Fables' New Socialist No. 11, May/June 1983.
17. Ibid.
18. Ibid.
19. Wicks op.cit. and New Society, 24 February 1983.
20. Lister, R. 'Family Policy: Alternative Viewpoints' Poverty, Summer 1983, p.16.
21. Ibid.
22. Ibid., p.17.
23. Ibid.
24. Ibid.
25. Land, op.cit.
26. Lister, op.cit., p.18.
27. Land, op.cit.
28. Poverty, Summer 1983, p.5.
29. The Guardian, 9 May 1983
30. Third Report of the Social Security Advisory Committee, 1984, p.3.
31. Ibid.
32. Hansard (Commons) 2 April 1984, Cols. 652-660.
33. Lister, R. A Budget for the Poor - Or A Poor Budget?, CPAG, January 1984, p.i.
34. Ibid., p.29.

35. Ibid., p.ii.
36. <u>1984 Changed Priorities Ahead?</u> CPAGs Evidence to the Social Security Reviews, Appendix.
37. Ibid.
38. <u>The Times</u>, 24 June 1984.
39. <u>Economic Trends</u>, 9 August 1984.
40. <u>1984 Changed Priorities Ahead?</u> Appendix.
41. Ibid.
42. See <u>Hansard</u> (Commons), 15 March 1984, col. 272.
43. <u>1984 Changed Priorities Ahead?</u> Appendix.
44. <u>CPAG Annual Report 1984/5</u>, p.7.
45. <u>1984 Changed Priorities Ahead?</u> - Evidence to The Review of Benefits for Children and Young People - Summary
46. Ibid.
47. Ibid. Evidence to the Supplementary Benefits Review - Summary.
48. Ibid. Evidence to The Housing Benefit Review - Summary.
49. <u>CPAG Annual Report 1984/5</u>, p.15.
50. <u>Financial Times</u>, 26 March 1985.
51. Lister, R. <u>Social Security Reviews: Countdown</u>, April 1985, p.3.
52. <u>Statement on Social Security Review</u>, Monday 3 June 1985, p.1.
53. Ibid., p.3.
54. Ibid.
55. Ibid., p.4.
56. See <u>Community Care</u>, 22 August 1985, pp.16-17 and <u>The Times</u>, 6 June 1985.
57. Lister, R., Roll, J. and Smith, R. <u>What Future for Social Security?</u> CPAG 1985, p.24.
58. For a recent analysis of the importance of child benefit to family income and its distribution within the family see Pahl, J. 'Who Benefits from Child Benefit' <u>New Society</u>, 25 April 1985.
59. <u>Burying Beveridge - Summary</u>, CPAG August 1985, p.4.
60. <u>Reform of Social Security: Programme for Change</u>, Vol. 2, Cmnd. 9518, June 1985, p.49, para. 4.50.
61. <u>Burying Beveridge</u>, op.cit., p.7.
62. <u>Poverty</u>, no. 61, Summary 1985, pp.14-15.
63. <u>Burying Beveridge</u>, p.9.
64. Ibid., p.10.
65. <u>Community Care</u>, 22 August 1985.
66. <u>A BASW Response to Reform of Social Security</u> - British Association of Social Workers, September 1985, p.9.
67. <u>Burying Beveridge</u>, p.11.

68. Fourth Report of the Social Security Advisory Committee 1985, p.2.

69. Townsend, P. Preface to Silburn, R. (ed.) The Future of Social Security, Fabian Society, October 1985, p.2.

70. The Guardian, 17 December 1985.

71. Hansard (Commons) 22 April 1985, Col. 624. (It is worth noting also that on 20 June 1984, the Minister of Social Security, Rhodes Boyson admitted to the House of Commons that 16 benefits had fallen in real value since 1979.)

72. Ibid. and see also Townsend, op.cit., p.6.

73. Potter, A. 'Attitude Groups' Political Quarterly, January 1958, pp.72-78.

74. See McCarthy, M.A. 'Pressure Group for the Poor' Social Work Today, 16 December 1985.

SELECT BIBLIOGRAPHY
(Place of publication London unless otherwise stated)

Abel-Smith, B. and Townsend, P. The Poor and the Poorest Occasional Papers on Social Administration No. 17 Bell and Co., London 1965.

Alinsky, S. Reveille for Radicals Random House, New York 1969.

Atkinson, A.B. Poverty in Britain and the Reform of Social Security Cambridge University Press, 1969.

Bachrach, P. and Barataz, M.S. Power and Poverty: Theory and Practice Oxford University Press.

Bacon, R. and Eltis, W. Britains Economic Problem: Too Few Producers Macmillan, London 1976.

Banting, K. Poverty, Politics and Policy MacMillan, London 1979.

Beer, S. Modern British Politics Faber, London 1971.

Benewick, R. and Smith T. Direct Action and Democratic Politics George Allen & Unwin, London 1972.

Bentley, A.F. The Process of Government (1908) reproduced ed. Odegard, P. Bellknap Press, Harvard 1967.

Berthoud, R. ed. Challenges to Social Policy Gower, London 1985.

Berthoud, R; Brown, J; Cooper, S; Poverty and the Development of Anti-Poverty Policy in the UK. H.E.B., 1981.

Birch, R. The Shaping of the Welfare State Longman, London 1974.

Bosanquet, N. After the New Right Heinemann, London 1982.

Bosanquet, N. and Townsend, P. Labour and Inequality Fabian Society, London 1972.

Bosanquet, M. and Townsend, P. Labour and Equality Heinemann, London 1980.

Brittan, S. The Treasury Under the Tories 1951-64 Pelican, London 1964.

Brown, G. In My Way Gollancz, London 1971.

368

Brown, R.G.S. The Management of Welfare Fontana, London 1975.

Bull, D. ed. Family Poverty 2nd ed. Duckworth, London 1972.

Bull, D. and Wilding, P. Thatcherism and the Poor CPAG, London 1983.

Castles, F. The Social Democratic Image of Society Routledge and Kegan Paul, London 1978.

Caves, R.E. ed. Britains Economic Prospects George Allen & Unwin, London 1970.

Cloward, R.A. and Piven, F.F. Regulating the Poor Tavistock, London 1972.

Coates, D. The Labour Party and the Struggle for Socialism Cambridge University Press, 1975.

Coates, K. and Silburn, R. Poverty: The Forgotten Englishman Penguin (Harmondsworth), 1970.

Commons, J.R. The Economics of Collective Action MacMillan, New York 1951.

Connolly, W. The Bias of Pluralism Atherton, New York 1969.

Cosgrave, P. Margaret Thatcher: Prime Minister Arrow, London 1979.

Crossman, R.H.S. The Diaries of a Cabinet Minister Vols. I, II, III. Jonathan Cape & Hamish Hamilton, London 1975, 1976, 1977.

Deacon, A. and Bradshaw, J. Reserved for the Poor Blackwell & Martin Robertson, 1983.

Dearlove, J. The Politics of Policy in Local Government Cambridge University Press, 1973.

Donnison, D. The Politics of Poverty Martin Robertson 1982.

Dorfman, G. Wage Politics in Britain 1945-67 Chas. Knight, 1974.

Drucker, H.M. Doctrine and Ethos in the Labour Party George Allen & Unwin, 1979.

Dye, T.R. Policy Analysis University of Alabama Press, Alabama 1976.

Ehrmann, H. Interest Groups on Four Continents University of Pittsburgh Press, 1967.

Field, F. ed. The Conscript Army Routledge and Kegan Paul 1977.

Field, F. Poverty and Politics H.E.B., 1982.

Finer, S.E. Anonymous Empire Pall Mall 2nd ed. 1966.

Foot, P. The Politics of Harold Wilson Penguin (Harmondsworth), 1968.

Gamble, A. The Conservative Nation Routledge and Kegan Paul, 1974.

Garson, D.G. Group Theories of Politics Sage Publications Vol. 61, 1978.

Gilbert, N. Capitalism and the Welfare State Yale 1983.

Hall, P; Land, H; Parker, R; and Webb, A. Change, Choice and Conflict in Social Policy Heinemann, 1978.

Harrison, M. Trade Unions and the Labour Party Since 1945 Allen and Unwin, London 1960.

Heclo, H.H. and Wildavsky, A. The Private Government of Public Money MacMillan, London 1974.

Heffer, E. The Class Struggle in Parliament Gollancz, London 1973.

Hill, M. The State, Administration and the Individual Fontana, London 1976.

Holland, S. The Socialist Challenge Quartet, London 1978.

Hutt, A. ed. British Trade Unionism Lawrence and Wishart, London 1975.

Jordan, B. Automatic Poverty Routledge and Kegan Paul, London 1981.

Jordan, B. Freedom and the Welfare State Routledge and Kegan Paul, London 1976.

Jordan, B. Paupers: The Making of the New Claiming Class Routledge and Kegan Paul, London 1973.

Kincaid, T.C. Poverty and Equality in Britain Penguin (Harmondsworth), 1973.

Kimber, R. and Richardson, J.J. eds. Campaigning for the Environment Routledge and Kegan Paul, London 1974.

Le Grand, J. and Robinson, R. eds. Privatisation and the Welfare State George Allen & Unwin, 1984.

MacFarlane, L.J. Issues in British Politics Since 1945 Longmans, London 1975.

MacGregor, S. The Politics of Poverty Longmans, London 1981.

Marsh, D. (ed.) Pressure Politics Junction Books, London 1983.

May, T. Trade Unions and Pressure Group Politics Saxon House, London 1975.

McCarthy, M.A. The Politics of Influence: An Analysis of the Methodology of an Environmental Pressure Group unpublished M.A. Thesis University of Keele 1976.

McNay, M. and Pond, C. Low Pay and Family Poverty Occasional Paper No. 2 of the Study Commission on the Family, London 1980.

Middlemass, K. Politics in Industrial Society Andre Deutsch, London 1980.

Miliband, R. Parliamentary Socialism 2nd ed. Merlin, 1973.

Miliband, R. The State in Capitalist Society Quartet, London 1973 ed.

Minkin, L. The Labour Party Conference Allen Lane, 1978.

Olson Jnr., M. The Logic of Collective Action Harvard University Press, 1971.

Perlman, S. A Theory of the Labour Movement MacMillan, New York 1928.

Potter, A. Organised Groups in British National Politics Greenwood Press, Connecticut 1975 (Faber and Faber ed. 1961).

Radice, G. The Industrial Democrats George Allen and Unwin, 1978.

Ricci, D.M. Community Power and Democratic Theory: The Logic of Political Analysis Random House, New York 1971.

Richardson, J.J. and Jordan, G. Governing Under Pressure Martin Robertson, 1979.

Richter, I. Political Purpose in Trade Unions George Allen & Unwin, London 1973.

Roberts, G.K. Political Parties and Pressure Groups in Britain Wiedenfeld, 1970.

Roos, Jnr., L.J. The Politics of Eco-Suicide Holt, Rinehart and Winston, Illinois 1971.

Rowntree, B.S. and Lavers, G.R. Poverty and the Welfare State: A Third Social Survey of York Dealing Only with Economic Problems Longman, London 1951.

Runciman, W.G. Relative Deprivation and Social Justice Routledge & Kegan Paul, London 1966.

Salisbury, R. Interest Group Politics in America Harper and Row, New York 1970.

Schattschneider, E.E. Party Government Holt, Reinehart and Winston, New York 1942.

Schattschneider, E.E. The Semi-Sovereign People: A Realists View of Democracy in America Holt, Rinehart and Winston, New York 1960.

Schmitter, P.C. Corporatism and Public Policy in Authoritarian Portugal Sage, London 1975.

Silburn, R. ed. The Future of Social Security Fabian Society, London 1985.

Self, P. Econocrats and the Policy Process Macmillan, London 1975.

Simpson, W. Labour: The Unions and the Party George Allen & Unwin, London 1973.

Smith, T. The Politics of the Corporate Economy Martin Robertson, 1979.

Spiers, M. Techniques and Public Administration Fontana, London 1975.

Stevenson, O. Claimant or Client? Allen and Unwin, London 1973.

Stewart, J.D. British Pressure Groups Clarendon, London 1958.

Taylor, R. The Fifth Estate Pan, London 1980.

Titmuss, R. Essays on the Welfare State Allen and Unwin, London 1958.

Townsend, P. Sociology and Social Policy, Allen Lane, London 1975.

Townsend, P. <u>Poverty in the United Kingdom</u> Penguin, London 1979.

Ward, S. <u>DHSS in Crisis</u> CPAG, 1985.

Wedderburn, D. ed. <u>Poverty, Inequality and Class Structure</u> Cambridge University Press, 1974.

Whitaker, B. ed. <u>A Radical Future,</u> Jonathan Cape, London 1967.

Wilensky, H.L. <u>The New Corporatism, Centralisation and the Welfare State</u> Sage, London and Beverly Hills 1976.

Wilson, H. <u>The New Britain</u> Penguin (Harmondsworth) 1964.

Wilson, H. <u>The Governance of Britain</u> Sphere, London 1977.

Wilson, H. <u>The Labour Government 1964-70: A Personal Record</u> Pelican, London 1974.

Winkler, H.R. ed. <u>Twentieth Century Britain: National Power and Social Welfare</u> New Viewpoints, New York 1976.

Wootton, G. <u>Pressure Politics in Contemporary Britain</u> D.C. Heath (Lexington Books) 1978.

Wynn, M. <u>Family Policy</u> Pelican, London 1972.